PAST LIFE TOURISM

PAST LIFE TOURISM
Gateway to Bridging Your Past and Future

Barbara Ford-Hammond

First edition
Published in Great Britain
By Mirage Publishing 2007

A CIP catalogue record for this book
Is available from the British Library.

ISBN: 978-1-90257-831-6

Mirage Publishing
PO Box 161
Gateshead
NE8 4WW
Great Britain

Printed and bound in Great Britain by

Forward Press
Remus House, Coltsfoot Drive, Woodston, Peterborough, PE2 9JX

Cover © Mirage Publishing
Design by Artistic Director Sharon Anderson

Papers used in the production of this book are recycled, thus reducing
environmental depletion.

For Mick and my family who are the best.

Introduction

I'm in a saloon. There are cowboys sitting about drinking and playing cards. It is noisy and the warm air smells of beer, horses and sweat. There is a mirror across the wall, behind the shot bottles, and spittons are in the corners. To the right of the bar is a wooden staircase leading up to the bedrooms. No secrets here.

I am thinking of the word 'doxy'[1] although I'm not sure what that means (I do now!).

As my story unfolds it becomes clear that I am a working girl and these men are my customers.

This was my first experience of being regressed to a past-life and certainly not something I expected. My fellow student therapist, RS, who was the book editor for a well-known Sunday tabloid; I was his first 'client' when I found myself recalling a past life as a prostitute in Louisville, Kentucky.

No matter how hard I tried, the ground refused to open up and engulf me, but when he realised what was happening he whipped out his pen and notepad and proceeded to interview me in true journalistic style. Equally fascinating was his own experience of being a soldier in WWI.

Nearly one-hundred and fifty years have passed since my time in Louisville but it seems like only yesterday. We are all the sum total of our experiences and lessons in life regardless of whether they are from this one, the last or the next - as you will discover, if you haven't already.

That first regression opened up a whole other world for me that I have since been able to share with many clients over the years for their healing or for pleasure. The lessons I have received from my clients cannot go unmentioned; the most valuable of which is to never assume anything.

[1]Doxy - an immoral woman; prostitute (source: dictionary.com).

I have learnt how we just 'have knowledge' without learning it from early childhood. Some people are able to speak a different language in their mother tongue or understand another without ever having taken a class. Others can compose brilliant music or have creativity that can never be taught. It is 'in' them waiting for the catalyst to trigger their moment of glory.

You can probably recall times in your childhood: happy thoughts of a birthday party, falling over and grazing your knee, getting into trouble, having a crush on someone totally inappropriate and many other moments. Sometimes you get a snapshot of a memory and at other times something may set you off on a trip down memory lane and you lose yourself in a daydream of reminiscence. All of these memories belong to you and are yours to retrieve and ponder on.

Finding out about our past lives is a very attractive thought. Many people visit psychics to be told who they were or what might happen, when actually it is very possible to retrieve our own memories and I believe that the answer is for everyone with an interest or reason to learn the techniques to regress themselves easily and safely.

The interest in past life regression has surged over recent years with more enquiries than ever before.

My own experiences started me thinking about sharing my knowledge in a book several years ago – maybe even in another life, but I didn't pay attention to the signs. As the seed began to germinate in my mind it took on a life of its own and the title *Past Life Tourism* burst forth. As with most brilliant moments it was that feeling of 'knowing'.

I wondered, though, if it said enough. We can just travel and explore anywhere that we choose for no other reason than we want to, but the title alone doesn't let you know that you can also go forward. Hence the subtitle, *Gateway to Bridging Your Past and Future*, which I believe says it all.

In this book you will discover the facts about past life regression and future life progression: by the end of which you will be able to self-regress and, if you wish, research your findings. You may use any of the techniques in this book alone or with a friend or get together with a group of travelling companions.

I have not written this book in an attempt to prove or disprove the reality of past life memories: I am sharing my stories, findings, methods and the amazing accounts that those included have been generous enough to share.

Are you living your best life? Can you imagine it? Would you know if you were?

If you are struggling or suffering, the solutions to heal are within you and with guidance from this book many answers can be found. Another rather cool thing is that you don't need to have a problem or any issues to be able to retrieve your memories from the past or to explore your possible futures. Desire is more than enough of a reason.

However, things can change; your wellbeing, aspirations and general outlook on life can be altered, quite dramatically, after a regression and often issues are resolved before you even know you have them.

1

I wasn't Cleopatra

Let's set the scene. It was the first evening at the beginning of the course. The teachers were going to show me the ways of becoming a hypnotherapist by being completely submerged in all things hypnotic.

I'll quickly share with you why I was there as it all connects very neatly together. In 1985 I severely hurt my back in an accident at work, which led to some major surgery to prop my spine with screws and bolts, followed by several hospital stays. For anyone interested, I started with a laminectomy and spinal fusion, which didn't quite do the job. I was then unravelled and redone with a transpedicular fixation of the spine.

During this time I studied all sorts of subjects, mainly psychology and counselling, but none of these really tickled my fancy. My interest was and still is in being able to help people to help themselves by supplying them with tools and resources. I hate the thought of anyone being dependent on another person for weeks/ months or even years of therapy or talking about their problems. As this wasn't for me, I found myself learning about hypnosis. I truly believe that if we work in the 'now' we can release debris from our past and create the futures we desire. We really can coach ourselves to freedom and success.

All these years later after taking classes, testing out and learning many ideas from my ever-obliging clients, I know it was right for me. Without self-hypnosis I am not sure how I would have coped with the years of back pain. Okay, violins away because now it is time for *your* journey of discovery to begin while you make use of the techniques and tools that have been developed just for you.

Returning to that first night of my training course. We had all popped out for a 'get to know each other' drink and had just ordered. Valerie, who is now a good friend and work colleague, asked for a sparkling water. When a large bottle arrived she giggled and said, 'I can't drink all that or I'll be on the floor'.

'Madam,' replied the hotel owner somewhat bemused, perhaps thinking she was drunk already or a little unhinged, 'it is only water.'

'Yes,' said Valerie patiently, 'but it has the same effect on me as champagne.' And, do you know what? It did, but she stopped drinking before slipping under the table. Sparkling water caused that reaction in her because of a hypnotic suggestion given to her when she had decided she wanted to experience the effects of booze without actually drinking alcohol. It made me think I was either about to learn about the most marvellous secret, or I was being set up and a secret film crew would appear any minute and say something like, 'You've Been Framed'.

This was the first but not the last time that I wondered if I should just make my excuses and return home. Luckily I decided to stay, and turned from a bewildered sceptic into a hypnotic diva.

The lessons we studied ranged from how to help people stop smoking to releasing phobias, eating problems to insomnia. My own phobia of flying was sorted, which I must stress was so severe that I would hurt all over just being in an airport. Each time I flew it was a white knuckle ride because I had to hold the plane up and level, which is no mean task, and resulted in me being a stressed out hysterical wreck and not the best of travelling companions. My smoking habit also disappeared in a puff of smoke.

We were then introduced to the fascinating phenomenon of past lives. This introduction into Past Life regression training was included to prepare us for clients who requested it and for those moments when clients spontaneously regressed to what they believed to be a past life.

At that time I 'knew' it would never happen. Good job then that I knew what to do when I had a client do just that in a smoking cessation session. He had continued smoking and in his follow-up session told me he felt afraid to stop. I regressed him back to the time when his smoking habit had importance; unlike the usual reports of wanting to look older, peer group pressure or rebelling against parents, he told me he was a soldier on guard duty and was so tired that the only way to stay awake was to smoke. Needless to say, he'd never been a soldier in this life and when he released the connection he stopped smoking immediately.

As with all good lessons, in order to get the most from them it is best to experience them firsthand. So, I watched somewhat nervously as a couple of other students and guests were regressed and, without any shadow of doubt, I knew my first regression would reveal that I was Boudica or Cleopatra or another powerful woman of note. Can you therefore imagine my astonishment at discovering I was working as a prostitute in a Texan bar?

I could see in my mind's eye the layout of the bar and knew it was in Louisville. Under the instructor's guidance, RS questioned me excitedly while I talked about the cowboys, who it seemed I did not like at all, sitting around being raucous, spitting chewed tobacco and drinking. I was in the business to support my little sister as we had no parents and although I didn't know what happened to them it wasn't an issue. To my horror I discovered I was pregnant. Not good when you have to make your money with your body.

RS took me forward to the time of the birth and asked me who was president. *Fool*, I thought!

My reply was, 'I'm about to give birth to a bastard child and you're asking me that!' As I gave birth, I told him the president was Lincoln.

It was quite upsetting to the 'me' in the now that anyone, let alone myself, would call a baby something so awful. This was a powerful indication to me about how different we can be in other lives.

I recalled that the baby turned out to be a girl, who I loved immediately, and soon after I was living happily with a wonderful man, my daughter and my sister.

At the time I was pretty sure that none of that would have been in my life script, but after I'd recovered it made complete sense. It was like a little bit of my own life's jigsaw had slipped into place. I'm whispering this bit - *deep down I've always thought I'd make a rather good Madam!*

Since then I have been regressed and recalled a couple of other lives that answered questions I didn't even know I had.

When I completed the hypnotherapy training, another thing I 'knew' was how to get clients swarming to me. We had been taught that adverts alone tend not to be cost effective. Mine would be. Into the local paper it went. My perfectly worded advert informed people how fabulous hypnotherapy was and that I was the one they should visit. I was pretty much the only one back in those days so I was even more convinced I would be swamped with enquiries.

In four days I had four calls. Three were from other newspapers offering to sell me advertising. The last one was a man who wanted to know if I provided extras with the massage?! I never really worked out how he got that from a hypnosis advert: maybe he picked up on something other than his own wishful thinking. Perhaps he knew about my previous life's work? I should have asked if he wore checked shirts and chaps over his trousers. Amusing really, so many threads that continue and, as you will discover when finding out about regression work, coincidences abound.

Theory

After my experience with the advert fiasco, I called a more upmarket newspaper and they sent a journalist and photographer. Philip was a charming man who wrote a lovely feature on me that really started my career rolling. He mentioned his fascination with past lives and, although very sceptical and convinced that nothing would happen, he wanted to be regressed.

During his session he slipped beautifully into another life and described being an army officer in India at the time of the Raj. He was staying in a beautiful hotel preparing for something important to do with Queen Victoria. He was so engrossed with his plans that he couldn't really be bothered with my questions. When he did deign to respond, he seemed to grow taller as he spoke. He was a small built man but in his past life he had an important role and was tall in stature. I asked his name but he wasn't sure. I asked what those around called him. His reply was, 'They call me Sir.'

He spoke in a somewhat condescending way, as if I was silly to be asking so many questions of someone so important. I had thought he wasn't able to get much information, but actually it was because he really couldn't be bothered with me; he even yawned at one or two of my questions, while I resisted the urge to slap him.

Afterwards, Philip felt invigorated and proud. He was also shocked at his ease in being rude and how normal that felt. The remainder of the session was spent with him apologising.

I immediately had a theory. Philip's past life experience was the complete opposite of what was happening in this life. That was what karma was all about. I had everything sussed. Why hadn't anyone else thought of it?

To confirm my rather brilliant hypothesis, my next regressee was Stella. Stella was very calm and feminine, but also doubtful about whether she could or would be regressed. The sceptics do make it more fun.

She immediately began to describe a boating accident and talked of the greyness washing over her as she sank under the water, far from a rowing boat. Stella went on to talk about drowning. She had gone straight to the end of the life, as the impact had been so powerful. I took her back to an earlier stage in the life. With a little investigation it became apparent that it wasn't an accident at all.

It was a suicide, planned in such a way that it looked accidental in order to protect the family name. In her mind a suicide would be the same as a confession of guilt.

Stella sighed deeply throughout the regression with her legs flopped open in a very ungainly manner while scratching and rubbing her chin. She described her life as an MP and her partner who had talked her into a fraudulent episode. I wracked my brain, trying to remember when women were first allowed to stand for parliament, but was distracted because the further she went into the regression the more she seemed to change. Her mannerisms, her voice and even her looks subtly altered.

I wondered whether the partner was her husband, but when I asked I got an emphatic, 'No!'

Taking her back even earlier in the life, she described school. I thought it strange that, for a girl, she knew far too much about Winchester Boys School. I slipped into a slow motion world: you know that pause, moments before a realisation when you get 'it'. She was a man in her past life. It was so obvious! Legs apart, scratching at whisker growth on her/his chin - lots of very masculine behaviour.

This was all brilliant. It meant that my theory stood: a gentle woman regressing to a brusque man.

Jean was a client struggling through life as a single parent. I visited her at home to help with her confidence, which had diminished after a troubled relationship. At the end of the treatment she asked if we could do a past life regression.

The previous life that we then visited was practically the same as her present one. Life for her was hard. She talked about a relationship gone bad and being so hungry that while walking through a market she stole fruit for her and her daughter. Although she got away with it, she was wracked with guilt and worried about getting caught and separated from her child.

Afterwards, she admitted to me that she had considered stealing a couple of times when the pennies were very low, but her morals meant she couldn't and wouldn't. Her regression shocked her into changing things so there was no chance of repeating the 'same old'.

However, my theory was dashed and has continued to be so over the years. There isn't necessarily any obvious correlation between this life and others. They can be the same, opposite, similar, merging, bits that match, bits that clash. You can change sex, colour and belief, or not.

One thing that does seem to be apparent is that unfinished business does need to be sorted. That might mean releasing, forgiving, accepting or just noticing. Remembering allows us to have closure and from that we can be free and move on.

Anyway, there I was doing my best to help people heal themselves, change habits or release something negative, when along came Jill and Sam.

Sam asked for a regression to a particular time and, much to my surprise, I discovered this was possible. She had a reoccurring dream and felt it was past life debris intruding on her life now. She was right.

Jill was an even bigger surprise. About to buy a bar in Spain, she wanted to go forwards in time to check its success before uprooting her family. I suggested a psychic might be best to advise her of a future event.

'Well', she replied. 'I figured if you can go back in time, why can't you go forward?'

Why not indeed? So we did. It all looked very good in her future and happened exactly as she predicted, or saw, depending on your perspective. I did wonder whether she had ordered it with the clarity of her thoughts and intentions, but when you are looking at something that has already happened, even though it is in your future (has your brain burnt out yet?) it feels different, as you will discover.

I'm not quite sure what I would have done at that time if her future had looked awful without the knowledge I have today. I now know that with our free will we can change and steer our lives.

I am sharing all this to demonstrate that moving through, in and out of time can be done with ease.

Think how easy it is to transport yourself back to childhood if your nose hairs detect the briefest whiff of school dinners. Or, remember a time from years ago: a party, a holiday or trip or perhaps a visit from a nice friend or relative. Are you remembering extra bits? Perhaps conversations, news, or receiving a present?

Have you ever spent time looking through old photos and immediately felt you were elsewhere?

Perhaps you can play the memory game with someone else and compare your thoughts. You might discover that even though you were in the same place at the same time, your stories will be different.

We remember and store everything that we see, feel or sense, but it is our own version of events that could possibly be very different from someone else's memory. Put yourself at King Arthur's Round Table with eleven others. On it is a huge globe of the world. It is so big that you can only see the people on either side, not those opposite.

As you look at the globe someone describes it. 'It is mostly water.'

Another joins in, 'It is mostly desert.'

Another, 'It is water and islands.'

Another, 'It is mountainous.'

What do you see on your bit? You see the bit only you can see. And it is the same in every situation. Nice as your bit of the globe is, it might be beneficial for you to walk around the table and look at another's viewpoint.

It is good to hear stories that others have and are willing to share from their experiences in this and previous lifetimes. Sometimes it helps us to learn and other times it is just fun. Often we discover things we hadn't even considered.

Peeping into other people's memories can in itself be the beginning of one's own journey, and is as intriguing in a similar way to reality TV shows. We all like to see what might be over the hill.

2

Lives Lies or Metaphor

Phobias

When I'm working with clients who have a phobia it is often necessary to return to the cause of the problem for them to be able to release it.

Phobic reactions seem to fall into various categories: someone else's, late onset, developed in childhood or no apparent cause.

Someone else's fear - of spiders, for example, usually forms in childhood from seeing another person, most often a parent, screaming or reacting in terror when an eight-legged beastie is in the vicinity. I've never met anyone who has been assaulted by a spider but the fear that spider phobics have can be very debilitating, and over the years can spread to other bugs and things that fly or creep. I can remember my mother standing on a chair, armed with a broom, because she thought she saw a mouse. Luckily, I thought that was very cool and secretly wished that I could catch one and keep it for a pet. That was probably one of my first delusions.

Another example of someone else's fear is thinking about how awful a reaction is in a particular situation and then replicating it. Some years ago, I worked with two male students. They were unrelated but their problems were identical.

One day, John was in a class preparing to give a talk to his fellow students. Everyone was nervous and rehearsing inwardly while trying to appear interested in all the others. One of the girls was so worried she had trouble breathing and had a full on panic attack. John felt sorry for her and imagined how awful it was. He stood to give his talk, still thinking about her, and had an attack himself. It was the first time in his life that anything like that had happened, but each time he tried to speak in class to the group he felt it coming on.

Peter's scenario was the same. He watched someone else hyperventilating and worried that it might happen to him - it did. Our imaginations are so powerful we must be aware of what we create.

Late onset is the sudden development of a fear: like flying. I have worked with people who travel constantly, yet seemingly without warning they get frightened. I say seemingly, but it is usually that there has been an incident or a particularly bumpy flight while they have been emotionally charged. Emotions get fired up when we are very stressed or tired, so what under normal circumstances wouldn't have any effect, at these times it can become too much to cope with. The mind then does a fine job of trying to prevent us from repeating the experience and the best way it can do this is to make us so anxious and worried that we don't do what the mind perceives as dangerous.

Developed in childhood is pretty much what it says on the tin. When I was about seven my parents took me and a friend swimming. I thought I'd look rather marvellous if I did the best dive in the world. In I went without checking the depth and smacked my head on the bottom. Seeing stars and the sun filtering through water when you can't work out which way up you are meant to be is rather scary: particularly when no one had noticed. That was that for me for many years. I forgot how to dive and worried for anyone else I saw planning a head first entry.

The thing with fear is that it feeds on itself. Instead of it just being about me and the actual depth of water, I was convinced that anyone diving anywhere would not only hit the bottom allowing their brains to spill, but also they might easily catch a body part on the side of the pool or the board. I had also grown a fear of flying when I was about two. I saw a boy fall from a rope attached to a log and, although he didn't fall far, he was covered in mud. My inner filing system decided to associate that with everything above the ground. I had no recall of the incident consciously and actually thought I'd made it up until my father verified that it had really happened.

The no apparent cause category is interesting. Early in my career I would come across people who had fears and phobias without a cause. Sometimes this wouldn't and doesn't matter as the mind will make a change and heal. Other times, however, that wouldn't or doesn't happen and in these cases past life regression is the answer to completely sort out their difficulties.

When I work with clients I don't start in the past in order to heal or change behaviour. I begin in the now and go to where the subconscious mind of the client takes us. A few times when their mind couldn't or wouldn't make a change in the 'now', I regressed them and they would slip back into the memory of a past life and describe the birth of a trauma that led to the phobia. Sometimes this would be a death scene. If your mind holds on to something potentially traumatic it will take you to the cause when it is time to heal or release. Even if a death wasn't trauma filled, the time just before and after the moment of passing may have been charged with emotions - yours or others.

Déjà vu

Jim came to see me after his holiday to Devon. He described fun and pleasure with his family as they relaxed, played and saw many different places. Although he had never been there before there was an air of familiarity - so much that he had commented on it to his wife. Jim had even contacted his mother to ask if they had visited the place on holiday when he was a child. They hadn't.

All was well until they stopped for a pub lunch, when he had what he believed to be a panic attack; he referred to it as an 'episode'. However, the 'attack' went as soon as he left the pub, but returned as he re-entered. He had decided to test it because of the very strange feelings he experienced and as far as he was concerned everything had a rational explanation. For several days afterwards he dreamt he was hiding in a cellar feeling terrified and would wake up sweating with his heart racing and a powerful need to check that his family were all okay.

There wasn't any content to the dream that he could grab hold of or recall and he began to worry before he fell asleep. His wife suggested that perhaps it was a past life issue and, although that notion seemed ridiculous, he gave it some thought.

Eventually, for a quiet life he decided to explore the possibility. I'm not sure which of us was more surprised as he described in detail an experience surrounding an incident prior to the repeal of the Corn Laws. As the regression continued, he developed a deep West Country accent. He was hiding in a cellar from soldiers and, although he wasn't found, there was an accident that killed him. The trauma of leaving his wife widowed with two small children was awoken by the visit to the pub.

Does this suggest a place or building might hold on to energies or memories, or do particular combinations set off memories? Like, for example, the smell of school dinners or particular perfumes?

Often people have told me that they 'knew' the layout of towns or buildings even though they had never been there before, and had no prior knowledge. It tends to happen when they arrive at a place and they think they are having a déjà vu moment, but then it develops into knowledge. Sometimes they share with others what is happening, but their accounts are usually dismissed as perhaps something they had read previously or seen pictures.

Can you remember having a déjà vu about a place? Think about what was happening, if you can. Take your mind back to the place and notice what happens now. Think also about places you would like to visit and why you think you might. What do you feel when you think about various locations? Excitement? Fear? Other people?

I have an obsession with Greece and everything Greek. The first time I travelled there it was as if I'd gone home. It is very hard to explain as I have a lovely home already and I have no desire to leave. The feeling in Greece was way down deep in my soul and I would have happily just stayed there. It was not the same as that romantic feeling we often have when we want a holiday to last forever so we don't have to return to normality - this almost hurt.

Children

What then of children? They are particularly good at describing places they haven't visited. You may have heard stories of children describing previous lives that have been researched and shown to hold up to the investigation. They begin by recognising someone and often talk about another family or how they 'died'. This can be very disconcerting for the parents and many stories are dismissed as child fantasy.

Jane remembered a time when her daughter was poorly and she said, 'It'll be okay, the last time I died it wasn't too bad at all.' She recovered and didn't remember the conversation. Jane put it down to a delusion from a high temperature, but decided to try out a regression for herself and recognised her daughter in another life.

Whatever anyone does or doesn't believe, hearing a child say such a thing would probably make you think for a while.

How often do we hear the term, 'He/she is an old soul', sometimes even after a person has gazed into the eyes of a newborn baby? It is as if their soul gazes back out in a way that shows they are not first-timers. These children often demonstrate amazing talents from a very young age.

My youngest son said to me, just before he was three, 'You're not the mummy who threw me off the cliff are you?' Not a lot I could say to that except, 'No.' Even after a little questioning, it was clear that he hadn't had a dream or heard a story, and there seemed to be no other obvious reason for asking the question. He just wondered and thought he'd ask.

Past Life researchers tend to agree that children's memories of past lives are present while they are young but diminish as they get older. They are still there but get buried under the life clutter until a trigger awakens them or they grow up and read this... Do you have thoughts about other lives from when you were a child?

Beliefs

Reincarnation for many is completely normal because it is as it is according to their religious belief. I don't think that those who believe are more likely to remember their other lives. I think it is because they are happy to discuss the subject and have been brought up to have an open attitude about the whole thing.

A fantastic example is Buddhism. Upon the death of each Dalai Lama, the monks search for the next reincarnation. When the child is found, he is taken away, to be trained in his role as Spiritual Leader. There's no debate - it just is.

Depending on the type of people you mix with and know, there are probably many things you would or wouldn't want to talk about. Past life information is the same. It's unlikely that you'd say to a stranger at the bus stop, 'I used to be a Pharaoh you know'. Unless, of course, you recognise the person as one of your eunuchs!

Talking of Pharaohs, according to a psychic, Tina Turner was Hatschepsut in a past life, and if you had to place her anywhere in history that would make sense, wouldn't it?

The Ancient Greeks and Egyptians embraced completely the notion of living several lives and the Greeks spent a great deal of time obtaining information on their past and future from the Oracle. Pythagoras claimed to have memories of his previous lives and Plato, who was a student of Socrates, believed we choose our incarnations in order to learn and progress toward perfection.

Towards the end of his life, Socrates said, 'I am confident that there truly is such a thing as living again and that the living spring from the dead.'

The Egyptians believed that souls migrated and the preservation of bodies through mummification allowed the journey to the next life.

Soul Mates

Have you ever met someone who you felt you already knew? Or had an immense attraction to another person in an almost obsessive way after a brief meeting?

Have you ever had a friend or partner where shifts or changes occurred in the dynamics of the relationship that seemed strangely familiar? You were probably unable to put your finger on what was happening but you knew there was a connection between you both.

Some people think that when you meet your soul mate he or she is the 'one'. Meaning the one and only. From my research it seems that soul mates come and go in our lives. Sometimes they stay a while and you have a good time. Other times might not be so good. In fact, they can verge on being hideously destructive and take much healing in order to recover. Some of my clients and friends have been in and out of relationships that follow a specific pattern of devastation and they know that each subsequent experience will be the same. They even say, 'I only ever attract bad men/women,' or 'All my relationships end badly,' or 'Everyone I have ever been out with has been unfaithful!'

It does seem as if we have to keep repeating a lesson or life experience until we 'get it'. Whatever the 'it' might be. Perhaps to learn not to be a victim or to grow more confident. Maybe to be ourselves and not the person someone else would like us to be.

Life lessons

We learn through experience. On a simple level, we can break that down to the practice it takes to drive, or how to cook. Having many lives gives us the opportunity to learn several lessons: poor to rich, happy to sad, success to failure and anything in-between.

Being reborn or having several lives is often bandied about in a very light-hearted way, usually referring to karma. We have all heard or said comments such as, 'I/he/she must have been good/bad in a past life.'

One of my clients said, 'At least next time round I'll know what to expect!' I expect he will. But I also expect he'll forget.

The solution to everything we ever want to know is generally right in front of us, if only we notice the clues. We do, however, like to be in a comfort zone. Many of us are, or have friends who are, stuck at a point in their lives but are complacent, believing they can't change things so therefore have to put up with them. Many suffer from lack of money, love, freedom or choice, but then something happens or they get a metaphoric kick up the backside and their lives change.

This frequently happens when exploring past and future lives. There is no need to keep on repeating the same old patterns - whether that is by the day or life and realising we can easily swap from same old different day to same old different life really does bring it home. How many times should we hit our head on the wall? Answers, please, on a postcard.

Coincidence, synchronicity or self-fulfilling prophecy?

Valerie was preparing to visit Langkawi in the early Nineties and carried out a therapy session swap with a newly qualified hypnotherapist, Elizabeth. Valerie wanted her session to be on feeling comfortable near dragonflies and Elizabeth wanted some help with a weight problem, which she thought might be a past life issue.

In Elizabeth's regression she described a very traumatic scene of being led to her execution. She was very thin from being imprisoned and was to be killed for what seemed like infidelity. She was totally enraged and professed her innocence and unfairness regarding the whole situation. Also, she was distressed, as it seemed her father was in agreement. Her final statement was, 'People will always remember this wrongness,' referring to the unjust way in which she had been treated.

Everything was sorted out beautifully, and the association of being very skinny just before dying was released. Her safety net was to seek comfort and she got a feeling of security by carrying extra weight.

Valerie then left for Langkawi with a girlfriend. They happened to go before the islands became the thriving tourist venues they are now and there wasn't much to do. On this particular day they went to the tomb of Mahsuri Binti Pandak Mayah. Her story goes something like this: Mahsuri was married to Wan Darus, whose father was the Chief of the island. When her husband was at war fighting the invading Siamese army she was accused of adultery. As it happened her husband had probably snuck home for some loving but that definitely wasn't allowed so she couldn't tell anyone.

Her father-in-law ordered her to be sentenced to death, and as she was led to be executed she repeatedly proclaimed her innocence and laid a curse on the island, 'There shall be no peace and prosperity on this island for a period of seven generations.' This was in 1819.

On her way to the tomb Valerie calmly walked through a cloud of dragonflies. There were so many similarities to Elizabeth's story it was almost laughable. As for Valerie, she felt completely at home with the island and had fabulous business opportunities given to her. She believed that if the island likes you then good luck happens.

Woe betide if it doesn't!

Now for one of my own stories. About 10 years ago I was invited to talk to the ladies at a very exclusive golf club. I parked my car and while I was walking to the venue I saw many women that I would later talk to. My stomach lurched so much I felt sick, and for a brief moment thought I might pass out. To say I felt terror would be an understatement. I couldn't work out what was happening. Each time I'd thought about this opportunity, which without a doubt it was, it had been exciting. But, here I was sweating, feeling faint, convinced they would think I was a fraud who knew nothing and with many other unpleasant doubts trundling through my mind. As it happens, public speaking is the number one fear, beating even death! Except I didn't have that fear, or at least I didn't think I had.

What could I do? Turn and go home and make up a tale of woe? Perhaps I could swoon, pass out in a drama queen way and get saved by the medics?

The time taken to moot these solutions took the same amount of time as walking to the door, and the organiser spotted me. I then heard my inner voice saying, 'Just do it. What's the worse that can happen?'

In I went, gripped the microphone so tightly I thought my arm might fall off. I had an absolute ball. It was brilliant. I loved it. Phew, all was well. They quite liked it too as I was invited back to talk to another group.

At this point I must emphasis the importance of being careful what you wish for! The Universe will, without fail, deliver your desires.

In the very late Nineties I was featured in the *Sunday Times' Style* magazine, in which I talked about breast enhancement with hypnosis (not now but maybe another book!). All hell or heaven, depending which way up you are, broke loose. I was flavour of the month with radio, newspaper and magazine interviews. Two TV offers floated my way after I agreed to the first.

It was an invitation to Nottingham to film at the Carlton Studios in a programme that was about Liz Earle. What a lucky bunny. Off I went to Nottingham and ensconced myself in the rather splendid hotel that Carlton had paid for. A delicious supper was delivered to my room and I lolled on the bed watching TV. All I could think was 'this is the life'

It then all went pear-shaped. I tripped over an imaginary step on my way into the bathroom and felt a twinge in my back. I laughed and thought 'That was lucky, I might have hurt myself.'

About an hour later I tried to get up from the bed and found I couldn't move. My whole lower back was in spasm and the pain was excruciating. Oh, not good. I lay there in tears, hours from home, all alone in a miserable hotel room that up until then had been bliss.

Being a hypnotist meant I could reduce the pain but I think we shouldn't remove all symptoms in case we cause more damage. As for the spasm, it was there to stay. I had the most miserable night and at about 6 in the morning I could bear it no more. Have you guessed the ending? I was carted off in an ambulance to be put into the care of the Nottingham General. It may well have taken a few years but I got my wish from those thoughts at the golf club!

After all these dramatics, I then developed an intermittent stage fright. Intermittent I hear you cry? Yes. A 'now and then' type fear. It was more stressful than having a full-on phobia. I didn't think that experience had given me the problem, it just reminded me it was in my psyche somewhere.

I tried various things on myself when, in a flash of inspiration, wondered if it was a past life issue intruding. I used the process that you will learn about a little later and recalled a memory of being a dancer. They weren't any specific dates but I could smell sweat and makeup. I had David Bowie's 'Diamond Dogs' playing in my head, and as I'm writing this it has just come on in iTunes. It all seemed overtly sexual and I could sense lots of red velvet, and I knew I was wearing frilly knickers. My name was Rose and the name Charles

Sidle (or similar) was in my mind.

In my memory I was given the chance to be a front performer, but stumbled and severely hurt my back. Useless, then, as a dancer. I was back selling my body; same old me again!

I know now the name I was sensing was Zidler and it was the Moulin Rouge. The music playing was a clue from this life - presented to me as a metaphor. Diamond Dogs was the name given to the prostitutes. And, after all, diamonds are a girl's best friend – it's not a dog, touch éclat or GHDs. Imagine if David Bowie was one of my customers in a past life. Excuse me a minute while I have a quick fantasy.

Who knows whether all of this was my creative imagination or I really did Can Can and land in the splits with my drawers on show. All I can say is that now I help people get over their stage fright and occasionally have the urge to lift up the front of my skirt.

The latest 'coincidence' in this story, which I had to be reminded of by my husband, is that we have just set up a new company to produce and sell self-help products and we've called it Lomburlesque. I had to get a bit of sensual glamour in somewhere.

3

The Regressions

Kayt and Penny

Those included here kindly agreed to be 'done' purely for you, the reader.

These regressions were carried out by me using hypnotic meditation. The regressee is in a cosy, relaxed state to allow the subconscious mind to be accessible in order for the memories to be retrieved. It is like being in a gently guided daydream.

As you will see, I have mixed and matched in that some have all my questions included and some are a précis of the experience.

This will help you decide which way works best for you: if you are looking for answers to particular questions or if you prefer to go with the flow and allow whatever will be to be. It will also depend on whether you are seeking answers or healing, closure or release. I did ask the regressees if they had anything in particular they wanted to find out before their journeys began.

I have used the same induction throughout to allow for continuity. The exact scripts are included later in the book. The recordings begin just over the bridge of time as they have 'arrived' in one of their memories.

Some of the regressees shared their thoughts afterwards. For all the grammarians reading this, it is written in the way they spoke.

Kayt
Let me introduce Kayt. A 'K' precedes her responses.

My bit begins, 'You are over the bridge now, and as you step off the bridge you step directly now into a memory of a past life, and just stand a moment, just wait a moment... just be... and as that mist clears you begin to get a sense of Self, a sense of your bearings. In a moment I am going to ask you to speak, and when you speak the sound of your own voice will help you to relax even more deeply' (you won't necessarily have the last instruction - that will depend on your preferred way of memory retrieval).

B: *Are you indoors or outdoors?*
K: Outside.
B: *Are you on your own or are there other people around?*
K: On my own.
B: *And how are you feeling?*
K: Calm.
B: *If you look around what do you see, what do you sense or feel?*
K: Just in an open space, with trees all around me and in front of me there is a big open space that I can walk through, it's just like walking through a forest, but I am not actually in the forest it is either side of me.
B: *And do you get a sense of where you are going or where you have been?*
K: I've just come off of a bridge and I don't know where I am going.
B: *Look down at your feet, get a sense of what you are wearing, describe what you are wearing.*
K: Brown pointed shoes.
B: *Do you have a rough idea of your age?*
K: No.
B: *Just go forwards a little in time, forwards a little in this life so we can see what is happening. What's happening now?*
K: Nothing.
B: *Are you still alone?*
K: I don't know.
B: *Can you hear anything or see anyone?*

K: No.

B: *Do you still get the sense of being outdoors or has that changed?*

K: I am not in the same place.

B: *Okay, where do you think you are now?*

K: It's night time.

B: *Are you in or outside?*

K: Outside.

B: *Can you see a building?*

K: I think there is one behind me.

B: *Can you have a look?*

K: I think it's a castle.

B: *Which castle is it?*

K: I don't know.

B: *Can you explore the castle? Is it all closed?*

K: It's night time there is no one there, there are lights all over it.

B: *Do you know where the castle is?*

K: Near a river.

B: *Do you know the name of the river?*

K: No, but there are trees either side of it, and stars in the sky.

B: *Have you been in the castle?*

K: I know it, but I don't know if I have been in it.

B: *Do you live near the castle?*

K: No, I don't think I know where I am.

B: *Do you know your name?*

K: No.

B: *Go forwards in time now to an event, drift forwards in time now, and again get a sense of Yourself, a sense of You bearings and just describe to me what's happening now.*

K: I think it's festival, it's like, it could be in the castle, it's like outside, but it's also like one of these films where you can see the castle walls and stuff. There are lots of market stalls.

B: *So you are inside the castle grounds?*

K: If it's the same castle.

B: What are you doing there?

K: Standing there in the crowd.

B: Do you know anybody there?

K: No.

B: Are you selling or buying anything or just being there?

K: Just being there. I think I have a purpose, like not meant to be there, like no one knows me. I am not friends with anyone. I am on the other side; I have just got in there.

B: What do you think you might be doing?

K: Gathering information, I think there is a king, and we want to get rid of him.

B: Do you know the name of the king?

K: No, it might be...no, I don't know.

B: Okay don't worry, you will probably know later - remember later. Do you know who you work with then?

K: I might be with a couple of people in there as well, but at the moment I am just in there on my own. I am just on the other side. I am not with any of the other people I am in there with the people that don't like these people, but they're not all there with me. I am just collecting information finding out where everything is.

B: Do the other people there have a name? Are they English, French, do you know who they are?

K: They might be English, I can't hear anything.

B: Do you know who you are trying to get information from? Or are you trying to get into the castle?

K: I am just walking around the festival to know where the king is, but we don't, I think we want to kill him, so we are just walking around and maybe something is going to happen during it, but there is a lady with pink, you know those people with a scarf and she is waving it around, and there are lots of people. We are just working out where everything is, so we know how to, so we can do something later.

B: Do you know what your role is, are you going to be responsible for killing the king, or are you part of a team?

K: I don't know whether I have got to do it, I am just with them, I have just got to help them.

B: Okay, let's just go forwards in time. Just drift forwards in time until this happening, just gather some more information. What is happening now?

K: Sitting by a river, I think, I don't think there are any buildings around, but it's the same scene, and there is a bridge and there are trees on the other side. I don't think I am alone, if there are people they are behind me.

B: Do you know if you got the information?

K: I don't know, it might be happening now. But I have gone away from all the noise, and I am not in the centre of it, I don't want to be involved I just want to get away once I get the information.

B: So you have passed the information to others so they can get on with it?

K: Yes.

B: And do you know the name of the king now?

K: Arthur.

B: Okay, do you know your name?

K: No, I don't need a name.

B: So where do you think you are going now, are you heading home?

K: I don't know, I think I have a family, but I don't want to go back to them. I just need to go on my own.

B: Are you in hiding?

K: No, I don't feel scared, people are not going to find me, it doesn't matter where I go I don't care, I just need to go away, people won't know who I am.

B: Go forwards in time now, until you have gone somewhere else and got away. There is some distance from that event. Where are you, what's happening?

37

K: I think I am in another country now, there are lots of different gold and yellow colours, I have got more money, I could be like a king, I have a lady, and she does things for me, but she is not my family from my other place because we don't have any money. So, I could be somewhere else, because I don't miss my family. I look the way I thought the king might look in the other one, but he had more reds and purples and I have yellows and golds. I have a wife, my wife does everything for me, I just tell her what to do and I don't really care, I don't feel for her, I just know that she belongs to me and she will do it. So I am separated from her emotionally. I cared for my other family but I had to go away from them, I had to get away from everything. The colours are different from the other place. I have got curly shoes on, and they are pointy at the end, and a hat with fluff on it, kind of purple, with kind of sheepy froth round the edges, and a gold stick, and grey curly hair and a beard. And a big bed.

B: *Are you happy here with your wife?*

K: I don't care, I have just got it all, it doesn't matter; I am not sad, or happy, I have just got it all.

B: *And the woman who does everything does she have a name?*

K: Marie or Maria, I think it's Marie, she has long black hair, she has tanned skin, and she wears plain simple clothing, and she reminds me of the woman with the pink scarf at the festival.

B: *What does she call you?*

K: She doesn't call me anything.

B: *Does she talk to you?*

K: She talks but we don't have conversations.

B: *And do you have an idea, or a sensation or thought of where you live?*

K: I think it's, not in a rich country, but there are lots of rich people and I am high up in my room and I can look out and see all my grounds, and I don't know what's beyond that.

B: *Okay. Go forwards in time, go towards the end of that life, near the end of that life and describe what is happening.*

K: I am in bed and there's a light beside me and there's a man that sits by my bed.

B: Who is the man?

K: Someone who is loyal to me, but, I don't think it's my son. I think my son and my wife have gone away and this man is the only person who always stayed with me. He has stayed with me because I can't get up again, I just stay in bed, he gives me drinks from a gold cup, he talks to me and holds my hand.

B: Are you ill or just old, what's happening to you?

K: I am just dying.

B: Okay.

K: And he is the only one who cares.

B: I would like for you to go forwards in time, beyond the point of passing. Leave that life behind until you feel comfortable and safe, and you have a message, or a thought, or a learning message. It might be in the form of a symbol or an idea but it's something you can use now from that memory. It is now uppermost in your mind. What is that thought or learning?

K: I need to think about it...You don't know who cares, no one really does.

B: Now you are just resting in between lives, would it be appropriate to explore the memory of another life now, yes or no?

K: Can do.

B: I would like for you to allow your mind to take you to another life, another life with something of relevance. Allow your mind to take you to another life in another time. 1, 2, 3 you are there, wait a moment, gather your thoughts, get your bearings, get a sense of Self. Are you indoors or outdoors?

K: Outdoors, but not in an open place, just somewhere we belong.

B: You say we, who is 'we'?

K: Me and my daughter.

B: Where is your daughter?

K: Beside me.

B: *Can you describe her to me?*

K: She's young. We are Indian but fair, not really dark, we wear jewellery on our foreheads and carry baskets.

B: *What is your daughter's name?*

K: I don't know.

B: *Do you know where you are going now?*

K: Back to where we live, we have just been out together collecting things.

B: *What have you been collecting?*

K: Things in a basket, food: possibly berries, things to make things with.

B: *Is there a man around? Do you have a husband?*

K: I think I do but he is not part of us.

B: *Okay, go forwards in time now until you have got to your home - where you live, describe that to me.*

K: My daughter is not with us, and he is on his bed, we have a big bed, but I don't know, he doesn't want to sleep in it, so he just stays in his bed. I talk to my daughter and fall asleep with her. He doesn't care about us, we just need him. We just live with him, we have to, it's the way it works, we wouldn't be safe if we didn't so we just act like it's all okay, it's like we are his.

B: *What do you need to be safe from?*

K: From being, it's the way we have to live, if we don't then we are not women any more we are not right we are just things if we don't have a man, so we don't, we are not whole, just not part of anything any more.

B: *Do you live with other people in a group or tribe?*

K: We live in a town, or a village, it's all the way around where we live, it's the way you have to live, there are other women we can talk to, they have to stay in their family and we have to stay with ours. And my daughter is all I have, we just have to live this life, and we can't escape from it, we have to be here, there is no way out. We are not poor, he has money and we are not his slaves, but he does own us, I have never cared for him, but I had to marry him, the other women had to marry their husbands and that's the way it works. But I have got my daughter, so it can't be too bad, until she grows up. I don't want her to grow up.

B: *Go forwards a little in time, forwards in time, until there is an event or a happening that is significant; get a sense of Self and bearings, what is happening?*

K: We are in a courtroom. My husband is quite important and he has got to give a speech. I just have to hold on to his arm, and then fade into the background.

B: *Is your daughter around?*

K: No, she is not here.

B: *Where is she?*

K: She, she is just not here.

B: *Okay, do you get a sense of how old you are?*

K: Not old, or young, I still look nice and my skin is good, I still look good, and that's what matters. I have to look good because he is important and people have to think I love him, he can't have a wife that makes him look bad.

B: *Can you hear his speech, what is he talking about?*

K: I can hear him talking, but I have gone somewhere else, because I am sad. I don't want to listen to him because I don't care.

B: *Why are you sad?*

K: I don't like him, he is not what I want, I don't want him, I know he is important but I don't care to listen to him or about him. I just go somewhere where it's dark and there is no noise, I just don't care about any of it, is not my values it doesn't match up, it doesn't mean anything to me, it's just all bollocks really.

B: *Go forwards in time; go forwards until near the end of that life. What's happening?*

K: He is in bed, I bring him food, he is dying and I'm glad. I care for him, I look after him, while he is dying, I think he has got a disease

41

or something, I know he is going to die soon. I am not sad about it, I am happy but I don't show it, I just look after him.

B: Go beyond the point where he has passed and then go forwards a bit more in time beyond that. What is happening with you?

K: I think I have gone away now.

B: Are you happier now?

K: Hmm, kind of but I can't do anything. I had to escape from everything; because once he was gone they would have done things to me, so I had to escape without them knowing. Now I am worried they will find me. I feel freer, and I think things will get better. I will be able to live a simple life, I don't have much money, I could be free, but I have no one to talk to, I don't really know what to do. If they find me they will hurt me, I don't even know if they are looking for me, I don't know if they care. I don't know if I am running away from anything. There's not much to do.

B: Is your daughter nearby?

K: No, she is gone, she married and is not allowed to talk to me.

B: Is that sad, or is it just the way it is?

K: It has to happen like that, that's how it works, I couldn't do anything, I just hope she is not hurt, I don't think they will hurt her, I think she is okay. I think she is happy enough, but I am on my own now.

B: Go forwards in time now, forwards towards the end of your life now, near the end of that life, what is happening?

K: I don't know, it's not there.

B: Have you already left that life?

K: There isn't an ending, it's all just possibilities.

B: I want you to just leave that life now, float away from that life now, it's in the past as a memory, but you have a learning that you can remember from that, something that will be useful now.

Find yourself on the bridge, bathed in that blue hazy mist, wait for a moment, and let all the memories float back to where they belong. You'll remember all you need to remember and may

remember other little bits. Snippets of information will float into your mind through the day and in dreams of the night.
And now cross back over the bridge...

Thoughts - Post Regression

It seems as though Kayt took a while to get going but she was actually only bothering to share what she felt like sharing. A lot of what is happening is never spoken about, in much the same way as you would describe an event but you wouldn't talk about every tiny detail. In Kayt's descriptions she was very accepting of the way things were – in this life she is single-minded and wouldn't tolerate anything if it wasn't to her liking.

***

Penny
Next up is Penny, who in this life is Kayt's Mum.

B: As before over the bridge, etc... Are you indoors or outdoors?
P: Outdoors.
B: Do you get a sense of being alone, are there other people around?
P: Don't know.
B: And how are you feeling?
P: Nervous.
B: Do you have any idea why?
P: I can't really see where I am. My skin feels very tingly, I am expecting something to happen.
B: Are you aware of any noises?
P: No, it's very quiet.
B: Are you aware of your surroundings at all, do you get a sense of being near buildings or open land?

P: Trees I think, feels like I'm in a wood, but I can't really see.

B: *Are you able to feel the ground underfoot?*

P: No it's almost like being suspended.

B: *Do you have any awareness of what you are wearing if anything?*

P: No not really, my skin feels really strange, there is a tingling going through my feet, then all over my skin. It sort of goes through my bones, it's very strange. I feel like I am not standing upright; I'm lying on something.

B: *Do you have a feeling that you waiting, on your way to something, on your way from something?*

P: I feel like I am in the middle of something.

B: *Allow yourself to just travel a little bit in time, you will become aware of what has happened or is about to happen. You are very safe and detached. It is as if a story unfolds to you. Are you aware of anything happening now?*

P: I am in a large room lying on a raised bed of some kind. It's like I am quite alone, but people are watching me, I am wearing some kind of robe, it is very loose and doesn't cover my feet or arms.

B: *Are you aware of why you are lying here?*

P: It's something to do with a ritual.

B: *Are you part of the ritual?*

P: Yes I am, I think I am lying on the stone, it's as if there is an energy coming up, all on the back of my body, coming up and going through me.

B: *Are you able to describe the ritual, do you know what is going to happen or be done?*

P: No I don't see any movement, I'm just there.

B: *Are you aware of any symbols anywhere at all around you or in the room, in the form of image, fixed objects, ornaments?*

P: There are lights; they are not in the room. It's kind of tunnels, coming out of the room that I'm in, there is light shining out of them, they are all round the room, although the room is quite dark, and I know that there are people waiting in these tunnels. It's like everyone is waiting for something to happen but I can't move, I just lie there, I don't think I am tied. Maybe drugged or something because I do feel very strange.

B: Do you have any idea of self, a name a title of yourself or of anyone there waiting?

P: I have the feeling that I have no name. I just keep thinking 'she'.

B: Do you think you are someone important or someone of nothing?

P: I think I am someone of value.

B: Let's just wait a while, let's just wait, and notice what is happening. Just describe to me anything at all that begins to happen.

P: Somewhere above me there is a light coming through and it shines directly on my body, it's almost as if the sky is opening, the roof. And now I am outside, surrounded by sunlight. I am still lying; I think I am being carried. I feel there are people below me, and I am being carried on some kind of litter. I am being taken somewhere. We are going up towards the top of somewhere. I have the feeling that I am going to just be left.

B: Left forever?

P: I think it is like an ending, maybe I am dying, I don't know, it's as if everyone has gone and I am just there in the outside. It's a very blue sky, there are clouds and things, the sun is shining, I can hear birds, but there are no people.

B: Allow a little more time to pass, and then you will get a feeling that you will die, or something else will happen, what do you feel?

P: I feel like I am sinking just going down and down. It's almost like, not falling, just sliding through the earth.

B: Do you feel you are passing from a life?

P: It's almost like passing through something, it's like a sort of limbo.

B: Are you between lives?

P: Maybe, I don't seem to be in one place or another.

B: *Are you aware of any colour or light around you?*

P: I feel as if there is light on me, but everything else is, not black, but sort of like nothing, it's like being suspended in nowhere.

B: *And do you feel as if you are a person or a spirit, energy or a light?*

P: I feel energy.

B: *Do you feel a male or female energy?*

P: Female.

B: *Are you aware of any sounds or noises whilst in this form of female energy?*

P: There is absolute silence.

B: *How has this formed? Do you have any memory prior to being an energy form?*

P: It is difficult to describe - there is a feeling of people running away from something and to something at the same time and there was some kind of panic. I think maybe I was a sacrifice, maybe an offering. I don't feel as if I was killed but something had to be given, the people don't weigh very much, mostly skin, mostly young people, it is a kind of agitation something had happen, something had to stop and it was an offering, I was an offering of some kind. And it's almost like, I think, I was just made into a deep sleep and then I was lifted and everybody went away but I don't know why. I can't get the feeling of why it was me; it is very vague it is more feelings.

B: *More will come throughout the day. Is there a message that you are aware of now, a message, a learning, anything at all that would be of use now, that might be good to know?*

P: All I keep hearing in my head is just 'be still'.

B: *Okay, you just rest for a moment now, allow yourself to just be bathed in blueness, feel secure safe and comfortable. Would you like to explore another memory? Yes or no?*

P: Yes.

B: From the blue mist from that form of being, an energy form from that in between area, of that complete feeling of nothingness, you can go directly from there to another life. Another life before or since, or from, or forwards, your higher Self will take you to another memory either past or future that would be useful for you to explore now. I am just going to count to three and click my fingers and you will find yourself in another place. One, two, three, 'click'.

Just take a moment. Now get a sense of where you are - thoughts, feelings. Are you indoors or outdoors?

P: I'm outdoors.

B: Are you aware of being alone or are there other people?

P: There are many other people.

B: What are they doing? What's going on? Can you describe what is happening?

P: It's night time, there are many people. There is a big fire, many people around it. A feast or celebration I think, I think we are getting ready to fight someone.

B: To fight someone?

P: They are walking backwards and forward with spears or weapons of some kind. There are men with beards, women. Women are going to fight too, all young people. They've made camp away from somewhere else. It's very, very dark.

B: What are the weapons made of?

P: From wood.

B: What are people wearing?

P: The men are just wearing kind of jacket things, heavy, men have beards and trousers but the women are not wearing so much. I think we may be black.

B: And how are you feeling?

P: I feel very strong and tall, shiny, kind of shiny, the light from the fire is shining on the skin, and I have straps of leather around my clothes, thin straps kind of criss-crossed around my body, and I have straps on my arms, but I am standing back and watching everybody. They seem like they are smaller than me, I think maybe I am watching them. I don't think I am with them; maybe we are going to attack them.

B: *Do you know who they are?*

P: They are just kind of wild people. They are just not important people.

B: *Who are you?*

P: I'm very strong, quite proud; I am just, they are just in the way.

B: *What is your name, do you have a title, what do people call you?*

P: It's something, it's like Ena but it's not.

B: *Okay.*

P: I have very short hair, and it has gold in it.

B: *Gold woven into your hair?*

P: Yes, like tiny threads.

B: *Are you important?*

P: Yes, I'm really important. I am at the front. I go first.

B: *So, going first, are you a leader of people?*

P: Where I go they follow.

B: *In your role as, as maybe queen, is it that type of role?*

P: It's kind of like that, but we don't have that.

B: *Right. You don't have that term?*

P: No.

B: *Do you have any type of term for yourself?*

P: The person who walks first.

B: *Okay, let's just wait a while, let's just see what's going to happen - if you are actually on the attack here, just allow time to unfold in front of you so we can watch.*

P: I have come out from the trees, I don't pay them much attention, they run to the fire, but there is no real fight because all these 'nothing' people just kind of run away and they do nothing, they have nothing. Why are they there, what was the point? There was no fun, no pleasure. I think, I think we come from a different land, we have crossed somewhere, and we were looking for something more than we had behind us, but there is nothing of real value to take here. The people have no spirit, they have nothing really. I don't know if we'll stay, and it's colder here.

B: *What's happening now?*

P: I feel really cold, I can feel the shivers in my body, it is not a good place to be. Even though the fire was there you can see they have to have fire and heavy coats because it's cold, it's a cold dark place and not a good place to stay. There is a bad feeling here, it's not good place to be.

B: *You had best head away, are you going somewhere new or will you head back?*

P: I think we will head back. I think we will return, we have boats.

B: *Do you know where you are returning to?*

P: It's west, just west.

B: *What are your boats made from?*

P: They are wooden boats, they are thin and tall, they go fast, but they are very long, we can get many people, but when you are on the boat it's hard to see over the sides, because the sides are high, but we don't have to travel very far. There are big rivers - these boats are very good for rivers.

B: *Are you on the boat now, are you rowing away?*

P: I don't row!

B: *Do people row you?*

P: Yes, there are people that row.

B: *Just go forwards in time now, forwards in time to a time of significance, an event, a happening of importance.*

At this point Penny popped to another life. This can happen and the memories often run in a random order. Sometimes there can be a tendril of similarity, but not necessarily. This shows Penny is very much a free spirit and her mind took her to where it might be useful.

B: *What's happening?*

P: We are out in the plains. I am riding a horse. I am a man, I'm an Indian man and I have one feather, which I feel isn't very many. I'm quite a young man. I am just riding out in the sunshine. I think I am riding by myself. I have a feeling of space, huge spaces. I am carrying some kind of short spear, a thin light thing, maybe I am hunting or something, it's just a feeling of space and there are trees, grass everywhere as far as you can see, I don't have any sense of purpose I am just riding.

B: *Are you aware at all of where you have come from or where you are going towards?*

P: I have the feeling I have been alone for some time. I think I may be on a quest - a quest. I don't know what it is I am looking for. I am looking for something. There's no real urgency. It seems to be important that I am alone; I have to do something while I am by myself and when it's done I can go back. There is a bird of some significance, maybe some kind of hawk or falcon, it's a small bird of prey, and I know it has some connection with me; it's just me and the bird.

B: *Go forwards a little in time in this life, forwards a little bit. What is happening?*

P: There are mountains in front of me. I have to find a cave in these mountains and I must spend some time in this cave and I can't return until a certain amount of time has passed. It's some kind of right of passage, I think I am to be some kind of holy man but I have to pass this test and until I have done this I will not have crossed the chasm or something like this. I have to cross something in mind, while I am in this cave. And it's years, it's lots of time but I will know when this time is finished and when this is finished and I have crossed this thing, I can return. Yes, that's it.

B: *Let's go forwards in time until when you know it is time that you can return, to an event or a happening or experience that you are waiting for. What is happening?*

P: I don't have any answers.

B: For yourself or for the people?

P: I feel I have failed, I don't have any answers, and nothing changes.

B: What is happening now? Are you going back to the people or are you staying?

P: No, I can't go back.

B: What will happen, what is happening? Let these feelings flow from you, let these feeling go, what is happening with you.

P: There are no answers (crying) endings cannot be stopped.

B: Is that not an answer in itself?

P: The way it has finished.

B: What will you do?

P: I just have to find new meaning in a different place. I cannot take this message back.

B: Will the people want to know what happened to you?

P: They will just think I have failed or been killed, it's not important, it's only one life.

B: Where are you going now?

P: Just away. I will go maybe to the mountains, different mountains. I will just go where my feet lead.

B: Okay, go forwards to the end of that life, near the end of that life now, where are you, what's happening?

P: I am an old man now. I am by a stream, it's simple.

B: Are you by yourself?

P: No, no, family, children, grandchildren. Now I am more at peace. There was nothing that could be done. Sometimes things must pass, things must change. Change will always happen - just live our lives and hope to grow a little wiser.

B: Allow Yourself now to just pass from that life, just pass from that life now. Beyond the moment of passing - leave that life behind and have that immense feeling of calm and peace and all the information that you have gathered is yours to keep. And you will find more pieces of your life - more and more pieces of the life's jigsaws will

51

now fit for you and you will be given more and more pieces in your dreams.

Find yourself back on the bridge now, very safe now, surrounding in the blue mist, very safe, leaving behind the past, keeping a hold of all memories that are helpful and useful, and beneficial. Come back from the bridge now, back to your door to your special place. The door can go now; it is only there when you want it to be there. It is the door of time.

***

Penny very kindly sent me her thoughts after the regression. Here they are, in her own words.

'Before my regression, Barbara asked if there was anything in particular I was looking for, and my reply was to see if there was some kind of theme, something that would help me with my current life.

'I experienced three very different lives and, having had time to think about them more deeply, I have the following observations:

'All three involved some kind of quest, or journey into the unknown, with no guaranteed outcome.

'All were to do with a perceived benefit to my people, rather than just myself.

'All involved a feeling of personal pride, or recognition.'

Life 1
'As a highborn maiden I had offered my life as a sacrifice. This did not involve me being 'killed' as such. I was proud to be chosen. The sensation was of being heavily sedated. I was taken from an underground location and left high on a mountain top. It subsequently felt as though I was being absorbed into the earth in some way. At no time was I aware of the identities of anyone around me.'

Life 2

'I was a female warrior, a leader. (I have since felt strongly that we were a tribe of powerful women where men were subservient.) Again, I was unaware of the identities of those around me, there was a strong sense that personalities were unimportant to me, neither those of my people nor my targets. I sense that I was extremely arrogant!

'I had left my own land in order to gain something for my people that was not available in our homeland. However, these people had nothing of value to us, not even any honour in taking their lives. I had to return humiliated.'

Life 3

'I was a young Native American travelling on a spiritual quest, or test, to find answers for my people who were threatened and despairing.

'I was very proud to go as I was sure that I'd return with strong messages from the spirits and our ancestors and receive a lot of recognition as a powerful medicine man. However, I received nothing positive to take back to them, our time was over and there were no answers for them. I felt a great sense of failure and despair, such that I couldn't face returning home. So I moved on to a different journey with no idea where I was going but quite unconcerned on a personal level. I ended up as no great medicine man, just an ordinary grandfather, but contented all the same.

'I thought about the themes, or messages, in these lives quite a lot for the next few days, to see what I could learn from them and these are my thoughts:

'I have a tendency to be self-sacrificing, to put the well-being of others above that of myself and this is not necessarily a good thing as it means I am not valuing myself enough. It need not be an automatic response to put myself last and doesn't always serve others effectively. And it's a form of arrogance. It's important to have the courage of my convictions and act on them but I need to let go of the outcome.

'I have been a very strong woman in the past and the memory of this life has made me braver, more prepared to stand up for myself and to take risks.

'Life is primarily a spiritual journey, part of which is experienced on earth. There are no answers because just living life is the answer. The whole point is live, experience and learn. It's all temporary anyway so keep a sense of perspective and just get on with it!'

A short while after her regression, Penny told me that this knowledge had given her courage.

There is nothing for me to add as Penny has shared the meaning to her of those lives and how they relate to her now.

**

Lizzie, Andrea and Kristian

Lizzie

Let us now find out about Lizzie's regression. My questions are not included but you will know what I've asked by the things she is saying. When Lizzie moves through time I have preceded the line with my instructions.

L: I'm outside on my horse walking through the street, a market place. There's a younger man on another horse. I'm wearing white. My horse is grey.

We've come back home. I see houses on either side and people in the market place, it's very busy. I've got a suit of armour, chains - oh, it's so heavy. I'm wearing a suit of chains. My horse has got a flag on it. King's men: King Richard. I'm the Commander. It's so heavy. We've been at war fighting the French. We lost many men.

I'm so thirsty, I need water. There's a well - I must get to the well, my horse needs water too.

My name is Richard. The other man is Arthur. They call me The Brave. We're at the well feeling a little better now. We are going to the castle, Leeds Castle. We're just going home to the castle. They've opened the drawbridge. I'm so tired: exhausted. Some people have come to get my horse – we've come straight from the battle. Others are on their way back.

I'm in the courtyard. People are welcoming me back. 'Welcome back, Sire,' they are saying.

I need to find Mary, my betrothed. She's waiting for me. She's with child. I'm going up the stairs in the turret. There is talk about Chichester - a great fire. I'm with Mary, she is kissing my ring. She's looking well. She's crying with happiness. I've got a dog. There's trouble in the West but for now I can rest.

B: *Drift forwards in time...*

L: I have a son. He is called Harold. Mary is well. She is a beautiful mother. I have to go away soon to the coast to fight the French. We will prevail. There is no word from the King of Scotland. I have sent one of my men to the border. We shall see if I get a response. He will follow me down with the reply.

I am on the way now. There are six hundred of us. We are travelling through the wood with some on foot. We must set up a camp and wait until daylight. We eat venison, mushrooms from the wood and chickens that we brought. My men cook the food.

Some of the men are not well; they are coughing. I am well though just a little tired and have an injured arm. I was struck with an arrow. It is healing.

B: *Drift forwards in time...*

L: (Utter despair in her voice) Bodies everywhere, my men and some French. My horse is down. I'm surrounded by men moaning – it's been a bloody battle. Hard to tell if we won over the French but I believe so.

I'm exhausted. I've lost many men. I've hurt my arm again and I have pains in my chest. I was hit with a sword. I'm badly injured. I'm cold. And there's still no word from Scotland. It's a mess but we have a few men left. I have survived but I'm wracked with pain. There is nothing I can have - I must go home. I must find a horse...

I've found a horse. It's exhausting but almost coming up to my horse. It's very difficult, I only have the use of one arm. There are bodies everywhere.

B: Drift forwards a little...

L: Going home. I am slumped on my horse, I must travel many nights and many days. I'll survive, just. There are a few men with me.

I'm back home in bed. My injuries are okay. Mary and my son are here. I can rest and recover for now.

B: Forwards in time...

L: I don't know where I am. I'm just floating, it's all white. I must have passed from that life. Scurvy! It was scurvy. I'm just floating in white. I'm in a beautiful garden. I've been here before. I'm a spirit between lives - just left that life.

B: Message, learning...

L: That no one should fight and take each other's lives for the sake of war.

A short while after the regression I asked Lizzie what she thought the relevance of recalling that memory might be in connection to her personal life, and her reply was, 'I can conquer all and get over something horrific.'

Again, there is nothing for me to add.

***

Andrea

Please now welcome Andrea. This regression is presented to you as an essay. As before you will know what I have asked by the things she says.

Andrea experienced a bit of a block to begin with so we used the disassociated TV screen method. Again, this is included for your delectation.

A: I can see a girl playing hopscotch. A little girl. She's wearing a blue dress with an underskirt. She's got red hair tied back: age 6 and happy. She's on the pavement outside houses. The houses are red brick terraced. Now, she's running down the street to her older brother who is calling her. He's picked her up and is spinning her around. She's happy. I can't hear them.

B: *You can turn up the volume on the remote control.*

A: I can hear them now. Her name is Sarah and he's getting her in for tea. She seems very happy and settled. Her brother is called Michael. Their house is on the same Street. They've gone in the house. The Mum is there wearing a green jumper, brown pants and an apron.

They're sat at the table. Mum is in kitchen and it's all brightly lit. They are having chips for tea and there's chicken in the oven. No Dad. Mum's humming a song. The kids playing at the table. It's a happy house although quite small.

Having their tea now - told to sit down properly. They are eating it quickly. I think it's a weekend. No TV.

I'm in the house with them now. The furniture is plain and there is a kitchen and front dining room. Table, chairs, bookshelf. There is red sauce on the table. It all seems quite old-fashioned - early Sixties.

There are two beds in the brother and sister's room that they share: not tidy, clothes and toys everywhere. It's very small. Just two bedrooms upstairs – I'm going back down. There's a toilet outside at the back. No bathroom but there is a tub in the yard and bucket. It's a small dark yard. It's getting dark now. The house very cramped. They read a lot in the evenings and there are children's annuals.

The Mum reads, sews and knits. I can see Charles Dickens' books and a knitting basket in the corner with needles sticking out and balls of red wool. There's a red jumper half finished for the daughter. Not sure if there's a dad. They don't seem to be expecting anyone as there isn't an extra plate.

B: *Forward in time...*

A: There's a carnival in the street. There is lots of bunting on the houses. Everyone's out, all the kitchen tables lining the street. Bottles of beer. Celebrating – it's something to do with the Queen. Blue, white and red. The name *Crowther* comes into my head. Party now and it's busy. The women are running about bringing out food. Lots of chatting. Children laughing and crying because they don't like getting nudged about. The food is bread, cheese, cakes and stew.

B: *Forward in time...*

A: There's a clearing of trees. It looks tropical. There's a waterfall. I've got my bikini on and I'm jumping in the water. It's like a deep canyon. I'm about 25. I'm alone at the minute, think I'm on holiday. It might be a jungle. Why am I in a jungle in a bikini?

I'm drying myself down. It's really warm. I'm walking though to some huts. Holiday huts. Definitely on holiday. There's a cocktail for me made by the waiter. It's a very private place. I must have a lot of money. I can see five huts here that belong to different people. There's a man in my bedroom - my lover. I should know his name. He's lying in a towel on the bed just had a swim as well. He's reading a blokey magazine. He's good looking. We're both quite glamorous and wealthy. He's wearing gold. He's rich. Probably there's a lot of stuff I don't need to know about. He doesn't tell me a lot about it. Up to no good. I'm brushing my hair, it's brown and I'm tanned. He's got champagne and mine's a Martini made with fruit. I like it here. We're here for a month. We get away a lot.

Then we go back to London but I'm a bit bored in London. Do you know I don't really think I like him that much. He doesn't like me to do stuff. He just wants me to be glamorous. He's older than me. I lunch a lot in places like the Savoy and posh hotels in London; the Meridian and private clubs. It's boring sometimes though.

B: Forward in time...

A: I'm in Piccadilly Circus, it's all very, very busy. I'm stood in the middle with everything spinning around me - like a whirlwind. I just need to slow it down. I'm sat down now with my head in my hands trying to stop things from going so fast. People are looking at me funny. I think I'm panicking, I'm not sure where I'm going. I've had to stop. There's a man coming over now, an old man. I think he's a newspaper seller. He's grabbing my hand and leading me to where he's got his papers and sitting me on a pile of papers. His hands are on my shoulders. He's saying it's okay. I'm crying. He's looking around for someone to help me.

I'm about 25 to 30, out on my own. I'm feeling better now and drying my eyes. The man's kind he has just got his hand on my shoulder but he's selling a paper. He's acting like it's okay, quite normal, like it's not really any trouble but not really any big deal: like he sees it all the time. I feel a lot better now.

B: Drift forwards a little...

A: I can't get out of Piccadilly. I'm still there, I can see the buildings tall in front. It's dark now, though the lights are on the car seems really fast. They're not really fast it just seems fast. I feel like I'm stuck here: like I'll never get out of here. I think it's the same day. I'm just going to walk across the road. I'm walking down the street, past Starbucks. I still don't know where I'm going. I'll go into Starbucks. I've had enough of not knowing where I'm going. I'll just go and have a coffee. I've been in Starbucks before. I'm getting a newspaper. Don't know which paper but there's been a plane crash. I've just had a horrible thought - thinking that maybe my husband would have been on the plane but I'm not that bothered.

Is that awful?

I don't think he was a very good person. He did a lot of travelling. Well, I'll do what I like now. Don't have to lunch with all those silly cows that were his friends. Or the wives of his friends. I feel really happy. I feel terrible. I only feel terrible because I feel really happy.

My phone's going in my bag (she had a 'silent' conversation). He was on the plane. It was my mum on the phone. I wonder how she's got to know before me? I think the police have called her, but they could have called me, they've got my number. Oh well.

I don't know now but I can do anything really can't I? I'm going to be very rich as he'll have left his money to me. I'm a bit worried as well though - who knows where some of it was and what was going on. I just don't know. I think I'll go away for a year – we had no children so I can do what I like.

B: Forwards to near end of life...

A: I'm writing letters, sat at my desk with paper and pens. My hair is tied back long and grey. The room is dark. I'm writing goodbye letters, I'm on my own. Writing to friends.

I think I know I've got an illness but I don't know what. Writing, sorry I have to go, I don't want to leave everybody. I'm a bit muddled. I'd quite like to live a bit longer really. I'm only young still, in my fifties. I've got a nurse and she's younger than me. I'm just in this one room like a study. I can still get about.

I'm just thinking of a song – can't remember who it's by but it's the one about the person that's dying and he says, 'Goodbye my friends it's hard to die when all the birds are singing in the sky'. I feel like writing it in the letter but feel like it's a bit, almost like a joke. My friends would think it was a joke, a bit naff but I still want there to be a bit of humour in there. But, I can't. I'm not sure how I feel. I never did have children; I think I wish I had. I think it's friends I've got more than family. I don't really want to wait though now. There's probably not much for me to do here now. I think I'll end my letters now and then lie down and go to sleep. Not even sure if I'll wake up tomorrow. I'm not in pain.

I've not got long. I think I've got cancer. Whispers - *probably because I was glad when my husband died.* I don't really feel frightened. The nurse has come in to pull the curtains like any other day. She doesn't stay over. She's going now. I'll just have a drink of water. I feel like I should have a last drink of vodka or something. I've not had anything for ages while I've been ill. But why not now? I wonder if the nurse has got some. I'll have a look in the cupboard. There's some whisky there, a nice one. I think I'll have some and savour it - mmmhhh. Feel a bit woozy now, I've not had a drink for ages. It's quite pleasant. I think I'll just go to sleep.

Then passed away.

B: *In peace - knowledge, learning or message?*

A: Lots of things: it's important for me to be a free person. I felt guilty because my husband had died but he wasn't a very good person and he didn't really treat me very well and then I was glad to be free of him. But, it would probably have been better if I'd never got in that situation in the first place. I need to trust myself. Trust my own instincts. I don't need to be lost I just need to spend some time thinking about it.

***

Andrea also kindly shared her thoughts, as follows:

'I think I was a little surprised at my regression, once it had unfolded. The first part, watching the girl and her brother, seeing the street decorated in bunting for the royal celebration (whichever that was!), didn't really mean anything to me. I couldn't make any sense of it, and I was quite glad to move on from it because it was boring me (can you be bored in regression?!).

'However, the second part was more interesting. When I first emerged in a beautiful exotic location, surrounded by tropical plants and trees in the heat, I was quite looking forward to what may ensue, expecting cocktails and fun with a handsome husband! However, in our beach hut/luxury accommodation, I soon realised that I didn't actually like him all that much and our marriage was a sham! This was a bit of a surprise.

'Moving on in the regression to being in Piccadilly Circus in London, I was having a breakdown by the newspaper seller (who was kind to me). I can only think now this was because I couldn't stand my life with this husband. When I walked on and had a coffee in Starbucks, and read the newspaper, I knew that he'd died on a plane and I was glad. I still am fairly puzzled by the regression.

'I can only think that it showed me that I do value my freedom and independence, and I would hate to be in a situation that I felt trapped by, such as a shoddy marriage to a man because he is rich! I'm not sure - because I've always known that I value my freedom and independence so that was nothing new to learn. I suppose I've always yearned for a little bit more luxury - although it's not a great deal in my life, but maybe the regression showed me that I wouldn't want this luxury at any price? Which I know as well!

'I suppose the regression has caused me to ask more questions rather than give me answers, as I don't feel that any answers were apparent for me. Maybe I'm left with wondering just why I was in that position with the rich (then dead) husband.

'I learned a lot. It's important for me to be a free person. I felt guilty because my husband had died but he wasn't a very good person and he didn't really treat me very well and then I was glad to be free of him. I need to trust myself. Trust my own instincts. I don't need to be lost I just need to spend some time thinking about it.

'And then how funny - here I say I learned a lot and now I'm not sure what I learned!

'What this says to me now is something about guilt - I went through a process of being in a position where I could have felt really guilty and didn't as much as maybe I thought I "should have" - is this why I have a tendency to experience guilt now?

'I'm not as riddled by guilt as a lot of other women.

'I think it also says something about what matters in life - definitely not being bogged down by material things, because they don't matter if you're not happy.'

***

Kristian

Please now welcome Kristian.

B: Are you indoors or out doors?
K: Outdoors.
B: Are you alone or with other people - what is happening around you?
K: *There are children playing in the woods.*
B: Are you in the woods or on the outside of the woods?
K: The edge of a clearing.
B: What are you doing there?
K: Walking back.
B: Walking back to where?
K: Back home.
B: Where have you been?
K: Walking a long way away.
B: How do you feel to be walking back home?
K: Tired…but happy.
B: Are you carrying anything, do you have anything with you?
K: Sticks.
B: When you look down at your feet what are you wearing?
K: Furs.
B: Do you have an assortment of fur or a particular fur?

K: Different.

B: *And how far away are you from home now?*

K: Very close.

B: *And, does your home have a place, where is it?*

K: In the clearing in the woods.

B: *Is there any body waiting for you?*

K: Yes lots of people

B: *Are they your family?*

K: Yes.

B: *Who of your family are waiting?*

K: My brothers and sister.

B: *What is your sister's name?*

K: Mira.

B: *What's your name?*

K: I'm not sure.

B: *And the children that are playing, are they children you know? Are they your family?*

K: Everybody knows everybody.

B: *And do you call people by name?*

K: Yes.

B: *And do they call you by your name?*

K: Yes.

B: *As you walk towards your home then, describe to me your home.*

K: It's timber…and thatch. And it's very strong and surrounded by forest.

B: *Does the forest have a name?*

K: It's all the forest.

B: *What time of year is it?*

K: Summer.

B: *Is it very warm?*

K: Yes.

B: *And the children that are playing, what kind of things do they wear? How do they play, what do they do?*

K: They are chasing each other, they are wearing skins.

B: And the sticks that you were carrying, what is the purpose of the sticks?

K: To make arrows.

B: Are they arrows, are they used for hunting?

K: Yes.

B: Hunting animals?

K: Yes.

B: Do you ever have to defend yourself with the use of arrows?

K: Yes.

B: Who do you defend yourself against?

K: Others.

B: Others who mean you harm?

K: Yes.

B: Who are these others?

K: Different people.

B: Do they look differently to you or the same?

K: The same but different.

B: What colour are their skins?

K: White.

B: Is your skin white?

K: Yes.

B: What colour is your hair?

K: Black.

B: Is it long or short?

K: Long.

B: Do you have hair on your face?

K: Yes.

B: And where are you now?

K: Outside the house.

B: As you go into the house just describe to me what happens?

K: Smoke stings my eyes.

B: *Is something cooking?*

K: Something is always cooking.

B: *What is cooking today?*

K: Deer.

B: *Who is cooking it?*

K: My wife.

B: *What is your wife's name?*

K: I can't remember.

B: *Is she there now - is she pleased to see you?*

K: Yes.

B: *What is she saying to you?*

K: That I have done well.

B: *And, how are you feeling?*

K: Pleased.

B: *Do you have anything else apart from the sticks?*

K: Yes.

B: *What do you have?*

K: My knife.

B: *Can you describe your knife?*

K: It is well made.

B: *Did you make it?*

K: No.

B: *Who did make it?*

K: Another.

B: *Do you have people or somebody that have specialist tasks, people who are very good at making things like knives?*

K: Yes.

B: *And when you eat the deer do you eat with your family and other people?*

K: Yes.

B: *And do you eat inside the building?*

K: Yes inside.

B: *What else is in the building?*

K: There are skins and beds. And a fireplace.

B: *And if you look out from the building or look outside, are there other buildings like that?*

K: Three.

B: *And who lives in the other buildings?*

K: Friends.

B: *Can you recall any of their names?*

K: Lots of names, yes…I can't remember.

B: *Are people known to you, by their first name or do they have a family name or a collective name?*

K: Everybody has a name.

B: *Do they have one name?*

K: Yes.

B: *What do people do with their time, how is time used?*

K: Busy.

B: *Busy doing what?*

K: Building, mending, cooking and making things.

B: What things are made?

K: Frames for carrying. A boat.

B: *Can you see a newly made boat, or a part-made boat that you could describe to me?*

K: Big enough for three or four. And it's heavy.

B: *And what is it made from?*

K: Wood.

B: *Is it all wood?*

K: Yes.

B: *And are you near to water?*

K: We have to pull the boat.

B: *And do you pull the boat to a river or is it the sea?*

K: A river.

B: *And then where would you go to in the boat?*

K: Sometimes up the river sometimes down the river, we have other boats.

B: *And do you meet other people when you go out on the boat?*

K: Not usually, no.

B: *Do you go out fishing?*

K: Yes.

B: *And would you go out one boat at a time or several boats?*

K: Just one.

B: *I would like for you to drift forward in time a little bit now in this life time, take yourself forward in time now to a significant time and event, a significant event. Just drift forwards in time, just take a moment to get a sense of self and place, and describe to me please what is happening.*

K: There's fire. It's bad.

B: *Tell me about the fire.*

K: It's everywhere.

B: *What's happened?*

K: The forest is burnt, everything's burnt.

B: *What are people doing?*

K: They are unhappy and running.

B: *How was it burnt, was it an accident, did someone do it?*

K: Yes.

B: *Who's done it?*

K: The others.

B: *Have people been hurt?*

K: Yes.

B: *Have people been killed?*

K: Yes.

B: *By the fire or by the others?*

K: Both.

B: *How are your family?*

K: They are hurt.

B: *And where are you all now?*

K: In the village.

B: *How's it looking?*

K: The roofs are burning.

B: Is there anything you can do?

K: No.

B: Are the others still there?

K: They are running.

B: Where are they running?

K: Anywhere.

B: Are your people fighting them?

K: Yes.

B: What are they using to fight them?

K: Spears and an axe, I haven't got my bow.

B: Where's your bow?

K: I don't know.

B: Oh dear, do you have a knife?

K: No. I don't know where it is.

B: Go beyond this memory now. Go beyond this memory, beyond this event, what is happening?

K: The entire village is gone.

B: Are you okay, are you all right, are you hurt?

K: My left arm hurts.

B: What's the matter with your arm?

K: My arm is cut and I'm burnt from ashes in the face.

B: What about other people in your family?

K: They're all gone, there is lots of pain.

B: Is your wife all right?

K: I don't know where she is, she's not there.

B: What about your brothers and sister?

K: Mira is there, brothers, some.

B: Where you live, is somebody in charge, is there somebody you look to for help or guidance?

K: No. No.

B: When you have to make choices and discussions would you all decide together?

K: Yes.

B: *How to behave, how to act?*

K: Yes.

B: *What will you all now do now that the village is burnt?*

K: Leave the place, it's not good.

B: *Where will you all go?*

K: Another part of the forest.

B: *Is that what's happening now?*

K: Yes.

B: *Is your wife about yet?*

K: I think so.

B: *She's just busy is she?*

There was a pause and then Kristian brought himself out of hypnosis. The following is the discussion that immediately followed:

K: Oh, that's weird, huh.

B: *Just take a moment, it's all right.*

K: What a peculiar experience (big sigh).

B: *Would you like a drink or anything, some water?*

K: No, I'm fine, thanks.

B: *Have you just made a choice to leave there or have you just spontaneously come back?*

K: I just came back.

B: *Just think enough is enough, eh?*

K: Yes, I still remember that.

B: *What are your thoughts?*

K: Wow, that's really weird, um...

B: *Shall I leave this recording?*

K: Yeah, sure. Phew, it's hard to collect my thoughts, really, it's like I just lived through that, good grief, wow, I'm quite amazed at the power of hypnotherapy. That was...a very strange experience... I was aware that I'm still who I am, but I also wasn't here, I was wherever I was. It was very, very odd.

B: How do you feel now?

K: I can still see it actually. I can see the buildings.

B: Are you able to put it into any context of time?

K: Yes. It was a prehistoric experience. Palaeontology is a particular interest for me in life. In fact I've always had an uncanny interest in it. There was no metal - pre-metal.

B: Are we in a chicken and egg situation? How do feel at the moment.

K: I feel a bit light-headed, like part of me is still there.

B: That is because you came back suddenly. Did it just switch off, Kristian?

K: Yes. Whatever was going on there was not good and I didn't want to be there, I'd rather be here.

B: What you can do later, away from here, is thank yourself inside and close it so you have the memories that you choose to recall. And, you may find that later an event in your dreams will lead to more information that will lead to closure on that.

And with that we finished.

Richard, Sylvie and Marusja

Richard

Let's find out now about Richard. Richard has a disincarnate Soul mate, Lorelei, who features, joins in and advises throughout his regressions. She also returns at the end of the book.

B: Are you inside or outside?

R: Outside.

B: Do you get a sense or a feeling, do you know if you're alone, and are there others around?

R: There is someone there.

B: Are you aware of how you are feeling?

R: Drifting.

B: *You say there is someone there. Who do you think might be there?*

R: Not sure, not sure if it's my guardian or not.

B: *Be peaceful. Take your time; allow your thoughts, feelings, imagery to flow to you, feel detached and very peaceful. Just go with the flow, allow what will come to come. And describe to me what is happening, as you relax more and more deeply.*

R: I haven't anything definite at the moment, it's just dark.

B: *Allow yourself to float to where you feel completely comfortable. Your mind will keep you safe, and will give you information that is available, that will be relevant to you now, information that is good to know. What are you feeling or sensing?*

R: I seem to be on a precipice, overlooking a pine forest. It's not... Oh don't do that!

B: *Just allow these images to come through to you, describe to me what's happening.*

R: It's as if somebody has guided me to jump off, and I am floating down through the trees.

B: *Who guided you?*

R: Lorelei, it's still indistinct. It's very dark, but it seems to be on a bit like a track or path, on a steep slope, angled up to the right with a lot of broken trees as well as upright trees.

B: *Are you still floating or are you on the ground?*

R: I seem to be floating a foot or two above the ground for some reason.

B: *Alone, or with company?*

R: I have somebody with me, but nobody visible.

B: *Sense who it is that is with you.*

R: Yes it's Lorelei. I don't know what she is up to, or what we are supposed to be doing. What we are meant to be seeing...

B: *Just wait a moment, allow yourself to be guided.*

R: I am up again; I am sort of floating over a forested landscape, not quite mountains but more than hill, bright blue sky and a relatively low sun.

B: Do you know where this landscape is?

R: Not really, no.

B: Is it familiar to you?

R: No, not seen it before.

B: Do you sense a time of year - a season?

R: Late spring, early summer. There is a building off to the right in the trees, but I don't know if we are going there.

B: Just let yourself go wherever you are going. And allow this experience to gently unfold itself to you and describe it to me.

R: It seems as though we have gone down, and it seems as though there is a building forming in images and now fading away, we are still there but it is indistinct, it's an odd mixture of being in a building and in a forest at the same time. I am sensing it's 17th century style, a large drawing room kind of place.

B: Become more aware of a sense of self.

R: (sighed) I have pulled back now, I am getting a sense of Self, there is somebody in front of me (myself). Wearing a frock coat type thing, with a goldie appearance I think mainly brown, with white frills underneath and a blonde curly wig, and a grey tri-corn hat.

B: What is your name?

R: Marcus, but that can link back to so many other things - thousands of years before, but just before you asked there was a woman coming towards him, sort of up a slope, yes he is outside now on the path, a sloping path, with a wooden fence to the right, it's like a thirty degrees slope, a single rail fence. The woman's got a huge brown and white skirt, mostly white top, puffy sleeves tight neat hair style, oh and a fan or something. Oh, I had another thought then; I think it is wishful thinking, something that came up a few weeks ago, about Countess Caroline.

B: Go with the flow whether it is wishful or not.

R: Oh yes, she is inviting me in. Okay, its still a sort of mixture of

73

inside and outside, but it's a large room, dark decoration, very large windows, has tables and lit candelabra, it's dusk, there are a few other people in frock coats, oh 1799.

B: *Do you know the names of any of these people, any of the Countess' guests?*

R: I am sitting down with a chap with a grey wig, tied at the back, his name is Robert, he is lounging back, looking out the window. Oh, I am Marcus come in. Marcus Browning. Nothing to do with Wimple Street I hope.

B: *So who are these people, what are they doing there?*

R: They are friends who have gone to visit. Oh, there is a coach carriage outside, mixture of coloured horses, white one, a grey one and a dark one.

B: *What colour is the carriage?*

R: Dark brown with a bit of gold painted on the main structures.

B: *Is there anyone in the carriage or getting out?*

R: Yes, she is wearing a dark dress and a plume hat, carrying a parasol type thing, saying, 'Hang on, wait for me'. I think it's Lorelei, and I think she was Emma then.

B: *Is she a friend, or are you related, are you a couple?*

R: She is my wife, she is calling Caroline the Countess Caroline. I don't know whether it's just a time slip or whether that was her name then as well. Because for the last few weeks I have felt there was a link.

B: *And you have gone to the Countess, possibly, Caroline's house, for a particular event? Or a celebration? Or just a gathering of friends?*

R: It's Caroline's birthday.

B: *Right, how old is she?*

R: sixty-two, no, oh well your hair is white I suppose. Sixty-two. Apparently!

B: *Lovely, are you having a special meal, is it a birthday meal, or a party, what's happening?*

R: It's quite a salubrious meal; I obviously wasn't a vegetarian then. Large fowls on the table.

B: What's the name of the house?

R: Ashbrook House, came to me as you asked.

B: Is this Emma giving you information? Or do you just know?

R: You know it's the Akashic don't you? We are all in it. That was Emma/Lorelei.

B: And has the countess received gifts, in celebration of her birthday?

R: Yes there seems to be a lot, a table full, on the dark back wall away from the window.

B: How lovely, are they open, or is she opening them, or are they wrapped?

R: Some are wrapped some are open, there is a mirror leaning against the wall, partially unwrapped.

B: What have you bought her, what have you taken for her?

R: Oh! Right, a couple of horses that were tethered behind the coach.

B: That's very lovely.

R: Yes, I must have had a bit more money then.

B: So what do you do, how do you earn your money?

R: Property, real estate, which sounds a bit American, it's just the terminology I guess.

B: You are very good at it then!

R: Yes, I seem to have been.

B: Let's just drift a little bit, in time, drift a little maybe forwards, in that life, that memory.

R: Oh! Oh!

B: Report back what is happening.

R: Oh, the coach went over a cliff or something.

B: Oh dear.

R: It was about two years later.

B: Who was in the coach?

R: I was.

B: *Alone?*

R: Not sure, I am feeling a bit mixed, I don't know if it was just me or both of us.

B: *Okay, come back in time, go the other way. Come this side of the moment of passing, the living side.*

R: Oh, this is something I have seen before; it's some kind of rolling green estate somewhere or other. It's a bit indistinct but large grassed area, and a house, and woods.

B: *Do you get an idea, a thought or a sensation that it is yours?*

R: I had the feeling earlier that it was. Oh, I am just trying to get over the feeling of pulling back from that crash; I don't think I have been through an end bit before, well not in one of these (regressions). (Big sigh).

B: *I think it would be useful if we left this memory. Take yourself now beyond the moment of passing, just drift beyond that moment so we can heal this and have some closure, go beyond now to where you are very safe. Perhaps receiving a message.*

R: (Laughing) You'll have to learn to drive better.

B: *Is that actually your learning and your message from that life, or is there something else?*

R: No, we needed to finish that one anyway, we had learnt enough.

B: *While you are in that blissful state, would it be useful to explore another memory or is this enough?*

R: Yes.

B: *Allow yourself to just go now to a memory or another past life, a memory of significance, allow yourself to drift to the memory, very calming, gently in your own time. And as before, get a sense of yourself, a sense of your bearings, notice what is happening, within you and around you, your surroundings and begin to report to me what is happening, what you are feeling, seeing, sensing and allow that imagery - that story - to unfold for you.*

R: Nothing distinct yet, except a feeling of an awfully long time before, completely different landscape, I haven't a clue where, more rocks, sand, and I think sea to the left, but I am not sure. There is shrubbery, but only about fifteen or twenty percent. Oh, I am up on the rocks and I see a figure down on the beach, hands in the air waving, come on down and have a chat. Loose white clothes, long dark hair, and what looks like a white headband or scarf around her head.

I am scrambling down the rocks towards her, there is some sort of boat, very clear water, and it's a blue, blue green, strange structure of strata. Alternating, very light worn rock, and sand and rock and sand; sort of almost separate layers worn smooth, slightly wavy surface to the rock, strange, almost like rock steps with sand in between, and some sort of boat with a sail and high brow but not a very big one. There is a bit more vegetation to the left, and palms, no they are not palm trees, there is too much green on them, Syracuse?

B: Why are you there, why are you on the beach?

R: Haven't a clue - she asked me down there.

B: What is your name?

R: Rafus or something like that.

B: What is her name?

R: Melanie or something similar, it was a holiday life time; it was a non-stressful one. We didn't do much, we just bummed around, or whatever the equivalent was in those days, we sailed around, did a bit of trading.

B: How nice, how lovely.

R: We made just enough to keep ourselves afloat financially and physically.

B: What were you trading?

R: Pots, glass, jewels, it was just a jaunting life time around the Greek islands and Eastern Mediterranean mainly. I was about to say we had a few hard life times, and they let us off on this one, we had a fun time for a few years or a few decades actually. We just about made our forties and fifties.

B: That is lovely.

R: We went down in a Mediterranean storm, you can't win them all.

B: So, from that memory again, is that the memory or learning for you now?

R: Yes. Relax and enjoy it, its better sailing from here, and we can always have a holiday some time.

***

Here are Richard's thoughts:

'Most of my regressions have been fairly vivid, real, actual, rather than symbolic. The 1799 session events had a degree of symbolisation, more unreality in terms of the "physical" structure. In contrast, the very early holiday lifetime was devoid of such "aberrations" and was closer to the "real" type of regression scene.

'Initially, there was the odd bit of "Western" lifetime or two but, for some reason, it felt wrong to go there, or I did not want to do so.

'I was in a wooded area, also seeing a lot of sky; then floating above the trees and seeing even more sky. I was seeing what, apparently, turned out to be me, in 1799, from outside my body, rather than through my eyes of the time.

'What was odd about all of that is that the room in which the Countess/Caroline's party was being held was a sort of room in the woods rather than room in a building.

'Initially, I was seeing a track, path, sloping down from left to right, quite steep; I said about thirty degrees but it probably was not that bad. The path was worn earth; no vegetation on it but quite a bit of dry, brown, woodland debris; the path worn hollow, a shallow "U" shape in the direction of travel.

'The path was across a slope that was facing me or, initially, appeared to be so. There was a fence on the nearest side of the path to me (the disembodied, viewing me) to guard against falling down the steep slope. The fence consisted of a series of posts, several feet apart (six to eight feet), with a rail fixed to the path side of the post, at the top of them, and was at hip to waist height. The wood was three to four inches thick and dark brown.

'The room was on the lower part of the sloping path, on the other side of it from the fence. The structure was brown wood, mostly stained, varnished, and glass; the lower two and a half feet solid wood and/or other construction; the double doors (French window type) were open, at least mostly.

'The overall impression was of a room having been taken from a large house, manor house, or similar, and transplanted to a sire beside one of those paths on Butser Hill, in Queen Elizabeth Country Park. However, at the top of the path, no more than fifty feet or so from the french doors, was a firm, fairly level area with grass and a clearly worn track, surfaced in some way, where the coach, in which we had arrived, stood. Even three months later, as I add to these notes, I still do not understand the reason for "the room in the forest" set-up during the regression, except that, as I write, other words come to mind.

'The Countess/Caroline came out of the doors and a few feet up the slope to meet us. She was mainly in white with a little black, dark brown, very full skirt, down to her ankles. "Fresh face" (comes to mind as I write) quite bright red lipstick, slightly orangey hue (again, extra detail comes as I recount). Her hair, as I saw it during the regression, was white and done up quite tight in a bun, bob; clear of her neck. Her dress/top had a low neckline and slightly puffy sleeves.

'In contrast, Lorelei/Emma was mostly in black with black hair and a full, long skirt to her dress but not as full, not as much bulk underneath her skirt; she was also carrying a black parasol rolled; it was too thick to be just a cane.

'What came to mind as I started to recount that last paragraph was Black Queen, White Queen, as in Chess, the two Queens being, of course, the two most powerful pieces on a Chessboard.

'The name that came for the house in the first regression, "Ashbrook House" is not as helpful as it first seemed, as there are a myriad of places by that name on the Internet.

'The Caroline/Countess connection is, of course, immensely significant, especially the "exchange of presents" over the centuries, the horses at Countess Caroline's sixty second birthday party and what Caroline has committed to doing to help me now; effectively the closing comment, as below.

'As Lorelei said, the second lifetime to which I regressed was a "Holiday Lifetime".

'The name I received for Lorelei in that lifetime was Melanie, which is, of course, of Greek origin.

'The name I received for me was Rafus. An Internet search shows that to be a valid surname, though I have yet to track down the origin of the name, or the region from which it originates. There is, of course, a possibility that my name in that lifetime was actually Rufus, which is of Roman origin.

'Either way, both names seem to fit with the Mediterranean area, apart from the Rafus/Rufus uncertainty.

'In the part of that lifetime to which I regressed, I was standing on ground, quite high above the beach, when Melanie/Lorelei waved and called to me to go down to the beach.

'The route down to the beach was, effectively, a series of rock steps; alternating light, warm rock with sand, rock, sand, rock. The rock was grey, smooth and soft, and felt a bit wet as even though high above the beach the ground could still be wet from a receding tide or rain. The layers were worn smooth with a slightly wavy surface to the rock.

'The rock steps were smooth and rounded at the leading edge, upward bulging convex edges with a hollow behind, in which there was sand. Cracks in the rock were visible but even the edges of those were rounded. The rock was soft and grey like that experienced on beaches in this lifetime; rounded when it had been washed out to sea and back again a few times, flat, somewhat sheet-like when it had not.

'Having thought about the rock quite a lot and discussed it with my wife, Jo, I believe it may have been clay.

'I was not sure what the trees were but they seemed a little green for palm trees; in general the vegetation seemed a little sparse, especially in comparison with the English countryside, or at least the "classical" English countryside.

'That is why it became extremely interesting when I came across a partial description of Mediterranean geography including, particularly, around Syracuse, which referred to alternate layers of sand and clay. Unfortunately, I have been unable to refine Internet searches to obtain the detail I want on Mediterranean geography for comparison.

'That is a pity, as the connection with Syracuse seemed to be definite. I am sure we spent that lifetime in many parts of the Mediterranean, but the Syracuse connections seems to be so strong that I feel we were based there, originated from there, or spent a great deal of time there for some reason or other.

'Several of the quotes, comments and "one-liners" Lorelei came up with struck a few chords as regards the feel of that lifetime:

"Bum around, or whatever the equivalent was in those days."

"Kept afloat, just, physically and financially."

"We had a few hard lifetimes and they let us off on this one."

"We went down in a Mediterranean storm, but you can't win them all."

'It was certainly quite a pleasant, very pleasant time. I feel the Caroline connection is extremely important. Perhaps that is why the explanation came up at the end, "The horses were my present last time. What Caroline is contributing is her present this time."

'In many ways two horses do not seem much for what she has done and has committed herself to but, presumably, there is more to matters than that and physical world values are different to spiritual values.

'Lorelei's comment, "Relax and enjoy it, it's better sailing from here," seemed particularly relevant.

'Everything seems to be getting better, after several difficult years, including many during which nothing much moved. Very many things now seem to be coming together.'

***

I think the varying experiences of the regressees show that there aren't any rules, so expectations mean nothing. It is also clear that information continues to flow after the sessions are over and a lot more happens than is shared.

***

Sylvie
Here is a story generously given to me by Sylvie. I have included the first part by way of introducing you to her life.

Richard and I
I chose (because I know that we choose each of our lives) to be born in Stockport in 1949, the only child of parents who were committed Spiritualists. I grew up in a house where Spirit people were part of the family and were regularly consulted and referred to for guidance. My mother had a succession of very pleasant women who had been sent to her to train as 'Guides'.

I was aware of Spirit friends from an early age, but I didn't really understand that they were Spirit. They told me stories. I lived half in this world and half in another world, which was in many ways Shamanic, since it was inhabited by talking animals – my Spirit friends appearing to me in a guise I could relate to.

When I was eleven, I became aware that a change had occurred. I had been looked after until then by one particular friend, and I knew him very well. Suddenly, there was a new character in my life, and this one was human. He was tall, rather gaunt, and dressed like a gypsy. He had black unruly hair and piercing blue-grey eyes, and he looked to be in his mid-thirties. I took one look and he instantly fascinated me.

He said his name was 'Rover' Sparks. He was called 'Rover' because he was a wanderer with no fixed home. He told me about where he lived and the people who were part of his life and, to me, it was a thrilling story. I thought he was the most wonderful, magical being I had ever seen.

Two years later, my dad took us to Sussex for the first time. Sussex had the same effect upon me as 'Rover' Sparks, and more – it felt familiar. After we left I yearned to go back there, with a kind of homesickness I didn't understand. The gentle Downs, the flint villages and the white cliffs and the sea all called to me. So the next year, my dad took us back, and this time we visited different places and, with a shock, I recognised all the places that 'Rover' had told me about.

By now, he was known as 'Richard'. That was not his original name – he had been Henry in his last life, but he hated it. As time went on and I got older and learned to know him better, I found out that he had been the illegitimate son of a 15-year-old girl and a Romany traveller. She then married a local carpenter, 10 years her senior. Richard was born in 1809 in Broadwater, near Worthing, but never baptised, although all the subsequent children were. He grew up with the stigma of being his mother's 'sin and misfortune'. He also grew up with his natural father's love of horses, looks, and Shamanic gifts. These gifts terrified him because no one taught him what they were or how to use them. If he went into woodland, the trees talked to him. He couldn't stand being confined, but was frequently beaten and locked in a cupboard. He developed depression, migraine and a deep fear of his visions.

He left home, tried to blend into society for a while, got married. That didn't work, so he left to become a wandering horse-trader, trekking from horse-fair to horse-fair, across the Sussex countryside. The land was his refuge and his love for it never left him. He drank, took drugs, gambled, got into fights. Eventually, the effects of all that left their mark. He became ill. He went to find his mother, to beg for her help; she had him committed to an Asylum, where he died of a fever not long after.

When he died, he realised that nothing had changed. He had been expecting punishment, damnation, or non-existence. Instead he was the same tormented soul he had been in life. He struggled to make sense of his life and himself.

I have memories of that time, because Richard and I have been together through so many lifetimes and the times in between. So I tried to help him. We came up with an idea, which we ran past our joint Spirit Guide, my Soul Brother, Seren. Richard did not want to reincarnate, but he did want to heal his past. So I invited him to share my next life, with the intention of returning to the places he had lived so that he could heal the memories.

I was born in Stockport, just south of Manchester, so a major relocation was called for. I wanted to be a social worker, so I trained as a social worker for the Blind and I secured a post in Hampshire. We moved here in 1971.

However, by then our relationship had taken a turn that horrified my parents. I had seen Richard as my Spirit friend; when I was 17 and going through a difficult part of adolescence, I had started to talk to him constantly. At 18, I began to realise my feelings ran a lot deeper than friendship, and so did his. He told me he loved me. I was at first troubled by this, but then I realised I loved him too. I still had doubts about how 'real' he was, although two of my friends, and my parents, were able to communicate with him. I asked him to prove his reality – we agreed upon a sign. At the next meeting of the Development Group of the Church, one of the members identified him for me and gave me the sign.

Knowing I loved him and that he loved me complicated everything. I grew up very quickly at that point. I had no interest in anyone else – no one could compare to Richard. We made the decision to live together as man and wife, knowing that we were doing it without anyone's approval. That was in 1968. Only Seren seemed to be on our side. We did it in secret at first, because I knew my parents so disapproved of our relationship. I could see why – Richard was older, troubled, and he wasn't even incarnate! He could hardly support me or give me children.

We moved down south and lived together. I won't go into all the details, but it was not easy at all. Richard suffered from depressive moods on a regular basis, which drained me as well. Seren did his best to support us, and we also found good friends who were healers and were aware of him. All through our joint life we have had friends who relate to him, too.

We did what we agreed, and visited all the places that meant so much to him. We finished with the worst place of all – the asylum. That was very, very difficult for him. And then something wonderful happened – he had a deep spiritual experience that turned him around and set him on the path to becoming a healer. I, too, had chosen this path. That was in 2000. Once again, we found people to help us both. We did Reiki 1 together, Reiki 2 – he has his own certificate – and we both became Crystal Healers. He had a very good relationship with our Crystal tutor, and used to visit her on his own when he needed to talk. He has a certificate for that, too.

In 1982, those who look after us in Spirit granted us a wedding. I was the only incarnate person present! Our little sanctuary at home was filled with loving Spirit people and I knew that at last our relationship was accepted.

Richard changed his name from Sparks to Lucas just before our wedding. Because my parents were still alive, I did not feel I could change mine, but in 1994, after they had passed to Spirit with six months of one another, I changed mine to Lucas, too.

My mum did eventually come round to the idea of us living together, a couple of years before she died. My father never did.

We have lived together now for 38 years. Our relationship has deepened and grown and we are inseparable. Richard has grown from being an embittered, troubled man into an amazing healer and teacher. He believes very strongly that you can walk from his dimension to ours just as easily as from one room into another, and that is what he wants to teach others. His healing certificates are an important part of that teaching.

He wants to tell our story – from his point of view. He wants to tell people that his world and ours are just different aspects of the same world and that no one is ever lost or ever 'dies', just transforms.

Our journey has not been any kind of romantic fantasy – it's been hard and I've had to live two separate lives for many years. But now the world is changing and people are far more ready to accept me and my life. Richard and I know that we need to share our vision, and that's where we're headed. It's been an extraordinary life, and not to tell our story would be not to finish what we started.

It's scary in some ways, but wonderful and exciting, too.

***

This leads beautifully to Sylvie's past life memories, as follows:

'This life was during the reign of Elizabeth the First, although I cannot tell you the exact dates.

'I know that my name was Frances, and I was one of the

daughters of a large family. I lived in a small town in the Midlands, somewhere near where modern Birmingham is now, and I lived in a timber-framed house. My father may have been some kind of merchant. The memory starts when I am in my teens, and I know that I loved markets, fairs, strolling players, minstrels, etc.

'It was the Midsummer Fair and it was a glorious June day. There were stalls, jugglers, tumblers, all kinds of entertainment, and food stalls. I was there with my family, a giggling girl with her sisters. There was a huge elm tree in the field and, leaning against it, was a young man, dark, good-looking. My heart missed several beats, and with a kind of inner understanding (I still have it – it's a kind of knowing that something will happen) I knew this man was my future husband. His name was Richard and his surname may have been something like Lansden or Langdon or Lansdown (can't remember exactly). He was a bit older than me and his father was a gamekeeper on a local estate. Richard was learning the craft from him.

'I can remember Richard made very sure he introduced himself to our family, so the feeling was mutual! We were married the following May.

'We moved into his father's tied cottage which became my home for the rest of our lives, and I can see it very clearly. I have walked around it often in my mind, looking at our furniture, mostly inherited from his parents, our deep wooden bed, our bare floors, the little leaded windows that looked out onto the herb garden. It was timber-framed and located up a rutted track. On one side of the track and further up, the woodlands stretched out for miles. Behind our little garden, there was an open field. Richard's father was quite a taciturn man, but his mother was more welcoming and she taught me about herbs and plants. She also warned me to be very careful about telling people I knew about herbal remedies, because they might brand me as a witch.

'We had two children – I do not recall more, because I think after the second, something happened, a miscarriage maybe, but I couldn't have any more. The first was our daughter, Elinor, who was dark like her father and a bright, vivacious girl. The second was born on St Crispin's Day, so we named him Crispin, and he was more like me in looks, but he wanted to be a gamekeeper like his father and grandfather. I can still hear them when I go back into this life, and they visited me in my present life; when I was growing up they were my companions, and later, they spent time with me, but I was torn between welcoming them and loving them and wanting them back. I haven't seen either of them for some time, but that's not to say I never will.

'My memories are very ordinary – my huge kitchen, baking, watching Richard return home from work, striding across the fields, hearing our children play, listening to the house creak, the local fairs, which I still loved.

'The next very clear memory is when Richard became ill. I do not know how old he was, in his 40's, I think. Elinor had married a local boy and visited with our grandchildren. Crispin was still living with us, but was training to be a keeper. Richard was becoming thin and gaunt – he was always so strong and lean and fit. He was beginning to feel pain. I used my knowledge of herbs to help him as much as I could, but I was aware that something was happening to him that I wouldn't be able to heal.

'My strongest memory is of our last night together, in our big wooden bed, with a fire in the grate. I held him close and a great wave of pain surged through his body. I knew now that he was dying, slowly and painfully, and I also knew that I was going to help him die peacefully and without pain. Whatever knowledge of herbs I had I was going to use. And I found that I had already made an infusion of herbs and it was waiting, in a wooden cup, ready.

'If I helped him die, and I remained alive, then questions would be asked. I could find myself accused of killing him; I might be hanged or I might be burned as a witch. In any case I knew without a shadow of a doubt that I didn't really want to live without him. Nor did I want to be a burden on our children. So I had made the decision – we were going to die together.

'We drank the infusion I prepared, lay down in each other's arms and listened to the crackling logs and the driven snow. It was January. We said what we needed to say to one another and then there was just silence until our limbs became heavy and our eyes closed. It was a very emotional experience. I knew that I had done it out of love, and that moment when we lay together, waiting for the poison to take effect, felt very peaceful and very loving. There was no pain, no fear, no regret.

'We woke to a bright May morning. The sun was warm and golden through the windows, the air was soft and the meadows were full of spring bloom. We woke to find ourselves changed; we were both younger and Richard was no longer in pain. We got up and our house was empty. We walked downstairs and out into the fields and there was a small church ahead of us, where there had never been one before. Hand in hand, not speaking, but each aware of the other's thoughts, we made our way towards it. Churches meant explanations; by now we had guessed we were both dead.

'Inside the church was a man dressed as a monk. He announced himself as a Franciscan Brother. The church was a little chilly but it did not feel unwelcoming. The Brother asked us many questions – I don't recall what. We were both ready to face Judgement – we had committed the sin of suicide. But there was no punishment, no censure, just love and acceptance and gentle understanding.

'I did not recognise the Brother then, but as I looked at him in my memory, I knew it was Seren, our joint Spirit Guide and my Soul Brother, come to welcome us both home.

'These are very intense and emotional memories. Every time I go back I end up in floods of tears, especially as we walk away from our home, up that hill and I know I am leaving it all behind again. I used to wonder if I'd made it all up, but I do not think the heart is so easily deceived – you cannot invent such powerful feelings.

'Every Midsummer's Day I am back in that life, smiling to myself as I walk through the Fair, feeling the intense joy I felt then as I recognised Richard again for the first time in that life, knowing that it turned out to be a blessed time, joyful, happy and precious. I am grateful that it has come back to me now to remind me that love is never lost, and that the people who are most dear to you never leave you.'

***

'There is another life that came back to me very intensely. Back in 1998, my friend gave me a book of the Runes with illustrated cards for each symbol. She gave the closed book to me and said that it hadn't meant much to her, but maybe I could help explain them to her. We both worked for the same company and I was just about to take my lunch break. So I opened the book (fortunately, I was on my own!) and took out the cards. Each one had the Runic symbol cleverly worked into the picture.

'Instantly I felt shock. It was so overwhelming that I was aware my pulse was racing and my breathing was fast. Energy poured in through my crown chakra, down through my body and I could do nothing but sit there, shaking. Then I was suddenly somewhere else – alone on a windswept hill, looking across to a group of standing stones. I looked around me and just below me was a village of roundhouses with a stockade protecting them. (Near to us we have the reconstructed Iron Age village and that has always called to me, too.) I knew who and what I was – the woman with the "sight", with the gifts of herbs and reading of the Runes. I had a special place in my village and I was respected. I realised that the Runes were my familiar friends and that all I needed to do in my present life was to remember them.

'I came back from lunch, white as a sheet and still shaky. My friend was deeply concerned! I told her what had happened and she decided I needed the Runes more than she did.

'It returned when I was training to be a Crystal Healer. I was attuning to the energy of Gold Topaz at the time. In fact all my life I have wanted that stone, without even knowing exactly what it was, only that it was deep gold in colour. When I picked up the piece I was meant to attune to, it almost said to me: "Hello, Sylvie, I'm back in your life again". I did have some very intense experiences with crystals, but this was a particularly deep past-life one and it haunted me for the whole week I was living with the crystal (part of the training is that you wear it for a whole week and keep a record of what happens).

'Once again, I was back on that windswept hill, close to my stone circle. A lot of things fell into place. I had always been attracted to stone circles, too. But this time I also realised that I did not always use my power with love. In fact I enjoyed the feeling of being in control of people's lives. They came to me with their fears and their hopes, asking for medicine, guidance and a glimpse of their futures. I was a huge influence in their lives, and that gave me my sense of power. I could manipulate relationships, and be very political within my tribe. I loved that.

'This other "me" was so powerful during that week that I even became more like her. I had a way of tossing my hair, and a way of looking at people with an intense stare. All that surfaced. All my life I have been a "nice" person, a people pleaser, to a fair extent, but that week I was nothing like my usual self. I noticed, too, that the Gold Topaz would have been on my finger. I knew that I had worn that stone in that lifetime. Gold Topaz is a Solar Plexus chakra stone and it intensifies your feeling of personal power. No wonder I had the feelings!

'I also had a fear of fire in that life, and I carried that into this childhood. I think the village burned and I burned with it, but I do not remember why.

91

One thing I have learned, however, is this: there is a link between these lives. I brought into this life a deep fear of all things Pagan. I was not Christian, either, but I was afraid of the Old Religion and its power. I did not know why. But now I do know that since that lifetime, when I so misused my gifts and my position, I have been afraid of my gifts. I have vague memories of embracing the New Religion as a nun, but with the same gifts and a great deal of inner conflict. When I was in the Elizabethan life, I was afraid of being branded a witch. It seems that in this lifetime I have the chance to resolve it all, because now I am more Pagan – I have learned about the sabbats, and I celebrate them, particularly Samhain. I have faced my fear, come to terms with my gifts and reclaimed my learning.

'I am sure this is why those two lifetimes came back to me – perhaps to teach me what I needed to remember in order to heal the past.'

***

Over the years I have heard the same question over and over and frequently get asked, 'Why is everyone famous in their past lives?' I even read as such the other day on a networking forum.

I hadn't actually ever regressed anyone who had been in the public eye in their past until recently, even if they were in this life, but thought it would be reasonable to, as most of us know someone in the limelight or have a friend who might. Can you imagine my excitement when writing this book to not only have King Richard visit, but to then meet Marusja, who agreed to be interviewed?

This is her story.

Marusja

Earlier in my life I lived in California for a long time and I studied psychology. Many of my friends were interested in things such as past life regression and one day we went to a psychic fayre. As

I walked through a woman, who used sound tuning symbols to psychically connect, stopped me and said, 'You were Jane Eyre'.

I felt a little worried and told her that was impossible, as that was a work of fiction. Her reply was that she was definitely getting something associated with Jane Eyre.

Throughout my life I have always written: stories, poems, my thoughts and feelings, and often used it as an escape from reality while I was growing up. I used to make miniature books with the tiniest of writing, I still have them actually. I always felt I'd been born into the wrong family - I just didn't feel that I fitted and usually felt unattractive.

When I look back at pictures of myself I am shocked that I had those feelings as I now see a very good-looking young woman. At the time I wanted to hide away.

I was always very good at English, so good that I was excused from wearing the school beret.

A few years ago I had a Canadian friend who was a psychic and channeller, and one day she offered to give me a reading. She reported on three of my past lives. The first revealed me as one of three reporters who worked on parts of the Bible. In the second I was an elderly man who died with all his writings tucked away in a box, never seeing the light of day. This particularly saddened me as I was beginning to think I was heading the same way.

She then informed me that I was Charlotte Brontë with the instruction that I would write the next book.

The memory of the earlier psychic talking about Jane Eyre popped to the front of my mind and I decided to do a little research and reading. The parallels between her life and mine are amazing.

The Brontë children were avid readers and writers and they created tiny little books with writing and pictures that were minuscule. It was written small enough for the toy soldiers to read while at the same time preventing adults from entering their world.

Charlotte's brother, Branwell, had red hair and died from TB following a relapse in the use of alcohol and opium. My husband had red hair and a similar excessive personality that meant he drank and took drugs. He was a very attractive, charismatic man but his habits forced me to leave.

There are many coincidental threads, including my illness at the same age that Charlotte was when she died. I've no doubt that I will write the sequel.

4

Memories R Us

Where do our memories live? If there is a trigger that makes you remember an event or a feeling, where does it come from?

What is the first memory that you can remember? Your birth? I'll guess probably not and surmise even further that the memories that you are consciously aware of are probably from early childhood. But, all our memories are neatly tucked away in our subconscious mind. I have had clients recall their births and some even discussed time in the womb. This is a good reason to keep births as calm and peaceful as possible to prevent the baby picking up any negativity. I haven't carried out any studies, but I have read of people describing events from their womb memory that actually occurred in the way they recalled. In their sessions my clients were in a hypnotic state to enable them to relax into the experience and gain access to their inner mind.

Likewise, remembering past lives becomes easier to do in trance. Sometimes dreams provide the knowledge while others 'know' of their past and have always been aware.

However, memories can just appear seemingly out of the blue and this is called spontaneous recall. Have you ever had a dream suddenly enter your mind when something is said or happens that triggers you to remember it? This is a similar experience but on a grander scale.

Being flooded with information can also happen when in shock, during illness or lost in reverie - strangely the two most emotive events being a church service and a moment of passion, but not necessarily at the same time! I have had quite a few clients describe 'visions' they've had while drifting off during a sermon or when completely lost in pleasure.

Kristian shared this memory.

Many years ago he was travelling home by car when he felt poorly and faint. He pulled over, stopped and then lost awareness of himself. When he came round he was sitting in the cockpit of a B-17 Bomber (Flying Fortress). He described the scene clearly and the memory remains to this day. Just as suddenly he found himself back in the car.

Something triggered that: perhaps the geography of the road, the combination of symptoms he was feeling or just his mood.

The dream state also gives many people information from their past. Jennifer has kindly allowed me to tell you her experience, as follows:

'My most recent lifetime before this one was as a six-year-old boy, or thereabouts. He lived in Amsterdam and was on a bus filled with other children. The city was under intense attack, and much of the city was being bombed. This little boy was caught in an attack, and the bus he was riding on was blown up. He died from a wound to his abdomen.

'His last moments were very clear when they came to me, and it wasn't something I relived intellectually. I could feel myself looking out at the world through that six-year-old's eyes. I experienced the horrific confusion of being in the midst of the bombings and felt the terrible sadness of being separated from my mother. I didn't know where she was or whether I'd ever see her again.

'Anyway, one particular night I had a dream in which "I" was a young 20-something woman in a bright, pretty dress that was of a style worn by middle-class women in the 1940s. I was somewhat excited because I was with a bunch of people taking a train trip. I had the sense that I wasn't someone who ever had the opportunity to travel and, while I didn't know exactly what was going to happen at my destination, I was excited to be dressed up in my nicest dress and spending time with other well-dressed people. I had the vanity that comes with being that age and wanting to see my image reflected back in other people's eyes. I had the sense of being someone who was bright but not highly intelligent, a nice young woman who had a people-pleasing personality and a somewhat conservative mindset. I was aware of having brown hair and being of medium height.

'The scene shifted, and I was disembarking with other people in a strange place. There was a flurry of luggage and a large crowd. And that was when the sadness hit. I don't know how much I was aware of at this point, but it suddenly flashed over me that maybe I would never see home again, and that I didn't entirely trust the people who were in charge. And I felt a real wave of sadness about family I'd left back home.

'That was the end of the dream. It felt like a vision but I couldn't at that time work out what it meant.

'Some time after this I was listening to Dr Gottleib's radio programme and his guests were talking about Holocaust survivors. At that moment the meaning of my dream hit me. I had dreamt about my mother from the life when I was the little boy and I knew she had been taken, never to return, to a concentration camp.'

***

Jennifer says she doesn't know how she might have had a remote viewing type of dream but the psychic connections remain through subsequent lives. But, she is sure that when that little boy died he was already an orphan and was put on the bus with the other children in an attempt to reach safety.

***

Pam told me about her memories:

'I am involved in a women's self-development workshop, which I staff from time to time. There are rituals we use which come from Native America and right from the start I felt a "knowing" about these traditions and ways of life.

'I never studied Native America and so would have no reason to have insight. We also use a technique of calling in our Wise Woman (who really exists as part of our Self) when we need to stand brave in courage, for instance, and for all this time my Wise Woman has come to me as a faceless Native American woman, wrapped in animal skins, feathers, shawls... I have a really clear image of her and, knowing this 'wise woman' is indeed part of me, this got me thinking about reincarnation and the sense that I had been in that life and had brought this wise woman through into my current body.

'The workshop I do perhaps triggered a memory deep inside my soul. I have another but don't know how this one came about, although I have sensed this longer than the Native American woman. I have never really been interested in history: geography has always been my thing. But, my sense is a specific attraction to 1930s culture. And my senses always bring up images of a house, with a two-seater sports car (like an original Morgan) outside, pearls, Charleston dancing. I am drawn to specific clothing which is from that era. I am quite a logical thinker and I like to be able to analyse things and the only conclusion I have for being drawn to this is having been there before. I am not a very religious person, but definitely spiritual believer.'

***

For others there are physical memories as in scars, birthmarks or discoloured skin that in a regression turns out to be a wound from a past life. We can also 'hold on' to emotional and physical memories that might be apparent in ailments that haven't a cause.

As every thought causes a reaction somewhere within us, repeating negative inner dialogues or thoughts can form programmes or behaviour patterns that become difficult to change.

The physical and mental reactions are the same whether we perceive danger or fear in the 'now', if we imagine something is going to happen or if we mull over experiences from the past. This doesn't even have to be conscious - it can bubble away just below our awareness so we keep on reacting again and again.

If you are holding onto emotional, physical or mental debris, past or not, here are a few symptoms you might encounter.

Head: headaches, vision problems, weak hair, early baldness, sleep difficulties, insomnia.

Face and jaw: congestion, sniffles, jaw clenching, bruxism (teeth grinding) that can lead to TMJ (temporomandibular joint syndrome - a painful condition that can affect the head, face and jaw like neuralgia), dry mouth, excessive swallowing.

Throat: sore throats, painful glands, earaches, difficulty in expressing self – 'holding onto' words, lump in throat feeling.

Neck and shoulders: pain, stiffness, headaches, slumped posture –hunching and round shoulders.

Chest: breast pain, chest pain, breathing difficulties - hyperventilation, lung congestion, asthma, bronchial problems, coughs, heart palpitations, high blood pressure.

Back: aches, disc wear, trapped nerves, sciatica.

Kidneys: 'fluidy', water retention – 'holding on', bed-wetting.

Tummy: indigestion, heartburn, ulcer, loss of or excessive appetite, empty hollow feeling, bloated-ness.

Reproductive system: conception difficulties, cysts, irregular and/or painful periods, excessive bleeding, hormone imbalance, PMS.

Bowels: IBS, spasms, wind, cramps, constipation, diarrhoea, haemorrhoids.

Genitals: impotence, vaginismus, inability to reach orgasm, libido loss, thrush.

Hips and thighs: hip tension, sexual problems, low backache, cellulite.

Limbs: aches and pains, arthritis, shakes, jumpy legs.

General: circulation problems, cramps, cold extremities, excessive sweating, low immunity.

The list does not mean that all those problems are only because of stress held from past lives, and I don't want a bunch of neurotic readers with a sore throat thinking they were garrotted a few hundred years ago, or any of you with a windy pain thinking you were run through...

Leftover grief, anxieties, injury, memory and such can result in themes of illnesses - back aches or upset tummies, for example. My example demonstrates this perfectly. When I hurt my back in Nottingham I had a prolapsed disc above the previous operation site. I truly believe if I hadn't 'dealt' with the stage fright issue relating to past injury I would probably have been crocked again and would continue to be.

As well as the physical, we can also experience 'feeling' stress: anxieties, fears, insecurities, boredom, and feelings of apathy, depression or helplessness. Unfinished business affects our feelings. Things left undone or words left unsaid. Needing to forgive and seeking forgiveness can also be felt.

We also have 'thought' stress: difficulty concentrating, self-doubts, forgetfulness, confusion, indecisiveness, distractions or monkey brain (where the mind will not switch off - usually at bed-time or in the early hours). These are left over 'should-have' and the 'why didn't I?' type of thoughts.

Then there is behaviour stress that is apparent by hyperactivity or slow reactions, extreme tiredness, clumsiness and twitching from repetitive limb movements; tics. Also empty habits such as nail biting and hair pulling that can derive from unchecked stress and can stay for years, lifetimes even.

Women in particular seem to 'hold' on to emotions in their cells that are apparent as unwanted fat and cellulite. Females seem more likely to hold words in - how often have we heard that they keep their mouth shut for a quiet life? Perhaps they didn't keep quiet in the past and suffered. But those words create a reaction: either emotional and/or physical somewhere within, so while word swallowing may help situations for a short while, in the long-term it becomes destructive. And, carrying negativity over several lifetimes isn't good.

Men generally hold on to stress internally, usually around major organs often manifesting visually as the beer belly effect.

Repetitive dreams that are unresolved in daytime thoughts may implicate past life debris and all encompassing unresolved sadness or misery can manifest as depression.

Jenny Smedley's depression ruled her life. She had nightmares involving being raped through to committing suicide. In her dreams she would call out the name 'Ryan' and he would call her 'Madeleine'. She often discussed her dreams with her husband, Tony, and they were both concerned.

Jenny also had constant pain low down on her left side. One day she had an urge to switch on the TV and onto the screen came the country and western singer Garth Brooks. At that moment Jenny experienced the most amazing turn in her life – Garth was in fact Ryan, when she was Madeleine. It was as if she knew all about his character and in that instant her depression was lifted.

Some time after, Jenny recalled during a hypnotic regression that he was Ryan Fitzgerald and she was Madeleine, his wife. Her depression had been a manifestation of grief as their lives had previously been torn apart.

Since that time Jenny has become a songwriter, author, columnist and TV presenter. I recently caught up with her to find out how she is now. This is what she said:

'Following the experience I got a sense of purpose which to me means following my life plan. I believe that when we follow that plan with passion and purpose it seems that doors open and you are given tools to move along. One of the tools I was given was the ability to read people's past lives and I do so in my magazine column. It began gently whereby I would see people but notice that they had different clothes. When I mentioned this to some of them they would confirm it and say they'd been regressed and what I was seeing was a past life memory. I can now also read auras remotely.

'I believe that once we get the trigger and focus in our lives we have access to the quantum universe where we can see everyone's energy. It is, then, no different going back on the time-line to the past than it is going forward.

'Immediately after my experience, I became very happy. It was a complete swing around, from being so depressed that I couldn't see the point in getting up in the mornings to finding absolute pleasure in everything. Even the mundane, like washing up, was enjoyable because I had a sense of wonder glowing inside me and I realised there was so much more to me than I ever thought. We are all here to achieve something. It might be viewed as small, like creating a beautiful garden, to something more like being awarded the Nobel Peace prize.

'My experience shook my subconscious into locking on to my reality. And for all of us, we just need 'switching' on.'

5

Research Pointers

For many, research isn't necessary as the 'knowing' is all that matters, and when you have that knowledge you may well feel completely satisfied.

You will know from the regressions shared already that sometimes we can't quite get enough information to even make research worthwhile. And, if you imagine your future Self just dropping into yourself now, you might not know very much about the 'you' in the now. The first time I was regressed, when I went back to Louisville, I didn't know how I looked until Valerie suggested I look in the mirror. When I did that I immediately rubbed my tongue over my front teeth to remove a bit of lipstick and marvelled at my magnificent bosoms. I had a mind-boggling cleavage, accentuated in a push-me-pull-you corset-dress. Interestingly, Valerie knew exactly how I looked which is why she wanted me to see for myself.

I have been in groups of people in a guided regression and we can sometimes pick up information from others. It is also possible to psychically detect other people's lives as in Jennifer's dream.

Not all of our memories are actually ours: remember back to the cases of panic attacks brought on by seeing another person have one. I have regressed clients and 'seen' very clearly in my mind their descriptions and felt their emotion so vividly it was as if it was mine. We're not always sure who did what in our childhood in this life, let alone previous ones. My children aren't always completely sure who did what when we talk about mischief. Unless they are just passing the buck…now, there's a thought.

You will find that more information will come to you after any regressions you carry out. Richard, for example, shared that as he was writing his thoughts he was gaining more knowledge. It's like if you write something – you might look at a blank page but once you get going the words flow unbridled as though they were released. Memories are there waiting and when you open the door for them they will burst forth. It might be slow to begin but your patience will be rewarded.

To start with, here are a couple of examples of research carried out.

Research

Mick very generously investigated the memories of Lizzie and Andrea. I didn't do it to avoid any thoughts of bias. I know you wouldn't have any, but some might.

Lizzie's regression was constructed around a reluctant warrior who could have been placed any time between 1119 to mid Tudor, but the most likely era would be in the reign of Richard III.

Lizzie answered 'Richard' when asked who was King (although she later called herself Richard), but which Richard? Trying to narrow the choice of which King Richard, there were several avenues to explore.

A good starting point, as ever, is 'Google'.

'I've got a suit of armour, chains - oh, it's so heavy. I'm wearing a suit of chains.'

The first search for chain mail showed links to historical websites, which agree that chain mail was in use in some form throughout the period. Further searches using Wikipedia for King Richard I, II & III have date ranges for their reigns.

Wikipedia is an open on-line encyclopaedia to which entries can be made or edited by just about anyone who can get online. The information can be flawed because of this. It is a good source to get an overview of anything and specific facts can be checked at other sites. All historic websites agreed date ranges for the 'Richards'.

How might these dates fit in with the other points?

'We are going to the castle, Leeds Castle. Just going home to the castle. They've opened the drawbridge'.

It's fairly certain that the 'Leeds' means Leeds Castle in Kent, as no mention of a castle in Leeds, Yorkshire could be found on websites. Tim Lambert's brief history of Leeds website describes it as '*a small and unimportant town*' in the Middle Ages.

Did Leeds Castle have a drawbridge?

Leeds Castle's own web site gives dates of construction and when major changes were made: '*A drawbridge and portcullis were added in 1278*'.

This would exclude Richard I as he died as a result of a fatal blow by a youth playing with a crossbow in 1199. On his deathbed he pardoned the boy, but they later hung him anyway.

Although each Richard had issues with the French, Richard I, when he wasn't crusading and being waited for by Robin Hood, spent time in France. He had skirmishes with local lords and seems to have used English troops, but this could not be regarded as war with the French.

Using similar search threads, Richard II seems no more likely a candidate; britannia.com states: '*Edward remarried in 1396, wedding the seven year old Isabella of Valois, daughter of Charles VI of France, to end a further struggle with France*'. They mean Richard, not Edward.

This is a good example of the World Wide Web having carelessly recorded information on it. Royal.gov.uk tells us that Richard II regarded himself as King of France and his reign was concurrent with a 28-year truce in the 100 years war with France. So not him then!

Richard III fits the bill for both his dealings with France and Scotland. Richardiii.net is packed full of information with references to its sources. It is interesting that Richard's name was blackened by Tudor propaganda as a hunchbacked bad guy following Henry VII's victory at Bosworth and the death of Richard after only two years on the throne, yet our narrator had nothing disparaging to say of him.

Throughout Richard's short reign 1483-85, there was a constant threat of invasion from Henry Tudor, exiled in France - but a truce with Scotland.

According to btinternet.com's timeline: '*1483 rebellion in Kent, Sussex and Cornwall*', and, according to Lizzie, 'There's trouble in the West'. In 1485 there was big trouble in the West when Henry Tudor landed in Milford Haven, West Wales, on his way to Bosworth.

As for other specifics: '*There is talk about Chichester - a great fire*'. The website british-history.ac.uk tells of a great fire: '*on 5 May 1114, the cathedral and city, it is said, were consumed by fire*'. While it doesn't fit with our story so far, it could be another starting point. There were many fires in the Middle Ages and most would be regarded as 'great fires' in the much thatched and timber cities.

To find out more about specific people before the keeping of records of births, marriages and deaths from Lizzie's regression, perhaps a phone call and visit might be a good idea, in this case to Leeds Castle, and talk to their archivist to find out if there ever was a son called Harold with a mother called Mary living there.

Andrea

Now for Andrea's story.

Andrea's journey into a past life didn't give enough detail to look for specific times, places and people, but there is a timeline that can be investigated.

Her character in the regression says, 'I'm only young still, in my fifties,' at the time of her death. Assuming that is more or less in the present, it would make her birth before 1956 but no earlier than 1946.

Some clues to the date and her age come with the description of the house, 'Seems quite old-fashioned - early Sixties' and

'Celebrating – it's something to do with the Queen'. 1963, being a decade on the throne, was celebrated with street parties. I confirmed the coronation date by checking on Google with interesting snippets on the BBC website.

Later in Andrea's regression, she is in her mid-twenties, on holiday and living a wealthy but boring lifestyle in London.

'I'm walking down the street past Starbucks.' A Google search *'First Starbucks London'* gives results with an extract from an article in the *Daily Mail*, May 2007, *'The first London Starbucks opened its doors on the King's Road, Chelsea, nine years ago'*. The earliest this could have been is 1998.

In this part she says 'My phone's going in my bag'. Although bag-sized mobile phones were not that common in 1998, it would be reasonable to assume that being well off she would have one. A Google image search goes to a picture of an early flip phone in an article on BBC on line news *'Education Teachers back mobile phone ban'* dated July 1998.

Towards the end of this life, Andrea says 'I'm only young still, in my fifties'. This is consistent with the earlier supposed birthday range if we come to the present day (2007).

***

Just this introduction into researching shows how much we can discover, depending on our start point. If you already have knowledge you might want to begin from there.

I was fortunate enough to speak with Dr Nick Barrett, historian. We started off with general information and then I asked him specifics. I'm 'B' and he is 'N'. Here is the discussion.

B: Can you suggest the best information for anyone wanting to research a regression? We know dates, names and landscape would make a good start, but what else is useful for searching?

N: Always focus on names and dates of events, as well as physical or geographical clues. These can then be followed up in secondary sources, official histories, archives and record offices.

B: Where does historical information and records come from? Online, places, societies, experts?

N: Depending on what you've found, you can always start online (Google or Wikipedia for example) and then expand your search into libraries. The British Library in London is the best place to start as it has an unparalleled collection. However, if you have some geographical clues you might also want to head to the nearest local study centre or county archive, as they will have specialist collections of books as well as primary source documentation.

B: How would one go about searching for older historical evidence?

N: How old is older? Written official records in the UK start in the Anglo-Saxon period, with one of the best collections at The National Archives (11th century onwards) though university libraries and museums will also have important documents. Indeed, the museum sector can help with even earlier periods of history, though it is unlikely you'll get names.

B: I would value your thoughts on how people get 'started' and from their starting point how to proceed. Although online seems the obvious starting point, there are limitations for non-experts.

N: Use the Internet to find offline sources, e.g. looking for useful books, then head to the library; read articles to locate key primary sources; go back into the loop once you've found the relevant documents and expand the context of the records by reading around the subject. It's going to be tricky to find a specific person with just a Christian name, so see if you can focus on surnames, dates of events, places - this will determine where you look for information (local, national, specialist).

I then put the following regressions by him to get a research 'start' point:

B: Limited information on a 'working girl' in a Louisville bar at the time of President Lincoln.

N: National Archives and Record Administration (NARA) in Washington DC should hold official records for this period, but depends on what sort of info you have.

B: Names, dates, house name, landscape details in the 18th century, UK.

N: There are no census records this far back, but you might be able to use parish registers or even land tax returns to locate information from an address or name linked to a specific part of the country.

B: No actual names but clear info on landscape, buildings (thatch style) and tools (no metal).

N: Vernacular architecture can limit to a region and time, but beyond that it's going to be difficult to make an effective search without a name.

B: Spontaneous recall – B-17 Bomber parked up - good descriptions of surroundings.

N: It might be possible to investigate the history of a military site, particularly an Airfield, and then track the movements of everyone involved in the missions flown from the base. Records at the National Archives, Kew.

If you are interested in researching your own memories this gives you a fantastic starting point. Please be aware that when you start off it soon becomes fascinating and totally absorbing.

There is a resource list for you to begin your researching at the end of the book.

6

Be your own Regressionist

You have now arrived at the bit where you get to discover, remember, or go looking and retrieving, your own memories. As you've been reading this book you might already have had or now have knowledge. Perhaps certain things have seemed familiar to you or you're already more aware of your dreams and any messages you might be receiving.

As thoughts, knowledge and memories are stored in your subconscious mind, that is where you need to go or allow them to come from. In our busy day-to-day lives it can be hard to get hold of information because the conscious mind is active – all the time planning, thinking and doing.

The easiest way to relax the conscious mind to gain entry to the subconscious is with hypnotic meditative relaxation. When you become aware of the ease and normality of these techniques you can use them in all areas of your life and you will find your thoughts become clearer and clearer – whether associated with past lives or life in general.

I would like you to have a clear understanding of the hypnotic, trance and meditative state including the familiarity of it all. You are already an expert; you just don't know it yet.

I will begin by telling you a story.

Once upon a time there was trance. When you lived in a cave dressed in your loincloth you would have been familiar with the experience of trance. The successful hunter would have been more adept by dropping down into a focused state. Tribal and group behaviour demonstrates the use of eye fixation, drumming and dancing, and the mind/mental states created are not new. Man has always been 'entrancing'. You can see an excellent example of this if you have ever watched a golf tournament. The audience is mesmerised and behaves as one physically, mentally and emotionally, willing the ball to stay in the air long enough to plop perfectly into the hole, all the time holding the one shared thought: that if they shout out, 'Go in!' it will.

History shows us that the trance state was used by the Ancient Egyptians in sleep temples for healing, as did the Greeks. Yogis, fakirs and shamans also induced trance using various methods but to the same end. Aborigines, American Indians, preachers and lecturers – yes, they all do. Information has always been passed on and down through trance. You only have to peek into any lecture hall to see that. Healing through prayer, hands on, spiritual, chanting, drumming and spell of intent, again, all induce trance. A child's bedtime story is another example.

Even the ringing bells that summon worshipers to church induces the alpha brain wave pattern that denotes a light trance. Several times throughout each day we all slip in and out of different mind states. When we are focused, bored, shocked, mesmerised, excited, or angry we access a different mind state or we drift off and hear phrases like daydreamer, head in the clouds or being elsewhere ('the lights are on but there's no-one in'). There are examples of people doing extraordinary things that afterwards they had no conscious recall of doing. I am sure you know the feeling of being on 'automatic pilot', possibly even saying that phrase about yourself.

You have no doubt experienced the irritation when supermarkets rearrange the shop in order to 'wake us up' and notice all the wonderful things on offer instead of functioning without thought.

Have you ever driven somewhere or sat on a train and been unable to recall the journey? Can you remember being totally absorbed in a book or film and become oblivious of your surroundings, so much so that maybe you jumped, laughed out loud or even cried? What about when you stop listening to someone talking to you – it's as if you 'zone out' and when your awareness returns you're not sure whether to nod in agreement, laugh or sympathise.

One day I was at Waterloo Station about to step on the escalator when it suddenly stopped. Most people on it stopped as well. It took some by surprise and they had to 'wake up' and decide what to do next. You could almost hear their thoughts and for a few they couldn't quite manage to work out a plan, so they stood still, shrugged their shoulders and waited for it to start up again.

Do you lose yourself in your thoughts? Ever had a song playing repeatedly in your mind? Do you replay situations in your mind or play the 'what ifs'? All these are examples of the everyday trances that we are all familiar with. Some people try to create (believing they will enhance) these experiences by taking drugs such as hallucinogens or using dance, music and light sequences that alter brain wave activity. If only they knew the secrets you are about to learn they would save themselves a packet and keep their health.

A trance is an experience of some of the things previously described, whereas hypnosis is the induction of a hypnotic trance during which you can decide to rest your conscious mind thereby bypassing to your subconscious mind.

The meditative state, while very similar, varies in that it creates an open-mind focus while the hypnotic state is focus with a narrowing of attention.

Meld them together and you get the blissful open-minded calm focus with the ability to put your attention where you want. All the while having access to your inner you.

I have used the description before as: meditation = flowing out and hypnosis = flowing in. When used together we can just flow.

Using hypnotic meditative states on and by yourself gives you access to your subconscious mind that is usually pretty much ignored while it just gets on with its job, which is to keep us alive and safe. It has no concept of right or wrong, good or bad. It acts automatically on instruction and will make us repeat whatever we practise doing. If we have fears or anxieties they will feed on themselves and become all-powerful. The subconscious mind, in its endeavour to protect, may well remind us of these feelings if it has associated it with an action. Whenever I used to think about flying I would get butterflies. When I used to think about performing I would go through the whole scenario of escaping by swooning.

All this doesn't mean that you can be forced to do things – it does mean you can choose. If you have decided you no longer want to smoke, for example, as soon as the old smoking programmes in your subconscious mind are brought up to date with your present desire, you are then a non-smoker with ease.

This is the same with phobias. My fear of flying was created by me holding onto an experience as a child that had nothing to do with flying, but I had attached it to planes and as my imagination is so brilliant I imagined myself into a state of terror.

If you have a desire to look at your past lives your needs will be met when you do so. If you have held on to an emotional memory that isn't serving any purpose likewise you will be able to release it. Any past pain that is part of you now can be set free and you can move forward in your life unshackled.

Brainwaves

Have you ever had a brainwave? Perhaps you might call it a 'eureka' moment, a split second of absolute brilliance; or, an awakening, trigger, light going on, flash of inspiration or a quiet 'aha'?

When you look at past lives you may well get an, 'Oh yes' moment. I did several times!

Your brain is a little hive of electrical activity and it is buzzing away all the time even when you are sleeping. You might be privy to this happening when you remember snippets of goings on in the form of dreams. Or even in the day when you get a seemingly random thought pop into your mind that hasn't anything to do with the moment.

For the more scientific among us, the activity can be measured and described in hertz per second. We have brainwave patterning that denotes the amount of activity we are experiencing. In the normal thinking, sometimes stressful state, we are in *beta*. If we relax and meditate, we are in *alpha* (you may have heard the phrase 'hitting the magic alpha'). In this state we are at our creative best. When we are predominantly in alpha our memories are easier to retrieve.

During the state of deep relaxation we go into *theta*. Here we dream and our imaginations can be vivid. Rapid eye movement (REM) is often occurring as in the dream state. Deep sleep shows the pattern as *delta* – not much going on just gently ticking over.

We mostly go through beta and alpha during the day and down to delta during the night. If we don't get enough calm or peace through the day by experiencing alpha it becomes hard to rest fully at night. When this happens we wake up feeling un-rested and cluttered with old stress. Over time this becomes habitual and damaging to health.

If you are taking exams or having to remember something you will be most productive and successful in alpha. This is because the conscious mind is not quite so interfering – the subconscious is accessible. People fail exams through being stressed because they are unable to access information that they know they know: the conscious mind gets in the way and stops the flow of answers. They remember everything the minute they leave the exam hall when the pressure is off. Have you ever tried to think of a word or someone's name and the harder you try the more elusive it becomes, but when your mind slows and is occupied elsewhere the answer pops in as if by magic. Any snippets of your past that you have been getting will grow when you become used to the techniques.

Recognising trances

Try this - have a look around and notice your thoughts. Are you thinking about brainwaves or trying to remember a time when you were trying to remember? Are you wondering if you were a Greek god or goddess? Or, do you already know?

Has the day of the week fallen from your mind? Do you need a drink or a trip to the bathroom? Spend a few moments thinking about something you enjoy doing very much. Really get into the experience and use all your senses to imagine how you feel. Do you feel any different after? Calmer, happier, invigorated?

Are you aware of the differing states you slip in and out of throughout each day? If you like you could work out exactly how many. Begin to notice the state other people are in.

This is invaluable if you are in sales, as it is no good talking to people if they aren't excited and motivated by your product or service. If they are in a dull mood they will be unimpressed and maybe even irritated. And, if you are boring, they will be become bored by you. It is important to be aware of balance – if you are over-enthusiastic and not in rapport, all you will do is make people want to poke you with a sharp stick.

As you begin to people watch you will notice that most are completely absorbed in their own inner world and often oblivious to everything going on around them, apart from those they are interacting with directly. Learning how to get into a connected state with others ensures you can slip into their world. Think then what might happen when you connect with yourself.

Sometimes hypnosis receives bad press because of unscrupulous baddies. Manipulation and cruelty occurs daily – you only have to spend a few minutes reading a newspaper.

Secretly people rather like the idea of power and control. Often I have clients ask me to 'make' them do or stop doing something and I often hear, 'Put me under your power'. The most relevant to this is the one who said, 'Take me to a previous incarnation!'

Very few suggest we do it together or ask if I can be their guide or assistant. They want to relinquish themselves and some are disappointed when I explain the normality of the experience, feeling almost cheated or deprived. All this though is another experience of programming. Even children play the hypnotist and say things like 'you are in my power. Sleep. You are going under. Give me your pin number...'

Senses

When you decide on a course of action how do you carry it out? Think about reversing the car into a parking space. Imagine that you had to describe it to an alien who could understand your language but who had no concept of cars, driving or roads. Consider other things that you do – crossing the road, using tools, changing a baby's nappy – things we do without thought but difficult to describe. And yet you can carry out many tasks at the same time quite safely without having to consider how. In fact, if you thought about it all too much it is unlikely you would ever do it again.

Remember the last time you went out for a meal. Did you know immediately what you wanted to order, or did you have to read the menu, think about the choices or maybe get advice from the waiter and allow his descriptions to entice and sway your decision – tempting your taste buds? If you think about flavours do you begin to actually taste them and remember when you last ate something that tasted of, say, garlic, hot and spicy or maybe sweet?

Do you talk to yourself or think things through? Would you have a discussion in your mind about the flavours of the food on offer or would you picture it in your mind? Have you noticed that most pudding menus have pictures to tempt you? If you were to think about opening a big new jar of pickled onions, getting one out and eating it, what happens to you? What about slicing and sucking a

117

thick juicy slice of a lemon? Are you salivating? Can you smell or taste it? And what is happening when you do that? Are you aware, conscious, or is it something else?

There are lots of people who complain about their thoughts and the way they behave as if they are not really part of them and they have come from somewhere outside of themselves. You may hear people say things like, 'I can't stop thinking about so and so', or 'I've got no will power', or 'Every time I try to stop smoking (or similar) I can't stop thinking about it'. Ask any dieter what they spend their time thinking about. The answer will be food and what they or someone else has told them they are not allowed to eat. The more importance put on not having something, the more desperate the need becomes. If you have gone without in a past life, for example food, love or comfort, you may well be obsessive about it in this life.

How and why do we do all these things? Where does the information come from?

The knowledge that enables you 'to operate' is stored very conveniently in your subconscious mind. So when you make a conscious decision to do something, i.e. 'I want to make a cup of tea', your subconscious mind makes a quick check to see if you have done it before and then it uses the stored information to enable you to brew up.

This process happens with everything we do. Crossing a road, knowing not to stick our hands into flames, driving and all the hundreds of thing we do everyday.

How we regard our subconscious is personal – I have worked with people who regard theirs as a computer, others who see it like a filing cabinet, tree of life, big box or maybe an instruction manual. The last in that list makes me think of what do we usually do with instruction manuals? Lose them, ignore them or throw them away.

The more we do something or the more emotion we put into it, the more familiar it becomes. Phobias typically take hold because of the powerful emotion going on at the time they were created. The fear of spiders, for example, is usually programmed during childhood when someone, usually an adult and most often a parent, screams in terror and is frozen to the spot, runs away or kills the spider. The child learns that spiders must have an amazing power or be very dangerous and therefore it is important to hold on to the fear to keep safe. In adulthood the logical mind can know it is irrational but that doesn't make the slightest difference.

We learn, it is stored, and we can then do things automatically without having to relearn regardless of whether it is something constructive or something debilitating. All this carries on until we want to alter something, at which point the subconscious mind seems to do all it can to prevent change. It doesn't want to let go of something that you have put so much focus and energy in creating.

If we are trying to change a habit, success is much more likely to happen if we are excited and motivated about the change. Something very simple like putting your keys in a different place can cause all sorts of problems and irritations because we suddenly have to 'think' instead of just getting them automatically, whereas changing something that is emotive is even harder than key storage because of that extra energy invested.

Smoking is hard to stop because smokers are fearful of life without their cigarettes and they believe they won't be able to cope or manage. This is the message that is constantly broadcast and that fear is stronger than the prospect of ill health through smoking.

Sometimes when people have phobias they are fearful of not having that fear anymore so remaining phobic is the better option. As soon as something changes we have to demonstrate that we can do the very thing we were afraid of, whether that is getting on a plane, have a spider walk up your arm or manage without forty a day.

When I was scared of flying I would do anything to avoid travelling and missed out on a lot of experiences, but when given the opportunity to be free from it I had to really think hard about whether I really wanted it to go. I knew that if I said everything was all right I would then have to get on a plane and prove it. This made me doubt myself and I played the 'what ifs'. You know the game? What if I only think it's okay? What if I am okay going but not when coming back? What if, what if, what if? I then rethought it all. What if I actually *could* get on a plane and enjoy myself? What if I *could* have the freedom to travel? What if I had the opportunity to see the world and meet many wonderful people?

At this point I realised that we have choices and that we can talk ourselves into and out of success with ease. When I was struggling with my stage fright, again I had a choice. Either I could deal with it or I could not.

This is where you are now. Having choices. If you want to visit somewhere, you don't need a reason you can just choose. If your journey takes you through time and you are ready to be a past life tourist, this is where you get on.

Language of the subconscious - internal imagery and self-talk

Our subconscious mind seems to be a law unto itself, doesn't it? Many believe that is where our 'will' lives. Do you know anyone with amazing willpower or someone without any? What makes one different from the other?

The one that seems to have the willpower is the one with the belief in their abilities, but what is this thing called *will*?

If we break it down it becomes the power of will. Surely that means that if you want to do or change something, then you will. So that's easy, you can now just stop smoking, stop being scared, overeating, getting stressed or anything else that is bothering you. Except *will* often doesn't want to. There is something else going on. Emotions get in the way, including other people's emotions. Reactions and behaviours are in the subconscious so does that mean that *will* is in fact in the conscious mind?

Often people tell me they have had their habit for so long because they haven't any will power. So the want is conscious but the action is subconscious – yes/no? Is there something you want to change or that you have been trying to change? Can you think through why you can or why you can't?

It is because of the internal naming system that we use: the inner programmes that run us or that we run. One person is struck with terror at the prospect of public speaking while another is thrilled and excited and craves to be vocal.

My 'fear' of flying changed when it got a different name that I felt completely happy with. My response to the feelings then changed. Whereas in the past I felt sick, had tummy ache and hurt all over with my new programme, these reactions became excitement and that wonderful feeling of not being able to wait. The rumbling of the plane at takeoff became thrilling instead of terrifying. The view out of the window was extraordinary. I had been unable to look before without feeling sick. Until that moment of change, I could come up with many reasons, or excuses, to not let it go. When the desire became so strong it overruled and that was it – time to be free.

Visiting the past can be like clearing out a cupboard. When you have something shiny and new you can throw away the old, scruffy broken stuff. But sometimes even after we have got the replacement we still hold onto the old stuff just 'in case'. Lots of us hoard negative memories and outdated emotions just as we do kettles and pieces of paper. We might be holding old grudges, dislike of others, scary attractions or crushes.

As every thought causes a reaction somewhere within us, repeating negative inner dialogues or thoughts can form programmes that become difficult to change. It is because of the effect that continual stress has on our bodies (this includes the mind) that we must do something about it before serious damage becomes permanent.

Our stress mechanisms - physical, mental and emotional - are the same now as they were when we ran about dressed in loincloths and lived in caves, the flight or fight response. Eat or be eaten.

The physical and mental reactions are the same whether we perceive danger or fear in the 'now', if we imagine something is going to happen or if we mull over experiences from the past. I realise that you might not have any issues whatsoever, but over the years I have learnt (the hard way or, should I say, the challenging way) that it is best to be aware and prepared. If all is hunky-dory with you, and I really hope it is, you can use all your newfound knowledge to help someone else.

Before we set off, please give yourself a quick scan. This is a bit like checking the oil, water and tyre pressures, only without getting mucky. You might like to make a note of anything at all that comes to your mind, even if it doesn't seem to make sense or hold any relevance.

Be aware of people who you are in contact with who might be depleting your resources. Even though we all want to appear nice and liked, most of us know people who act like leeches - draining us or using us. You might not be aware but if you think about your friends you will know which ones make you feel good, your true friends. This might be apparent in the feeling of unconditional love or that they always leave you with a feeling of contentment.

Think of those you love, care about and admire. Think of friends who you always enjoy seeing with, regardless of whatever else might be going on. Be aware of whom you would contact in an emergency or that person you know you can rely on come what may (it is quite likely that these people are soul mates).

Now think of people you instantly felt comfortable with as if you'd always known them the moment you met. Have you ever fallen in love in a split second or felt a wave of familiarity to someone?

***

Now that you are ready and prepared, here are various techniques for you to try out. You may find you like them all, or you have a preference to one or the other. It may be that different methods reap varying rewards. Information might begin to become apparent in dreams that you can use as a starting point, or if you use another method successfully your dreams might complete your journey.

Dreams

If you don't remember your dreams, start to have a pen and paper next to you and when you wake, either during the night or first thing in the morning, immediately write down your thoughts. It doesn't matter whether it makes sense at first; soon it will. You might not even remember that you penned a message to yourself until you read it, but after a while it will become second nature and a pattern will form, even if you write in code or symbols that your sleeping mind understands. A voice recorder works perfectly as well to store your dreams, but if you share a bedroom it might be best to warn your partner; in case they think you've lost the plot or that you're giving them a running commentary on your night-time activities.

Instructing yourself about wanting to have memories come to you in your sleep is the first step. This can be as direct as you like. Focus your mind and your thoughts on time periods, places, feelings, desire to explore or whatever feels comfortable. Or use direct suggestion to yourself, 'Subconscious, as I sleep please bring to my awareness memories from my past lives in my dreams'. Of course, you may prefer a different instruction, for example, 'Let me dream of the past' or similar.

Another option is to meditate during the day and instruct or ask for dream memories, as the subconscious mind is happy when tasked. Generally when my clients have been regressed they often get more awareness during their dreams.

If you believe you are holding onto an emotion attached to your past, put your awareness there as you drift off and expect the answers you are seeking to come to you. You could try, if you like, focussing your thoughts on wherever you think you might have a past life memory you wish to retrieve, in a similar way to daydreaming except the intention is to fall asleep with the scenes from your inner movie mind playing.

A nifty little way to fall asleep, while thinking about the journey you wish to take, is to stare straight ahead. Of course it will be dark so you aren't actually looking at anything, just staring. After a while you may notice you can't quite tell if you're eyes are open or closed or you might fall asleep before that happens.

Before doing this, as with any other method, remind yourself that you are safe and that you are just observing - trust that your own inner healing mechanisms will work for you at all times.

As you continue to read this, you may mix and match the other techniques for your sleep dreams.

Although you are making use of your dreams and sleep, there are two very wonderful natural hypnotic states that happen to us all. They are the hypnagogic and hypnopompic sleep states. What fantastic words they both are. They refer to that little twilight zone, seconds before falling asleep, and that cosy first few awakening moments. We often have brainwaves, amazing thoughts and intense feelings of exhilaration during these times.

Daydreams

It is possible to daydream into your memories if you aren't too distracted by your environment or thoughts, and this will often induce a relaxed state that you can then drift into fully. You can pick a starting point for yourself and then allow your thoughts to free flow to wherever your mind takes you.

Say, for example, you think you have an association with a particular person or time period. Begin by imagining that – create a picture[2] in your mind of how you would have dressed, where you might have been and who you would have been with or known. This is just the jump off point to get you going.

Imagine then that you are a casual observer and allow the images to unfold to you as you sink into the experience. Please don't be concerned if you think you are making it all up, as you most likely will be in the beginning. The idea is to awaken your subconscious memories by giving them a helping hand.

Pendulum

I mention this part before the hypnotic meditation, as some of you will prefer it, while others might use both together.

There are some very beautiful pendulums available to buy, but it is fine to make one: it can be as complex as you like - with beads, stones, a chain or a ring on a bit of string or necklace.

In the first instance you need to 'tune in' to your pendulum by holding it for a while in your less dominant hand until it feels just right. If it is bought and has a bead at the top hold this in your dominant hand. If it is a homemade version, drape the chain or thread over your fingers while keeping hold of the end so the pendulum part can move freely.

In your mind or out loud, say, 'Show me a yes' and then wait and notice which way it moves. It might swing, spin, vibrate or be still. But, when you sense that you know, ask it to then show you a no. Yes and no is enough, but sometimes the answer might not be available and so in those instances a not at this time movement might be pertinent.

When you are ready, all you need to do is ask questions and the pendulum will respond. It reacts to miniscule triggers, signals and messages from your subconscious mind and your hardest

---

[2] Some call this creative visualisation, but if you aren't visual use the sense or the mixture of senses that feel most comfortable to you.

job will be to trust it. This method might seem slow at first, but like everything the more you do it the easier and quicker it will become.

To get started ask general questions like, 'Am I a man (or woman)?' 'Am I blonde?' 'Am I addicted to cheese?', etc and you'll ascertain how the pendulum works for you. In between your probings, gently rest it on your other hand for it to still and settle.

For past life questions you can follow the plan that comes later or make your own.

Hypnotic Meditation

We automatically drift into a trancelike state if we do anything repetitive or boring. When we concentrate, fix our attention or bombard ourselves with too much information, then away we go.

Hypnosis is a recognised discipline within the medical and complementary therapy fields. People from all walks of life use it for as many different reasons that you can think of. These range from stress management to creating abundance, phobia removal to past life healing, along with everything in between. Although it is not a panacea for all ails, it is quite probably the best tool you can have at your disposal in preparation for anything life may throw your way.

Millions on a daily basis practise meditation worldwide: for many it is their way of life and they couldn't do without it, but when you combine the disciplines together it gets even better.

From reading the previous chapter you now know about different states of mind, so all that is left for you to do is learn how to let out your expertness.

Sometimes when people first start trying out hypnotic or meditative techniques they think they 'can't' do it or they haven't 'got' there. If you experience these thoughts, I want to assure you that very soon you will recognise your own individual trance states in the same way that you are aware of all your other states. It will become as obvious and natural to you as it really is.

Preparing for your sessions

Some people like to dim the lights and use candles, joss sticks and soporific music while others like darkness, silence and no smells. There are those who enjoy a meditative place like woodland, for example, and I know of several who snuggle into bed.

A walking meditation doesn't need to be excluded as it is entirely up to you how associated you are with your experiences and it is then like a controlled daydream.

You do whatever you prefer – drum to your own rhythm – rule free. But most importantly, have fun with it, enjoy the bliss and reap the benefits.

Choices you may want to consider
1. Write notes or key points to trigger your actions or include these if you are preparing a recording. Think of your desires and then create a representative symbol that you recall during your session. Read through, then remember how to induce trance. Record your instructions and play them back to yourself.

2. Prepare a 'seek mission' beforehand. Say your plan, write it or think it. As you read through the inductions you will notice that some are more suited to a read 'script' while others are easy to remember and then just 'do'.

3. First we have the induction. This is a state of wakeful relaxation for some, a focussed mind in others or a bit of both. Your experience may vary depending on your mood, tiredness levels and what your goal might be.

4. Methodically using rhythm of words, breathing, sounds or experiences, or through 'overloading' the mind with instructions as well as under-stimulation by focussing on one 'sound' or thought, are all natural ways that you can use in a controlled way.

5. The next bit is deepening. This isn't always necessary as it depends on the induction, how deep you choose to go or if you are just having a quickie: for instant calm or perkiness. When you have learnt the techniques you may well want to explore other things such as inner peace or pain removal, for example. The techniques are variable, plus you can mix and match, and you are free to create your own versions, as it is fun to try out different ways. Visualisation, counting down, creating the sensation of sinking, drifting or floating, imagining walking down steps or stairs all create excellent results.

6. The deepening is followed by your 'session' that you either gently float into or as a definite step or stage in your process. This part will vary depending on whether you are using a script or going into an emotion as the starting point of your regression or progression.

7. Lastly is the finishing off and 'awakening'. Although this is a misnomer as you aren't actually asleep, it tends to be the best word rather than coming back, returning or arousal. You do this by counting, having an alarm, just awakening or, if you like, after you've had a little snooze.

Inductions

Inducing a hypnotic meditative state is more successful if it is personal to the way you think and process information. If you were told to picture a beautiful day and you don't particularly see images in your mind, you may be disappointed and think you can't do it. A good way to cover all eventualities is to use 'see, sense or imagine'.

Better than that, though, is to pay attention to your inner processes and use the induction that suits you the best. If you are:

Visual – you see pictures in your mind. They are usually in colour and are most often moving pictures. Do you see what I mean?

Auditory – you hear your inner voice; you self-talk instruction or you have a running commentary going. Are you hearing me?

Kinaesthetic – you feel experiences and emotions attached to incidents and memories. You may take longer to respond to questions because you have to remember the feeling. How does that feel?

I have also included the following and will explain why after.

Gustatory – taste. Are your experiences flavoursome?

Olfactory - the smell has it. Did you slow down and smell the flowers?

I have included these as I once did a whole course of hypnotherapy with a woman who only used her sense of smell. It was a challenge but we managed. Most people are bits of all the above, but a few are more dominant in one or another.

We all operate in cycles and rhythms so please remember this when creating your inductions: the waves lapping on the shore in time with your breathing, slowly breathing in and out…in…out… in…out. Gently rocking, sinking, drifting, or whatever terminology you are using.

Methods to try

Progressive relaxation
This is useful to learn and experience because of its stress reducing properties and healing.

Make yourself comfortable with you arms and legs uncrossed. Focus your attention on your feet and imagine they are relaxing. Focus on all the muscles in and around your feet and allow them to rest. Now, do the same with your ankles and calf muscles. Do this slowly in a controlled way, right up your body until you reach the top of your head. If you are very tired or stressed you might fall asleep, and if you have difficulties dropping off to sleep this technique it may help.

Some instructions for this suggest that you clench and relax each muscle as you go. I personally think this is unnecessary and it might disturb your rhythm if you suddenly have a little discomfort anywhere that you were unaware of before. A tight muscle is a tense one and this is far from our aim.

You can imagine each body part resting, or say the instruction to yourself as you go, 'My feet are relaxing', 'My ankles are relaxing', 'My calves are relaxing' and so on.

Counting techniques

In your mind, count (see, imagine, sense) backwards from 100, rhythmically in time with your breathing, and relax a little with each number. You might like to say to yourself after each number, 'relax', 'deeper and deeper', 'calm' or a word that you associate with being relaxed. Do this until you lose count or forget where you've got to and can't be bothered to start over.

Count to yourself: 1, 2, 3…1, 2, 3…1, 2, 3 over and over and try to prevent thoughts nipping in between the numbers. If they do manage to squeeze in, say the numbers quicker so they are closer together. The aim is to only have the numbers in your head with big gaps between them, but it may happen that you forget where you are or forget to remember to count.

Eyes

Fix your eyes on a spot slightly above your natural line of sight. Breathe into that spot and imagine there is nothing else but that spot. You may find that your eyes get tired and want to close: if so, let them. Or, you might end up not being sure whether your eyes are open or closed. Years ago I worked with a young tennis player who described his trance as having his eyes open on the outside but closed on the inside during the game but when resting it was the other way round.

A quick way to trigger relaxation is to roll your eyes up as high as possible without making them uncomfortable as you breathe in and let them gently close as you breathe out. Repeat this twice more and after the third imagine or pretend your eyes are so relaxed they can't be bothered to open. When you feel that, just let the relaxation spread, flow and ooze all over, in and through you as you relax more and more deeply with each breath.

* * *

Here are a couple of scripts that you may wish to play around with and jiggle to personalise to your desires. Pause at the ellipses regardless of whether you are recording your instructions to yourself or just carrying it out. I am aware that they are grammatically incorrect but that is the nature of the hypnotic beast.

They can work perfectly well as reading meditations; you can just ignore the bit that says close your eyes, unless you want to read first and then when you are ready close your eyes and take yourself on your trip.

Make yourself cosy and comfortable.

Take a slow breath in and, as you breathe out, you may let your eyes gently close or wait a while until you feel ready to close them.

Begin to notice your breathing ... You don't need to alter your breathing pattern...just breathe gently and regularly, noticing how you feel as you breathe...if you feel differently when you breathe in to when you breathe out...allowing yourself to become more restful each time you breathe out.

Begin to notice thoughts in your mind. Thoughts coming and going. Some thoughts staying awhile and some being sorted or filed before you notice them...

Become aware of noises and sounds coming and going. From now on during this meditation just ignore all sounds that you hear while you are resting, apart from an emergency; just remind your mind that you are relaxing more and more...

Now, think about your feelings – in your mind and in your body. Feel those feelings...feelings of tension can begin to be replaced by calmness...

Thoughts come and go... Sounds come and go... Feelings come and go...

Breathing regular and slow...as you relax deeply into yourself where all is well...

Put your awareness now into your hands... Notice how they are feeling – if they are warm, cool, heavy or light. Imagine how your hands would feel if they were completely relaxed. Only you know how your relaxed hands feel...

And all the while, thoughts coming and going... Sounds coming and going... Feelings coming and going...

Breathing regular and slowing...

Think now about how your feet are feeling. Notice if they are warm, cool heavy or light... If they feel the same as your hands...

While you are thinking about your feet, allow your hands to relax... Only you know how your relaxed feet feel.

And all the while, thoughts coming and going... Sounds coming and going... Feelings coming and going...

Breathing regular and slowing.

Focus your attention now on the back of your neck. Imagine your feet are relaxing the same as your hands... Relaxing more each time you breathe out...

And now slowly and gently allow the relaxation in your hands begin to flow up now into your arms... At the same time the relaxation in your feet can spread up your legs...

Resting... Slowing... Calm and comfortable...

That restful feeling can spread now from your arms, across your shoulders and down your back… At the same time from your legs feel it flowing up, up though your hips, pelvic area, tummy and chest…

Calm peaceful waves of peace and relaxation flowing through your whole being…

All that relaxation can flow up now through into your neck, up the back of your head and through your face, eyes forehead and scalp…

And now…slowly, gently but very thoroughly back down your body like little waves on the sand.

Calm… Peaceful… Relaxed… Soothed. Taking yourself down inside yourself to where you feel comfortable. That cosy feeling way down deep inside – where all is well. This is your time now – time for you.

Any tensions, anxieties, worries or fears are mentally massaged away. Draining away from you.

As you relax, more and more deeply, I am going to count from one to ten and you can allow the passing numbers to help you to rest even more…even more…

One, resting… relaxing…

Two, breathing gently… relaxing more and more with every breath… with every gentle beat of your heart…

Three, feel your whole being soothed… caressed in peace…

Four, breathe away any tensions or anxieties…

Five, rest… relax… calm…

Six, calm… breathing easy… soothed…

Seven, resting more and more deeply…

Eight, inner peace washing over you and through you… calm… peaceful… relaxed…

Nine, each breath taking you deeper and deeper into calm and peace…

Ten, continuing to relax…

Special place

Now, in your mind, create a special place. It can be somewhere that you know or somewhere that you make up. It can be inside or out. Use your imagination as best you can. Have your special place exactly as you like...colours...textures...everything perfect...

All that matters is that this special place is yours - it belongs to you. You choose who or what you have there. Relax now in that special place within you, that you are now in. Spend some time looking around...enjoy the feelings and inner contentment...

When you are in your special place, all is well. You can begin to release anything that isn't serving a purpose and you discover that you can make choices and experience freedom.

Spend some time now in your special place and know that you can return whenever you want.

Your thoughts can be clear, calm and focused and whenever you think of your special place your mind replicates calmness.

You can now become aware of your desires and goals, and your inner mind is now creating the programmes for you to achieve exactly as you wish. Create it now in your mind.

Fill yourself with success.

You can visit your special place if you want to relax, if you are looking for answers, or for no other reason than it is lovely.

Find somewhere now where you can rest – a chair, hammock, bed...and snuggle down into slumber. In this special relaxation your mind is able to access anything that you desire...ideas, memories, plans, goals...anything...

From here you can rest, continue your journey, sleep or gently awaken.

Relax along a rainbow

This method makes use of colours and anything you may associate with each one.

As your awareness is in each colour, focus on the sensations you experience and specifically what you might want to happen in any particular area of your body. Release any and all anxieties and tensions into each colour.

Imagine a rainbow floating in front of you. See the colours swirling and flowing and notice each colour become clearer.

The separating colours of the rainbow are becoming clearer and clearer - notice the red, orange, yellow, green, blue, indigo and violet...all the colours are going to flow through you so that you can experience the calming power of each colour.

Imagine yourself sinking a little deeper into comfort as you think, sense and feel the red of the rainbow flow in and through your legs as you fccl at ease. Allow the red colour to swirl around you and feel it in and around your legs, bathing them in comfort...

Imagine yourself sinking a little deeper into comfort as you think, sense and feel the orange of the rainbow flow in and through your pelvic area. Allow the orange colour to swirl around you and feel it in and around your pelvic area, bathing you in comfort...

Imagine yourself sinking a little deeper into comfort as you think, sense and feel the yellow of the rainbow flow in and through your tummy. Allow the yellow colour to swirl around you and feel it in and around your tummy, bathing you in comfort...

Imagine yourself sinking a little deeper into comfort as you think, sense and feel the green of the rainbow flow in and through your heart. Allow the green colour to swirl around you and feel it in and around your heart, bathing you in comfort...

Imagine yourself sinking a little deeper into comfort as you think, sense and feel the blue of the rainbow flow in and through your throat. Allow the blue colour to swirl around you and feel it in and around your throat, bathing you in comfort...

Imagine yourself sinking a little deeper into comfort as you think, sense and feel the indigo of the rainbow flow in and through your forehead just above your eyes. Allow the indigo colour to swirl around you and feel it in and around your eyes, bathing them in comfort...

Imagine yourself sinking a little deeper into comfort as you think, sense and feel the violet of the rainbow flow in and through your head. Allow the violet colour to swirl around you and feel it in and around your head, bathing you in comfort... Spend some time enjoying the colours as they dance and swirl in and around you. Notice you can direct thoughts, calmness, relaxation and inner healing power to wherever you desire.

Allow the power of the colours to continue to work their magic. Become aware of one particular colour that you associate with comfort and focus your mind on that colour. Be soothed, peaceful, relaxed.

Just by thinking, saying or hearing this colour reminds your mind that you can rest into comfort.

And as before, from here you can rest, continue on your journey, sleep or gently awaken.

***

Here is a complete journey that is taken from my CD. At all times you are in control and you will get the most benefit if you use your imagination as best as you can. If I ask you to look at something and you aren't physically seeing anything, just use your senses and imagine what you might see, hear, feel, taste, smell or sense.

Okay. Get cosy and make sure you are warm enough. This meditation is gentle and calming. To begin, you will physically relax and then as your mind rests you will be able to focus your thoughts more and more to retrieve your memories. From now on during this process, all noises and sounds that you hear, apart from an emergency, just remind your mind that you're relaxing. If you need to awaken you can do so at any time. But, for now...

Let's begin. Imagine that as you are breathing - gentle calming waves of relaxation are rhythmically flowing through you.

Beginning at you feet. As you breathe in, imagine the feeling of relaxation flowing into your feet. Really get into the rhythm as you gently breathe in and out, the relaxation washes through, in and over you like waves on the sand. With each breath the waves flow higher... your breathing controls your relaxation. As you breathe out fully you rest even more, even more. Allow the wave to flow now... to your knees... thighs... hips... tummy... chest... up your back... neck... shoulders... everything resting, slowing down and now the calm and spread up into your face and head...

And now... slowly, gently but very thoroughly, back down your body like little waves on the sand.

Calm. Peaceful. Relaxed. Soothed. Taking yourself down inside yourself to where you feel comfortable. That cosy feeling way down deep inside, where all is well. This is your time now – time for you.

Any tensions, anxieties, worries or fears are mentally massaged away. Draining away from you.

Think about floating with relaxation as you sink deeper...

As you relax more and more deeply I am going to count from one to ten and you can allow the passing numbers to help you to rest even more... even more...

One, resting... relaxing...

Two, breathing gently... relaxing more and more with every breath... with every gentle beat of your heart...

Three, be soothed... caressed in peace...

Four, breathe away any tensions or anxieties...

Five, rest... relax... calm...

Six, calm... breathing easy... soothed...

Seven, resting more and more deeply...

Eight, inner peace washing over you and through you... calm... peaceful... relaxed...

Nine, each breath taking you deeper and deeper into calm and peace...

Ten, continuing to relax...

And now… in your mind create a special place. It can be somewhere that you know or somewhere that you make up. It can be inside or out. Use your imagination as best you can. Have your special place exactly as you like… colours… textures… everything perfect…

All that matters is that this special place is yours - it belongs to you. You choose who or what you have there. Relaxing now, in that special place within you, that you are now in. Spend some time looking around… enjoy the feelings and inner contentment…

When you are in your special place, all is well. Your thoughts can be clear, calm and focused and whenever you think of your special place your mind replicates calmness.

You can visit your special place if you want to relax, if you are looking for answers, or for no reason other than that it is lovely.

In your special place there is a door that leads outside. The door is only there when you want it to be there.

Go to the door now, and if it is closed gently push it open and step through it, onto the small safe step that leads onto the bridge of time. You are safe and in control as we slowly cross over the bridge to your past. Sense the swirling pale blue mist that you are walking through and pause when you are half way.

Now slowly continue over the bridge and notice that the mist is gently clearing on the other side. As you step off the bridge you have travelled back in time to a memory of significance in one of your past lives. Take a moment and wait for the mist to clear.

Take your time and get your bearings.

Allow yourself to tune in to where you are. Remember you are just looking... in a safe, detached way.

Begin to notice things now - are you inside or outside? Is it quiet or is there noise? Are you male or female? What season is it? You can explore while I continue to prompt your thoughts, but you don't particularly need to listen to me.

Become aware of your thoughts and feelings associated with

whatever you experience. Are there other people about? What are you wearing - can you sense colours, textures, temperature? Do you know your name?

Take your time to really allow your senses to detect everything. If there are other people about, are they familiar to you?

Now you can travel in time through the memory to events or happenings that are relevant to you. Perhaps you are receiving an answer or an indication of why something is as it is. Do not be concerned if the chronological order of time is muddled - you will be able to sort through later and it will make sense.

If you are seeking something in particular that you would like resolved, go now to the time where that answer awaits. You are safe and detached. If you are not seeking anything in particular, just explore.

Gather the information you desire, but know you don't have to do it all in one go, and it may well be that knowledge comes to you in your daydreams or dreams of the night.

If you find an emotion attached to a memory that isn't useful or productive, detach from it now. In your mind acknowledge it, thank your mind for enabling you to discover this and then imagine separating from that emotion. Knowledge is very valuable and often just knowing is all that we need.

Take yourself now to near the end of that life. Become aware of all that is happening. Your location, your thoughts, feelings, emotions. Are you alone or with others? What is happening around you?

Now go beyond the moment of passing from that life - be free. Sense the clearness. Look or think back to that life you've just been recalling and know that there is an important message or learning for you. Wait until you have that valuable insight...

You will bring that back with you. Be peaceful and restored.

It is time for you to return now. Find yourself back on the bridge of time and slowly cross back towards now. Feel safe and calm. As you step off the bridge, leave the past where it belongs - in the past - just a memory like any other memory. Keep hold of the valuable message that you have.

Come back through the door and into your special place. Find somewhere to rest while you assimilate whatever you have gathered.

Make sure all your inner filing is done and know that you can return whenever you choose or you may retrieve other memories.

It is now time to awaken - bring yourself awake as I count from ten to one.

Ten, nine, eight, seven, six, five, four... more and more awake... three, two, one... eyes open and have a stretch.

Let your thoughts clear.

Thank you for taking this journey with me. You may find you recall snippets of memory throughout the day or dreams of the night. The process can take you as long as you like.

***

When you create your own journey you might like to consider that you go into a memory through a tunnel, pass through a cloud, watch a clock's hand turning backwards or you just arrive - perhaps on the count of three. For example, 'On the count of three I will be in the memory of one of my past lives... one, two three.'

If you are very kinaesthetic you can sink into a memory by focussing on a part of your body where you might be holding a memory or an emotion.

I once watched a regression whereby someone had stiff arthritic hands. By only thinking about his hands, any messages they might have for him he recalled hanging on to a ledge while trying to escape with his life from a traumatic event. He didn't share anything else but immediately felt relief in his discomfort.

You can try the more direct approach as well. For example, 'Subconscious, please show me the reason for my panic attacks, fear of water, men in hats...' or whatever.

As I said before, always remind yourself you are safe to begin and make sure you are finished at the end. If you feel fuzzy or muddled, take a quiet moment while your subconscious carries out its filing and sorting.

The Journey Planner or the past life protocol

Regardless of whether you are touring or seeking a solution, it is best to stick to a plan. I have included my plans for the regressions that I carried out in the exact order so you know how I do it.

The client arrives and we discuss their ideas and thoughts about regression generally - your equivalent is reading this book along with you answering your own questions as you've progressed.

I ask about any previous experience they may have including dreams, spontaneous memory and holding patterns. We discuss these but do not analyse. The process is explained along with the method of inducing a relaxed state. As the hypnotic meditation is pretty straightforward everyone understands what will occur.

When we are ready for their journey I ensure they are completely satisfied with the plan, and I begin the induction followed by the deepener.

They are then taken to their special place and through the door, pass over the bridge of time, through the blue mist – the remainder is as per the script.

Creating your own special place is a valuable tool to have. As well as being your own Regressionist, you can use the techniques for all sorts of reasons: reducing stress, healing, sleeping well and self-therapy.

Research questions for PLR

If you particularly want to do some research, here are some things for you to be aware of during your regression. Some of the answers you will already know, others you may have to look for even though you might not always find the answers the first time. You will perhaps have other thoughts and ideas if you are seeking something in particular. You can guide without leading.

Married - maiden name/own name/known as?
Most important building/place/person?
Who you are dependent on/or on you?
Senses of taste, smell, sounds?
When - season/date/year?
How/where travelling?
What is to left/right?
Where water/food?
Time of day/night?
Where – location?
Any fears?
Pleasures?
Weather?
Children?
Food?
Sex?
Age?

And then all you need to do is put it all together! There are various scripts for you to try out later.

7

Future Lives

We have touched on the possibility of progressing to the future in this life, but I have also had people travel to far future lives.

When we look forward we may well be glimpsing a mind creation, as it projects a possibility rather than inevitability by using what is known now. We can then make choices in our actions if we don't like what we see.

If we can travel back in time can we also go forward? Can we visit what hasn't happened?

For those who like to be mind boggled, how about the thought that it is all happening at once anyway and there is no past or future, just the now? Depending where you are in the world at this moment, for some it is yesterday while others are in tomorrow.

Is the future already planned, waiting for us to take up our role and place, or are probabilities of what might or might not happen changing by the minute? If we alter something does it have a knock-on effect? Possibly. If you heal from a childhood trauma, changes occur in your 'now' which then creates ripples that then affects people around you. We all live in causality, so everything we do causes an effect in us, others and our environment.

My client, who was moving to Spain, wanted to know the outcome. Who knows whether her wishful thinking created the success - her hard work definitely did, but when she came to me she was nervous about the potential effect on herself and family. From that viewpoint I would have expected her to make a negative future picture as a possible escape. Miserable negative people expect the worse and inevitably get it. Their language is, 'I knew it would go wrong. Nothing ever goes right for me'. It is the same story again.

The only difference is, it hasn't happened yet.

Andrea experienced a regression and progression for a magazine feature. In her past life she was a patient in a mental hospital recovering from a breakdown. We then worked our way forward and she visited her son's wedding. When we are looking forward are we actually creating it, or only our expectation and therefore result?

To finish, Andrea went to a future life where she found herself working as a brain surgeon, or doctor of the head, with the name of Doctor Blake. At the time of the progression she/he was aged in the mid-forties and on a ward round. The post carried, or will carry if we're being pedantic, a lot of responsibility.

From one to another the contrast was clear. She felt helpless in the past and then moved on to being strong with many responsibilities taking care of those with vulnerabilities. Andrea was able to 'chat' with Doctor Blake and get some advice for her present Self. Coincidentally (if there is such a thing), in this life she is interested in everything relating to the head and healing.

Did her past trigger the route to her doctor persona via her fascination with psychology, or is it a metaphor of extremes? Does it matter?

After Lizzie's regression, she travelled forward to a time whereby, after much sadness, she was sitting on a Welsh mountain recovering and planning for her future. The amazing thing about this particular case is that it has now happened exactly as she saw.

I think it's rather a nice touch to visit the future as an end to visiting the past or vice versa.

Denise Linn describes in her book, *Past Lives, Present Dreams*, how as a small child she had felt a sense of someone being present when there was no one actually there. Thirty years later she took herself back in time to visit her childhood and to offer love and support to herself as a child. She wrote, 'Not only had I travelled back and visited my younger self (sic), but as a small child I remembered the visit!'

Richard Craze had spent time mooting the possibility of leaving a legacy for his future Self that lead him on an amazing story, whereby he discovered historical facts about his home and many threads tied neatly together. During one of his regressions he discovered that his past Self had attempted to travel forwards in time using ether and he had come face to face and met himself. The past traveller coming forwards was very shocked by this because it had actually worked. This aroused Richard's interest in the subject matter even more and so he decided to go forwards. The following is taken from his book, with kind permission of Roni.

'I'm in a room, a very, very white room. I am in it and watching me in it at the same time. It is like an operating theatre, but it isn't, it's very, very white.

'There's something – ahh – this hurts, they have put some thing here (pointing to behind right ear), something here, this ridge behind my ear, there is something in there, an electrode, an implant or something. It is something new - I don't know...

'White desks, and on the desks there are things like computers but they are not computers, the keyboards are too big, they are almost oval – big. And the keys aren't keys, they are colours and something else – symbols, I can't see and there is no screen and there is nothing else, just keyboards. Four rows of keys, the top keys are colours and then the symbols not on the keys, they are above the keys and you have to...they are like 3D keys, you have to put your fingers through the symbols to operate the key, the keys are flat, strange, very strange.

'They know what I am trying to do.

'I am very young. They don't think I can do this. They are surprised when I say I can do this and now they know I can. I've told them what I am doing and they were expecting this, expecting me.

'I'm getting a lot of information that I do not understand. They

145

are talking to me in data.

'They say – oh it's something to do with dream research and the name "Metis". Metis is doing this consciously. He is giving them his dream. They are monitoring his dream, my dream, our dream.'

The notes written by the therapist after his session were thus:

'You described yourself as very young (13–14) – blond, humorous and laughing. Wearing a white shirt and white trousers, very casual. The room felt white. You were teaching them to use – cross between keyboard and organ keys.

Metis was not your name – he is Metis, doing Metis. Metis wanted to know what my computer was. Don't need that stuff to do what you want to do.

Given this opportunity just once will not be allowed to return.'

Is your mind boggling? Would you like a little more?

In 2005 I was involved in an idea for Discovery Science and a film crew toddled over to film a future life progression. I did a couple and Joylina was sweet enough to send her thoughts, as follows.

Recollections of Future Life Progression

'I drifted gently for a while in a kind of limbo which was really nice, full of love, and went into the future and found myself on a planet which was full of only feminine energy - the individual souls, i.e. individual people, were all female and we worked together as a group beaming feminine energy into the universe. It was to balance the universe but there was another planet somewhere else that was working with masculine energy. Our role was to keep the universe in balance between the two energies.

'It was really interesting there; the light was ever changing through the different colours of the rainbow, but was very muted as if it was all dark as well, yet the colours were there in a kind of swirling kaleidoscope. They faded, they went from one colour to another, whichever one seemed to be needed most to keep this

146

balance that was the main purpose of being there.

'It was very strange because I was aware of my own individual soul, if you like, and energy, but I was also aware of being part of the larger group. I could move in and out of being one and being part of the whole at will.

'I was aware that I had no body, I was pure energy but there was a sort of container - containing the energy until I joined with the others. We did get time off but it was more around when the extra energy was necessary.

'It was a really pleasant feeling, very caring, very much being a part of something, whereas I think in this life I have always kept myself very much out of groups and alone. This was very much being part of a whole.

'Another thing I was very aware of, was that though I did not seem to have a body, I could teleport to wherever I wanted. If I thought of something, I would instantly be there in a different space. There was no walking, no floating. It was instantaneous like teleportation. It was the same with the energy as a group; we would just focus on different parts of the universe and the energy would follow. Also I seemed to be aware instantly of where it would be necessary to send the energy and when. It was as if part of me just knew. I came into my mind or realisation without conscious thought or scanning of the universe.

'There was as background hum of this feminine energy being beamed out but if something started to go out of balance we would just change part of the focus. It was if it was just part of a subset and move it to a different area, a different direction of the universe wherever it was needed.

'I was certainly very happy and felt what I was doing was important and I didn't really want to come back. It's quite nice to know that at some point in the future that's the sort of thing I will be doing. Certainly that there is definitely life after death, if you like, but I was aware of that anyway, and have always been since I was a very small child, believed and known that there is something after death.

'I think the other thing that was most striking was that there was a tremendous amount of just general acceptance and knowledge, an inner knowing, of what is and that everything is good. Yes there is negative energy, but it's balanced and the negative energy was purely for people to experience rather than the fact that it is malignant of its own free will – it's not – it is just about people (or species) being negative as humans and as other species on different planets, but generally the main energy was just good and love and acceptance.

'There was no judgement on that planet at that time and I got a sense that there is no judgement in the universe either, it was just experience and those colours were quite extraordinary, incredibly vibrant at the same time as being muted, really weird. I know it sounds strange because of the contradictions, but then the universe and life does seem to be made of many paradoxes - good and bad - light and dark - joy and sorrow, etc.'

Would you like to visit your future? You will soon.

8

Scripts

Here is an ensemble of scripts and ideas for you to use as inspiration or to trigger your creative juices. There is no definitive right or wrong way. Remember that you own your memories, whether they are in the past or future, but the words you use to get them should be in the language in which you are fluent. By this I mean don't address yourself in flowery romance or rhyming slang if you haven't got a didgeridoo[3] what it means.

Exceptions - if you are working with someone else, either on your past or theirs, guide rather than lead in the questioning. From the regressions you will see that asking either, or types of, question is fine. For example, 'Is it hot or cold?' If it isn't either, the subconscious will reply to such. It is important to not jump ahead or assume something is there. An example would be finding yourself in a kitchen and assuming there is a table.

The questions would be, 'What is in the room?' Not, 'Can you see the kitchen table?' Or, 'Tell me what's on the table', unless you have ascertained there is in fact a table.

A guiding question is, 'In the kitchen is there a table or anything similar?'

Let's talk about dates and time-span. I was once regressing a man, with a group of onlookers. He was working very hard on a building and told me it was about 200 BC. Well, we almost had a riot. Predictably and correctly the group couldn't understand how anyone would know that such dates existed if they were living then. We maintain the knowledge that we know now so he was able to deduce the most likely time. Often, clients will have a running

---

[3] Reference to rhyming slang - didgeridoo = clue

commentary with themselves while some are totally absorbed and know more afterwards.

James was describing his time in the war and, without any discussion with me, gabbled away for about five minutes saying to himself things like, 'That isn't right. Surely that won't work.' But the best was, 'Cor blimey, O'Reilly, who would have thought that would be a success?' At that point he had merged his past and present Self.

It might be that they need to 'think' through the experience or wait for more information to become apparent.

I will also mention amnesia before I forget. It is rare, in my experience, for anyone to completely forget their whole regression. When people are working together they might not want to share out loud if they find themselves in a compromising situation, with someone they know in this life, during a past memory. You might look at your wife a little differently if you recognise her as your child or discover your most hated teacher at school was once your lover. It is most likely you will spot people you know from your soul group, but if you don't that's okay too.

If you are recording your instructions you must decide whether you address yourself as 'you' or 'I'. I think it is easier to not work in the first person unless you are daydreaming and free-flowing, as otherwise it doesn't always make sense.

Your Most Perfect Life

Instruct yourself that you are going to travel back in time to one of your perfect lives. The meaning of perfect is very personal, but it will be special to your past Self even if your present Self doesn't quite 'get it'. Sometimes it takes a while for a semblance of reason to appear and we are often given examples to help us balance.

Here is a very general script for you to play with, with guidance along the way. Use your favourite induction and deepener, or this one.

Make yourself cosy, comfortable and warm, ensuring that you will be undisturbed. Count rhythmically as you breathe in and try to breathe out for a little longer. Breathe in 1... 2... 3... and out 1... 2...3... and repeat.

Keep it easy and restful (gasping or choking is not good!), gently sinking into comfort is what we're after. If you prefer to slow count, that works very well. Breathe in 1... 2... out 1... 2... 3... and so on... slowly... gently...

You will reach a point whereby your breathing is perfectly co-ordinated with your relaxing and you don't need to bother or remember to count. It is natural and peaceful.

Inwardly scan yourself for any tensions, anxieties, worries or fears and mentally massage and soothe them away with your breathing and inner peace.

Create the sensation of sinking deeper into comfort by imagining it is happening or count, imagine steps, an escalator, floating on water or floating upwards. Sinking down while imagining that you are floating up has a hypnotic effect very quickly. Contradictory self-instruction is very powerful in the world of hypnotic mediation. Sinking down as I float higher, the higher I float the deeper I relax... mmm, bliss!

Be in your special place and spend time making it all exactly as you like. Colours, textures, sensations - make everything just so. Imagine a time portal that you feel compelled to pass through; be as vivid as you like. It might be a swirling ball of light and movement, a doorway or lift even. Personalise it totally. This is all about you, and as the language of the subconscious mind is imagery, let yours flow unbridled.

As you go though the gateway, feel that you are leaving the present behind for a while as you take yourself on a journey to the past.

Use whatever sense you like - all of them if you choose - and just allow yourself to drift into your memories as they awaken for you. Be comfortable all the time.

As always you can be as associated or as disassociated as you prefer. Spend as much time as you wish in your perfect life, just observing or gathering information. When it is time for you to return, you can come back into the present time remembering all you choose.

Then awaken in your preferred way.

If you really want to be completely disassociated it can sometimes be easier to start off in a detached way, as follows. In your special place you have a television and you have the remote control.

Choosing whichever way you prefer, you can put in a DVD or video or just have your life you are visiting on the screen. As you have the remote you are only observing and you have the ultimate protection or security: the off button.

It is unlikely you will want to switch off but it is a good way to end your session.

During Andrea's regression we set off but then she wanted to come back to her special place, where she felt secure, and we used the TV method. When she couldn't hear what was being said she adjusted the volume. After a little while she felt more comfortable and did associate herself in the experience, but you may decide whether you do or not.

Please play around with your own scripts and try them out, recorded or written. It is fine to test out alone or with friends. You may find that you end up in the same past life as whoever you are with and then you can compare notes.

You will get answers to questions you did and didn't know you had. It happens every time.

If you take a while to get warmed up in the practice of regressing, don't be concerned. It might be that you are trying too hard. Just tell yourself you are happy to experience whatever and you will relax into it.

Here is information for you using chakras as the starting point. It is similar to the earlier colour meditation, but more defined.

The word 'chakra' is the Sanskrit term for wheel. We tend to think about, balance and heal the seven main ones. They are the body mind link: the energy centres of your life force and if you are feeling off colour, balance or kilter, it is because your chakras are blocked or mucky. I think of them as the crossover point of the physical to the etheric where you could be in either/or, or both.

As an aside, I see auras. The colours that I see emanate from the chakras, so if I see a mucky blue I know that the person has throat issues, for example.

You will notice as you read through, the similarities to the holding pattern list from earlier, but I'm sharing this as a clear method for you to use. Understanding your own chakras will help you and in turn, if you wish, you can help others.

You can probably feel if you are off balance - whether emotionally, physically or mentally.

The seven main chakras for our purpose are as follows.

The *base* is Red and is responsible for grounding, stability, stamina, motivation, self-confidence, drive, passion, and excitement.

The *sacral* is Orange and is responsible for joy, respect for oneself, release (of stored negativity), creativity, cheer, pick-me-up and happiness.

The *solar plexus* is Yellow and is responsible for cleansing: physical, emotional and spiritual, happiness, feeling uplifted, ego, strength of will (power), energy, focus, enthusiasm and self worth.

The *heart* is Green and is responsible for balance, harmony, inner peace, abundance, love for yourself and others, release of heart related emotions: grief, unrequited love, new growth, starts and beginnings.

The *throat* is Blue and is responsible for the release of physical

153

tension, communication, peace, healing, honesty, calming, cleansing and the ability to express oneself and one's needs.

The *brow* (3rd eye[4]) is Indigo and is responsible for wisdom, protection, vision of the psyche[5], responsibility, understanding, seeking, power.

The *crown* is Violet/white and is responsible for clarity of mind, clearing negativity, being at one with the universal energy and pure thought (pure as in clear, not as in not mucky).

The easiest way to balance and discover if you have past life issues stored on a cellular or psyche level is actually to whip out your pendulum, but if you would rather not a meditative technique will work.

If you are using a pendulum on yourself just hold it comfortably over your lap or other hand and focus your mind on each chakra in turn, starting at the base. Again, before you begin, set your intent by thinking or saying to yourself, 'As I work through my chakras, any of my past lives that would be useful for me to know about can come to me.'

The aim is to have it turning in your yes, or positive, direction. At the same time clear your mind and allow any imagery from the past to come to your awareness, maybe in thoughts, pictures or symbols.

If you notice anything negative in your feelings, imagery or the pendulum movement, wait for it to clear and change to a positive direction. Also notice the imagery and know that even if it doesn't make sense during this exercise, it will do either in your dreams or during another meditation.

Perhaps nothing at all will happen until afterwards, when you notice your thoughts are focussing on something in particular or a

[4] Sometimes when people tune up or balance their chakras they become aware of the opening of the 3rd eye. It is the centre of your psyche and I have had clients describe that they have become aware of it during meditations. This is useful to know if you are using cosmic ordering.

[5] Psyche is the Greek word for Soul and also refers to spirit and mind.

certain colour keeps appearing.

Jesse felt 'blocked' in her red and orange chakras. There were no imagery or particular thoughts to accompany the sensation. She described it as a feeling of being clogged up or congested. For days afterwards she had urges to eat oranges and bought an orange jumper (unheard of), she also noticed the colour red everywhere: cars clothes, furnishings. After a week or so she began to dream and slowly but surely pieced together her story.

In a past life her husband had an affair while she and he were hoping for a baby. The other woman got pregnant and that is when she discovered his adultery. She was from a rich important family and 'they' paid off the other woman (or perhaps frightened her) into disappearing with the child and beat the husband severely with the threat of hobbling his legs if he contacted the mistress or ever strayed again. They also said if he left his wife they would attack the child.

None of this made Jesse happy. She felt sad for him when she realised that he had really loved the other woman and that he only remained with her under duress. She was upset that he never saw the child and wept that the child didn't know who he was. As it all became clearer she felt much better. Months after, she told me she'd always had achy, jumpy legs and hormone problems. All this was becoming better. After so much sadness and grief, we visited a perfect life and she found herself playing happily on a boat with her two brothers. They were the husband and other woman from the sad life.

Sometimes soul groups just have to work things out and go through stuff. It is unlikely any of this would have come up if she hadn't had problems that needed dealing with and it all worked out perfectly in the end.

If you are working with someone else it is best if they lie down while you hold the pendulum over each chakra. Ask them to focus on each colour and notice anything that comes to their mind. You may find, now that your skills are awakening, that you get imagery and ideas relating to them, their health and their past or future lives. What you do with it all is up to you.

If there is negativity anywhere, wait for the pendulum to change to the positive direction. You might like to discuss beforehand if there are any issues. It is always best to ask, as we must never assume we know what is best and we must never inflict ourselves on people.

***

Issues

If you come across a problem or something that needs healing in any of your or other people's regressions, here are some techniques that I know work very well.

I will do it in the way I deal with actual problems, but you will see how the methods can be changed to suit the situation.

Mary always chose to have relationships with abusive men and went from one miserable relationship to another. If there had been an award for attracting mean men, she would have won it. Her regression revealed that she had accidentally killed her husband when he tried to save her from a fall. They were high up on a cliff and he grabbed her as she stumbled, but missed and fell onto the rocks.

Was she punishing herself in this life, was she not worthy of a happy life?

In the regression she spoke to him after he had passed, and he explained to her that he in no way blamed her for his death. He knew it was an accident and he told her to let go of the unresolved grief.

She is now happily married to a lovely kind man and they even enjoy cliff walks.

Jim was fed up with neck pain and insomnia that was put down to stress. In his regression he was hanged and, although cut down, he wasn't quite dead. He hung on for a long time believing that if he fell asleep he would die.

I suggested to him that letting go in death and sleep were very different and we changed his memory slightly, in that he rewrote it so he died before he was cut down.

Immediately following his session his pain began to subside and he was able to sleep.

Oh, I hear you saying, is that allowed? Can we change events to suit ourselves? Does that mean we can rewrite history? No, I don't think so. But, we can change our interpretation of events and happenings and make them more comfortable, and therefore release anything that isn't serving a positive purpose.

Elise wanted a have a baby very much but was terrified to even try to get pregnant. She recalled having a forced botched abortion in a past life. Her explaining to the baby what had happened and how sorry she was completed her healing and release. As the trauma was released, so were her fears.

Peter was terrified of water, but his wife wanted them to go sailing together. His previous Self remembered being sent to Australia as a prisoner for a crime he didn't commit. He was distraught at leaving his family and spent the whole journey sick. All he did to release the trauma was to forgive those who condemned him. He realised that they did what they believed was right, given the evidence available, and in that moment he knew he didn't need to continue to hold on to the fears any more. His family hadn't blamed him as they knew he was innocent and they survived. He is now a happy sailor and his wife is thrilled.

If you find something you don't like, what would make it more bearable? Think about how you might advise a friend who was going through a similar experience. What would you suggest to someone who was suffering?

The You in the 'now' can always advise or share knowledge with the 'past' You, and likewise the 'past' You can do the same. Work together and all will be well.

This might all seem very simple. Let me assure you - it is!

Don't over complicate things. If you make a mess you clear it up. If you cut yourself, you clean it and put a dollop of cream or a plaster on it. If you pick at it the healing is delayed and you end up with a scar. It is exactly the same with past lives, as in the reality of day-to-day living.

Forgiving, releasing without blame and accepting freedom is your right. Holding onto guilt is never productive and usually debilitating, causing illness or disease over time.

Future scripts

Going forwards is almost the same as going back. You are just travelling to another time.

This method is a good place to start.

Relax. By now I'm sure you are an expert, but if you are only going forward until you find reverse use one of the inductions and deepeners included in this book.

Then either imagine the bridge of time, but now it is to the future, or a gateway to take you forward. Or you may prefer to create or pre-plan your whole journey.

From your special place you can go to wherever you choose. There is a special lift that travels through time and as you can step into the lift your journey begins. You feel calm and comfortable. The movement of the lift is subtle and it will travel in the direction that is right for you. When you arrive in your future the doors open and you step out into a beautiful place of brightness and peace. Directly in front of you is a door to the library of all.

As you enter the door you notice the shelves are lined with books, except one book which is ready for you on the table. Sit down and just allow the images to float up from the book. This is your book. It contains everything about you. Your past, present and future. In here are answers, ideas, suggestions, solutions, experiences... everything.

You may only look in your own book and you must treat it with utmost respect. A lot of information will come to you quickly and you might not assimilate it until you have returned to the present. When it is time you can either find yourself back here, in your special place, or return in the lift.

***

If you wish to go into a future life you can use the same technique but set your intent differently at the beginning. Another way is to prepare a complete journey beforehand and then take yourself on it. Here is an example.

Relax, etc. On your journey you are walking along a path. It is your life path and if you stand still you know your past is one way and your future is another. After a while the path widens and you come to a crossroads or signpost. One of the signs points to the future. Go that way and you find yourself easily and gently going into a future life. Just go and look. Watch it unfold. You can ask the future you for advice or suggestions, or anything you might wish to know that might be useful now.

As always go with the flow and allow what will be to be. Don't stop to analyse what is happening or you might get analysis paralysis and feel stuck or trapped.

If you wish, you can remain completely detached and just be a casual observer of yourself by using the TV technique. Everything you have learnt can be mixed and matched, jiggled or rewritten, edited, chopped, increased or used verbatim.

***

In your planning stage before you regress or progress you might like to think about yourself and note your likes and dislikes. Be aware of the following:

- Times in history you are interested in or already know about
- Food types or styles that you enjoy
- Things that make you happy
- Places you feel drawn to
- People you admire
- Styles of clothes
- Your job or career
- Or, the type of work you are attracted towards

As you become more experienced you can then check out things that aren't quite so good, such as:

- Tasks or a job that drives you to distraction
- People you dislike or who irritate you
- Things that made you sad or fearful
- Food you dislike or refuse to try
- Places you loathe

***

I'll briefly share what occasionally happens when people unearth an emotional attachment to a memory – it is called an abreaction.

These emotional outbursts are always much worse for the onlooker than the person experiencing it. Some people sob seemingly uncontrollably while others maybe shake. They sometimes occur during a 'healing crisis' – the mass clearout before the healing moment of freedom. It might seem strange to have crisis and healing in the same sentence, but in China the word *weiji* means 'crisis and opportunity'.

If you have one yourself, my advice is to let it out – think of it as the opening of a dam's valve. The flowing out is generating powerful energy for good.

If you are with someone who abreacts, just talk to them softly and assuredly until it passes. When they are calm, a serenity will come over them that is truly thrilling to witness.

After every experience, past or future, ensure you are perfectly grounded. You can do this easily just by stamping or rubbing your feet on the ground or, if you prefer, imagine you have roots that go down from you into the earth.

Carry out a mundane grounding task like making a drink or food to eat, or even something like washing up, and you will easily be fully aware in yourself in the here and now.

With regressions and progressions it is useful to make notes as, even though we think we'll remember it all, we don't. Recording becomes second nature and some people keep a time travel journal that they put everything into like a scrapbook.

So, now you can explore and if necessary heal or repair your past. You know how to visit your future so what is left?

How about designing your perfect life?

Scripts - for use verbatim

If you don't want to create you own scripts, here are some that you can use without changing anything. They are suitable for you to read, record or have read to you. Enjoy.

Significant life

Make yourself cosy and comfortable.

Take a slow breath in and, as you breathe out, let your eyes gently close.

Begin to notice your breathing… You don't need to alter your

161

breathing pattern… just breathe gently and regularly, noticing how you feel as you breathe… if you feel differently when you breathe in to when you breathe out… allowing yourself to become more restful each time you breathe out.

Begin to notice thoughts in your mind, thoughts coming and going. Some thoughts staying awhile and some being sorted or filed before you notice them…

Become aware of noises and sounds coming and going. From now on during this meditation, all sounds that you hear while you are resting, apart from an emergency, just remind your mind that you are relaxing more and more…

Now, think about your feelings – in your mind and in your body. Feel those feelings… feelings of tension can begin to be replaced by calmness…

Thoughts come and go… Sounds come and go… Feelings come and go…

Breathing regular and slow… as you relax deeply into yourself where all is well…

Put your awareness now into your hands… Notice how they are feeling – if they are warm, cool, heavy or light. Imagine how your hands would feel if they were completely relaxed. Only you know how your relaxed hands feel…

And all the while, thoughts coming and going… Sounds coming and going… Feelings coming and going… Breathing regular and slowing…

Think now about how your feet are feeling. Notice if they are warm, cool heavy or light. If they feel the same as your hands…

While you are thinking about your feet allow your hands to relax… Only you know how your relaxed feet feel.

And all the while, thoughts coming and going. Sounds coming and going. Feelings coming and going. Breathing regular and slowing.

Focus your attention now on the back of your neck. Imagine

your feet can relax the same as your hands… Relaxing more each time you breathe out…

Now slowly and gently allow the relaxation in your hands begin to flow up now into your arms… At the same time the relaxation in your feet can spread up your legs…

Resting… Slowing… Calm and comfortable…

That restful feeling can spread now from your arms, across your shoulders and down your back… From your legs feel it flowing up, up though your hips, pelvic area tummy and chest…

Calm peaceful waves of peace and relaxation flowing through your whole being…

All that relaxation can flow up now through into your neck, up the back of your head and through your face, eyes forehead and scalp… And now…slowly, gently but very thoroughly, back down your body like little waves on the sand.

Calm… Peaceful… Relaxed… Soothed… Taking yourself down inside yourself to where you feel comfortable. That cosy feeling way down deep inside, where all is well. This is your time now – time for you.

Any tensions, anxieties, worries or fears are mentally massaged away. Draining away from you.

As you relax, more and more deeply, I am going to count from one to ten and you can allow the passing numbers to help you to rest even more… even more…

One, resting… relaxing…

Two, breathing gently… relaxing more and more with every breath … with every gentle beat of your heart …

Three, feel your whole being soothed… caressed in peace…

Four, breathe away any tensions or anxieties…

Five, rest…relax…calm…

Six, calm… breathing easy… soothed…

Seven, resting more and more deeply…

Eight, inner peace washing over you and through you… calm…

peaceful... relaxed...

Nine, each breath taking you deeper and deeper into calm and peace...

Ten, continuing to relax...

And now... in your mind create a special place. It can be somewhere that you know or somewhere that you make up. It can be inside or out. Use your imagination as best you can.

Have your special place exactly as you like... colours... textures... everything perfect...

All that matters is that this special place is yours - it belongs to you. You choose who or what you have there. Relaxing now in that special place within you that you are now in. Spend some time looking around... enjoy the feelings and inner contentment...

When you are in your special place, all is well. You can begin to release anything that isn't serving a purpose and you discover that you can make choices and experience freedom.

Spend some time now in your special place and know that you can return whenever you want.

Your thoughts can be clear, calm and focused and whenever you think of your special place your mind replicates calmness.

You can now become aware of your desires and goals and your inner mind is now creating the programmes for you to achieve exactly as you wish. Create it now in your mind. Fill yourself with success.

You can visit your special place if you want to relax – if you are looking for answers – or for no reason other than it is lovely.

Find somewhere now where you can rest – a chair, hammock, bed - and snuggle down into slumber... in this special relaxation your mind is able to access anything that you desire... ideas, memories, plans, goals... anything...

Now, as you relax deeper and deeper, you are going on a journey... a journey into one of your past lives... when you are in a deep meditative state you can access memories from your subconscious mind... memories that will help you now in this life... by giving you an understanding or answers that you are seeking.

When you are remembering your past life you have a sense of detachment but with a deep understanding of self.

Trust that your subconscious mind protects you at all times... this journey is going to be to a past life where the memories you retrieve are useful and beneficial... a significant life...

Imagine now that you are bathed in a blue mist and you are standing on a low safe bridge... the mist of time is comforting and protecting, you feel safe and cared for... the mist is all around you while you slowly cross the bridge... this is the bridge to your past...

Pause for a moment when you get about two thirds over the bridge while the mist clears a little... and as it begins to clear a little on the side of the bridge that you are walking towards, you notice the light changing... it is a welcoming glow that you feel drawn towards... you feel excited as you now continue to walk over the bridge into a life from your past... a significant life...

Step off the bridge now directly into your past... take a few moments to adjust while the remainder of the mist clears...

When it has cleared begin to make mental notes. Look down at your feet and get a feeling of your age and notice if you have anything on your feet... Are you a male or female? Notice the ground beneath your feet to see whether you are inside or out...

Now look at your legs and up your body... What are you wearing? Make a mental note of colours, textures, the feeling of the material... Whether you are warm or cool... What colour your skin is...

Look if are wearing or are adorned with any jewellery, anything on your head or anything in your hands... look at your entire person and get a feeling of self...

Now begin to have a good look at your surroundings... are you alone... if there are people about, who are they... what do you see... hear... feel... think... get a full sense of what you are doing... where you are or where you are going... are you aware of your name? Perhaps someone speaks to you and calls your name...

Get a sense of time... the season... maybe the year...

In a moment you are going to move to a time in this life of an important event or happening... I will count to three and it will then be just before this important event - one... two... three...

Wait a moment to get your bearings... get a clear understanding of what is occurring... your involvement... your role... your experience...

Allow these memories to flow without interruption or interpretation... There is a reason that you have recalled this memory and you start to become aware of that reason now...

Let your thoughts now go to just after the end of this life... It is a few moments after you have passed from that life... What wisdom can you bring with you to your present life?

What message would your past self have for your present Self? What knowledge can you now use to the good?

With those thoughts it is now time to slowly begin your journey back... Find yourself back on the bridge in the blue mist of time, and as the mist clears you are back in yourself in your special place.

Rest awhile and allow your mind to do whatever it needs to do...

Now... I will count from ten to one and with each number you can bring yourself gently, slowly, awake... ten, nine, eight... becoming aware... seven, six, five, four... more and more awake... three, two one... eyes open wide awake in the here and now on the (present day, date).

Take a few moments to gather yourself and take notes if you are keeping a record. Now, please ensure you are grounded.

***

Some people prefer and find it comforting to make use of their higher Selves, spirit guides or angels. If your belief lends itself to this, you don't have to travel alone, either back or forth. They can take you from your special place or just be waiting when you are at your destination.

If you wish, you can use an invocation at the beginning of each regression or progression by asking for guidance and protection.

***

Future Self Script

This future life script includes your higher Self.

Look straight ahead of yourself and notice all that you can see. Keep your head still but become aware of everything right up to your peripheral vision. See everything: the colours of objects, textures... everything. When you have a perfect impression of it, close your eyes but keep the image in your mind. You will find that it fades or drifts away... let it go, and as it floats slowly away allow yourself to gently sink down into relaxed comfort.

Feel waves of calm and peace wash over and through you. Create a wave of inner peace, and for the next three breaths increase your relaxation.

Imagine that you are standing outside in a garden at the top of five safe steps. We will go slowly down the steps together and on each one you can be doubly relaxed.

Let's begin.

Down the first, second and third step, sinking, resting... fourth, fifth. At the bottom of the steps you find yourself on the grass, feeling so relaxed now you can walk across the grass to a gate on the other side of the garden.

Walk through the gate. Now imagine walking alongside a stream on a perfect day. Together with the soothing sound of the water trickling by... and the gentle warmth of the sun dappled through the leaves of the overhanging trees... you feel safe and soothed...

You might want to stop a moment and look into the water... Notice the colours and shapes formed and unformed by the movement of the water... Perhaps you want to dip your fingers in... Notice its coolness and the sensations...

Continue your stroll now and a little way ahead is a gate. As you approach the gate, you see it is slightly open and you are keen to peep through the gap.

The gate opens into a courtyard, and as you step inside you are filled with a sense of awe and inner peace... on the other side of the courtyard is a building... a very special building... it looks like a magical castle... nestling... waiting... welcoming... make your way across the courtyard, noticing all the features as you pass...

The big door of the castle is open and you are able to walk straight in... You are safe and welcome... inside you find yourself in the most beautiful hall. There is a huge stone stairway in the middle, sweeping up and all the furnishings, pictures and wall hangings seem very familiar to you... enjoy these feelings as you now begin to go up the stairs...

Hear your feet on the stone steps... at the top the landing opens out to reveal several doors... you are drawn to one in particular that you know to be the library...

Go through the door and into the library... there are rows of shelves with every book there ever was lining the walls... walk along... touch them... notice the smell...

On the other side of the library is a large table – go now and sit at that table...

Become aware of a book opened out on the polished table in front of you... This is the book of you... It contains your past, your now and your future... your higher Self has opened the book for you to see your future Self... Spend a few moments getting comfortable so that you may lose yourself in your dream of you...

gaze into the book and drift into the images that float up from the pages while you allow thoughts to come to your mind... it is like you are watching a film... with you as the star... you are a casual observer of your own future life.

Watch it unfolding before your eyes now. Let the images, thoughts, sounds and feelings be present without judgement – let it all flow. Make a mental note of anything and everything that you chose to remember... and remember this is the life you are creating... think of your dreams, plans and goals and trust that you can create your desires...

As you drift further away into your future, your mind and body work together to create a template for you... for your success, health, well-being and happiness (add anything here you think is pertinent to you).

Dream awhile...

You are viewing your future self and creating happiness and success. Know that you are able to create and design your perfect life by being clear in your instructions to yourself.

Remember all that you need to know and begin to let the images fade away and drift back into the book...

Close the book and spend time with your higher Self, sharing knowledge. If you are seeking an answer, you may ask and you may receive the answer now or later through clues, symbols or dreams.

When you feel the time is right and you have completed gathering your information, leave and thank your higher Self. Then, with the knowledge that you have gained...retrace your steps down the stairs and out through the door...across the courtyard and back through the gate...

You know without looking that the magical castle has disappeared, only appearing to you when you need to access the library of knowledge.

Be back by the stream and gently, slowly, in your own time, bring yourself back to the here and now and then start to come awake (count here if you like, ten to one, becoming more awake with each number)

Take a few moments to adjust and let your mind finish its filing.

Now is a good time for you to write notes about your experience or feelings. Looking forwards in time can set off interesting thought processes and, if you choose, you will be able to seriously consider all of your options in regards to what you now know.

If you feel in any way muddled or confused trust that your higher Self will guide and help you. You are always free to return to the castle to gather more information as the special library is there for you whenever you please.

9

Bits and Bobs

The bits here are those that don't quite fit anywhere else. Actually they might, but never mind they're here now.

I wanted to mention two of the best-known pioneers in the world of past life regression: Edgar Cayce and Henry Bolduc. Bolduc learnt from Cayce and the following is a short excerpt from Bolduc's out of print book, *The Journey Within: Past Life Regression and Channeling*. As you will read, he talks about Cayce and travel and it pretty much could have been written for this book. I had planned to précis it, but his words read so well I have left them as is.

In 1964, the Cayce Foundation headquarters were in a big white building that had been donated by Cayce supporters as a hospital that used procedures in the Cayce readings to heal. The building is a Virginia Beach landmark, perched high on a hill overlooking the Atlantic Ocean. In 1964 it contained offices, a small rack of books for sale, and a library that housed thousands of books on topics that paralleled the Cayce readings. It was and is one of the most important libraries in the world in parapsychology. In addition, the library contained all 14,253 readings, cross-referenced for anyone to read and study.

The upper floors of the building had a number of rooms where members of ARE (Association for Research and Enlightenment) could stay while doing research and study. Hugh Lynn kindly arranged quarters for me there. An adjacent building housed a print shop and an auditorium for conferences. (Since then, the guest rooms have been turned into offices; the library has been moved to a new library/conference center; the single rack of books has grown into a large and active bookstore. The presses are still rolling and computers help ARE keep in touch with a membership of more than 65,000.)'

The Cayce Readings *(extract continues)*

The more than 14,000 Cayce readings are a fascinating but difficult study.

The technical language and vocabulary were far beyond my high school comprehension. Also, the flow of subconscious psychic channelled material was a whole new world for me. I could not just sit and read it as I would a story book. It was hard even to understand most sentences. I am good reader, but the material was very deep and unfamiliar, and it has a complicated syntax.

I also read just about every book in the library on hypnosis and age regression experiments. I averaged about one book per day, reading late into the night, during the month I stayed at ARE.

Here are some of the key questions I explored.

Can we remember past lives?

I answer, "Yes, we can recall past lives."

But if I could prove it absolutely there would be no need for this book.

Reincarnation, which is what we are talking about, would be accepted by everyone - or almost everyone, as almost everyone now accepts that the world is round.

We use electricity every day, but no one can define it. We fall in love, and who can define that? We accept many beliefs we cannot prove, and that does not affect their reality.

Here is a parable from Kahlil Gibran that illustrates my point.

Other Seas *(extract continues)*

A fish said to another fish, "Above this sea of ours there is another sea, with creatures swimming in it - and they live there even as we live here."

The fish replied, "Pure fancy! Pure fancy! When you know that everything that leaves our sea by even an inch, and stays out of it, dies. What proof have you of other lives in other seas?"*

Are we making it all up? *(extract continues)*

I remembered my youth and the Santa Claus myth that all adults seemed to be in conspiracy to protect. I wanted real answers. I did not want fairy tales. I had peeked on Christmas.

So in the library I read books by other serious researchers who had done regression work that paralleled my experiments. Answers began to unfold slowly. There was no great flash of light nor instant revelation; it was not like that. But slowly, bit by bit, things fit together. Some things did not fit well and I put them aside. As it turned out, it took a few more years of living, learning, and growing before I proved to my own satisfaction that people just didn't make up past lives.

Meanwhile, I delved for the answers in the Cayce readings. In his conscious state Cayce was very wary of reincarnation. In his subconscious state he was an outspoken advocate. He said that in past lives we "find talents and strengths" (Readings 30222-1 and 2002-1) and that our recollection "brings peace that passeth understanding to inner turmoils" (105-1). The readings said that recall is for "soul development" (2121-2); it "helps others and brings them comfort" (764-1); and, most important, that the recall itself "brings awareness of the continuity of life" (1641-1).(5).

These were fine explanations of the advantages of understanding past lives. But I could not find anything by Cayce that said we could prove their existence to anyone but ourselves. This dilemma led to my biggest question.

What role does imagination play in past life recall experiences?

In past life exploration, many people worry that their experiences are "only imagination". At times, I suspect this is so. Nevertheless, further research may reveal that even simple imagination may have strong messages embedded in symbols, as in night time dreams.

Cayce suggests that imagination is the avenue to the visual faculty of the mind. My own experiments suggested that hypnosis enhances the image part of the mind; that is, people who could consciously visualize, imagine, or daydream seemed to be better subjects for hypnosis. Years later I was to understand the reason for this: hypnosis stimulates and enhances right brain activity and visualization is a right brain activity (little note from me - if you are interested in this to find your preferred side please see the quiz).

There is a definite link between the part of the mind that stores and retrieves images and past life work. The processing of visual information is one function of the mind; we do this all the time when we recall anything from our experience.

The creation of visual fantasy is another function of the mind; we do this whenever we daydream. The functions are separate and distinct, but they are often confused. Fantasy is fantasy. Retrieval of a stored image, whether the image is conscious or unconscious, is retrieval of a stored image.

But there is a fuzzy border between the two. That overlap is what causes confusion in many people - thinking that all images are fantasy. For instance, consider two Walt Disney movies. Real-story, true-event "imagination" would be like the movie, The Living Desert, while fantasy - imagination would be like Fantasia. My own regression experiments had shown me that most people recalled events through scenes, pictures, and images, though the other senses can trigger recall of past memories. A few subjects said they "heard" the information in their minds and repeated it. A few others said they "felt" or "sensed" the information that came forward. One said she "smelled the ocean", and much of her recall was triggered by her sense of smell.

But for most the image facility was the key or the doorway to the past life memory. Most of their recall was of images and scenes, and because they had not consciously "seen" these images before, I could understand that some thought of it, or mislabelled it, as imagination. But this imagination stayed with them long after the session. With time comes the realisation of what is valid and meaningful. Time separates the wheat from the chaff in past life recall; the impressions that last for a long time are more meaningful than passing flights of fantasy.

When I searched the Cayce readings on this question I discovered an entirely new link of the imagination with past life study. Cayce said, "The ability to imagine other places [is] because of the past there" (379-3). I responded to this statement with a surge of enlightenment. The imagination is not in conflict or opposed to past life memory; it is a helpful tool.

"So that's why my subjects can describe a particular place or time period so vividly," I thought. "Because it is actually remembered from their own past!" People are always so quiet in libraries, but I wanted to shout for joy when I found this nugget. In fact, Cayce told a person specifically to "Use your imagination to fill in details of past life" (1468-1).

A reading told another person, "Turn to the mirror of life and ask yourself, What do you suppose was served as supper then?" (1179-2). Another person was told, "Visions and odors harken back to past life in the desert" (2662-1). (This reminded me of the woman who started her regression by smelling the ocean.)

What are the warnings about recalling our past lives?

Cayce said, "Beware unless you are balanced in purpose" (5399-2).(6). Also, "Don't abuse the talent for recall" (340-15) and "don't dwell on it, rather abide in love" (1608-1). One person was cautioned that past life exploration could cause him to be "side tracked" from his present life (3360-1).

I heartily agree. My concern was not that a person would

175

get "stuck" in the past, because that has never happened in my experience (7), but that someone might dwell on the past or, worse, take it too seriously. I was beginning to realize that we are given a series of lives specifically to be able to start anew that we are born again to be free of the past, not sentenced by it.

Insight and self-knowledge of our pasts can bring benefit, sometimes can help us change and grow. But the past is past. The readings encourage people to study themselves and their past lives and caution only of the "abuse" of recall. I had faith that if my intent was unconditional love in helping others there was nothing to be afraid of.

Why can't everyone recall past lives?

In one reading, Cayce said, "Doubt" (1152-9). To me, that summed it up in a neat one-word package. But really, there are many more factors than that.

Some people are afraid of what they will uncover. Some people still think hypnosis is like a truth serum that will cause them to blurt out some deep secret (they won't unless they want to).

Perhaps a bigger block than either of these is over-anxiousness. Some people are too eager and try to rush the process. The best subjects are neither too apprehensive nor too zealous. The qualities I value most are honest skepticism and an open and honest mind that is willing to accept new experience.

What are other recall techniques?

If using the imagination can help recapture past life experience, are there other methods?

Looking into water, a mirror, a crystal ball, or one's own mind can be good tools for meditation. But a more practical method to enhance past life recall is to study the time period. The readings told one person, "Study Grecian period to recall lifetime there" (1732-2). Another person was told, "Study geography, scenery, windmills, etc., will give the person proof of experience there in Holland" (114-1). Another was told, "Study and vision monuments to recall

Egyptian experience"(311-2).

When I read this material in the ARE library, I wondered how many people already subconsciously study a certain era or place because of their earlier ties there. The readings gave sound advice; anyone can get insight into themselves by studying times and places that deeply interest them.

To me, this gave clues to why some friends only read a certain era of history and others studied only certain places. And the opposite: Why some people dislike a particular time or place - because of negative experiences, perhaps? One young woman I had recently regressed had had a sad and tragic life in China. After the session, she confided that she hated Chinese food and disliked everything Chinese. In her present life she had no ties whatsoever to the Orient.

Travel can also help us get in touch with past lives, Cayce said. He told one person, "Travels to Williamsburg will stimulate recall [of] lifetime there with present husband" (578-2). To another, "Travel to Jamestown and the sense of familiarity what will come over them" (268-3). One person was told to "travel to Palestine to recall both the crusade experience and earlier" (341-8). Another: "Sit on the sands [anywhere] and remember Persia" (1837-1). And: "Travel to coastal areas of Connecticut to recall early settlement there" (1825-1).

The readings even suggested travel and activity combined to re-experience events: "Go to the fort on the August moon and listen to your voice which was raised there" (3377-1). Many readings recommend meditation. Cayce suggested meditation "to recall details of life in Jerusalem" (853-8 and 1486-2). For another he recommended "Entering into the silence for the visions that may be brought from the Grecian experiences" (858-1).

I loved the suggestions for travel. I took the advice and launched a new career of extensive travel. Studying was a nice, passive approach to past lives. Actual travel to other lands suited me better.

There are feelings and vibrations that can only be lived; I do not find them in books. Little did I realize it then, but I was destined to fill a number of passports and to live in and travel to many countries. I love travel and recommend it as an exciting, if sometimes difficult, method of stimulating inner experience. *(End of extract.)*

***

I have left the American spellings and the reference numbers relating to the readings just in case any of you fancy a bit of light reading.

Thanks to Henry Bolduc, who has given his work freely to humanity for us all to share.

I thought it might be useful for you to know what actually happens when you think your thoughts, for no particular reason apart from it's very interesting and perhaps useful to know if you want to make changes or have different kinds of experiences. It is relevant to cell memory and chakras. Everything is connected, even if we don't always think so.

Notes on the biological functions from thought to cell

An example of thought making changes in the body is of imagining you have hot hands. This is sometimes an experimental game played by medical students. How they do this depends on their individual visualisation and imagination. They may think of warming their hands in front of a fire, they may think of increased blood flow or perhaps just imagine a feeling of warmth.

I can make my hands hot or cold by thinking about them being in hot or cold water. I have to imagine something happening rather than just willing them to change temperature. The results are the same for all. Our hands do indeed change according to the temperature. The warm technique is very useful for anyone who suffers with headaches and migraines, as it enables the blood vessels in the head to relax as it diverts the blood away from those that are engorged. When this happens, the pain subsides.

Much work has been carried out on investigating the body/mind on a cell level. Most notably by people such as Dr Deepak Chopra, Dr Wayne Dyer, Denise Linn, Louise Hay, Louis Proto, Dr Richard Bandler and Dr Candace Pert.

In the past it was generally believed that everything that occurred within us was because of electrical activity created by us. Medical science now knows that the body and changes within it are due to the production and use of chemicals, and the electricity is only part of it. Our cells work in harmony with every other cell, but each has its own complete intelligence. Every thought creates energy that causes a response, so if we direct our thoughts we can direct that response for our own benefit.

Positive thoughts create 'good' chemicals' whilst negative create the opposite. People who are happy with a positive outlook tend to not only be more successful, but are usually healthier, and if they do fall ill they recover much quicker than a misery guts (who probably suffer with a 'miserable gut'). As all thought causes reactions, we have to be careful with our minds. How often do we hear of people who feign illness for a day off work actually developing that imagined condition? Be very careful what you wish for.

Cells react to stimulus from our inner awareness, behaviour and circumstances that are not always within our control, i.e. being surprised or frightened. Of course, sometimes we do control the circumstances - an athlete in preparation for an event alters diet and behaviour to bring about change. A long distance runner's cells need to be able to store and slowly release fluid very differently from someone sitting at a desk.

Recapping, you know the subconscious mind 'runs' our bodies. It is in charge of everything automatic, it looks after memories so we don't have to keep re-learning, it holds on to habits (good and bad), it adjusts our emotions and generally does everything it can to protect and keep us alive. We are able to access our subconscious minds using techniques such as self-hypnosis and thereby bring about mental, emotional and physiological change. A good example is when someone stops smoking in a hypnotherapy session. Within an hour the subconscious mind can accept a completely new programme that every cell in the body understands. All dependency is removed and the person is happy and free from cigarettes.

When we think, we fire a small electrical discharge from a neurotransmitter in the brain. This jumps across a synapse and travels along the correct pathways, joins other instructions, releasing chemicals or hormones, in fact whatever is needed in the exactly correct amount, directing and finally squirting them into the cells in areas in our bodies where they need to be.

Just the act of lifting an arm or having a scratch needs this to happen, but we don't need to know the processes involved in order for us to do so, we can just do it. This is because the body is finely tuned to release exactly what is needed at just the right time. Feeling an emotion - be it fear, love, jealousy or excitement, is actually a chemical reaction somewhere in our bodies.

Because we can access the subconscious mind we can direct these processes and, if we want, we can bring about change.

If we are hungry we receive messages that let us know it is time to eat, but if we are busy or on strict diets we can ignore these messages. When we eat the hypothalamus receives messages from fat cells via neurones to say 'switch off' hunger now, but again we can ignore it and keep on eating.

Fat cells are the ones that can most easily accept change. Throughout history we have passed through times of plenty and times of lean and our bodies need to be able to adjust accordingly.

When excess unwanted fat is sitting around in the body, it can be from a build up of bad eating habits or confused emotions that send inappropriate messages to our cells and brain. The fat cells in women are distributed around the outer layer of our bodies, and in men the cells are around inner organs. So the build-up in women becomes visibly evident as cellulite and squidgy bits, whereas as men grow in girth they develop a weakness in the organs affected.

We have talked about this earlier during the 'holding on' part. When memories are released the chemical make-up changes following the release of emotion.

In between lives

The knowledge that something happens after death is comforting for many, while some people think dead is dead - cease to be, no more, final. As I said at the beginning, I do not want to prove anything, it is all about the sharing.

We do therefore need to mention the 'in between' bit from one life to another. The gap, if you will.

When I was a child a family friend died and I remember asking my mother if he had been through the mist yet.

Her reply was, 'Yes'.

That was the only reference we ever made to death and dying, as we had not previously discussed it and didn't afterwards. I knew though that somewhere a blue mist was involved.

How, or in what context, I wasn't sure until I got older and learnt (or remembered) the time spent in between lives. There are many names for this time or place: the Tibetan Buddhist term is Bardo, the state between life and being reborn - it lasts between 7 and 49 days depending on variables.

Others are: heaven, nirvana, spirit, where the soul rests, the holding area, afterlife, paradise, temple, garden and more.

Lizzie talked of being in the most beautiful garden during her regression and said she remembered it from being there before. Some of these 'places' are permanent. I think when you're there it's for eternity, you don't return.

During one of the first regressions I carried out, I instructed the client's mind to take her to a moment in a past life of significance. When I asked her to describe what was happening she looked serene and calm and started to talk about the sensation of floating. She said she wasn't 'of body' but was living on. Her conscious interpretation was of it feeling 'cloud-like.'

Her reason for seeking regression was to address her fear of dying and her mind sorted that out in about two minutes.

Here is a little add-on for your mind's pleasure.

Andrea's past life was contemporary, which may suggest it was a metaphor or a tale made up in her imagination. There is another theory, which I discussed at length with Lizzie, and that is the phenomena of a soul splitting.

Lizzie told me about twins who were regressed together and in the past life they were the same person, one person. This is not to suggest that all twins are split souls.

Not much of a thought jump for Andrea to be sharing a soul with the woman who was having a breakdown in the middle of Piccadilly, especially when you consider her other life as the mental patient and her future one as a doctor. Maybe we all have another aspect of ourselves.

Jenny went to the place of Madeleine's death and collected what she called a fragment of her soul. This enabled her to feel complete.

How often have we heard the phrase, 'Pull yourself together' when aspects of ourselves aren't quite whole? Maybe that familiar feeling or the déjà vu experience in particular places is a little bit of our souls left behind that we recognise when we arrive. Or that feeling of 'going back home' that I got when I visited Greece the first time. It was as if some of my essence was there and it was very comforting; as I felt whole. I realise that might sound as if I didn't feel whole before or I was experiencing a sense of loss - I wasn't. But, often we don't now we need something until we have and we don't appreciate what we've got until it's gone.

After the regressions I didn't particularly think it necessary for me to analyse what happened, apart from the odd comment, but I love to get other people's thoughts and opinions. And, do you know, I don't mind whether they are incarnate or disincarnate.

Earlier we had Richard's regression and I mentioned his disincarnate soul mate, Lorelei. She agreed to share her thoughts on Andrea's past/present life and here they are, dictated to Richard, as follows:

'Andrea is not so much a split soul as a multitasking soul.

'It comes down to impatience, or as near as you can get to that in a timeless existence, which is out of the physical, closer to what Real Reality is, of course.

'In an earlier conversation with Richard, I referred to her as an impetuous kid, or something like that; not meant as a slight, just that young Souls, or relatively young Souls, tend to do that sort of thing.

'Whereas old stagers, like you and me, Barbara, have seen it all, or, at least, rather more. Hence, in part, our rather off-beam senses of humour. You don't get warped senses of humour like ours without the knocks of many lives, not usually anyway.

'Back to dear Andrea.

'She is overdoing it a little, certainly for the last few lifetimes, though I feel she is about to calm down. Not a lot of choice really, she is wearing herself to a Soulless frazzle.

'I feel that the energy drain is what led to, or contributed to, the cancer which ended the lifetime to which she regressed. That seemed a bit of salacious experiencing but we all do it. Good luck to the girl; I'm all for a bit of fun, as you well know.

'Okay, now my thoughts. Yes, more of them.

'Andrea had trouble tuning in to that life because of the overlap, physical time-wise, and the energy drain. She needs to learn how to take her physical lives more gently as she does not seem to realise, at least on the Soul level, how wearing and challenging they can be.

'Let's clear up the young Soul thing, as it might be taken the wrong way. You know what it is like for a physical person in the late 'teens, early to mid twenties; a bit more get up and go, more impetuosity than, say, a forty year old; also, they do not listen to advice so much. In the Soul sense, Andrea is more like the former, we two, as well as others around us, more like the latter.

'It all fits; trouble coping with trying to do too many things at once, confusion and tiredness, at least on the etheric level, though it does not necessarily show in the physical, at least not obviously. The "conventional" earthbound approach always misinterprets these things, well, usually anyway.

'I don't think it is appropriate for me to go drifting off into the ether for this sort of thing. I need to keep to what you present to me, so to speak. After all, we need to keep to the book and people are going to think of us as mad enough as it is, though I am out of it really, I can sit and watch and have a giggle. I hope you lot have got thick skins.

'Besides, rules are rules. There is a limit to how much we should interfere with the Earth side. Most of this is "preordained" in that we agreed it before we started, this lifetime, your lifetime(s) that is; I always was going to contribute from this level, this time round, within limits which you also agreed to; you in the general sense rather than any one person.

'Okay, back to your "parallel stuff", Barbara. It is only parallel in the earthbound sense. Timelessness, on this side, means the parallel notion does not fit as well as it does in the physical. It also makes it pretty difficult to drop in at the right time, though I am getting better with practice.

'Andrea is one of those people who try to do too much at once, as we all, or many of us, have thought of doing at one time or another. In a sense it is "getting the physical experience bits over a quickly as possible". Okay, so that doesn't make much sense from a "timeless" point of view but it is a matter of perspective. It conveys the intent, the thought, the thinking out of what to do with these physical lives.

'Uh, oh, I'm rambling; bad habit. Let's try to be more lucid.

'Andrea is trying to get her lives in the physical world over in double quick time, for want of a better way of putting it. There is more to what is than physical lives of course. And some try to get that part, the physical life part, over with as soon as possible to move on as quickly as possible. Andrea has been trying to do that and falling over her own feet to some extent. Even so she has made remarkable progress. She has made mistakes, as we all do, but has learned from them. Onwards and upwards, my dear. Overall she is doing very well.

'Does this make any sense? It does "up here" but not sure about "down there". It is a little while since I had to cope with physical thinking and have got out of the habit somewhat. If not, let me know and I'll give it another shot.

'Happy writing.

'Lorelei.'

***

Let's have quick chat about the importance of the language we use, as it is relevant to us whether researching our past or not. If we use negative words or phrases, it will affect us in a detrimental way. By describing yourself or another person using terms such as 'soul-less' or 'gutless' is not good.

If a task is dull please do not say it is *soul destroying*.

One very positive message is the ability we all have to transform and you have probably done that lots of times by now.

185

10

Final Thoughts...Maybe

Let's begin in the past - which could be now or in the future.

You may well have discovered that the retrieval of memories alone is sufficient to answer a curiosity or question.

Before my first regression I didn't have a problem or 'issue', it was done purely for the experience and learning. But, it answered many questions that I didn't know I had. Often clients tell me how the experience of their journey to the past has given them a lot of insight into themselves, how they live their lives and the people they attract or repel. For them that was more than enough. We certainly don't want to go on a search and destroy mission for problems that don't exist

If you have held on to unwanted memories in any form you can release them. Awareness is often enough, but if you have anything at all that doesn't work or isn't useful you may as well get rid of it. You might like to think of it as Feng Shui of the mind, body and soul. Clutter is clutter in whatever shape or form, and if we hold on it takes up space and might remind us of stuff we'd be better off forgetting, or, at least releasing.

I remember a client in her mid-fifties who suffered with insomnia and had done for almost as long as she could remember. She told me that her bedroom was always trashed but she refused to tidy it. It was so awful she had trouble getting into her bed, let alone sleeping. During her therapy she remembered how cross she was as a child having to clean her room for when her grandmother visited, as she slept in her bedroom. She had loved her gran but begrudged the intrusion and annoyance of having to share and therefore tidy away toys. My client had held onto that cross-ness all that time – her grandmother had been dead nearly forty years!

She started laughing out loud during the session at her silliness. But, it was only silly when she knew. Before that it served a purpose for the little girl in her.

If you have issues or difficulties to work through the easiest way - as with most healing techniques - is to make use of what you know, whether is it from your past, present or future Self. Andrea talked of Dr Blake offering advice and we know that going back and comforting the child 'within' can be profound and more effective than any amount of therapy.

Holding onto anything, even if you don't know why, can easily be cleared if you get a little helping hand. Ask your future Self for guidance or suggestions and comfort or laugh with your past You. Remember you have free will and can make it all up as you go along if you don't like the way it is panning out. Not sure how it might end? Have a look. You will get an idea even if it isn't the definitive end result.

A successful technique to release, create or reap whatever you desire is to write your own life in the form of a story. You don't have to literally write it: imagining it or recording are perfect methods. Create your story, beginning wherever you wish: in this life or a past one. Pretend it is the exact set of events and circumstances that you would love. If it is in the past, imagine learning whatever you needed to benefit your life now. Imagine you have the knowledge necessary for your perfect life of bliss and design the future of your choice.

You can do this as often as you like, changing, tweaking or rewriting as you go. It's your story, you have control. The beauty of being in charge of yourself is that the subconscious mind can't actually tell reality from imagination and so if you change an emotional hold from a stress filled one to a happy one, the mind will change your physiology and you will feel different.

As you design your life you will automatically be giving yourself ideas, affirmations and suggestions of success and abundance. Because you've cleared away anything at all that might be in the way physically, mentally, spiritually or metaphorically, it will become your reality. And, if you don't like it, you can change it.

But, if you are troubled beyond self-help and can't manage, please get guidance or treatment. I'm certainly not proclaiming we can do everything ourselves, but believe me when I say we can achieve a huge amount when we have the knowledge.

How much easier it is when we actually look in the manual.

Cosmic Ordering

We sometimes hit blocks or can be surprised that even if we are doing the whole shebang of deliberate creation, positive thinking, healthy living, taking care of ourselves, etc, we still seem to get dealt the rubbish hands.

Most often it seems to be about abundance: in love, money or health. We send out our Order and back comes…nothing or something else entirely. If you have held onto to the expectation of lack from a past life, your desires to the universe are muddled.

Imagine you are seeking someone to love, who will in return love you unconditionally. Why then do all the relationships end in tears? Mel had this problem.

She came to see me after yet another awful break up. Men were very attracted to her and there had never been a problem finding gorgeous guys. Telling me very succinctly the theory and what she did, it was clear that Mel knew how to ask.

In recent years her Ordering had resulted in a fabulous job, home and plenty of money, but in matters of love she failed miserably. Convinced it was past life debris, we went off to explore. Immediately the answer arrived. During a moment of illicit passion with a lover in the 18th century, his wife had appeared and the shock caused him to have a heart attack and die. The Mel from the past was unable to cope with the grief and guilt and soon afterwards killed herself by jumping out in front of some galloping horses.

Her mind had held onto the belief that bad things happen to men if they fell in love with her, so for their protection and hers she managed to destroy every relationship as dramatically as possible.

Being armed with this knowledge freed her from the manacles of grief and guilt and has enabled her to have normal relationships. She laughed when confessing her hatred of horses, as she had always been terrified of them from childhood. Her mother later confirmed that they had attempted to sit her on a tiny pony when she was a small child, but she had screamed the place down and remained distraught for hours. They never tried again. She had two very different things presented and cleared for her in just one session.

Her story shows that even if we think we are clear thinking, if we're holding onto debris deep in our psyche we send out muddled requests. Or, the requests are perfect but we can't receive our abundant life, as along the way we are blocked or have decided we are unworthy.

These thoughts always come from us. The universe doesn't ever decide what we can or can't have. We do! Always every time without fail!

Claude had a gambling problem. He bet on the horses, cards, dogs, anything and everything, even betting on the bet by saying that if he won over a certain amount he would give it away. He earned plenty of money but had very little to show for it. Surprisingly, his problem was nothing to do with gambling. During a past life memory he recalled being a wealthy and successful landowner who had been killed accidentally during a bungled robbery.

Where was the logic then in gambling? Well, if he didn't have any money no one would try to take it. Gambling was his guaranteed way to lose it and therefore never have any to worry about.

If you don't seem to be getting what you want out of this life, maybe you are sending out muddled thoughts and confusion in your

Orders that is preventing clearness and receptivity.

If you are running an inner programme expecting bad fortune and loss, that is what you are sending out and that is exactly what you will receive. It will come to you perfectly every time. Clear out the junk and you too will be free to receive the abundance that is rightfully yours.

My 'Journey Past' story illustrates my experience. I grew up with knowledge of past lives, auras, chakras, intuition, that old blue mist and with psychic abilities that I didn't even have the language for. I was often in trouble for questioning adults when the rubbish that came from their mouths was very different from what they were thinking. After a friend of my mother was talking about a cat flea problem, I told her to use paprika. I was four years old.

As I reached my teenage years it became clear that people generally didn't know the things I knew – I now know that they do but have forgotten or suppressed it all. I too made a decision to keep quiet after getting one strange look too many.

When I had my own children, I seemed to know a lot of what we might call 'old wives tales' like using rosemary for sore throats along with various other treatments, and much of my childhood knowledge came back to me.

It was strange then that for many years after I became a hypnotherapist. I 'hid' all evidence of the more 'esoteric' and tried to stick to the conventional, often dull, side of the coin. I wasn't a 'healer' I was a 'stress manager'. I didn't help people with Cosmic Ordering, I did career or life-planning. I certainly didn't sell spells or teach anyone psychic development. Despite hiding away from my truths and realities, I had clients asking for past life regressions, healing, to have their chakras balanced and so forth, and I did those things but somewhat secretly.

From when I first started seeing clients, they nearly all told me their star signs. The first time it happened was very shortly after I had opened my practice. After the client had gone I couldn't think

191

why he had mentioned it. Really, I should say I pretended to not know why.

I never, for example, mentioned anything that might be misconstrued as 'out there' in any press interviews.

After my past life came back to me I knew why. At that moment I came out of the witch's broom closet and have never looked back. Well, actually I have but you know what I mean. It was a moment of amusing irony, shortly before my recall, when a surgeon who had developed an intense aversion to the smell of blood found the answer in a past life.

Where will you go from here? Wherever it is, there must be no regrets or should haves. Be free and reap the pleasure.

***

We are now reaching the end of our journey together, or maybe it is just the beginning. Perhaps we've done it all before and will do so again. Possibly next time we'll do things differently but then again, maybe not.

It has been a pleasure sharing this with you and I hope you have much fun on your travels and explorations from this life to the rest.

11

Journey Past

Here is one of my past lives that affected my whole career. It came to me after I self-regressed about 13 years ago. It didn't all come in one go, but during the regression and for a few dreams during the week that followed.

My sister Lizzy and I lived on the outskirts of a village. I knew the year was 1590. Our mother had died some years ago, quickly followed by my father who died of a broken heart. His last words were, 'I'm sorry to leave but I need to be with your mother, you have each other. I leave you both our home and my love.' He then slipped into a peaceful sleep from which he did not wake.

Lizzy and I lived a happy settled life for a few years, growing flowers, making and selling bread. We had been schooled by our parents in herb lore and tended to the sick. Many visitors would come for healing potions. We helped at births and used herbs and prayers to ensure those who passed went in peace.

One day in October, the village men had a meeting. From that day our lives changed dramatically.

We never found out what the meeting was about and who exactly was present, but from that day the people in the village averted their eyes and whispered to each other whenever we passed by.

Lizzy and I were on our way home one afternoon, having visited dear old Sarah who passed over from a weakness of the chest, when four men approached us. Two held me back while the other two attacked and assaulted Lizzy in a vile, cruel way. They didn't attack me - only her. I found out later they were fearful of me.

I helped Lizzy home and tended her wounds. She never recovered and soon began ranting incoherently writhing in agony. I made a concoction of Belladonna and relieved her from life. I would have gone then as well had I known what was in store for me.

That night after I buried Lizzy, Henry arrived to see me. Henry and I had been dear friends since childhood and I'd helped his wife during the birth of their son. He came to tell me that he had been threatened with death if he came near me ever again. The men had said all my family were witches and as I was the youngest I was the most powerful and the one to watch. That must have been why they didn't attack me when they hurt Lizzy.

I told Henry to hurry away and protect himself, but the men were waiting. He was severely beaten and died before he reached home. In the night there was banging on my door, but I hid and whoever was there went away. They didn't attempt to break in. The next morning I found my cat nailed to the door. The only crime he'd ever committed was to kill a few mice.

They really believed I was a witch. I would have laughed if it hadn't been so terrifying.

I had to act fast and rushed into my garden to collect more plants for a poison, but they saw me and grabbed me before I could get back in the house. They dragged me away, breaking my shoulder. Twenty came - safety in numbers. I can't imagine what they thought I might do to them.

I was taken to a dungeon type building where I was fully examined from head to toe. After that they pricked me and laughed at my pain; how brave they were now.

Days passed, I was kept in my cell and every day people, men and women, came to watch me suffering. They all wanted to know how much pain I could stand before I died. As I grew weaker I begged for death to swiftly take me in her arms.

They tortured me in groups of four to six. Not for me a fair trial. I was guilty of whatever they wanted to lay on me. They were murdering people daily. Mainly women, but a few men as well. It seemed that anyone who had ever been kind or helped anyone was now being punished.

They stretched me backwards across a small table with my legs splayed far apart, while they laughed at the pain of my degradation and humiliation. After examining every inch of me, sticking pins in me and dropping boiling wax onto my breasts, they took turns to rape me.

They had bets to see who could cause the most pain without actually killing me. They drank of my blood. How brave they were now. No one came to me. Friends had been threatened and were fearful for their families and lives. After five days I had weakened so much I could no longer cry out or speak. I constantly prayed for death.

All manner of things and body parts had been rammed down my throat, that I couldn't have confessed to anything even if I'd wanted from the damage they had caused. They only thing I could taste was my own blood. They untied me and threw me to the ground. My feet were black-dead. I couldn't stand. One of the kinder guards offered me water, but I refused. I wanted to die.

I heard whispers. I heard shouting. I heard screams. I was dragged out into the yard and the smell of burning flesh engulfed me.

'Witch. Witch. Witch,' was all I could hear.

A woman pushed her way through the mob to me and insisted she moisten my lips – she ministered a brew.

'It won't be long my lovely...' She sounded like my mother.

They tied me to the post and lit the straw but I knew I'd be dead before the flames reached me. I felt a wave of comfort wash through me as I slipped away and I heard the voice of someone from another world.

12

The Quiz

You know that the left-hand side of the brain works in a literal and sequential way, while the right-hand side is your creativity and imagination. Balance is perfect for day to day living with the ability to trigger action from either at any time.

Here is a little quiz for you to determine which is your preferred brain side.

Preferred Brain side
1. Change BULL to GATE changing one letter at a time in as few goes as possible.
2. Work out the seventeen times tables - backwards. Do this for two minutes.
3. Imagine being a flower. Notice everything about yourself. Where are you? Are you in bud or blossoming? How are your roots? Check out your colour, size, and strength. Really try and get into being the flower. Is the earth dry or wet, warm or cold?
4. Imagine in your mind's eye that you are a bird. What bird are you? Are you small or large? What colour are you? Do you fly, walk or hop? What do you eat? What noise do you make? Are you male or female?
5. Being your imagined bird, fly over the top of your house and see how it looks from above, all around the outside and then go inside and explore the whole building, going from room to room.

How was that? Numbers 1 and 2 predominantly use the left hand side. Numbers 3 and 4 predominantly use the right. Number 5 uses both as you have to be creative and at the same time think logically to move around your house.

Which numbers did you find the easiest or the most preferable?

Have you ever heard the saying, 'Not in his/her right brain'? Some people call the left side the thinker and the right the emotional – that's a pretty fair description.

When you are regressing and progressing you will mostly be in right-brain mode. But, your left-brain will join in and quite likely analyse, comment, disagree or agree knowingly as you go.

It might be that the left side is mostly the conscious mind and the right, the subconscious.

This is often surprising to many people who expect to be 'out of it' when in hypnosis or a meditative state. I cannot tell you how many times I have been told, 'I heard everything you said. I remained conscious throughout.' Well, that's a relief then.

The other frequent comment is, 'I didn't seem to go under'. I always ask them, 'Under what?'

The common misconception is that when we go into the hypnotic meditative state, we slip under the level of consciousness. However, we don't even do that when we're deeply asleep. We might when we're dead until we come back for another go.

If your quiz results show that you are more left-brain dominant, by using your imagination and getting in touch with your feelings and emotions, you will be able to enhance the abilities of your right.

Too much right brain activity might make you seem fluffy or with your head in the clouds. Some serious right-brainers seem to bypass reality totally (maybe that's not such a bad thing?!). Logical thinking or doing things like working through a puzzle book or Sudoku will boost your left side. Some lefties seem narrow minded, as it might come across as though they are lacking in imagination and devoid of any emotion. If you are completely balanced please come and work for me.

13

Quotes of Note

Here are some of my favourite quotes. I have a lot more but had to draw the line somewhere.

Those who cannot remember the past are condemned to repeat it
George Santayana (1863 - 1952)

The unconscious psyche believes in life after death
Carl Jung MD

Life can only be understood backwards;
but it must be lived forwards
Soren Kierkegaard (1813 - 1855)

I think wholeness comes from living your life
Consciously during the day and then exploring
your inner life or unconscious at night
Margery Cuyler

For certain is death for the born
And certain is birth for the dead;
Therefore over the inevitable
Thou shouldst not grieve
Bhagavad Gita (250 BC - 250 AD), Chapter 2

If you live to be one hundred, you've got it made.
Very few people die past that age
George Burns (1896 - 1996)

Past Life Tourism

For three days after death hair and fingernails
continue to grow but phone calls taper off
Johnny Carson (1925 - 2005)

The average man, who does not know what to do with his life,
wants another one which will last forever
Anatole France (1844 - 1924)

The soul of man is immortal and imperishable
Plato (427 BC - 347 BC)

Millions long for immortality who don't know what to do with
themselves on a rainy Sunday afternoon
Susan Ertz, *Anger in the Sky*

The first step to getting the things you want out of life is this:
Decide what you want
Ben Stein

The point of philosophy is to start with something so simple as not
to seem worth stating, and to end with something so paradoxical
that no one will believe it
Bertrand Russell (1872 - 1970)

The face is the mirror of the mind, and eyes without
speaking confess the secrets of the heart
Saint Jerome (374 AD - 419 AD)

The best way to predict the future is to invent it
Alan Kay

Gateway to Bridging Your Past and Future

*A preoccupation with the future not only prevents us from seeing
the present as it is but often prompts us to rearrange the past*
Eric Hoffer (1902 - 1983)

I have seen the future and it doesn't work
Robert Fulford

*Time is just something that we assign. You know, past, present, it's
just all arbitrary. Most Native Americans, they don't think of time
as linear; in time, out of time, I never have enough time, circular
time, the Stevens wheel. All moments are happening
all the time*
Robin Green and Mitchell Burgess

*Not only is the universe stranger than we imagine, it is stranger
than we can imagine*
Sir Arthur Eddington (1882 - 1944)

*When we remember we are all mad, the mysteries disappear and
life stands explained*
Mark Twain

Life is just a chance to grow a soul
A. Powell Davies

Life is a progress, and not a station
Ralph Waldo Emerson

*We do not believe in immortality because we can prove it, but we
try to prove it because we cannot help believing it*
Harriet Martineau

Past Life Tourism

I don't believe in an afterlife, so I don't have to spend my whole life fearing hell, or fearing heaven even more. For whatever the tortures of hell, I think the boredom of heaven would be even worse.

Isaac Asimov

***

14

Research Sites

Starting off is not quite the hardest point. Getting waylaid with the information available is the most difficult thing, as you'll find. Although it is important to not make your story fit the research, you may find that as you get more information you will have more understanding and things will tend to make sense.

The information you have will determine where you begin your research. You can research like a genealogist, historian, archaeologist, interested person or mix and match.

Here are some places to begin. You will probably find people keen to assist you, regardless of whether you tell them where you've got your information from.

www.google.co.uk
www.british-genealogy.com/resources/census/index.htm

Museums: www.museums.co.uk
The museums, libraries and archives council:
www.mla.gov.uk

Archives:
www.nationalarchives.gov.uk/www.historymole.com

All newspapers have their own archives. Some are online but a start is:
www.bl.uk
www.mediauk.com

Never underestimate local knowledge. This is the British association for local history:
www.balh.co.uk/tlh/index.php

Most places have local Tourist Offices and the worldwide tourist information portal is: www.towd.com

If you have a name or names these can be useful:
www.englishgenealogy.co.uk
www.county-surnames.co.uk/index.php
www.search.ancestry.co.uk

National Archives and Record Administration (NARA), Washington:
www.archives.gov
www.whitehouse.gov

The British library: www.bl.uk

Local study centres - see local library/colleges and universities. Each university has comprehensive libraries and usually websites

Parish registers: www.parishregister.co.uk

Land tax returns - each town city or county keeps records some as early as c1692:

Census: www.nationalarchives.gov.uk/census

War records – this is a good 'how to' starting point:
www.genuki.org.uk/big/BritMilRecs.html

These places are mentioned and were used in the book.

Wikipedia – www.wikipedia.org
www.britannia.com
www.royal.gov.uk
www.richardiii.net
www.history.ac.uk
www.bbc.co.uk

The national archives, Kew: www.nationalarchives.gov.uk

Each country will have its own variations on the theme and once you know your direction the route will become clear. Be prepared to be sucked in, as it is all fascinating.

Please keep me posted! You can do so via my website:
www.barbaraford-hammond.com

Acknowledgments

Thank you to everyone who agreed to be interviewed and/or regressed. The following have websites for you to browse at your leisure.

Martyn for his help in transcribing the regressions:
www.thebesttheworst.com

Andrea: www.andreawren.co.uk
Henry: www.henrybolduc.com
Jennifer: www.lipstickmystic.com
Jenny: www.jennysmedley.com
Joylina: www.joylina.com
Lizzie: www.lizziefalconer.com
Nick: www.nickbarratt.co.uk
Richard: www.richardspsychicrealm.com
Richard Craze: www.richardcraze.co.uk/e_books.htm
Roni: www.whiteladderpress.com
Valerie: www.theaustintechnique.com

Some Other Titles From Mirage Publishing

Cosmic Ordering Guide
Stephen Richards

Cosmic Ordering Connection
Stephen Richards

Cosmic Ordering: Oracle Wish Cards
Stephen Richards & Karen Whitelaw Smith

The Butterfly Experience: Inspiration For Change
Karen Whitelaw Smith

*The Real Office: An Uncharacteristic Gesture of Magnanimity by
Management Supremo Hilary Wilson-Savage* - Hilary Wilson-Savage

*Burnt: Surviving Against all the Odds – Beaten, Burnt and Left for Dead
One Man's Inspiring Story of His Survival After Losing His Legs*
Ian Colquhoun

Prospective titles

Cosmic Ordering: Oracle Healing Cards
Stephen Richards

The Tumbler: Kassa (Košice) – Auschwitz – Sweden - Israel
Azriel Feuerstein

Occult: Dispatches From The Shadows
Jonathan Tapsell

Mirage Publishing Website:
www.miragepublishing.com

Submissions of Mind, Body & Spirit
manuscripts welcomed from new authors.

FOR THE LOVE OF VINES

FOR THE LOVE OF VINES

N. L. HURTIC

Matador
9 Priory Business Park,
Wistow Road, Kibworth Beauchamp,
Leicestershire. LE8 0RX
Tel: 0116 279 2299
Email: books@troubador.co.uk
Web: www.troubador.co.uk/matador
Twitter: @matadorbooks

ISBN 978 1838591 021

British Library Cataloguing in Publication Data.
A catalogue record for this book is available from the British Library.

Printed and bound in Great Britain by 4edge Limited
Typeset in 11pt Adobe Jenson Pro by Troubador Publishing Ltd, Leicester, UK

Matador is an imprint of Troubador Publishing Ltd

For Edin & Azra,
Always remember and never forget the magic of the Vines.
Love Always

Chapter One

⚜

Up Until Now

I sat waiting, my hands clasped in my meager attempt to look older, more mature and collected. Not a chance on the inside, but I sat appearing somewhat poised with my back against the padded bench of the Moosic Diner. The table, a laminate 1950s style, that was probably the exact booth that stood here some sixty years ago when they built the place as a stop for travelers off Route 84 and the locals alike. The place had seen better days, as it had the obvious wear and tear of visitors stopping in off the highway on their way to bigger places like Scranton or further on to New York City. Somehow it still appeared neat and clean and ready for business after all this time. Wishing I was more like the booth, at least it was where it belonged.

I don't know where I originally came from, as I was raised in and out of foster homes in Lackawanna County since as long as I can remember. In the fifth grade, I was officially taken in by an older woman, Mrs. Elouise Vendor, and I stayed with her until her death.

That was almost five years to the day from next Friday, my birthday June 1st. Yep, I'm a Gemini. It's funny that Geminis are supposedly ruled by their intellect, purely logical individuals. I can't say that I see myself as this great intellect. I mean, I'm not dumb but there is more of a void in me that has kept me alive by leading me through the motions than to say I am someone who masterminds everything and plans it out. If I were to go on that, I would say I don't really think about anything but that I sure wished I was more like what my sign says I am. I kind of just have been trying not to think or feel anything and have been 'just winging it' and hoping it works out. I don't have a plan but I try to make decisions that will keep me ahead of the game, or at least safe. I'm not really into astrology in the sense that I follow my daily horoscope, as that's a bunch of hogwash, but I did have my astro chart done once by a woman who claimed to be a seer at a church picnic, of all places. I think for me it was more of a curiosity about myself; a real desire that drives me, as the only people who could have told me about who I am are dead. That I was, and most likely still am, searching for any information that anyone can tell me about myself, no matter how strange, insignificant or even unlikely. I am not sure what religion my parents were or are, since I have never met them and am not even sure if they are alive or dead, but Mrs. Vendor was Catholic. She was, like just about everyone in Moosic, so I kind of go along as it doesn't seem to be a bad thing. Honestly, I kind of like the ceremony of the robes and the procession, the incense and candles and singing together. It was always one of the few places I could be in a crowd of people but yet be totally alone and feel at peace, safe.

Mrs. Vendor had her mind set on saving me from the horrible misfortune she said was my life and that I had potential to be a somebody. She enrolled me in St. Mary's School of Avoca from the time she took me in until the eighth grade. I think of that time as the best time of my life. Sure I was different than the other kids. I wasn't raised from birth in their little community where everyone knew everyone else, everyone had a station and acted it out proudly, married each other and died in that little town just as everyone had before since the time their ancestors came over to America and settled. I couldn't follow that direct lineage and had no idea who I was or what my station should be in the scheme of things, but somehow I was happy there. They were all good to me and didn't ask too many questions; they just let me be. Most of their ways were due to their beliefs, and it was really hard to figure out coming in as an outsider and to know what to ask, as everyone else seemed to know what to do. For the first time, I could settle. Maybe start to heal and even make sense of the world. I learned more than the basics of Catholicism at St. Mary's, but also manners and really just how one was supposed to be, things I wasn't given from foster care. I loved Mrs. Vendor for it; she was the only one who ever invested in me. The sad thing is I started to believe and see all the things she saw in me as we went through just the daily and mundane things of life in Moosic.

It happened on my walk back from Jitty Joe's. I was enjoying one of their famous hard ice creams. I got banana this time and was finishing off the pretzel when I got the call from Moses Taylor Hospital; Mrs. Vendor had a stroke and I should probably come down. That day at Jitty Joe's was my reminder that the universe wasn't going to let me have happiness or the kind of life I believed I could have from what I saw at St. Mary's. After Mrs. Vendor got home, I never started that following year at Seaton Catholic like I was supposed to. With Mrs. Vendor's disability, it just wasn't enough to pay someone to come and stay with her while I was in school, so I just never went on. I ended up taking a job at the convenience store under the table, stocking shelves in the back. It was on the corner of Minooka Ave so I could just walk home, which was across the street if she needed me. I was never away for long. When I turned sixteen, I got my G.E.D. and took a job waiting tables at the Blue Oyster, the gay bar around the corner, as they felt bad for me, I guess, and they let me work. People in town started to look at me different but I didn't care. They were good to me when I needed it, so whatever those guys did with each other was their business.

Then one day it happened. I came back from my shift at the Blue Oyster and as usual went into the bathroom to shower and get into my sleeping jogging pants, and I looked into Mrs. Vendor's room and saw her hand grace the floor. There she lay, so peacefully in her bed I knew she had to have passed. I took her arm that hung off the side of the bed and it was cold, all the life had left her. She was gone. I asked God to take her, pleading with him, saying in my mind that if the only reason was because I knew enough to talk to him now and it was because of her, that should be a good enough reason. Like always, I never got an answer like so many people of faith claim to, but for whatever reason, I believed in that moment my prayers were heard and I didn't feel so alone.

I didn't cry; I just checked to make sure she was decent and called the rectory. I knew the number from my days at St. Mary's. The voice who answered was Father Frank's secretary, who cooked his meals for him and did the housekeeping. She was a devout Catholic and believed taking care of 'the good father,' as she called him, was considered a good deed and her way into Heaven. She informed me that Father Frank was no longer with the parish. He had met a woman on a cruise and had married her, and it was love at first sight and quite the scandal for Avoca. That he had actually moved out of the district but she was sending the new priest, Father O'Kelly, over to help me make the arrangements. I had to sit down; the news was just so shocking. I was actually happy for Father Frank and that he had found someone. As I had not been raised Catholic except for Mrs. Vendor's influence, I was more open-minded about the things a religious person should do and was confused sometimes as to who could marry and who couldn't. I knew rabbis and imams married and some Baptist preachers but respected the way Catholics did things and almost felt like I was one of them for a while, until Mrs.

Vendor's stroke changed everything. I sat next to her for a minute, just thinking about her and being grateful I got to see that life had more options than what I had been shown before her and called the police to report her death.

I don't really remember what happened after that; it is all kind of a blur, foggy. I know Tommy, the Moosic constable, was one of the first people who came by to pay his respects. I believe it was him who handled a lot of the official things and made the necessary phone calls to handle her affairs, as I was a minor. He also arranged for me to get the apartment in the government housing when Shannon, the woman everyone knows is strung out on drugs, was convinced to stay in the halfway house in Scranton to get treatment. It was Tommy who got me her apartment. I don't know if there was any paperwork done to secure me as the official resident, but I had a place to stay. I remember people leaving me food and putting their arm around me or patting my back gently, but I can't place who they were or envision their faces. I felt their kindness when I needed it but it's all a blur.

So, for a year, I stayed in what the kids at St. Mary's would call the projects. When I first went in, I just locked the door and slept on the bed for two days. I woke up so hungry that I took a quick shower and made my way out of the Lackawanna Housing Authorities little house they let me live in and made my way down Main Street to see if anything was open. That night, I found a little diner, and for eight bucks I had coffee for two hours, had scrambled eggs, home fries, toast and two slices of bacon and left her a tip. Not bad, I remember feeling like a human being again and thinking thoughts a kid shouldn't have to worry about. At that point, I had to come to terms with the fact that I had to decide for myself what I should do, and I had no direction since the only direction I ever had was gone. For the first time since I got the call at Jitty Joe's, I looked around at the people around me. I actually looked at them and took recognition of their faces. That night at the diner, no one I knew came in. I can see myself sitting there like a scene from a movie; the memory is still so fresh and clear in my mind. I was so thankful to be alone for a moment, since I didn't think I was ready to engage with anyone. I was still too sore, and maybe I was in shock or angry that I just couldn't get a break. I think it was mostly that I was hung up on what should be, as I was still a kid and shouldn't have had to deal with all this, let alone on my own. Nonetheless, there were some really good people who just did the right thing for me, if only because it was the right thing to do, and here I was. Fortunately, I was not homeless and had a good meal. So *what now?* I thought to myself.

That night, I made my plan. I knew I would never be able to do as good for myself as Mrs. Vendor intended, but the sad thing now was I had seen what she had intended and it was a good life for me, and I just couldn't go back to foster care. In having decided I could carve out a better situation for myself than group homes and social workers could think up, a small voice inside me began to emerge. I was angry. For the first time, I questioned how I was treated and the hand I was dealt. It asked me how some lady from Scranton, with a degree in social work or not, could know what is best for me. After all, she didn't even know my parents or ask me what my dreams were, what I wanted for myself. I felt a wall build up between me and the world as in that moment I loved me. Even if it was just as a duty, because there was no one else I had to be better for me. I had seen something different than what I was given and I wanted it for myself.

I ended up smudging the year on my birth certificate and made myself a year older and got hired on at Topps candy factory and made a decent check. I worked there for a little more than four years and made line manager. I got myself a car, an old Subaru Forester, which surprisingly ran pretty good for a car that was older than I was. It was great on gas and I didn't worry in the snow and on the icy hills we call roads in the winter. I had almost forgotten my hurt and stopped cursing my life, because it had become steady and good, when I got the call.

I should have been more careful not to let the world see me relax, I told myself, but was excited by the curiosity of the man who said to meet him at the Moosic Diner that Friday at 5 pm. The call was so strange anyway; all he said in this professional deep voice was, "Aurora Rose Kohl?"

It was so official; of course, I just immediately said, "Yes, speaking." He didn't sound young and it wasn't any voice from the neighborhood that I could recognize. So I didn't think it was someone who would have business with me or a guy who may be interested in me for a date, then I would imagine he would have addressed himself and have said how I may know him or at least how I would have heard of his family. I mean, maybe because I skipped out on high school here there were a couple of kids or families I didn't know, but I was pretty sure he wasn't from Avoca, or Pennsylvania for that matter. Plus, he had a strange accent. It was faint, but I could still detect something odd or different from how we spoke in Lackawanna County. I mean, I noticed it.

I understood him perfectly but was left with a lingering curiosity about the mysterious caller, as his call was so brief. He was definitely in charge of the conversation and to the point, so much so that the call was over before I knew it. Now I was just left with all the feelings and questions that kept going through my mind as I tried to focus on my daily tasks throughout my days that led up to my birthday. So here I was, nervously waiting to see what this was about. He did name a public place for us to meet, so if it turned out that he was crazy, I had some options or at least witnesses. Growing up in foster care, I was pretty sure I could handle myself or at least get away if he turned out to be bad news. I knew from watching enough crime T.V. shows such as my favorite, *Law and Order*, that if I was smart, I would be less curious about my meeting with the mystery caller and more cautious about meeting a total stranger who knew a little too much about me. I just couldn't help it. For the first time in forever, I was excited. Like something inside me had woken up. I tried to remain grounded so as not to get my hopes up to possibly be disappointed or let down. *Who knows, he may not even show up. It may be a prank after all.*

Chapter Two

The Visitor

I sat facing the door, taking in every feature of the silhouettes that entered the diner. No one new, no one strange; oh, where was he? This mysterious caller who knew my full name, even though I had gone by Rose since I could recall, who called and told me where to meet him four days ago. Some way to spend my birthday, work a full shift at the warehouse then sit in the diner waiting for someone I had never met. I dazed off into a contemplative daydream of what people who turn twenty-one usually do. I was envisioning a massive rave party being held in my honor by one thousand friends I didn't know or have, when he walked in and gracefully, yet affirmatively, slid into the seat across from me in my booth.

He was nothing like I could have envisioned, yet he looked exactly like he should be expected to, if that made any sense. He wasn't extremely tall, about six feet in height with a muscular, yet lean build. He had red hair like me; just his was so red and thick it may as well have been black. His features were sharp with his high cheekbones and slender nose. Except for his eyes; they were large and a blue so light they were like ice yet not cold. His mannerisms were controlled and masculine yet somewhat smooth and comfortable. He had awareness about him and he carried himself like he was used to engaging with people and all types. He gave off an odd vibe because he came off as warm and welcoming, yet he was extremely rigid and almost soldier-like. That would make sense; people in the military sometimes get deployed overseas. He would have to work with all different kinds of people. Maybe he was a soldier, but his clothes didn't give that impression. They weren't new clothes, but worn. He was definitely from a city, a big one. He seemed comfortable in them and they appeared practical; a maroon tee shirt with a buttoned collar and worn-in light blue jeans that were a little faded in the hips and knees.

I noted he must hang his hands on his pockets or put them in and out of his pockets a lot to wear the hips like that. That in itself was unusual. *Well, I guess I shouldn't be surprised. This mystery guy is unusual*, as the whole thing was. I mean, I didn't know anyone except for the few people I had made acquaintance with over the years around Lackawanna County, and it's not that large of a place. He gave me a big smile, revealing perfectly straight, yet surprisingly large off-white teeth. He introduced himself and I detected a slight accent, which I couldn't really place. It was definitely foreign, overcast with a proper New England speech pattern in his spoken, "Aurora, hello." I corrected him quickly with Rose and tried to look polite and interested as I held myself back from fidgeting from the eagerness of my curiosity. I tried to place where he might be from through listening to each sound as he pronounced the words, but I hadn't met many people outside of the area and I hadn't traveled at all really. My basic assumption was that it wasn't Scottish or German, but definitely Germanic. It was sharp and smooth like his features; it suited him. I noticed the lack of lines on his smooth, ruddy skin, but he had to be ten to fifteen years older than me. He had large, square hands like me. It was odd to see the would-be male version of my hands. I wondered if he was a relation to me, maybe some long-lost cousin or something like that.

The prospect of having a family surprisingly appealed to me, which shocked even myself as I had gone so long trying to convince everyone I was so strong and independent, tough, and that I didn't need anyone, especially the poor excuses of people they shuffled me to in my group home days. That day, I found myself different and wanting to connect and extend myself to my possible would-be family. Maybe it was because they would be my actual people and not strangers who were paid for my care. I didn't know but was so excited I could barely stand the suspense, and this mysterious stranger got more comfortable in his seat as the waitress approached our booth. He and I both ordered coffee and a water. I added a slice of Dutch apple crumb pie to mask my nerves and hopefully settle my stomach. I hated that about me, that whenever I get excited or nervous, I have to eat; not a lot but just enough to comfort me. I don't know how I managed to stay under my 110 lbs. even during the holidays, with the older women of the Avoca parish baking up a storm for the plethora of church fundraisers, but I had never had to worry about my figure. I noticed I was slim and muscular, more athletic like him. I had in my pre-teens wished to have more of a girly body, more chest, but as I got older and especially in the sometimes taken pride in holding my own at work, which was more difficult for some of the other girly girls, and I was definitely glad I wasn't built like Rhonda, the second shift forklift operator who really was built just like a man. I was defiantly a woman, just not your voluminous type.

I got up the nerve to ask him if he was the one who had called; he said he was. I couldn't tell, not sure if it was just the shock of the call that I was distracted and didn't pay attention as much as I should have to his voice, or if his striking appearance was distracting me now. He went on in conversation after the coffee came taking two creamers and no sugar to my four, making my coffee very light. "As you know, today is your birthday and also you have legally become an adult."

"Yes," I said, "but how do you know that?"

"I'm Anders Anderson; my friends call me Andi. I am your cousin through marriage.

"Originally from Denmark, your cousin Asta is my wife, and our family is just trying to settle these last matters since your grandmother's death. I am a lawyer and have agreed to take care of all the arrangements and help you get settled now that you are of age, Aur... Rose." His smile could have melted all the ice in Scandinavia. I could easily picture him handling important matters and heavy negotiations.

"So my family's name is Kohl and I'm Danish?" I asked.

"Yes," he said. "Kohl was on your father's side, originally from Northern Germany. They migrated up from the islands that are between Denmark and Germany and stayed in Denmark." I tried to remember islands off of Germany, but not having had much schooling, I didn't know much geography, so I just tried to pay attention to what he was saying. "Your mother's side can be traced to Denmark since the time of the Vikings, give or take a couple stolen Irish brides during successful raids."

I looked at him with such utter shock and said, "You are kidding, right?" He just kind of smiled and said no with such a casual inference, as if I should already be familiar with the tales of my lineage, as if there was nothing wrong with stealing brides during a Viking raid. "Be as things may, I guess we do things differently now," I said.

He just said a hearty "Yeah" and seemed amused at my naivety. I couldn't tell if his attitude was because he was older and had seen more of life, so what I found shocking wasn't so much for him as life had exposed more of itself to him, or if he just thought I should know about our family. "Your grandmother Lauren Lorensen Kohl left you her home in Loganville, Georgia, when she died three years ago. She also left some money with a stipulation that you live in the house and attend the college she selected for you and graduate before you can collect the full sum in its entirety."

"What!" I cried out. Everyone in the diner looked at our table for a few seconds and carried on back to their business. I intentionally closed my mouth, as I realized it was still open from the shock of what Andi had said.

Chapter Three

Minooka Ave

What else could happen? This was beyond what I ever thought could happen to me, yet somehow it felt right. I walked into my small loft apartment that was initially built as a mother-in-law suite over my landlord's garage, but she died the day before they finished it. Sad really, but at least she knew what they were trying to do for her. Not sure how she would have made it up the steep, wraparound steps that led to my loft apartment, but it worked for me. It was basically a big open kitchen/living room with a large island clad with two stools instead of a traditional table and chairs to eat at. My bedroom was just big enough for my full-sized cast iron bed I found at a thrift store in Scranton, and my dresser. I hated to leave it but there was no way I could haul that thing all the way to Georgia, and to be honest, I really didn't feel like taking it apart and carrying it down the twenty-three stairs to my Subaru.

I couldn't believe how excited I was about going, let alone leaving the only home I could remember. I didn't really care about my job at Topps. I mean, the pay was good and I had learned how to work in an office and be professional; and before that, warehouse work was everywhere, so for that I was grateful, but it wasn't where I saw myself forever. The good thing was that I had gained the title Manager, and that looks really good on paper. Who knew, maybe I could land a good job down there. Funny thing is, I had never met anyone from Georgia and couldn't really recall any T.V. shows depicting people from there; the only thing that came to mind was from the film *Gone with the Wind*. Not exactly the setting I wanted to move to, and I'd heard a lot of good things about Atlanta from the business section in the newspaper, but I didn't think Loganville was anywhere near the city, or at least it didn't sound like it would be.

I felt foolish getting all excited about a place that I knew nothing about. Who knew; this so-called cousin could have been a scam artist or serial killer. My mind was putting up a good fight, but deep inside somewhere, I knew way down from the bottom of myself that this move was right. How crazy was that! How crazy was I?

I needed to get out and get some fresh air. I started walking and ended up in Avoca, right in front of St. Mary's School. I must have dazed as I was walking. I really must have been losing it because I got a good two miles from my loft and had no recollection of my walk to my old school. I made the old familiar way up the drive path to the small walkway in between the old convent and the school. The nuns had already moved out when I attended school here; we just used the building for storage by then. Now it was all abandoned, and I began to feel sad that no one else would receive what I did from St. Mary's. I leant against the old 1919, a marker that told when the building had been built. I had never been sure why old builders used to do that, but it was a comfort to me now as I reflected on all the times I played right by its side; games that were old and outdated even when I played them all those years ago. The world had changed, I guess, and now there were iPads to amuse kids with. I just sat there for the longest time before I realized I should be walking back before it got dark. This was goodbye, I guess, on to my new life and a new start. I was making good time. I was past the tavern and on the bridge toward Main Street before I could even form a thought about what my plan for Georgia would be. I hoped they wouldn't all be small-minded, small-town-going-nowhere rednecks. I guessed I could always move again if I didn't like it.

The stipulations in my grandmother's will were that I enroll and finish my four-year degree at some nobody's-heard-of college in the next town over. Worst case scenario was that I finish up school and take the money and leave. How bad could it be that I would have to leave and couldn't bear four years? If I kept myself busy in school and found a job to amuse myself, the time should pass. I had a sudden fear of flunking out of school. I wondered what would happen if I did. I guessed I wouldn't get the money but I thought the house would still be mine, no matter what. I'd have to go back over the fine details of the will. It was way too overwhelming all at once when Andi was explaining everything to me. I had another fearful thought as I passed Bolugas' convenience store, the small mom and pop that had been there since Mr. Boluga came back from World War II and opened up the place. I was almost home when I started thinking about the movie *Mississippi Burning*. I wasn't a fully vested Catholic but I was pretty sure in the film, the Ku Klux Klan targeted Catholics too, and definitely Yankees. Well, that was supposed to be a long time ago, before my parents even, and a lot had changed since even I was a kid, so hopefully I'd be okay. Even with my little pep talk to myself, I had only managed to change my mind; the nervous feeling in my stomach was calling for food to settle me down and the rest of me wasn't so sure if this was a good idea. Just when fear began to re-emerge, I told myself the worse that could happen was that I'd have to find another warehouse job; so what? I had already turned in my resignation letter at Topps, so I should just take this as a little dip of excitement. I mean, I was still young and had the ability to change my life. I should at least see what it was; maybe an opportunity I wouldn't have here. Who knew?

I sat, as I planned, the rest of my night so as to make sure I got everything done off my checklist. I wondered if I was a weirdo being so efficient with my time management or if everyone carefully planned out their activities the way I did. I wasn't the kind of person to really open up and share a lot of myself to really have any way to compare myself to others. I only had to go on what I heard from others here or there and make my own comparison. I guess I was like that because I was shuffled around so much as a kid; those in my life either had their own problems or weren't really invested in me, so the opportunity to open up wasn't an option. I guess people can turn to books or movies to kind of figure things out. In moments like these is when I wished I had read more or maybe finished school. Maybe I could; I had been given this crazy option I never thought was possible by a woman I had never met, had never known even existed. I guess I should have been angry or upset that I had family all this time and that they knew about me, even knew where I was and I was left alone. I made it back; I decided not to go up the twenty-three stairs to my apartment, even though I had to pee so badly I just got in my Subaru and drove to the Moosic Diner.

The place was full of just a couple of the usual locals. After using the restroom and washing up a bit from my walk, I slid into my favorite booth and ordered up a storm. I told Nina, one of three waitresses who worked there, I would be leaving and that this was my last supper with her. She gave me a hug and ripped up the check. "It's on me, hon... good luck down there."

Old Barney, another local, put down his paper to yell out, "Don't let the heat get to you; ya know it affects people. Don't come back all crazy... heh heh heh," as he gave me a hug. I felt good and said my goodbyes; it was official now. I was on my way to my new life. I was excited and eager to get on the road the next morning. I planned to leave by five in the morning so I raced home, took a shower and got in bed.

This would be my last time sleeping in my big cozy bed. It was perfect really, big enough for me, and soft. I heard it wasn't good to sleep on a soft mattress, but it was so comfortable I slept well, and I didn't see any point in spending a lot of money when I was happy with what I had. Sometimes I found that growing up poor gave me a certain practicality that I may not otherwise have possessed and appreciated in myself. I drifted off into the strangest dream I had ever had. In the dream, I was in a deep forest of green and somehow was walking easily on a path. I looked up and there were two large yellow-green eyes staring at me. Whatever it was, it was just staring at me, acknowledging my presence, watching me but it didn't move or come out and reveal itself to me. I was somewhat afraid but still aware that it was supposed to be there just like I was. Then I woke up to the buzzer of my phone, it was 5 am time to get up. I had put my bags and packed boxes in the Subaru the night before. Just had to wash, put on a little black eyeliner and mascara, which was my signature look, my favorite knee-length yoga pants and a thin summer hoodie, which is perfect for summer mornings because you can push the sleeves up as it gets warmer in the day. Slipped on my pair of slip-on teal and black Sketcher sneakers, grabbed my purse and I was out the door. I left the key with my landlord and said goodbye and didn't look back until I was in Virginia somewhere.

I really didn't want to stay there for the night, so I just stopped at a truck stop which surprisingly was really busy, well-lit and appeared a lot safer than the two no-named gas stations I passed within the last hour. I used the restroom, got a water, large coffee and pound cake. I filled up my tank with gas as who knew, from what I'd seen from Virginia so far, when I'd have the option to get gas again. Don't get me wrong, the state was absolutely beautiful; green with hills and mountains, but the people, although nice, seemed a little behind, and this was from my Avoca perspective. What would I think if I was from a big city like New York? It wasn't that they were just moving at a slower pace but they also looked at me, and I got the feeling they thought I was strange and definitely an outsider but were too polite to ask. My most concerning observation was that there were no guard rails along the mountain side and there were some really steep drops. If I was off the grid and camping or something, it may not have been concerning, but I was on the main interstate, which also, by the way, wasn't well lit. I wondered where their tax money was allotted to as I pulled back on the interstate and made my way further south. I made it past the Virginia/North Carolina border when I found a Best Western next to what looked like a diner called Waffle House. I pulled in, got a room and crashed. I must have fallen asleep as soon as my head hit the pillow of the huge double bed. I woke up at five fifteen in the morning.

I guess my body thought that's what time I woke up now, before six. I showered and amused myself with the tiny soap and shampoo the hotel provided for me. I lotioned up with the bottle of lotion they left on the sink. I usually hated to smell generic and preferred my four-dollar bottle of lavender Baby Magic body lotion, which surprisingly softened my skin well and gave it a healthy glow, but also with my unique smell which I think are called pheromones, it smells great on me and no one can ever guess what I'm wearing. It's light, subtle and still feminine without smelling like a jar of potpourri. Just changed my underwear and threw back on the same clothes, which were so comfortable to travel in. Don't think I could have sat in the car that long in a pair of jeans, not to mention it had gotten more humid since I made my way further down past the Mason-Dixon line. I wondered how much warmer my new home would be than Avoca, as it was something I hadn't really thought about until I began to really perspire in the car.

I packed up the Subaru and went back inside to double-check and make sure I hadn't left anything behind and closed the door behind me as I made my way over to the office to return my room key. I had to ring the bell a couple times before a young guy about my age took the key and gave me my receipt. I got in my Subaru and drove next door to the Waffle House as I did not feel comfortable leaving my car in front of the room since I already checked out. I wasn't familiar with the rules or local customs and just believed it to be easier to jump right into my car after I ate anyhow.

There was a wedding going on as I walked in; I am not kidding. Apparently the bride was a waitress there and met the groom while on duty, so they decided it was the most fitting place to get married, of course. I thought the culture in the south so far was a little uncouth, even for a foster kid, but I kind of liked its unconventional ways too. It did lift my spirits. I drank at least four cups of coffee, which wasn't terrible coffee, and the food was better than I expected. When she called out my order, I realized there was some kind of subculture associated with Waffle House as she read… "Cheese egg plate, scattered covered, white." Maybe I'd catch on as I lived there longer. I did hope Georgia had more to do and more of a sense of community like Avoca did as I looked out the window and saw nothing for a while but darkness, no cars on the road, nothing but my motel.

Hey, seven bucks, including my tip! Wow, living in the south may have its perks, so far so good. This meal would have been at least four dollars more in Avoca, and I would have gotten home fries, which I think are a little heartier than hash browns, but when in Rome… do as the Romans do, the saying goes. I was just happy driving on Highway 95 en route to Atlanta. I had never been out of Pennsylvania before, well, not that I knew of or remembered, so I was really enjoying the drive. I had always wanted to travel, but circumstances in life never gave that opportunity until then. That day, I was starting new, and maybe I could travel more once I got settled, see more of the world.

After Mrs. Vendor passed away, I just tried to be an adult, never really thought about life or what I could do with mine. I just generally woke up each morning and went to work, tried to make money. I knew I needed a job and I didn't want to end up bad or as a scumbag as they say in Avoca. I had a little taste of St. Mary's and knew I wanted to be better; I just wasn't sure how to be like those girls who had moms and grandmas to tell them how. Well, I guess I did and I was on my way now to being at least what my grandmother wanted, not sure what that was yet, but it couldn't be bad if she had money to leave me. She seemed to be okay, insisting I go to school. Inside, I felt excited, as I never wanted to be ignorant. I mean, I knew after Mrs. Vendor was gone, I'd never have a chance going to somewhere like Penn State or Marywood College; I thought maybe I'd eventually go to Lackawanna College after I had saved up some money. I had eight thousand dollars. It wasn't a lot, but definitely more than anyone else I knew, and secretly I was proud of myself, coming from where I did and having enough sense to save at least that much. I never told anyone, mostly because I felt fake, like a sham, as if someone like me shouldn't even have that much, even though I knew I was the one who worked and saved it in my PNC savings account.

I knew I should be doing more for myself but I wasn't really sure what. I'd catch that finance guru Susie Orman sometimes late at night before I'd doze off, but I had no idea how to get started, but I knew ya needed money to do whatever it was; I'd just keep saving until later. I couldn't really think of all that right now. I was happy to find out they do have PNC branches in Georgia, none in Loganville, but there was one in the next town over. Thank goodness for the internet because I couldn't remember the name of that town if my life depended on it. I surprisingly wasn't annoyed at the inconvenience of having to travel to do banking, as maybe it would encourage me to save more since it would be harder to go and withdraw my money. When I say inconvenience, one town away wasn't too terrible. Well, probably not, since just about any store allowed you to get cash back with a purchase, even the Dollar Store. I guess I just had a romantic notion about my move; I hoped I was right.

Once I got settled, I could go into a bank and see what they had to offer. I was sure they would have someone in the branch who could advise me or tell me about options that maybe I had that I just didn't know about or at least set me on a track so I could get there myself.

Chapter Four

The New Georgia Peach

I couldn't hold back my big grin as I flew past the giant sign that read *Welcome to Georgia*, but of course my grandmother had to live in the middle of nowhere so I still had a long drive ahead. I hadn't had to turn on my Google Maps yet, as the trip had been a straight shot so far, just stay on Highway 95 south to Georgia, then get on 85 south toward Atlanta then after a while, you need to get the specifics from your directions. As I came out of the city and was passing the King and Queen Buildings, I was pretty sure I would have to do something soon, so I turned on my phone and gave it a minute to adjust. It directed me to get off at Beaver Ruin and then make a left on Club Drive. Whoa, this area was not nice and there is no other way to say it. All the plants were molted from the heat, there were a lot of people walking around but there were no sidewalks, traffic was so crazy, often bumper to bumper. I realized real quick that the traffic lights were not synchronized, which only added to the congestion, which, by the way, was a lot.

Most of the locals appeared to be Mexican and I started looking
with the intention to see if they were the only locals. I counted one
older black woman and a small girl I assumed was her granddaughter
at the bus stop on Club Drive. Everyone else I passed was Hispanic
and, I was almost certain, Mexican. The area looked run-down and
poor. Avoca was poor but everyone took care of their stuff and there
wasn't garbage all thrown everywhere. I began to fear what kind of
house mine would be since I was supposedly only a half-hour from
Loganville. If there was garbage in the front, I could pick it up, but
what difference would that make if the house next to mine looked
like they didn't care? That would be the best description of the area:
nobody cared. No one cared enough to invest any money or time
in the area. They seemed to have the same stuff everywhere too:
Waffle House, CVS, Walgreens, Zaxby's – whatever that was and
McDonalds. It all looked so generic, as if it was a rural area and
someone came in, flattened it, then just dropped a CVS down in the
grass with no thought, plan for the infrastructure or aesthetics of the
area. What I'd read about the south is they had a lot of land so they
built out instead of up. I understood what they were talking about
now as I saw a Waffle House then drove for two minutes to see a
CVS. I hate to see the wilderness destroyed, as I would prefer a city,
a community or farms; not a weird blend of all possibilities. Not
really sure how to describe this. What a shame. In Pennsylvania, you
could visit great cities like Philadelphia or Pittsburg then go explore
the wild forests and national parks. I drove by a neighborhood
before I turned onto Ronald Reagan Parkway and you could tell
the homes were just thrown up to sell. I get it no one wants to
invest anymore; I mean, it's not as if the contractors or builders
hired are working on their own homes as was the case when a lot
of the homes in Avoca were built over a hundred years ago. In some
historic areas like Stroudsburg, some homes were there during the
Revolution, and you could see the time and craftsmanship that was
put into building their future residences. It didn't seem like that was

going to be the case here as I drove past home after home of the new constructions as the sign advertised. It seemed like the builders were mostly concerned with making a profit and not the quality of the homes. They looked so cheap and paper-thin. I know the homes here don't need to be built to weather through a winter storm, but they shouldn't look as though my meager 110 pounds could kick a hole through the siding. I wished it was just a small case of culture shock at my new state's appearance, but I am a pretty logical person and not one to get all caught up in emotions. I let out a deep sigh as I knew it was probably a true assessment of the area. Well, I didn't see my own house or Loganville yet, and like I said, I could endure this until I graduated; how bad could it be? No worse than the projects and group homes, I was sure, as I tried to comfort myself into staying positive about my decision to come down here.

As I veered onto the winding parkway, my mood changed as I saw nothing but green for about four exits before I saw okay-looking apartments overlooking the parkway. I hoped that the Beaver Ruin/ Club Drive area was like the area I grew up in when I was in the foster system and that my grandmother's home was in more of an Avoca-type community. I was going to meet Andi for supper at a local place before we went back to the house together. He said he would give me a tour of the house and the keys. I came to a red light right at the end of the parkway at what seemed to be an important intersection for the town, Scenic Hwy 124. To my delight, there were shops and a Starbucks. I'd have to take note of this place for future reference as it seemed to be much cleaner and there weren't any people walking around. In the bumper-to-bumper traffic, everyone seemed busy getting home from work or school as it was rush hour. There were a ton of fast food restaurants, Target, Publix and then what seemed to be the signature stores CVS, Walgreens across the street and a QuikTrip gas station/convenience store on the corner. I passed over the intersection and drove for a while in what was a really nice group of homes, all well cared for; not quite farms, but they all had a lot of land. I was directed to another shopping center with a Kroger, McDonalds and a bunch of small specialty shops. Looking at the people shuffling through the parking lot, I watched my new neighbors, which thankfully were a good mix of people. The Kroger parking lot had everyone: white, black, Hispanic and Asian, from all different backgrounds and social classes too. I began to ease up a bit as all of these people just seemed like regular, normal people just out doing their shopping. Well... all except the black bodybuilder-looking guy whose Chihuahua's purple painted nails and tutu matched his purple sparkling headband, extremely too short shorts and purple sequined sleeveless shirt. That pair made my whole trip, but I was glad to see them. At least I knew my *Mississippi Burning* fear of moving to a small, closed-minded town where the mentality is 'it's like us or get punished' was disproven.

This was a relief as when dealing with the 'in-crowd mentality' or I guess 'this is the way it's always been' kind of place, or the people who decide what kind of place they want it to be. Who is okay and who is not and by what credentials or standards...? I guess if I knew what my template was or should have been, it still would seem wrong to exclude people. I mean, no one can help where or how they were born, what family they were given to, how that family would raise them to think or believe. Heck, in my case, I didn't even get a family, and there are all kinds of stigmas associated with orphans and people like me who grew up in group homes and government housing. In a way, I was glad, at least so I'm not a snob and think I'm better than others just based on where they are from or who they were born as. I really try to be discriminative on the person they are, or choose to be. I laughed at myself as I hoped I wasn't hypercritical in my fear that my new town would be some backward hick town. Whew. I don't bother anyone and would prefer to live where people lived and let live, but if you wanted to get out and meet people, there were places you could do that. We had the American Legion; kids took dance lessons there, played pool, basketball, and the seniors had bingo and pottery. It was nice and safe too. Not sure what to expect now about my new home but I was hopeful again. The directions said I had arrived but I didn't see a diner. I saw the Kroger gas station to my right and the shopping plaza to my left. Behind me in the parking lot, a bank and an auto shop. Huh, got out of my car, looked around again to see an ice cream shop across from a playground across the street, and I saw it. The Grayson Diner; geez, it looked so small. There was a glass door in the cream-colored brick of the shopping center, the size of one of the shops. Why, there couldn't be more than two tables inside. The address and name were correct. Guess this was the place, as small as it may be.

The shopping plaza looked clean and busy; all of the sidewalks were swept and cared for. There were plenty of garbage cans placed sporadically around the parking lot and on either side of the sidewalk, as if to say you really had to want to litter because they made it so easy to discard your trash. As nice as the plaza looked I felt a disdain for it, maybe a small fear, as I had never been anywhere where I wasn't familiar with the shop owners or had at least heard of the store's reputation. It sure looked nice, though, and I took a small conscious breath and made a determined focus to walk toward the entrance of the diner. It was hard not to smile as I walked past a set of two carefully arranged flower patches that were overflowing from stone holders that lined either side of the entrance. Someone had made a real attempt to say they took care of this place. So when I'm wrong, I say I'm wrong. My spirits cheered a little and my nervousness slowly eased as I walked toward the door; and to my surprise, it was just a little smaller than the Moosic Diner inside. I immediately thought of that scene from the Harry Potter film where he goes in the tent, and because of magic it was quadruple the size inside, but on the outside it appeared to be a one-sleeper.

Georgia has been full of surprises, I thought to myself as I walked toward Andi in a small booth in the corner. "Good evening," he said as I approached.

I gave him a weary smile and said, "Well, I made it. Thanks for meeting me to get me situated."

"Yeah, no problem. I have to make sure my cousin gets taken care of, it's Lauren's wish," he said. I took in his smooth and refined accent and the silver band that flashed from his hand as he took a sip of his coffee. It wasn't a smooth metal ring. The design and engraved carvings in the metal made it look more attractive and masculine somehow. It was a squareish band that had some kind of etching on it that was too small for me to really take in the details without asking for his hand to examine, which didn't seem appropriate. Glancing again, without trying to be obvious, I would think they were Celtic knots or some kind of Gaelic writing or something, which couldn't be right since Andi wasn't Irish. If he was American, I wouldn't be so curious, as we tend to wear stuff because we like it and not necessarily to advertise a brand of meaning.

He looked right into my eyes, so confident and in control yet warm somehow. I wished I could be more like him; maybe some of him would rub off on me. I enjoyed my French toast with powdered sugar and turkey bacon. Andi commented with amusement that I must be the only Dane he'd ever heard of who didn't like pork. Maybe, but I'd just found out I was Danish and it's less greasy and better for you… plus it has more protein so you stay full longer. It just made sense to order turkey. Off in my thoughts, I realized that I had no idea what Danish people ate or anything about their culture for that matter, other than that they were Vikings. Andi filled me in on some basic details to get me started on my new life here.

He apologized that he would not be able to accompany me back to my home tonight, as something had come up with a client and he had to mitigate, pronto. He handed me a black leather notebook. It would have looked very professional, like something a businessman or someone would carry to a meeting, if it hadn't had my name sketched in a silver sparkly script inside a large square on the front of it. I liked it immediately and began going through the contents inside its pages. Andi was very thoughtful and thorough, which surprised me, as we just met. I guess in his line of work, being able to accurately assess people and their situations in great detail was necessary, so I shouldn't have been so surprised that he was good at it, thinking about it. Maybe it was that I hadn't really ever met someone like Andi before. I'd seen people like him on T.V., or could picture a character like him, but never met anyone like him, especially not in Avoca. I'd run into a fancy lawyer or business type passing through from New York City in a diner here or there, but Andi still had a uniqueness about him that I couldn't quite put my finger on. Almost like a contained wildness that had been trained. I flashed back to the circus I went to one time with the group home. Some do-gooder from Scranton gave the home free tickets and all of us got to go. Thinking back to the memory of a giant lion sitting so calmly on a stool, taking orders from a shabbily dressed circus performer... that was it, I thought to myself. It was like when you see a lion in the circus doing tricks. You are watching him perform all of the necessary motions perfectly but it looks odd, somehow you know he doesn't belong there and is supposed to be doing something else. Like he is too powerful or majestic for the tent or stool he is sitting on, yet he does it gracefully without disagreement. Anyone who met Andi would see in a short time there is so much more to him than the moment of their exchange. Funny, even as a lawyer, I mean, that's a big-time job, right? It still seemed too menial for him. Odd, well, maybe it was just that I was from a small town myself and hadn't met anyone or been anywhere much myself, so who was to say what was the standard? I really hadn't been out enough in the world to accurately gauge anyone. I had to admit to myself that I found all of this exciting and that was the most probable explanation of me noticing these tiny details about my cousin. I mean, I had never met anyone from Denmark before. For all I knew, he could be perfectly normal and he just seemed larger than life to me because of the newness of it all. I mean, the other people in the diner barely glanced at us, so he couldn't seem as different as I was imagining him to be. Maybe I was longing for a family more than I wanted to admit. Inside, maybe I'm not as tough as I play off to the rest of the world. I looked down at the notebook, and embarrassingly at the peeling polish of my fingernails. I looked past my imperfections to focus on what was written down.

Inside on page one was a list of phone numbers; everything I might need from Andi's cell phone, Walton County Water and Gas Utilities, Georgia Gwinnett College, handyman and Emma, whoever she was. I found this was very thoughtful of him, as it would take me some time to become acquainted with all the things I would need and the area, without help.

The second page was a mini version of my grandmother's intentions and what I needed to do to honor my part of the bargain or to fulfill her wishes and to allow me to receive my inheritance.

The third page had a small manila paper envelope clipped to it which enclosed my application and acceptance letter from Georgia Gwinnett College, my financial aid award letter and a sheet that showed the four classes I was registered for starting in August. Wow! That was only two months away. Perfect really, it would give me time to get settled and learn my way around before I started something like college. I asked Andi about the financial aid and he said I was eligible since I wasn't employed and on my own, in addition to there being special grants for students who were in foster care. It's like the government's way of encouraging those who came through the system to hopefully end up as productive, contributing members of society. If somehow the system had failed them, they would still have a chance. Also, I would not receive the inheritance until I graduated, so currently I was unemployed and alone. He ended the statement with yeah, in his accent which I thought only Germans did. He had such a precise and direct approach to speaking and looking at things. I would be afraid of coming off rude and getting into an argument if I spoke as directly as he did, but he didn't come off that way; funny. Not sure how he does it, guess that's why he's the lawyer.

Page four had a job posting for the Uncle Remus O'Kelly Loganville Library. Boy, if there ever was a bumpkin-sounding name, it was that. Andi said he knew the people over there and had settled me a part-time job if I wanted it. He said it would look good on paper that I worked at the library; it was only part-time and the manager over there said he would look after me. It would be an easy job, just sit at the front desk and scan books; his wife did all the filing. It was also really close to the house and he would be accommodating to my school schedule. Something to think about; I didn't know anything about books, as I don't read much for pleasure but I really appreciated what Andi was trying to do for me. If anything, it was a job for now; it might be good until I learned my way around. It didn't sound like a terrible job and my would-be boss sounded like he was nice and he knew Andi. It sounded like they still operated on the 'good ol' boy' system of hiring, so I guessed I had better take it since this was the only connection I had down here so far and may be the only one I could manage. I wasn't an avid reader but I was pretty sure the Uncle Remus books were considered racist and very controversial; not sure how they got a library named after them, but okay. Maybe I misunderstood, as if I did decide to read them, they probably wouldn't be my type of books. I don't like to label stuff unless I have experienced it myself, but fat chance of me reading that stuff. Guess I'd never know for sure.

Andi stood and extended his hand for his usual proper handshake. After we said our goodbyes, we walked out and I made my way toward the parking lot and he called after me with a wave for me to call him if I needed anything as he watched me get into my Subaru from the sidewalk that lined the shops in front of the Grayson Diner.

I drove past in between the bank and auto shop and made a right onto a small tree-lined road that took me past the park I saw from the diner. What a picturesque park, and it was far nicer than any I had seen from Pennsylvania. The city really invested in this one. It had a pavilion clad with picnic tables, two separate play areas – one for the older kids with monkey bars – a climbing rock, swings and a suspension bridge that led to a slide. Wow! In Avoca, we had an old, rinkidy merry-go-round from our parents' time and a swing set clad with two swings. This was floored with wood chips to pad the children's fall from the monkey bars or slide. The whole park was lined with trees that looked older than the town. The trees looked ancient, as well as the homes that surrounded the park and, like the trees, they seemed sturdy and stronger because they were there for a while. The park was clearly added after. I was amused as I drove past the toddler's playground with its whimsical rides of the ladybug and bee bouncer and the mommy swing, which allows the parent to sit with the baby and swing.

A small fort with a little plastic slide and tunnel made me want to pull over and explore the park, but I was more eager to see my new home before it got dark. It was almost seven but since it was summer, I still had time.

I observed an old house that had been converted into a new age coffee shop, and next door was a similar house that was now a music studio, advertising piano and guitar lessons. It all looked very homey and comfortable. I went through the intersection and drove a while before I ended up in a small downtown area. It was so small I would have missed it if it were any later and darker. The street was clad with a row of a couple small brick two-story buildings of the essentials for the town, or at least they were back in the day. One was a barber's shop, the other a Masonic lodge. I missed what the other one was as I had to watch the road and couldn't really sightsee, not that I assumed I would miss anything that I needed or was of importance. I made a left as directed from Andi's directions and passed a small house with garden gnomes and statues all over the front yard, noting a sign that said, *For sale, lawn ornaments.* The gargoyle looked really creepy and would seem far out of place on any of the homes I could see around the area. As I drove around, all of the homes were old, mostly Victorian and small. They needed some love; well, to be honest, the whole area seemed to, but they appeared to have good bones and be well built, if not taken care of. They varied in size; some were two stories, others seemed so small they may have been able to fit possibly one bedroom inside their structures. There was no apparent rhyme or reason to the plan or style of the town proper's initial layout other than it was thankfully in blocks, which was more like Avoca and what I was used to. There were no sidewalks, but it seemed too hot to walk anywhere anyhow. I slowed down so as to pay more attention to the numbers on the houses. They consisted of about four houses to a block and they seemed large enough to be comfortable, but were not too big where you didn't want to clean your own home. The excitement began to build as I knew I was nearing my own and would be looking at my new place and life in any minute. I slowed down, almost crazy with anticipation as I read each address on the mailboxes that lined the street. Some were old and worn and took more time as I read over the numbers.

Chapter Five

Home Sweet Home

They were lined up next to each other in rows, similar to Avoca and older neighborhoods in the country. I pulled up to the address that should be mine from the marker on the mailbox and noticed the address was also painted on the glass on the door, so I pulled in the driveway that was next to the house. The small detached garage that was next to the house at the end of the driveway wasn't open, so I just parked in the driveway. There was a small stone path marked by a trellis of vined white flowers and an old-looking metal gate that guarded the path to the house. I immediately liked it because it was old, but it looked cared for. The stone path led up to three very wide stone steps made of the same material as the walkway. I guess they were efficient back in the day and used all the available resources. It made the entrance into the yard homey and more welcoming yet distinctively the personality of the owner. The porch was as long as the front of the house, white, and the wood had been recently painted. There was an old fifties-style metal lawn chair with a table on one side and a wicker bench and rocker clad with cushions on the other. The porch was just what one would imagine a grandmother would sit on in the afternoon. It was a perfect little Victorian, old and well-built but not ritzy like the Victorians I had seen in Scranton in the Marywood College district. No, this one was perfect. I stood in front of the heavy oak door with its huge glass middle. I loved the black cast iron doorknob. I almost knocked, enchanted by the house and forgetting it was mine. *My God, it's mine! I live here.* This was crazy and too good to be true. It hadn't sunk in yet. I knew I'd attached my Subaru key to the set of keys Andi had given me, throwing out my old keychain in exchange for the unique one he had given me with the keys. It just hadn't registered that I had the key to this house. I felt the knob of the ball of the old knotted rope that Andi said was handmade in Denmark that made the bottom of the keychain. It looked like a soccer ball made of rope that gets long like a finger then loops for the ring to be attached to. Surprisingly, it comforted my nerves as it massaged my hand as I turned the key in the lock.

Inside, the house was dim and cool. Thank goodness, because it sure wasn't outside. I had sweat dripping off my forehead at the hairline from just my short drive here. My bra was soaked through and I was eager to get settled in so I could take a shower or at least freshen up from my trip. I was tired but the eagerness of exploring the house was overwhelming. As the door opened, I took in my first good look at the house. It looked as I thought it would inside, yet unfamiliar as I scanned the interior. It wasn't humongous but it had high ceilings which added a lot of depth to the space. The floors were solid wood, like I was used to from back home and the windows were big, classic for the period it was built in.

It opened up into a foyer and a set of stairs on the left side, with a table and mirror above set next to a door, which I assumed was a closet, and it was. A small closet with an old metal bar pole to hang a couple coats on, maybe your usual everyday jacket and a small amount of room for one or two guests to put away theirs. To the right was a narrow hallway which I made my way down past a small living room, then formal dining room. The hallway ended at a swinging door where thankfully I found a cast iron cat door opener to brace it open to avoid the near hit in the face I just encountered. I was surprised the dining room wasn't conjoined with the kitchen, maybe it was at some point and the room was closed off later to suit the owner's needs. I was kind of glad, as I preferred defined spaces and really hated the new trend of an open concept or one giant floor plan. I mean, I am coming from humble means, and for me, a single girl in a studio apartment, an open floor plan made sense, it's cost effective and it was only me; I didn't need to define any space. In a house, though, I was glad to see the defined areas. Moving into the kitchen, I had to take a minute to soak it all in, because it was beautiful.

One would properly define it as shabby chic, but for me it was perfect. The kitchen was defined by the cream cabinets that went all the way around the room and were rectangular, having a good size. She had updated the knobs and appliances in a matted stainless steel and had done the countertops in a white stone; not sure what it was, maybe quartz or marble. The walls were a dark teal which matched the bench cover that lined the built-in bench that was in the corner. A small cream-colored round table was in front of it, guarded by a round-back cream chair that had a round seat cushion covered in a matching teal cushion. It looked very comfortable and for a moment I could see someone sitting there for a very long time, relaxing after a meal or talking to guests over coffee. There was a small octagon-shaped island in the center that had some storage underneath with a single teal-painted stool that looked like it was older than the house itself but appeared surprisingly sturdy. My grandmother was surely eccentric if she was the one who designed this kitchen, but it was clean and modern, yet old at the same time. It was beautiful. Adjacent to the island was a sink that sat in front of a good-sized window that opened like a small door. I had seen windows like that in old medieval movies and I always liked them. On the ledge in between the sink and window sat a couple small plants that seemed to be enjoying the sunlight that was streaming in. Above were some hanging silver lantern-like lights, and there was one above the table and the island. To the right led a doorway which was a mud room of sorts, with a bench to sit on and remove your shoes and a washer and dryer. The walls were a dark blue, and the color extended straight up the wall and onto the ceiling! She had actually painted tiny gold stars on the ceiling too; she surely was a special lady. Broad oaken shelving was above the bench and complemented the trim of the door frame. The washer and dryer were a dark grey. I didn't know you could get your appliances in different colors, and thought it was pretty cool, especially since an older woman was selecting all of this stuff. The light switch was brass with ornate swirls in the plate that matched the thousands of gold stars. Grandma must have been a hippie or something, I thought, as I tried to remember what years that movement took place in an attempt to match up the age my grandmother would be to try to make sense of the eccentric house. Somehow it wasn't too much; it kind of had a flow to it, one which I surprisingly liked, although I would never have been able to come up with this stuff on my own. I couldn't make head nor tail out of it as the average person just didn't find this stuff and throw it all together in such a beautiful array; it must have taken her a lifetime. Maybe it had. The last thoughts silenced my mind a little as I continued onward to view the rest of the house. The excitement left as I felt somber yet curious as to whether my parents had ever seen it or had even known about this eccentric little gem that was tucked away in nowhere Georgia. Were they eccentric too? I thought most likely not; living in Scranton. The glass door led outside but I wanted to explore the rest of the house, so I backpedaled to the other side of the kitchen, which had two closed oak doors. The one straight ahead of my path led to a small walk-in pantry that shelved some food still. Wow, I'd have to go through it and see what was still good and if anything was out of date. The other door was locked. I rattled the old cast iron doorknob again just to make sure it wasn't just stuck but to no avail. Just then I saw it. A single black skeleton key hung by a string from the inside of the door's threshold. It was hung exactly at my eye level off a small nail that was hammered in exactly between the wall and the wood of the casing of the door. Pretty clever hiding spot; and I found it fit the door perfectly. I became a little excited as I heard the click of the door unlock. To the right was a light switch which, surprisingly, the light worked. Andi had successfully transferred the utilities like he said he would, so good, one thing I didn't have to worry about and I was glad, because there was no way that I was venturing into a creepy basement of an old house alone, in the dark. I'm pretty tough, but some things are just smart to avoid. As my hip accidently bumped the door, a bell jingled and I jumped so high in a spook that I almost lost my balance, had it not been for the sturdy metal bar rail that had been securely screwed into the wall. Oh, my word! I composed myself in a kind of amusement of my fright at a row of tiny brass bells that had been secured on a long, dangling rope and knotted so they hung down the door. An archaic alarm system, I gathered. I held the end in my hand to further admire them. Someone had painted blue paint on every single one of them in such a way that the brass shone through the paint to resemble tiny gold stars! Wow! Grandma surely liked blue paint and gold stars. Well, at least she was true to herself and consistent. I suddenly realized I had grown affection for this woman I had never met, a respect and love for her strength to be unique and still be successful in the world. I was different, weird, I guess. I never felt like I fit in and always attributed it to not having known my parents or who I was, and trying to form myself from nothing, really.

I just chalked it up to accepting that of course I was different; everyone else had parents and I didn't. After coming in contact with Grandma, well, of sorts, I began to realize maybe it wasn't just growing up in the foster system that made me different. I felt that hope creeping up again as I thought to myself, well, Grandma made it, maybe I will too. She definitely helped me out, if anything; I have a really cool place to live, which was way nicer than I could have ever had on my own. Well, at least now, I couldn't have afforded a place like this, and this home is probably rated as middle class. Who knew, maybe I'll even graduate. I lost my fear of the bell chimes, but was still happy that whoever crafted the staircase included that sturdy rail and put backs on the stairs. Every horror movie I had ever seen with a dreadful basement scene, the stairs were open so the monster could grab the main character from the back of the ankle from under the stairs, and get them. Not this time; these stairs were against the wall and closed off, to the relief of my nerves. I read one time that I should fear the living and not the dead, and it seemed like really logical advice; but to not be so hard on myself, I was in an unfamiliar basement alone. When I made it down to the bottom, it was a paved floor that had been tiled with stone, a grey-blue color with a random white one every now and again. The walls were brick but had been painted white. It looked clean and empty. To the right was a sheet rocked wall that had been painted white, with a new door, which was also white with a matching trim. You could tell it was a new addition, as the door was composed of a cheaper quality from the sturdy oaks that were upstairs. It had a shiny, round nickel doorknob which I turned and led myself into a small lavender-painted room with the same tiles as the rest of the basement. It had a small bathroom with a small corner shower that had a really modern glass door that was curved; it made me think of an elevator I saw at a mall in Wilkes-Barre one time. It had a tiny pedestal sink and toilet. Just a basic bathroom, this would be a perfect guest bedroom, if I had a guest.

It would also have been perfect for me to live in here with my grandmother, had she still been alive. My mind flooded with questions and I began to feel a pang of regret for not having ever known her. My thoughts were racing with the mystery of her when the door slammed.

I jumped so high I would have hit the ceiling had I been any taller than my 5 foot 3 inches. I immediately opened it and peeked out; nothing. The wind, no way, in a basement! Come on! There were no windows open or possible drafts, as I would have felt it too. I ventured left, which led to a steel white exterior door which I unlocked. It led to a tiny stone room which had a large metal sink and a flight of very large, wide and thick stone steps that led to a roof of storm doors. I pushed open the latch and pushed up to open the doors onto the backyard. Wow! It was beautiful, green and I took a quick glance at another trellis of more white flowers, a metal fence that was overgrown with vines and flowers, a small table and a single chair and a stone pathway to a small shed. It could have only been a minute before the heat got to me and I started to sweat, so I turned around and locked up the storm doors and then the exterior door and made my way back into the kitchen, being very sure to lock the door with the skeleton key after my gust of wind experience. I secured the key back on its nail and took a bottle of water from the fridge before I checked the house out some more. I was super excited to see what else was in the house and explore but the heat, traveling and my nerves being all jumbled from my overactive imagination were telling me I needed to sit down for a minute.

After my little break on the stool at the kitchen island, I made my way upstairs and decided to take my shoes off as my feet were getting tired from my trip. My bare feet felt so good against the cool waxed oak floor. At the top of the stairs was a door that led into a small room that had a large window on the left side. It peered out into the top of the street that led to the main Athens Hwy U.S. 78.

Wow, the house must sit on a hill and I didn't realize it; otherwise, you shouldn't be able to see past Brand Street and onto the main road. The room had a full metal bed, a nightstand, closet, dresser set with a lamp on a white lace doily and upholstered lemon-colored cat claw chair that was the same color as the floral wallpaper that lined the walls. I was contemplating the classic feminine and very surprising décor after the mud room as I made my way down the hall. The hallway was clad with a beige and blue floral runner that led to the next room. The hallway had no furniture, although it was wide enough to house a bookshelf or something. The room was amazing. It had wood paneling made of little vertical boards that went halfway up the wall and were stopped by a chair rail, all of which were painted a cream color. The top half was painted a rich blue. The light fixtures and doorknob and plates for the switches were a dark metal. It had a beautiful window seat straight ahead that overlooked the backyard, and on the left side of it were built-in bookshelves that went from floor to ceiling; and on the right a small closet. In front of the bookshelf was a small cat claw desk, painted in the matching cream of the room's wood. It sat catty-corner to the entrance way and was placed so there was just enough room to squeeze in to sit down in the chair and sit at the desk. It had a soft, really detailed octagon-shaped Persian rug with a base of cream and little blue flowers. It felt so good on my feet. I would have to come back here the next day to really go through the desk and closet, to see if I could learn any more about my family and the house, as I was beginning to get really sleepy.

I felt so sleepy that a nap on the window seat looked really appealing, but it was now dark, and if I allowed myself to doze, I may mess up my whole schedule and wake up at 3 am or something and not be able to fall back asleep, which had happened in the past. No, I determined my pace to a quick peek in the bathroom that was at the end of the hall. It was also a charming classic, with a cat claw soaking tub, white and black small marble octagon-shaped tiles on the floor and the same half wall cased in the same wood and chair rail as the study, but only painted black, with the top part of the exposed wall being painted cream. It was clean and didn't appear to need any maintenance, so that was a relief. I had never seen or would have ever thought of painting wood black, but it looked good.

Boy, she must have been something, I thought as I passed a door that led up to the attic. I heard the click and made my way to the last room upstairs. It was a pleasant and basic room that must have been her bedroom. It was medium-sized and no way a standard master by today's expectations. It had the similar features of previous rooms with the cream-colored wooden bead board paneling and chair rail but it had purple walls above. It had a queen-sized cast iron bed, similar to the one I had in my loft but only of a better quality. It was covered in the thickest mattress I had ever seen, making the bed high up off the floor. I had no idea how Granny could have gotten up there unless she was at least six feet tall; then I saw the stepping stool at the edge of the bed. Funny, she would go through all the trouble instead of just getting a thinner mattress. Next to the bed on the left was a small oak nightstand with a marble top, housed with a lamp. Along the wall were two big windows which ended at an en suite bathroom. It was an average size with small white stone tiles on the floor and grey subway tiles up half the wall. It had light grey paint on the top half of the room. It had a full-sized walk-in shower. I guess it was added so she could easily step in and out, as the glass door was wide and modern. The sink had enough counter space with its cool grey granite for any girl to spread her hair supplies and makeup out upon to get ready in the morning. It was a practical and nice space and I was already happy to be in it. I decided to take a quick shower and also it was as good a time as any to see how the plumbing worked.

Happy not to have encountered any issues during my shower, I felt like a million bucks, or at least like myself and not all grimy from the heat and long drive. Exiting the bathroom, there was a shoulder-height oak dresser with four drawers that housed a T.V. and a door on its other side that led to a small closet with two shelves over a single pole for my clothes. It was a pretty basic setup for older homes, really not much different than the turn-of-the-century builds that were common in Avoca back home. I was aware older houses didn't have much closet space, so this was a godsend really to even have closets, but it was tiny. I wasn't one of those girls that had a ton of clothes and who occupied all her free time consuming at the mall, but modern women definitely had a lot more clothes and stuff than they did back in the day, for sure, for someone whose entire possessions could fit in the back of a Subaru should never have to downsize to make room. I began to feel myself get more and more comfortable on the oversized bed. I was ready to relax for the night. Unpacking would have to wait until the next day or until I got some rest.

Thinking fondly of my new house, I couldn't have picked a better one for myself if I had tried; crazy where life can take you. I mean, I had worked hard, and with the help of some people from town just trying to do the right thing in a bad situation, I wasn't destitute or anything. I had a job and a clean, nice apartment loft and had secured a future as a manager, but this was like a dream that was just given, or more like, carefully planned for me. My mind daydreaming my happy thoughts as I went through my unbelievable good luck, I found myself dozing off on the bed, and before I knew it, I must have konked out from the exhaustion of the trip.

Chapter Six

Loganville

I woke up as the sunbeam continued to dance on my face due to the wind chime of hanging crystals that was slowing, catching every ray and reflecting them back in a prism on my face. I would have been irritated had I not been amused by the certainty that she had to either be a witch or a hippie; that was for certain now as eccentric only goes so far. I glanced at what had to be the tiniest alarm clock I had ever seen, whose hands were about to join together at 7:45 when the little hammer on top of the clock between the two silver bells began to ring. I jumped so high that I nearly fell off the bed, and I caught the clock that I had knocked off the nightstand and miraculously caught before it hit the floor. *My God, this house is going to be the death of me!* I knew my hair had to have gone grey at least some since I got here with as many times as I'd been spooked, by bells and wind. No need to go to a haunted house this year, I amused myself with... "I'll just stay home," I said out loud... "enough spooks around here." I made sure the bedroom door was locked and checked the handle with a pull, even though I heard the click of the old cast iron doorknob; guess I was still a little wary of my new home and neighborhood.

I left the bathroom door open, which had been a habit of mine since I had grown accustomed to living alone, but still needed that bedroom door locked, even if to ease my mind. I found the water got nice and hot and was relieved that my cousin had taken care of everything for me so far. He said I would receive an email from all my bills, confirming their payment every month as he would use the estate's money to pay the bills but left my email as the recipient of the electronic receipt. When I graduated and received my inheritance, then I would take over full responsibility, but Andi said not to worry about any of that now. I appreciated the way he set it up, as I am somewhat wary of people and like the level of transparency that comes with the way Andi handles everything. We'd call him a straight shooter in Avoca; well, whatever he is, he's been my Angel if you believe in that sort of thing.

I found some rose-scented lotion in the bathroom which I used, since I forgot to bring in my bags from the Subaru the previous night and certainly didn't feel comfortable going through the house in a towel; it still felt like I was visiting. It wouldn't make any sense to get fully dressed to get undressed just to lotion. Also, it absorbs better after you just come out of the water. Normally, I would feel weird using a dead lady's personal effects but oddly, I didn't. Honestly, normally, I didn't feel comfortable using or taking anything from anyone. Not sure if it was because of how I grew up or just an oddity of mine, but ever since Andi told me about my inheritance, it was almost as if I knew this would happen and it's been the most natural thing in the world for me to accept. As if I was supposed to be here. Well, I guess under normal circumstances, people give their children and grandchildren stuff. That's the thing; I'm not used to being normal. Well, I guess from what I'd observed about my family so far... they weren't exactly what ya'd call normal either, but I guess that did explain a lot, I smirked to myself.

As I saw more of the house in the full daylight I was pleased to find either was Grandma. Clad in a clean pair of yoga pants and long cotton V-neck tee shirt, I made my way to the kitchen to see what I could come up with for breakfast. I unplugged the coffee maker and brought it over to the sink to clean it out, spraying the inside with water and being careful not to saturate the electrical parts.

I placed it back and plugged it in and brought the glass pot and coffee filter over to wash those with soap, when I couldn't help but admire the soap dispenser. It was made out of some blue stone cased with a silver stand and dispenser. Neat, as I just squeezed out what I needed from the plastic bottle it came in back home. I told myself I had to stop referring to the loft as back home, reminding myself that this was my home now. I cleaned them out to my satisfaction and found the can of Folgers in current date and unopened so I was happy to make my first pot of coffee in my new home. I stood there at the counter, just taking in the wonderful smell of the brewing coffee as I looked at my hands pressed solidly on the smooth stone. It was almost as if I somehow needed the aroma and touch of the cool stone to believe I was standing there. The first cup I had at the island, just sipping and taking in my new surroundings. My second cup I had on the front porch. It was getting warm outside, but it was still before 9 am, so it wasn't unbearable. Gosh, it was only the first week of June, what was July going to be like? I knew it would be unbearably hot. Too bad Grandma didn't install a pool, but then come to think of it, her garden was really nice. I probably wouldn't be able to enjoy it until the winter, as it was so humid, but it was nice that it was there. The porch wicker couch was really comfortable and not a single car or person went by as I enjoyed my coffee. I enjoyed the quiet and wasn't ready to meet any neighbors yet. I found it strange that I was living there myself and didn't want to talk about it or answer any questions until I felt comfortable with my situation, which would be who knew when. I put my coffee mug down on the small table, which I just realized had a star on it, when I saw the same markings etched in the top of the wood frame of the threshold of the door that were on Andi's ring. Strange, it was barely noticeable but it was there. It didn't look odd or draw too much attention, as it was an older house. It must be some whimsical thing between them, or maybe not. Maybe it was our family name or the name of our clan or whatever you called Vikings or Danes from long ago. I suddenly hated that I knew nothing about myself or my family and realized the last time I had this feeling was in the sixth grade when Molly O'Brian was telling a secret at the lunch table and all the girls in the class knew it, except me. You'd think I'd be used to being an outsider by now, used to not knowing or belonging.

Guess I wasn't and I hated wanting and longing for it. I tried to clear my head and focus on what I read one time in one of those trendy self-help books: *Just believe what you want to be true, create your feelings, decide how you want to feel and make it so.* Maybe it could be that I just simply decided that this was where I belonged and that was all that was needed to make it true. I felt a little better and convinced myself I was being a brat for not being crazy happy that I had been given this house. I tried to think of all the kids I had met in the foster homes and how fortunate I was, as I was sure none of them landed something this good.

As I was grabbing the last box from the back of the Subaru and making my way up the stairs of the house, I saw him. As I crept toward the giant yellow-flowered bush that offered some privacy to the porch, I saw his big, almond-shaped yellow-green eyes. He didn't appear afraid of me and I scooped up what had to be the dirtiest, most underfed black kitten I had ever seen or could have imagined. I carried him into the house and up the stairs to my bathroom. I put a towel on the base of the bath tub as a liner of sorts. I had once heard an old woman say she did that when washing her cat, in the

Moosic Diner. I never thought eavesdropping could help, but the kitten seemed to appreciate having something to sink his claws into as I soaped him up with my shampoo and conditioner. Now that my mind was at ease that he wasn't filthy and going to bring fleas or something else into my home, I thought that he would need to eat. I was pretty sure there wasn't any cat food in the house, but there was no telling; maybe Grandma was feeding the cat. Maybe that was why he was here and so close to the house.

No way to know for sure; it was faster to just go out and buy some instead of wasting time. The poor kitten was probably starving; otherwise, why would he seek me out? Off I went and a half-hour later, when I came back from the Dollar General I found on Hwy 20 with a bag of kitten food, he was surprisingly somewhat fluffy. I guess before he was washed, his fur was caked down with dirt so bad you couldn't tell, poor thing. I was glad to see him eat the full bowl of Friskies. I'd heard cats were skittish when in a new environment, and he definitely needed to eat. I'd never had a pet before, and somehow when looking at him in that bush, I knew he was going to be mine. I was happy to find the company and glad he wasn't a person with a million questions I wasn't ready to answer; he was perfect. Just there and ready to hang out and be loved, just without all the prying most people do when they hang around enough. I couldn't decide where to set up the litter box; I chose the hallway bathroom instead of the mud room because sometimes I closed the mud room door. Now what to name him? It was a toss-up between Jade, reflecting his eyes, or Nox, describing the color of his fur. I tried calling him Nox and got no response, so Jade it was. Jade fell off the tongue faster anyway, I thought, as I gave him a once-over glance with a smile. I was starving by this point so I crafted up an American, Swiss and provolone cheese on white bread sandwich, with one slice of turkey and mayonnaise and lettuce. I was happy to find Jade didn't judge me, as most people found it strange I preferred more cheese and lettuce to the one slice of turkey on my sandwiches. I also found it odd that the stuff was fresh, and that Grandma had exactly what I liked stocked in her refrigerator. So either Grandma had the same taste that I did or she was watching me to see what I preferred. I had mixed feelings about her watching me. On one hand, it was very considerate that she cared enough to investigate what I liked and to make sure it was here so I would be comfortable, on the other hand, kind of creepy to have someone spying on you, even if it was your own grandmother. If she was, why not just reach out to me and try to have a relationship? The whole thing was just strange. Well, I wasn't exactly normal either but I didn't watch a person, that's like stuff you'd see on *Law and Order*. Things like that were done by either criminals who were up to no good or by the detectives who were trying to catch them. Not by grandmas.

I washed off my plate, which I suddenly really noticed, and it was beautiful. I was so lost in my thoughts that I just made the sandwich but wasn't really seeing what I was doing. I wondered how much of my life was like that, just as Jade rubbed against my leg. Well, at least I noticed him. I was happy again. The back of the plate said, *Made in Copenhagen*. More Danish stuff. Well, at least Grandma was true. I thought initially she liked it because it was blue and white; it seemed like her theme. Now I saw there was more to her methods. I put it, the knife and blue glass chalice in the stainless steel dishwasher and decided to search the study to see if I could find anything else about Grandma or my family.

After three hours, I found nothing. This woman was so tidy, there was really nothing personal. It was almost dark but I felt really antsy, so I decided to go for a walk. I told Jade to watch the house until I got back, and locked up behind me. I made my way toward the opposite side of the street away from Athens Hwy 78. I walked until the road took me out of the series of streets that formed the couple of old blocks that housed the handful of old houses that made up the old Loganville, where I now lived, and ended up at a

Dunkin' Donuts on a curved corner that wrapped around to a post office and tiny strip of stores. A subway, UPS store and nail salon. How weird they put a UPS store next to the post office, like they built a Lowe's across the street from Home Depot and CVS next to a Walgreens. I was already tired of their odd way of competing with rival businesses; it seemed like an excessive way to ruin the landscape and kill trees. I finally ended up at a small cemetery, oddly across from a white gazebo, which sat in the middle of the road. It looked almost as if whoever expanded the town had no intention of placing the main Athens Hwy right there, but let it happen anyway. I looked through the couple of markers; some elaborate, most just marble inscribed with the date and family name of those who had lived and passed from the town.

Then I saw it: Lauren Lorensen Kohl. Underneath, it was scribed, *One Great Lady*. I felt the tears swell up in my throat. How silly for me to cry, I hadn't even met the woman. Why was I so upset? More importantly, how weird to put a cemetery in the middle of a busy road, or allow the poor planning to build around this place of rest. Not sure if this was backward, tacky or just plain disrespectful. I just sat at her marker for a while and allowed myself to cry. I finally finished my lag in composure and surprisingly felt better, and made my way toward the house. I uncontrollably allowed one whisper to release "Grandma" out loud as I looked back at her marker. Well, at least I got to see her, even if it was now after she was gone. As I made my way back past the ridiculous Hardee's restaurant toward home, I wondered if this was our first time together or if I had known her when I was a baby, before I was given up for adoption.

Chapter Seven

Rosa

I woke up at 6:01 am and found myself on the worn mauve chaise that sat in front of the window in the living room downstairs. I couldn't remember coming in, even sitting on the lounge, let alone falling asleep. I began to simply accept the comfort the house seemed to give me as I acknowledged my lofty behavior and time lapses that had become the norm since I came to live in this old house. I must have been really worn out from my good sob and long walk outside the day before. My fitness level had seen better days; it had mostly been affected by the long drive down here and the change in environment, as I have always been sensitive to even the slightest change in my routine. I was never a complainer; well, even if I had been, I wouldn't really know as I never really had much of anyone to complain to. My practical nature just never saw much sense in griping; if I didn't like something, I just didn't bother with it or found some way to get it out of my life and make it go away. I usually got more tired and stiff and just felt an overall icky feeling until I got into a regular routine; it's just always been how I am. By going to bed a little earlier, drinking lots of coffee and long walks are my chosen methods of getting over it. I walked into the kitchen to start a pot of coffee to brew while I took a nice hot shower and got myself ready for the day.

By the time I had my eyeliner on, had jumped into a pair of yoga pants and had my coffee in hand, the doorbell rang. Who would be calling for me at this hour! It wasn't even 7 am yet; in Avoca, that would be considered rude. Plus, who did I know around here? I barely knew anyone where I was from, let alone in Loganville. Wondering what could be so urgent that someone had to call at the crack of dawn, okay, I was exaggerating as it was summer in the south so the sun had been up for a while, but still. I could see a small silhouette of an older black woman, wearing a small floral printed sundress and loafers. Her hair was white and clad in a tight bun at the back of her head, not as I wore mine today, high and loosely piled upon my top. I opened the door and leaned in the doorway and looked at her.

She smiled and said, "You must be Aurora. I'm Rosa. I live next door and knew your grandmother, she was my friend."

I said, "Hi, call me Rose; I don't go by my first name." She smiled again. She had smooth, fair skin with high cheekbones and a small, sturdy build. Her nose made me think she may have been part Native American but I knew it was rude to ask. She was quite pretty for a woman who must have been at least sixty. She talked about it being Wednesday and that was the day her and my grandmother would garden. She came by to see if I wanted to honor the tradition and make an old lady happy. To be honest, the idea of gardening seemed boring, but I had nothing else to do and Rosa was quite charming. Plus, I was curious about my grandmother and about myself. It seemed everyone knew I was her granddaughter, except me until lately. *How odd*, I thought to myself as I followed the graceful old lady through my trellis and into the backyard.

She opened the little gate that led to the small garden that housed cucumbers, tomatoes, corn, lettuce, sunflowers and a few plants I couldn't identify. I hadn't noticed until she opened the latch that there was also a small gate that opened into her yard and matching garden. So, they must have worked like this for who knows how long. It was beautiful and practical, as they didn't have to go to the store for these items. If anything, they always had a salad to eat, and it seemed like it would be good exercise. How nice that they had each other to share this with. I hoped to have someone too to spend my days with.

Rosa showed me a couple of garden tools and how to use them. She gave me the tour and explained when we should pick each one and how to remove the vegetable so as to not damage the plant. She said it wasn't time to pick any of these yet, but she would be happy to help me keep up the garden until I got the hang of it. I quickly liked Rosa and saw why she and my grandmother were friends; you couldn't help but like Rosa. Some people were like that, you just appreciated them. I was never one of those people but glad I found one, as I was getting a little lonely in my new home. I know I had just gotten settled in and it hadn't even been a week and a half yet, but I was missing company. It was true that I was more of a loner, but I still liked engaging with people on a regular basis, even if it was only a brief exchange.

At Topps, there were a couple girls I ate lunch with from time to time and spoke to make the days at work pass. I had gotten used to seeing the same familiar faces at the A&P grocery store or Convenient Mart. I guess I was itching to get out. I asked Rosa if there was anything I needed to know to become familiar with. She suggested I drive to G.G.C. and have a look around, since I'd be starting school soon. She said there were a couple restaurants and places to eat at on the drive home that I might like. It seemed like a good idea, as I had enough against me as far as academics were concerned, so becoming familiar with the area would at least prevent a new environment from adding to my ability to learn the material. She gave me some, what seemed to be, straightforward directions to the school and she closed the gate behind her and made her way toward her cute little white steeple-shaped cottage, with its high peaked windows and overfilled window boxes that were stuffed with various flowers.

I felt good, like someone was watching out for me. Odd, since I just met Rosa, but I felt as though she cared about me. Maybe it was just that she loved my grandma and that love just passed on to me. Who knows? I definitely wasn't used to it but it seemed right, if that makes any sense.

I poured Jade a generous bowl of kitten chow and was on my way down Grayson Parkway, which was a single-lane tree-clad, occasional-house-on-a-lot-of-land road to Hwy 20. I had no idea why it was called a parkway, but to what used to be Loganville, I guess it was. I always thought a parkway led to a highway, not that Avoca was anywhere on the map of places to visit. This led through to the neighboring town of Lawrenceville. If I went in the opposite direction, it would take me to a town called Monroe and then on to the larger town of Athens, which also had a college. I followed her guide which led me just as she directed to downtown Lawrenceville, which was still a small nobody town, but it was definitely larger than Loganville and had a couple cute shops, mostly food and antiques. I made a left onto University Lane, and there it was: Georgia Gwinnett College. It was a small group of buildings. It looked nice, was very clean and well maintained. It was mostly composed of brick and glass, one building in the back had a giant G set in the middle of its roof as an immense logo of sorts.

There were a couple flags doting the college logo, and one of the streets had a giant bear statue, which I was guessing was the school mascot. Okay, it looked good. It was small so it wasn't exactly intimidating, but it didn't look run-down or like a place you would question its credentials. Actually, to my surprise, it seemed perfect.

This was so crazy, as if someone had looked into my heart and made my secret wishes and dreams, that I didn't even know I had, come true. I kept driving down a small road that went past the student parking, a daycare and set of apartment buildings. I came to a sign that said left was dormitories for the college, and I didn't want to drive around the college anymore. I'd save further exploring for a day I'd plan and come visit the campus on foot to find my classes and bookstore. I went left, which ended at a stop sign, so I made a right, which led me to a giant shopping center. I passed an IHOP and what had to be the biggest Dollar Store that I had ever seen, a Home Depot, Ross and a movie theater. When passing the Panera Bread Company, I decided to pull in instead of going home as some coffee and a cinnamon crunch bagel sounded divine, as I didn't have a chance to make anything with Rosa stopping by so early. I sat in the booth and took in the crowd; the place was packed with students doing homework and little crowds of study groups which must be from the nearby school, my school!

Wow! I envisioned myself coming here in between classes; maybe I would be studying with them. It must still be summer semester here. I knew larger or Ivy League schools were off for the summer. Some of my nerves about my academic ability began to pass as I saw the students, all people my age, talking and discussing the problems together. I knew I wasn't exactly popular or fit in well with others, but I could get along if I had to. I thought to myself, I'll just make an effort and find someone who seems to know the stuff and get them to let me tag along. Suddenly school didn't seem so far away and impossible. I got a refill on my hazelnut coffee, which was free, to my astonishment, and realized when I got to my Subaru that I had no idea how to get back home. There were entrances and exits all over the parking lot, which was huge, and all of them led to roads that were not the one I came in at. Thank goodness for Google Maps, which I enjoyed as it took me home a different way than I came. I was a little excited about exploring and seeing what was in the area now that I felt safe from getting lost with my auto map. It took me down Sugarloaf Parkway, yet another parkway. This one at least was large and seemed more like a mini highway than the last one. It ended at Hwy 20, which took me back to Loganville and to my street. When I made my left turn and saw my house next to Rosa's, I relaxed for the first time in a long while. I released my first big exhale since I lost Mrs. Vender all those years ago, and it seemed as if a heavy burden left me and was let go into the sky. I hadn't realized how sad I had been; I'd never really thought about it. I had just kept moving and doing what I knew, to keep going and I had up until now never stopped for a minute to really look at things, make plans or to feel anything. For the first time in forever, I had a little peace. I guess being in the south had affected me already, as I was already doing things a little slower, and I chuckled to myself as I released the thought and made my way up the big stone steps into my house.

Chapter Eight

Grandma

I got in and opened up a can of minestrone vegetable soup from the pantry, which surprisingly was still good from the date on the can. I wondered if she had stocked up and then suddenly passed away unexpectedly, or if the house had been set up for me to come and take over. It strangely seemed as if someone, Grandma or Andi had stocked it for me. I mean, that was more believable than assuming my grandmother, whom I had never met, had all of the exact taste as myself in food and décor. Well, they say blood runs deep and is thicker than water, and I know biology does play a huge part as to how we are, even in our likes and tastes, but to find out she liked my favorite soup, it was getting a little hard to believe that all of this was some strange coincidence. The whole place really was hard for me to take in, even more so as Jade jumped up onto the smooth stone countertop to face me as I sat at the island and ate my soup. Even he just appeared, right when I needed company. Without this place, I would just be another lonely foster kid who lied and landed a job at a factory. Here, all my dreams were coming true, even the ones I hadn't admitted to myself. It was kind of scary; it made me feel like I did my first night with Mrs. Vendor; afraid to get comfortable, that in any moment someone would come and say I had to go.

Also, I wasn't from a big city like New York, but I was smart enough to know that I was here on trust alone, and how good of an idea was that! I mean, how many women end up getting raped or end up dead in a ditch because they just trusted what someone told them? I was the perfect candidate for that kind of stuff to happen to; I fit the typical young woman alone. No family, no one to enquire after her, to check up on her. I came down here, drove over one thousand miles on trust that the papers Andi gave me were legitimate and the keys were really mine. I mean, I heard of people getting thrown out on the street because they paid their rent money to their landlord, but it turned out he broke into the house and changed the locks while the owner was out of the country on business. He came back and the supposed landlord had accepted two months' rent and now was nowhere to be found, and those poor people were thrown out on the street after having to initially prove they weren't squatters. I guess I was afraid because I wasn't some wiz on the computer and wouldn't even know how to begin to research if Andi and my grandmother were legit. To find anything about the whole situation, I may have to hire a private investigator. Logic told me, along with my gut, that Rosa, being enrolled at G.G.C., the potential job at the library were all signs this was okay, weird but okay. I guess I was just afraid that this was everything I ever wanted and would probably take years of hard work at Topps, if ever, to accomplish. Who knows if I would ever have gone to college, and I most definitely would have never left Avoca. I would have wanted to, but life would have most likely led me to nothing because it can be really hard to build from nothing without help, or at least someone to tell you how to get there. I washed off my bowl, small saucepan

I used to warm the soup, spoon and glass I used for my sweet tea, and put them in the dishwasher. I didn't start it yet, as it wasn't full and I didn't see any point in running the machine until it was full. I took a nice warm shower and put on some comfortable yoga knee-length pants and a loose long-sleeved tee shirt for bed, as the house was somewhat cool with the air conditioner on, but comfortable. I preferred to sleep in a cool environment anyhow, yet another thing Grandma had in common with me, I assumed. Instead of going right to bed, I went into the study and turned on the computer. I typed in Lauren Lorensen Kohl and got nothing from Google Search. Well, why would an elderly lady be on the internet anyhow? I typed in myself, and nothing came up either. I put in Andi's name, and there was an image of him in a suit and tie, very professional-looking, and the name of a law firm. A couple articles about properties he was handling and a case his firm represented. So he was legit. I wasn't surprised really. I knew inside that this was all as it was supposed to be, and that I could trust Andi. Well, at least my instincts were assuring me that this was the right path for me, but my mind still needed that reassurance. I guess some of the kids I met through the foster system, who were just products of their bad environment, and all the episodes of *Law and Order*, make me a little skeptical of most people. I am not usually a go-with-your-feelings kind of person, I am usually very practical. I guess that is what is so scary, that someone just handed me an answer to my prayers, a way out of Lackawanna County and onto a path that should have been for me all along. In my wildest dreams, I never would have guessed that I'd own my own home, well, not anytime in the near future and not one nice like this one. Well, it actually looks like a lot of the old homes in Scranton and Moosic, just smaller and as if someone had cared for it. I mean, really invested in it. There were more expensive homes, of course, but this one, you could tell that someone lived here and cared about the place. There are so many small little touches that really are a witness to the time and care someone, Grandma, I suppose, put into the place. From the tiny gold stars on the ceiling in the mud room, to the garden, she loved the place. Thinking about it made me sad and happy at the same time, as I wished I had known her and that she had invested some of that devotion in me.

I guess she did, and now I'm here. I was going to go crazy from the mystery of her; it was all so strange and yet seemed right at the same time. I thought for a moment that maybe Mrs. Vendor and her were together, looking down at me, but I quickly washed the thought from my mind as it was made clear in Catholic school that there were no such things as ghosts or spirits. Once you leave your body, your soul goes either up or down or waits in Purgatory to go up if your soul was still heavy from some sins and it wasn't ready for Heaven. That if in a saddened grief you made contact with a loved one or ghost, say a prayer because it wasn't really a loved one but the devil or one of his demons messing with you in your time of weakness.

They used to put such emphasis on guarding yourself from the evil that is allowed to pass in our world. I never saw why there was such an emphasis on it, as none of us were really bad at St. Mary's, or at least to the point where one had to worry about us or our souls, well, at least I didn't think. As I got older, I saw the rise in paranormal shows and the like and saw why we were warned so often. I know myself, when I was grieving Mrs. Vendor, I was more impressionable. I was just going through the motions and was lucky no one came along and led me the wrong way. No, I was very fortunate to be in Avoca when I was going through that time as it's a small community of mostly good people. If you had told me I was going to be living in Loganville, Georgia, I first would have said "Where?" and then laughed, but the world has changed with technology and the internet so there is really no place on Earth now that is so shut off that one has to fear being turned into a bumpkin or left living in conditions so backward one can't function.

Compared to other places like Boston or New York City, Avoca was a little nowhere that you might find if you had to stop, passing through to somewhere else. I guess Loganville is like that too, but for the south. I guess I am not very good at researching as I found absolutely nothing on Grandma on the internet. Heck, this was her house, wasn't it? There had to be some clue in here somewhere about her. I had hoped this wasn't going to be like our teacher's answer as to why there was no mention of dinosaurs in the Bible. At the time, we were so happy at St. Mary's to have lay teachers instruct us instead of nuns like they had as faculty at the neighboring St. Ann's, as my class didn't feel we were getting an expert response from Miss Cimensky. As a sixth grader, it was really hard to just accept that the purpose of the Bible was not to go into detail about the animals but to serve as a guide for us to have the best life possible here and make it to the intended next life. Not a good answer for an eleven-year-old. If Grandma took that approach, I should just say thank you and accept that all the information that I needed was provided to me by Andi. Again, not a good answer, and yet I kind of felt like that was where this was going. I was all wound-up now and excited, with my mind thinking of these unanswerable things and wishing I could find some clue about her and my family and the whole situation. I should have been relaxing in bed, but I just found it so hard to believe that this was her home and there wasn't anything about her in it. Did she have someone clean it up? I guess the only thing that could be done now was to wait until the next day and go next door and ask Rosa. She knew my grandmother; they were friends. Maybe she could tell me some more about her and myself and the whole situation. I was a little uncomfortable with approaching her, as she was really a warm person who, for whatever reason, even if it was just out of the respect and love she had for my grandma, seemed to care about me. I just didn't know how to start up the conversation and I was never good at getting personal with people. Plus, what if Grandma was like me and didn't share?

From my inability to find anything about her so far, that seemed like a real possibility. How awkward would that be, asking

Rosa about my business and she didn't know either? I could just see myself standing in front of her tomorrow all awkward and uncomfortable with her giving me the look of "You should know your business, why are you asking me?" Just in that moment, a warm feeling washed over me and I had a vision of Rosa in my mind and I saw her smiling her warm smile at me and I knew the thoughts I was tormenting myself with were foolish.

Jade began meowing from his spot on the corner of the Persian rug he sat upright on. How weird, just sitting there on the corner of a rug, meowing. "Jade, what is it?" I asked in my sweetest baby talk voice. He didn't stop until I got up and approached him. As soon as I got close, he hurried out of the room. How weird, that cat! Just then I felt a bump under my foot. I ran my foot over the soft carpet that covered whatever was under the rug. I threw the rug back to find a large skeleton key on a silver chain. Very cool necklace. I wondered if it actually opened anything or if it was just a trendy vintage accessory. Happy it wasn't a mouse; you never know with cats, especially this one apparently. I put it on and felt relieved, as if I was safe and that all my questions would soon be answered. I never took a psychology class but assumed this must have been my subconscious telling me I was capable of finding all the answers I needed and to trust in myself and my abilities. Whatever it was, I was off to bed.

I turned on the T.V. in my bedroom and went back and forth between the *Steven Colbert Show* and *Jimmy Fallon*. I loved Colbert but he was talking about Trump again and I just wasn't a political person; I had my own problems and everyone seemed to be talking about this election and I was so tired of it. Fallon was really funny; I liked him on the old SNL reruns. He wasn't as good as Colbert, but he didn't talk politics the whole show, so I settled.

I don't remember falling asleep, but when I woke up, my new key necklace was hanging on the doorknob of my closet and I had no recollection of taking it off the night before. Now this was getting weird! Another memory lapse that I couldn't allot to jet lag or whatever you call one's travel assimilation to their new environment, what was happening to me! Strange, but it wouldn't be the first unexplainable thing that had happened to me, especially in this house. I was quite sure there was some logical explanation. Maybe I should get a physical or some blood work done, I chuckled to myself, or see a psychologist was probably more like it. I would probably have laughed out loud but I was alone, so no need as I was not sharing this moment with anyone else. Crazy as it was, I did feel as though someone else was acknowledging my moment and had maybe even led me to it. I guess I was still overwhelmed from the trip and all that had happened so far and in finding out I had a family and now owning this beautiful house, in starting a new life. *I'll try to relax more, maybe take a nice long walk.* I started a pot of coffee before I jumped in the shower. I tried to pace myself so I was dressed and had my eyeliner and mascara on before my coffee was finished brewing. I never made it but I was still done in less than ten minutes, and for the average girl that's pretty good. I ate a bowl of Grapenuts, which is actually pretty good for an old lady's cereal. I locked up and made my way over to Rosa's, who didn't answer but had left a sticky note on the door addressed to me! *Aurora, gone to church, will come by later. Love, Rosa.*

How on earth did she know I would be coming by today? This place! Perplexed, I started down the street toward the house on the corner with all the stone statues, across from the cemetery. I sat down in the white gazebo and tried to count how many cars went through the Hardee's drive-thru. Only in Loganville would they build a Hardee's next to a cemetery, it just didn't seem right. It's not like they didn't have the space to build further down. It was just another oddity about my new home. I looked across the street and I saw it: the library. I decided today was as good as any, so I made my way over there.

Mr. Avery was very kind and said he could use me to start next Friday, which I was happy to agree to. I signed some paperwork and let him make a copy of my driver's license and was on my way walking back to the house. I passed through the cemetery and thanked Grandma for the job and everything as I passed her grave and made my way up the street to my home. Strangely, I saw Jade waiting for me on the front porch as I walked up the steps. I didn't remember letting him out. "How did you get out? Bad kitty! But thank you for waiting until I got back." I hoped he didn't need to be washed again.

We walked back into the house and I poured him some kitten chow. I got the small Dirt Devil from the pantry and did a fast vacuum from what we must have just dragged in and sat down at the table and looked out the window to see Rosa working in her garden. I took a sip of water from my water bottle and went out back to try to catch her and ask her about Grandma. We talked for the longest time and hugged and laughed and I didn't really find out specifics other than what I surmised: my grandmother was a good woman who found out about me after the fact, and the only way she could make sure I got everything I should have was to wait. Rosa said it hurt her to not contact me, but she knew I was safe and taken care of and would be ready to take over since I was used to taking care of myself. She said most young people my age would lose the house or be thinking about parties or stuff that would distract them from the responsibility of this house. My grandmother knew I was very special, so was this house, and that we belonged together, so she started making the arrangements for me. A lot of people in town said my grandmother was a witch, but this was before the big influx of people that moved into Gwinnett and Walton County over the last twenty years. I was secretly smug with the thought of being right about Grandma; she was a witch after all! Hah!

Loganville used to be smaller than Avoca, she said. It was mostly farms, just a handful of families and then this strip of old houses in the Loganville proper. Back then, everyone knew everyone else, their kids and their business. "Your grandmother was Catholic and attended at St. Oliver's in Summit Chase. Yep, she sure did… every Sunday. Yes, ma'am."

"Wow," I said. "So why did they say she was a witch?"

"Well, you's got to know Miss Lauren had moved here before all them people came in, ways before them Katrina people flocked here after FEMA screwed all that up. She came here and she wasn't from here and had her different ways, her Yankee and Danish ways before that from her country," said Rosa. "And folks 'round here weren't used to outsiders and didn't understand her or her ways.

"But, ya know, it was hard to judge your grandma wrong as she had a lot of sense and just about everybody had come to love Miss Lauren. After that, folks kept coming and moving in and a building; pretty soon, Miss Lauren didn't seem so strange." I let out a smile and a 'huh.' Rosa began to walk toward her house and looked back. "Ya know, you're a lot like her… you and Miss Lauren," and she went into her house as the door closed behind her. I wanted to ask her why she went to church on Wednesday morning. Maybe she had left that note since Sunday and I wondered if she was Catholic too, like me and my grandma. Well, if I was anything, it was that, and it seemed more official now since I knew it went beyond just Mrs. Vendor's influence of St. Mary's, but my family was Catholic too, so I guess I was.

I made a mental note of Summit Chase and St. Oliver's and planned on checking them out before Sunday. I was suddenly famished and decided to kill two birds with one stone and find food and then check out my grandma's church. I Google mapped St. Oliver's and sure enough, Summit Chase was not even five minutes from my house. So I cleaned up a bit and was out the door, this time making a right onto Athens Hwy 78, which I knew if I stayed on for an hour I would reach Atlanta but fortunately I only had to travel five minutes. On the left, I spotted a small diner that said Open, so I pulled in and ordered my favorite French toast and turkey bacon. It was good, not as good as the Moosic Diner, but the serving was big and the waitress was nice and kept the coffee coming. All the customers seemed local and ancient. One table of old men had to have at least six hundred years between all of them. I glanced at my phone and it said I was two minutes away, huh. I could walk to it. A lot of people used to walk to St. Mary's, but we had sidewalks and it wasn't so hot. I would hate to go to church all sweaty; it would seem disrespectful. Plus, I'd feel bad if someone was distracted from their prayers because of my bad body odor. I paid my bill and headed out again on Hwy 78. My phone told me to hang a left on some windy road that bent around a small old antique store. The sign said *Dirt for sale* and was placed on a huge stack of hay. The place was decorated with various old metal works that were shaped and welded into various whimsical animals. It seemed like a place I would enjoy checking out, but I remembered the place having a big sign that said *Summit Chase* and it was lined with roses. I was also skeptical of traveling down any old small roads off the highway especially alone and definitely not until I learned my way around. *Mississippi Burning* may have just been a movie, but I was staying on my planned course and there it was, just a short distance past the antique shop. I made my left at the light which was lined with the roses I saw from the website. It stood in front of a very large, nice-looking daycare that was on the corner and marked the entrance to the neighborhood. As I drove on the road, lined on one side lay a heavy forest, the other a unique fenced-in play area for the children, which housed a dinosaur and plastic palm trees, slides and a swing set. I came to a four-way stop and Google Maps said to keep going so I drove on. The corner house on the left had a large, whimsical garden and various benches. I looked down further and could see a small white church and graveyard. It sat way in the back, cased in by two big sagging weeping willow trees. It looked picturesque and eerie at the same time. It was like something out of an old film. A person couldn't have built this to look in the way that it did with any sort of intent. No, this old building had aged this way, forming its shape and image over ages and the experiences of the people who attended here. I didn't know why my Google Maps kept telling me to stay straight, but I made a left toward the church. I drove down the curving road that lent away from the church, guided by woods on both sides, past a giant weeping willow, or no, maybe an oak tree with Spanish moss.

I wasn't really sure what the immense tree was called, but it cast off such an atmosphere that it was a structure all on its own. As I came closer to the building, it sat further back than it had appeared from the four-way stop, another strange encounter with Loganville that could only be explained as, well, happenings in Loganville. My phone kept telling me to make a U-turn and head back toward the road I turned on when I saw the sign. It wasn't St. Oliver's! Well, how could that be true, and how many churches were in this neighborhood! Just then, the small olden double doors jumped open and outburst a congregation. They were all black and mostly middle-aged or some elderly, a few children, and were dressed well. It gave a new meaning to Sunday best, even though it was Wednesday! I guess whatever church this was, they worshiped on Wednesday. I had never heard of people going to church on any other day but Sunday. I mean, we went in the morning for daily Mass at St. Mary's before school, but the official worship day was on Sunday. The two little girls gleamed in their little dresses, and the fabric was of good quality, one bright pink and the other bright yellow, which shone in contrast to their dark skin. All the ladies wore hats and they looked so clean; even their patent leather shoes were scrubbed clean with not a spot on them. They were all smiling until they saw me, and they just stared. I got the feeling you get when you accidently notice a rabbit in your yard at dawn or dusk; it just freezes and takes the entire scene of you in, all the while standing perfectly still, just waiting to see what it is you are going to do now that you acknowledged it. As if you weren't supposed to know that both of you coexisted in the same yard and found out, and now it was waiting to see what you were going to do now that you saw it. Awkwardly, I was unsure what the correct custom was in the moment. I stuck with friendly and smiled. I waved and kept driving past to try to appear natural, as if I had business there, and made a left at the break in the road which led me back in front of the daycare. I drove on the little road which led into the daycare's parking lot and observed the little padded bench and the various arts hung on the big glass windows of the classroom of the children who attended there. So the neighborhood had its own daycare and church, like an exclusive community, but it didn't seem ritzy or snobby and they didn't seem out of place. Actually, the church was obviously older than maybe even the town of Loganville itself. I had to look that up and took a mental note to research the church and town when I got home to my computer. I hated people who just stopped what they were doing and started staring at their phones. Directions, okay, but people walking around with their faces glued to their phones not only looked ridiculous, but honestly, you'd probably be a lot more efficient looking at a larger screen in a comfortable chair. I definitely wanted to make sure I had my wits about me and was paying attention, as who knew what could happen around here? But the mystery of this place was almost too much and I could easily have been tempted to pull over and look up the area had I not made the firm decision to drive on and stick with my carved-out plan for the day. The daycare was definitely built within the last ten years or so; it was bright and cared for. It seemed like a nice welcoming place and new; a huge contrast to the little church. I didn't blame them being watchful of people driving by slow who weren't part of their congregation. With all the stuff going on today, ya just never know when someone is up to no good. I would think I wouldn't be a likely candidate being a young woman driving an old Subaru, and it was in the middle of the day, but it's always good to be cautious, I guess. I drove straight this time and admired the scenery as I passed over an old stone bridge that allowed me to pass over a small river that flowed through the neighborhood. The way the large, old trees hung over either side of the bridge gave it the feeling of some of the old covered bridges we had back in Pennsylvania. Back home, they protected the bridges from snow and ice so they wouldn't cave in our winters, here it was just beautiful and seemed to serve no purpose other than for me to say so. To my left was a small playground for the residents, and on the left the river opened up into a mid-sized lake and sidewalks. Wow! They were civilized here. I thought what a nice neighborhood. Someone had definitely taken the time to carve out and plan every detail. As I drove on further, I saw a sign with an arrow pointing left to a county club. Well, that explained it. The residents all belonged to the club and paid their monthly dues, which paid for the upkeep and maintenance of the area and neighborhood. I'd seen some like this in Scranton in the Marywood district, with their manicured lawns and model houses, but those homes were much older. Those neighborhoods were established. These homes, I acknowledged as I drove past them, had to be around twenty years old, nice and clearly built for a certain kind of client but not wealthy people, still in the middle-class range, but every yard was well maintained and cared for. It was obvious the people here all wanted to be here and invested in themselves and in the surrounding area. These people who lived here had purchased a type of lifestyle and wanted to be part of a certain type of community, and not necessarily a type of economic bracket, but rather a type of living, maybe to raise a family in.

It could easily be the type of neighborhood you would see in a movie or T.V. sitcom, marketing the perfect suburban American landscape. I definitely got that serene feel as I coasted along and drove further in. I admired all of the homes that faced the lake, some with their screened-in back porches and decks facing the water, others with fire pits and lawn chairs for their enjoyable outside space. The road came to another four-way stop and my phone declared that I had arrived at my destination.

There it was: a small, modern Catholic church on the left and a soccer field across the street with a house on the grounds that I assumed was the rectory. I pulled into the church parking lot and parked. Oddly, the door was not at the front of the church, so I had to walk around the building to find the big glass double doors. I went inside but wasn't in the church! *Okay, this is weird,* I thought to myself. At the end of a long hallway was a glass window; seated behind it was a pleasant middle-aged woman at a desk. She explained they locked up the church unless it was confession or Mass times, to protect the church. I thought to myself that what she said made no sense at all! What, who would vandalize a church, and from the neighborhood I just left, come on! From the looks of what I just drove through, I would be surprised if they had to lock the doors around here. I just nodded in acknowledgement of what she had said and thanked her for allowing me to go in and say a quick prayer. I felt that instant peace that had always accompanied me when I sat in the pew of a church alone. I would prefer just practicing my faith like this but everyone puts an emphasis on the Mass on Sunday, so that's what I did, well, what I used to do. All that signing and stuff was nice but I felt the best and a connection, I guess, most when sitting quietly at times like this. I guess I was a heathen after all, but maybe it wouldn't hurt if I started to go on Sunday here. I thanked the secretary again and looked at the Mass times for Sunday and made my way out of the church toward my Subaru. The Father must like to walk as I noticed the sidewalk stopped at the church but went through the neighborhood. Maybe whoever built it was Catholic and a member of this parish. Most likely, the developer had a vision of a community and the church was part of the lifestyle he envisioned. More curiosities for me to research, I thought, as I made a left toward the road, so I made a left again which led me past the Rosebud Kroger. It looked like a nice place to shop, and it was close. I was surprised they had built another Kroger so close to the one I saw my first day in Loganville, which was less than five minutes from here. There seemed to be a pattern of building and rebuilding the same stuff, without much demand for it. I have to admit, Loganville would have been really beautiful with all of its big old trees, had they not kept knocking them down to replace them with the same old stuff. Maybe it was just farms that were struggling to survive, so when a big investor came in, the families were so desperate for a way out, they just took the offer that was made, figuring there wouldn't be another one. Who knows, it's just a shame whoever bought up all the land didn't have a better vision. Sure, the stores are making money but it looks ugly.

I guess I'm old-fashioned, from another time even, in my thinking that a developed area in one patch of land would have been better overall for the environment and still have met the needs of the residents. Maybe it's that I'm coming from a developed area and would have liked to have seen a vast forest and not a small patch of one, then a CVS. My thoughts were interrupted by the discomfort of the heat. Why, even in the blaring heat of this summer day, which made even the small walk to my car from the church break me out in a sweat, I could see how pretty the scenery must have been before, as Rosa put it, "they all came and built." I had a fantasy on my way home that I had somehow acquired a vast amount of money and was able to buy up all the land that I saw and convert it back into a forest.

Just as I was importing wolves from Yellowstone National Park, along with a few mountain lions, my daydream was interrupted by the traffic light changing from red to green. Strange, I never had these kinds of thoughts before and I wasn't one to daydream. Not sure if it was the heat down here that was getting to me or the strain of the move, but I needed to get it under control. For one thing, it was dangerous; distractions can lead to accidents. Plus, I always prided myself on being very grounded and practical. On being the

71

kind of person who had their head here and not lost in the clouds. Maybe it was that I never had the opportunity to dream as I had to grow up fast and always had the serious troubles that usually plagued the middle-aged. Lazy thoughts were a privilege of the privileged, and up until now I didn't have the luxury. I made a right off of Rosebud onto Hwy 78 and was headed home. I made my left past the tiny house with all the statues and was home in no time. I paid my respects to Jade and plopped down on the pink chaise in the living room and fell into an afternoon nap.

Chapter Nine

Vines Park

I awoke to Jade kneading and purring on my stomach. It was four o'clock and I made my way into the kitchen to brew a pot of coffee and put together a beef bologna sandwich on white with Colby and Swiss cheese and spicy brown mustard. After my second cup of coffee, I rinsed out my dish and cup and put them in the dishwasher and washed out the coffee pot. I brushed my teeth and decided to head outside for a nice walk. I went left out of the house and up out of the row of houses that engulfed my neighborhood. I walked forever at my own leisurely pace until the road ended at an IHOP, passed the post office and kept on past a Bojangles, which seemed to be a chicken restaurant. Besides its odd name, it sat like a residence in the middle of a plot of land, like a house would have. If it wasn't a commercial building, that is exactly what it would look like, that someone had decided to turn their house into a restaurant. It seemed busy for being an oddity that looked as though it would have trouble passing a health inspection. Hopefully for its patrons, looks are deceiving. There was almost no parking lot, and the small paved area in the back had a basketball hoop. I kept on walking, curious as to what else I would find but not really expecting to see anything appealing. I arrived at a Lowes and Dollar Store shopping center which led me back around into a small alley behind a RaceTrac gas station. I decided this was enough for today and was going to do a U-turn at the carwash and walk back when I saw them. A group of guys, about my age; maybe some in the group were a tad younger at fifteen or sixteen, but at least two were in their late teens or early twenties. Most of them were black but two of them were white. I felt afraid, funny as they hadn't even noticed me yet, and I really hoped that I could avoid them somehow as inside I knew with every part of me they would be a problem. I didn't see any way to avoid them at this point. If I could have seen over here when I was behind the corner from Lowe's, I could have went around, but now there was nowhere for me to go but the direction I was going. The more that I got a look at them, the more I realized my intuition was right. They didn't look like good guys; my gut was telling me to get out of there but there was nowhere for me to go. Internal guide, intuition or just plain common sense, whatever it was or why, I knew enough to know it had saved me in the past and to just trust it. Some people who haven't been in my shoes may think it's profiling or judgmental; heck, look at me... I've gotten a bad rap before just from being in the group home. No, I trust me. That's for sure. I've met all kinds from all classes, good and bad, and I knew this was a bad situation that I needed to avoid. I could continue on past them, which from the looks of them it didn't seem like a good idea, especially since one of them just threw a bottle at one of the large green boxes you see outside to cover electrical wires. The bottle broke with a loud crack and glass sprayed all over the beginning of the alleyway that began at the main road and curved as a double entrance for the gas station. The guys began laughing so loud at this possible cause of driver's flat tire that they just sprayed all over; a pack of hyenas came to mind when I got a good look at one who seemed to be the leader. The brooding mannerisms of the figure as he turned to face me sent chills down my spine to the point where I had to consciously command my legs to be firm as I walked with a determined purpose toward the entrance of the gas station.

He was large, stocky and somewhat chubby but held some solid mass to him. He was white and had a large nose that reminded me of the cartoon Elmer Fudd's nose. It was definitely his predominant feature as it seemed to take up his whole face. He had a cruel appearance, with expressions that scowled often as he spoke, and he seemed dirty, with his greasy light brown hair and worn green army jacket that had to be from the Vietnam era, as the army wears desert colors now. He would hurt me if he could, there was no doubt about it, and his friends would just go along with him. At this point, if I turned back, it would be obvious I was avoiding them and there was no help for me in the little strip of road between here and Lowe's. Plus, even if I made it to the Lowe's parking lot, they could catch up to me. I could try to turn into the RaceTrac but I'd still have to pass them, crap. God be with me. Maybe I could quickly grab a big piece of that glass and defend myself; a quick unexpected cut to their arm or face may give enough time to get a head start and make it into the RaceTrac. No dice. A quick glance down let me know they did a pretty good job of smashing the bottle, and only ground pieces lay on the ground in front of me. I walked at a normal pace with my head somewhat down but making sure my body posture and language was strong but minding my own business. I learned this from the groups of kids that were bussed in from the Bronx into Scranton's projects in Sister Mary Clarence's attempt to offer these lost inner-city kids a chance at a good life. All it seemed to do was bring down Scranton as they just did what they knew how to do, which wasn't good. Sister Mary Clarence had the right intentions, but it still wasn't good for Scranton other than giving social workers and the local police job security. These guys here weren't from the city and they look bored and destructive, as if they had no direction and would end up doing something just because. At least the kids that were bussed into my old area grew up tough, and they were like that because they had to be; maybe they just didn't know any better. I wouldn't go as far as the good sister to say they just needed our local God-fearing love, but these guys just seemed out of place and choosing to be destructive. There seemed to be a big difference between Frankie Rodriguez robbing a liquor store to eat and just giving people flat tires. Maybe there wasn't, but Frankie never gave me a bad feeling, I just knew to stay away from him because I didn't want to get mixed up in any trouble, I never thought he would hurt me or that he wanted to. Don't get me wrong, I heard Frankie stabbed someone on the subway in the Bronx, that's how he ended up with the Church, but he was from a rough neighborhood. The groups of guys in front of me lived in Loganville, Georgia, and were choosing to break stuff and scare me for that matter, instead of doing something else. I stayed in my position as I continued to walk toward the entrance of the RaceTrac when I heard "Look at that bitch." They saw me, not sure what the best thing to do here was so I kept walking, pretending like I didn't hear them. Then they started walking after me, pushing their lips together to make a kissing sound, one of them saying, "Wait up, sexy, where are you going? I'm right here, baby," as he grabbed his private area in a lewd gesture. I could hear some of the others laughing at the younger one's comments. The black kid had such a young, handsome, almost pretty face. If I had seen him anywhere else, I would have thought he sang in the church choir at St. Mary's and never would have envisioned this. His hair was shaved short and he looked the cleanest of all of them; his Nike sneakers looked new and expensive. His eyes weren't cold like the others but checking him out allowed him to get closer. Crap! In realizing my mistake and stupidity, I almost ran for the door at the RaceTrac. Whew! I made it inside and was safe for now. I went into the ladies' bathroom and locked the door behind me. I used it and then washed my hands, allowing the cool water to run up to my elbows. I put some behind my neck too. I felt much better and was almost recharged. I drank some water from the sink after letting it run for a few seconds from my hands and sat down on the floor against the wall for a good ten minutes, hoping the guys were gone. I peeked out the door and didn't see them, so I sneaked out into the small hallway that encased the bathrooms when I saw him, the leader. It was too late. He made eye contact with me and before I could turn around, I saw one of the other guys, the younger black kid, was next to him.

Crap. I backed up and ran out the emergency exit door. I ran as fast as I could but was going the wrong way in my panic. I lived up the other direction toward Lowe's! I ran across the tiny main street toward the car wash when I saw them, and they were crossing from Hwy 78 toward the car wash. I dashed in between cars and ran toward the woods in front of me. God, this was like a horror movie gone wrong. You know, when the girl runs into the woods, she dies in the end. How stupid. I ended up cursing myself, but I didn't seem to have a choice now, and there were so many of them that they had cut me off. I had to hide, that was my only chance, but where? I was never in the woods in my life and wasn't sure what to do.

The thick pine straw beneath my feet seemed to be slowing me down and crunching beneath my footsteps that getting away seemed unlikely; as I knew once they got inside these woods they would be able to hear me. I kept running and running, saying to myself, please, God, help me, please. There was something honest and unpretentious about my faith when I realized my fate may not be in my hands. This could be it. I wasn't sitting in a church for the sake of what someone in the neighborhood thought about my reputation. No, this was the transparent view into my soul that knew I probably didn't have a chance in Hades without some help. Also that I always believed someone was there, listening and watching. Not sure if it was the Catholic God of St. Mary's but I believed, and I just hoped he heard me now. It was getting dark and I felt the fear and exhaustion driving me at the same time. My lungs were burning and sweat was dripping off my head and face. My legs felt tight and light as though they were going to give out and collapse from under me. No, I needed them to get me away. I needed them to run faster. I pushed them on unbelievably, as I was never the athlete, but I knew what stopping would lead me to so I just kept going past the burn and fear that I would hurt myself. I came to another road which I ran across to a meadow that led into deeper woods. I heard one, who I was pretty sure was the leader command "Get that cunt" to the group. I felt the fear creep over me as I heard their intent to harm me. I hoped that he was just making a general statement and that he hadn't seen me. If I had any doubts about them or how this would go down if they caught up with me, I was certain now. The ugliness in the tone of his voice went through me, encouraging the tears to well up from my throat and start dripping down my face. I put my hand over my mouth to try to remain quiet and hidden as I scanned the forest for a place to go. *God, please help me, show me what to do,* I pleaded with all of myself, hoping if there was a God, he would have pity on me now. I knew with certainty that was my only chance here for survival, as they were too close now for me to make a run for it; they would either see or hear me. Odds were these guys knew this area and I didn't. I could just as easily run right into their backyard, into some abandoned warehouse or even back onto the highway. There were a lot of them so eventually they would find me and could just grab me and make it look casual, force me to walk in the middle of them until we got out of sight. It would most likely be well into the night, when there was no chance of anyone else being around. Even if someone did notice would they help me? There was no guarantee that someone could or would do the right thing. How could I place a bet on a stranger to come to my aid against this pack of animals? No, I had better chance of a miracle. Just then I saw a red-furred doe peak out of the brush that lined the trees of the back of the start of the woods. She was so calm and aware. She must also be hiding from them. Something told me to copy her movements. I looked around and didn't see my pursuers, so I quickly made my way toward the bushes she was in, trying to be as quiet and as light as I could as I walked over the pine needles that lay all over the floor of the forest. I saw the opening in the bush and went inside.

When I was in deep enough inside, I crouched down and held onto the trunk of its massive base. My guide was nowhere to be seen now, but I was thankful. In my dark clothes, hopefully, I would be unseen like she was. I saw them pass me a couple of yards away; they were headed left and along the street side of the trees. I waited some time before I slowly crouched out. I felt just like my guide, eyes large, attempting to scan the woods for danger, creeping out of the thickets into the forest. Good thing I was wearing dark clothing as I guessed it hid me. I thought maybe I should go back to the thickets, as I had no idea where I was. I had become confused and focused on just escaping from my pursuers and didn't take in much of the environment and was lost. I just kept on walking until I came to a small hill. Unsure I was making the right choice, I began thinking about turning back around and trying to retrace my steps. I heard the sound of running water. I listened and walked toward the direction, assuming the guys would be too loud if they were anywhere near, so I kept walking. The sound led me to a small stream which I followed then leapt across and kept going. I leant against a thick tree and looked back and didn't see them, so I continued on thankfully at a quick walk forward, which led to another grassy meadow that opened up like a path in between a thick surrounding forest. I stood back to take it all in; even not in the best of light, I was overwhelmed by its size and vastness. How could this have been hidden within walking distance of my house and off a main highway? I tried to listen for the busy sounds of cars from Athens Highway; nothing. That didn't make any sense. Looking around, there were a lot of trees. I could maybe even assume this was a large forest, but I should still be close enough that I could hear traffic. I mean, there can't be enough trees within walking distance to be that good a sound barrier. My path ended at a small sign that said *Butterfly Garden*, and I looked and there was a tiny garden of flowers, surrounded by a man-made wooden fence.

Where was I? I wondered as I came to a four-way stop of sorts for pedestrians. To the left was more meadow that ended in a forest and the road seemed to wrap around and come back, straight curved to the left, and became a paved road. Left went toward some kind of brick structure and I was uncertain which way to go. I was relieved my pursuers seemed to have given up so now just to find my way back home before it got dark. I decided to go left and was led up three yellow brick steps toward a red brick road that was paved on both sides with all kinds of roses, types I had never heard of or imagined. They had a faint smell but it was pleasant and exactly what I needed after my encounter with the local boys. It was such a beautiful scene as the brick path led me between rows of the flowered bushes. Roses are, to my knowledge, hard to maintain and they were clearly designed and arranged with intent to create a magnificent garden. Someone had clearly done this, but who? Was this someone's property or a museum or something? Not likely in Loganville, another strange thing to note about this place. I wish I had found this place on another night, as it really was quite beautiful, but my nerves were still shot and it had only been a moment ago I feared this place is where my short life would end. My heart was racing, so I couldn't really take in all that I was seeing. It was eerie, yet I wasn't afraid. I looked up as I walked further down the carefully created path; I saw what could be in the beginning of a very gothic horror film. They were magnificent but definitely out of the ordinary for one's average daily encounter. I looked to my left and saw a row of white statues, carved in detail and lifelike. They were women, frozen still. Trapped and cemented in their daily pose as great statues.

There were four of them and for some reason I couldn't look them directly in the eyes as I took in the features of their faces. They were beautiful and dressed as though they were imported from ancient Greece with their feminine flowing robes. Something you might see in the garden of a mansion or in a museum, not in the middle of a forest in podunk Loganville, Georgia! What the heck! I wasn't sure if I was surprised or in awe, but I still felt the internal drive to get back home to safety, far away from the possibility of running into those guys again. I knew they had to be nearby somewhere, they most likely had no other plans for the evening and were smart enough to assume that being on foot, I was probably still around here somewhere.

Even being in the unfortunately dangerous and stupid situation that I was in, I couldn't help but stare at them in wonder and astonishment, as I had never encountered anything this cool or out of the ordinary in Avoca. It was like something out of a good fantasy novel or movie. It was as though they were watchers, or guardians of some sort. Scanning over from the way they stood watch from above as if they were locked in place in their protective towers. The first one had animals, a bird, on her shoulder; she represented the fowl. The second one a jug of water she was pouring into a basin. The third lady held a bowl of fruit and the fourth a basket of grains. Each held something people needed to survive or things most certainly part of life long ago. They were not scary but seemed powerful, as if they were the protectors of this place. I guess those things would have been relevant not only in ancient Greece but also on any plantation or farm in the Americas. Animals, grains, water and vegetation were definitely necessary for survival. Protecting them would have been vital. I guess making a statue to show their importance makes sense. Art usually reflects daily life; it's odd they weren't depicted or carved to represent the Colonial or Civil War era, though. Maybe they were imported, or a local resident was in art school and copied some great ancient masterpiece. Someone had to know the history of this place. I was getting so caught up in the mystery and beauty of the garden that I almost forgot why I was there in the first place. It was curious how the setting had an almost tranquil effect on me, as though it had an essence of its own. Even now, consciously acknowledging what danger I was in that very moment, I felt calm. How oddly at peace in this unfamiliar and wondrous place I was! The very air seemed to have a presence as it entered my nostrils. I could easily have drifted off again in thought, forgetting the real imperilment of my situation. Few times in my life had I seen true beauty. Once I was on a school trip to the Archdiocese St. Ann's Monastery, in Scranton. We were preparing for our Confirmation and I remember the first time I stepped into the church; the beauty and the craftsmanship of it literally took my breath for a few seconds. With its massive white columns and green and white marble floors that beamed clean and the sunlight escaping in through the stained glass, I believed for a second that I was in Heaven as the light hit me in reflection. It was truly glorious and I marveled that it was all made by man. Today was the second; even in the darkness, the white faces of these beautiful women who seemed so real, that for a moment it would be believable that they lived but were only cased in stone. Truly remarkable they were. I liked the animal one in particular.

For some reason, I was drawn to her more than the others, oddly, as the lady holding the grain seemed to have more strength and the water more grace and somehow the guardian of the fruit seemed prettier and more feminine, her fingers delicate in their pose. I stood under her gaze as her carved eyes glared down at me. She represented the animals she cared for, wild and free yet existing in the civilized world that was created and kept for them. There was something earthy and womanly about her strength that I admired. She was young, about my age. An adult but not yet wise in her years. She was obviously a female yet athletic in stature, much like myself. Maybe it's true that we are attracted to things like ourselves, but up until Jade, I had never been into animals. Maybe it was that I hadn't the opportunity, living in group homes and government housing, but I find that I do enjoy having a pet. Thinking about it, I was much like Jade, and Mrs. Vendor took me in. Having a pet allows you to just love when ya have nowhere else to put it. I thought, as I stood under her watchful shadow, acknowledging her hair that was pulled up into a small bun on top with the rest of her hair loose down her back and unkempt. The rest of the women had the loose buns piled atop of their heads like the fashion of the period, with the Lady of the Grain having an extra string of curls to surround her face in the now moonlight. I felt a peace and wonder about the world and this place as I walked further through the garden toward another large statue. The road ended at a giant statue of a mermaid surrounded by three tiny male sea nymphs; her children, I suppose, who were blowing horns. It was beautifully placed inside a small circular brick encasement that housed a flowerbed of various flowers. She was staring down at the medium-sized lake the road overlooked. I walked toward the edge and there was a flight of rather steep brick stairs that opened wide. They looked like the perfect place to sit with a friend and chat as you overlooked the water. From my high vantage point, I could see shadows moving in the distance. It was them entering the area on the other side of the lake.

I ducked behind a potted tree that marked the entrance of the stairs and saw the group of guys walking on a trail of sorts on the other side of the lake. *Crap, okay, where do I go?* I had no idea where I was. *Help me, God, please.* It was so dark and I almost began to panic. I closed my eyes for a second in an attempt to let my eyes adjust to the total darkness I found myself standing in. What an idiot I was, strolling along like I hadn't a care in the world under the charms of this place that I left myself vulnerable. Unable to describe the power this place had over me that I had lost my thoughts for a moment. That was so dangerous and unlike me. More reason to get away from here, but how? I felt a slight breeze and a sudden calm.

When I opened my eyes, it was still dark, but I could at least make out shapes to guide myself a little. I walked toward the four ladies and looked up at the Lady of the Grain. Her face seemed amused and kind, knowledgeable. I wished I was like her and suddenly saw the path in front of me. Oddly, even though logically I could hide less and would be more visible on this road than in the forest, I felt somewhat safer on the path, even if only because I knew people had at least been on it or it may lead me to people at some point. I knew nothing for certain about the woods; anything could be in there.

Thank God my eyes became a little more accustomed to the night and I made a dash for it and weaved around with it until it opened up into a gravel road big enough for a single car to drive upon. I was still somewhat relieved as I didn't hear them and felt somewhat protected and hidden by the row of large bushes or maybe they were small trees that lined the dirt and somewhat rocky road to my left. Clearly, someone had made this path, but who and for what purpose? I hoped it would lead me somewhere safe as I followed along in fear and solitude, listening for them and hoping for concealment as I walked on. It opened up at the end with some picnic tables and a small porta potty. I had to pee so bad at this point; all that running and fear does it every time. It seemed weird to have a porta potty in the middle of a forest but I guess with the picnic tables maybe people do events here or something. If this was a park, though, the statues didn't make sense but then again, nothing about Loganville so far did. I got in and locked the door and just as I finished my business, I heard something outside; it was them. I pulled up my yoga pants as quietly as I could and tried to breathe in and remain still. I decided that to sit back down on the toilet was the best option to be silent as the floor of the porta potty seemed shaky and I wanted to remain quiet. I looked up at the windows of the tiny plastic shelter, and it didn't seem like they would be able to see me if they tried to look in. Just then, I heard footsteps and distant laughter; it was the same sounds as before. They must have been on the road right in front of the potty. I looked down at the locked latch of the door, which didn't offer me any comfort as I knew if they knew I was in there, they would find a way to get me out. I just sat there listening and waiting, hoping they would just pass and go home or wherever they go. I heard a loud bang, which caused me to jump up and catch myself in a thankful effort that I still remained quiet.

They must have kicked one of those metal garbage cans I saw that lined the road. I heard him, the leader, say, "Forget that bitch; she probably wouldn't be any good anyway."

Then another one chimed in, "Yeah, what about Cindy?"

Another voice said, "Nawh, I'm tired of that ho." It was then I realized they did intend to rape me. I just sat with my hands over my mouth and allowed the relief of silence to come in, as I couldn't hear them anymore. I sat in there for at least an hour before I had to pee again, so I did, and cautiously opened the door after to complete darkness. It had become night as I waited in the small enclosure for my tormentors to leave. Now I had no idea where I was, and it was dark. I never thought of myself as a stupid person but this evening may change my mind.

I decided to continue on the path the way I was headed before and got back onto the road and began walking in the new direction away from the porta potty. I saw two glowing eyes emerge from the dark bluish-black shape of what must be thickets. They moved slowly, almost floating out over the bushes, and were gone, almost vanishing out of sight. That must have been a deer, I hoped. It seemed to be the right shape and there was no way a human could jump that high or do so gracefully. I saw something white like a beam so I walked toward it and it was a little house surrounded by a chain-link fence, enclosed by what seemed to be a miniature town and railroad, like the ones you see people put around their tree at Christmas time. This place was getting stranger by the minute. I thought of trying to go inside the house to sleep in until the morning as it seemed empty, but then I thought that is exactly where the guys would look for me, so I kept on walking.

I passed more picnic tables under a roof of vines which led to a small sign that said, *Children's Maze*. There was no way I was going in a maze by myself in the dark, especially since I wasn't sure where those boys went off to. I made a right up a steep set of wide wooden stairs that were covered by vines and flowers, causing a covered tunnel effect as I climbed them. Such a powerful and sweet smell encompassed my journey up to the road, which caused the first sight you see to be moving waves of water as it led you to be eye level with the lake on your third step from the top. It was beautiful. I felt such peace, and somehow inspired by this place, this magical place. I wondered what it was. Did someone live here? It obviously had some landscaping and structures placed here by people. Unsure of which way to go, I went left and in the dark I fumbled around until my foot hit a huge rock, which I decided to sit upon and think of what to do next. As I allowed my hand to fall down to rest, I felt a long curvature that felt like an ear. I jumped off the rock to get a good look at what I was sensing and almost screamed. I quickly realized my eyes were just playing tricks on me in my dark and foreign environment; it was only that someone had carved and painted features out of this large rock to resemble a giant troll emerging out of the ground. They even planted grass and moss on the top of his head to resemble hair. My nerves couldn't take much more of this place or Loganville for that matter. Maybe under other circumstances it would be really cool and I would appreciate this creative masterpiece, but tonight I just wanted to go home and for my journey to end. I saw the entrance to the maze so I knew I had to be on the other side of the large patch that sat in the middle between the road of the porta potty and the lake, so I went left and eventually, as I surmised, hit the lake. Okay, I looked up and there was no moon. I decided that my best bet was to walk along the lake, which I knew would lead me to the road where the boys came in, and toward the direction of the RaceTrac. Sure enough, from just following the path, I eventually ended up at a brick structure that had two doors; one for ladies and one for men. It had to be a restroom. I walked past an old water fountain which had to be as old as Mrs. Vendor, with its curved and detailed features and brass handle. I wondered if it worked. I went over and tried it and it did work! I took a big helping just to be sure I was hydrated, for who knew when I would make it home? The water tasted better than my bottled Evian, so cool and smooth. Like life itself. I was so surprised the water tasted so good from an old fountain like that. I walked under a massive metal threshold shaped in a peak that served as the opening of the fence that seemed to go on and on through the trees and past the forest. When I passed through to the other side, I looked up and saw a giant V in the middle on top of the gate. It led out into a mid-sized parking lot divided into rows, each headed with trees and flowers. What a place, still no indication of what it was. It had to be a public park, but with all the statues and beautiful and eccentric touches, it didn't seem like the right assessment either.

I turned back to look at the entrance again and saw a large squirrel sit in the middle of the walkway and put its hand on its hip and cock its head to the right and just look at me. I have never seen or heard of squirrels coming out at night. It sat there for the longest time, just taking me in, it seemed, and then off it went down the paved road. I faced the dark and larger-than-would-be-expected parking lot of Vines. It was empty, thank God, and it was lined by the occasional street lamp, so at least I could see where I was going. I walked toward the left closer to the woods so I could dart in and hopefully hide if I had to. I came to a four-way stop of a road and kept going, which led me to eventually pass a Christian school, Methodist, I believe, and eventually onto the road of the car wash. I made it. Relieved and fearful to walk down the alley where I encountered those guys earlier that day which started this whole nightmare but I kept walking, determined to get home. I realized

For the Love of Vines

that someone had cleaned up the glass from the roadway as I looked down in relief that it was gone.

An hour or two later I arrived at my house. To my relief, Jade was waiting for me at the door. I found myself looking back behind me to make sure I had arrived alone.

Jade circled around at my feet as I scooped him up into a big embrace, so happy to see him and be home. He didn't seem to appreciate it as much and immediately began grooming himself when I put him back down. "Fine... lick off my coodies," I said, unable to not express my happiness to see him. "You wait until you want to be petted," I said to him as I walked up the long oaken staircase toward the bathroom. I realized that I still had some remnants of the fear from my experience as I found myself neurotically for a second thinking they were still after me, maybe even the possibility that they were in the house. I quickly shook it off, assuring myself that they would have had to be inside the house already when I came home for that to be possible and then how could that be, as they had no idea who I was before this evening, so it wasn't possible that they could be here waiting for me.

Also, if they were following me still, they wouldn't have waited until I got home to get me. Either way, I didn't see them and plus, Jade seemed completely normal and that should mean something. Feeling somewhat relieved, I eagerly turned the knob to let the water warm up. I took a long, hot shower, taking longer than normal to use my exfoliating brush to scrub myself clean, fully enjoying the safety of my home and the moment. Exhausted, I went to bed so happy to have made it home.

Chapter Ten

The True Vines

I opened my eyes and I was back in the dark at Vines. I had fallen asleep on the bench seat to the picnic table on the patio that was covered by pergolas and ropes of vines. I could see now, as the moon had revealed itself and hung like a personal lamp over the lake. Something approached me from the thickets behind. Feeling and acknowledging its presence, I slowed myself to turn and face whatever it was. My thinking was that if it was dangerous, it would have already pounced on me instead of choosing to gently observe me from the safety of the shadows. As my eyes scanned the bushes for its shape, it emerged, and shockingly it was a large red-coated deer! She was a beautiful doe with the same yellow-green eyes I had seen earlier.

Gosh, I had no recollection of coming here. Maybe walking home had been a dream, or I was so tired that I didn't remember coming back out here. As she walked closer, I admired the strength of her form and grace as her muscular legs guided her graceful glide through the grass. A shimmer of golden light engulfed her form as she grew more slender and began to take the form of a lady, a female human. She continued to walk toward me with her thick, long hair that was so red it appeared black in the night. She had strong and slender features and greenish eyes. Her legs occasionally flirted with me from under her long sheer gown, showing their muscular shape and slender curves. A ghost, she must be a ghost. My mind tried to make sense of what was happening, as seeing a deer was magical enough, but now my mind was playing tricks on me in the night. It must be like it was earlier with the stone troll. I'm sure my eyes were just mis-focusing as they grew accustomed to the dark and I was mistaking a branch or something for her image. I was certain it had to be that the deer moved just at the right angle to confuse my eyes and my mind. I blinked and there was no deer and no lady; she was gone. I stood up and walked toward the table to see a large red-furred squirrel that seemed to be talking to a tiny glowing light that was hovering above the table and was about its size. When the squirrel acknowledged me, it cocked its head to the right and placed its little hand on its hip just as it had before. I said, "Hello there," and it made some movement with its mouth as the glowing ball floated toward a brick path. I stopped as something on the squirrel's waist caught my eye, and peered in earnest only to confirm what my mind didn't want me to see: a tiny bag hung over its shoulder and sat at its waist! A tiny leather satchel or purse! The squirrel was wearing a bag! I made a conscious command for myself to get over the shock of my realization and to close my mouth and locate where that floating orb went before I lost it. I could think about what I saw or thought I had seen with the squirrel later. I followed the light the best that I could, which led me past a bird bath in the center of a large brick-paved circle which stood in the center of four paths. Great, this again; I'd have to choose which way to go, as I lost sight of my floating sphere. I went left on the stone path, winding around some tall shrubs, and ended at a large glass gazebo which served as a sunroom for various plants. I continued on, which led me to a windy path along rows of tall flowers. The road ended at the corner of the lake and a massive tree to my right, so I went right and heard running water and singing. There on the right was a small waterfall against an earthen wall and on either side were small ponds. Floating above the rocks that encased the pond was about twenty or so of those floating balls of light. I tried to get close to one to see what it was, a bug or something, but they kept their distance. Finally, I sat down on the bench that faced the small river. The river seemed to be flowing down into the small waterfall, which fell into the Lake of Vines Park. As I sat there at peace, just following the flow of water with my eyes to take in my environment, one of the globes slowly approached me and began to float in my direction and then came very close to me, hovering so close to my face that I could feel the wind that was created from its tiny wings. It would best be described as a blue ball of light that had a greenish hue around it, much like the light of a flashlight has a kind of ring.

As it approached, I focused on it, afraid it would leave again before I could figure it out, but I didn't dare lose sight of it and I focused on it with intent, as I tried to remain calm and still in its presence. Still somewhat afraid and unsure of what they were or if they could bite or were harmful, I tried to seem still and assure it that I meant it no harm. Looking and trying to focus on its shape and features of what was inside the ball. How were they moving? I could see the small details of a tiny face emerge. In shock, I realized it wasn't that of an insect but a human face. They were human! Tiny little humans with wings! Delicate and lean was the outline of the tiny form that emerged. I looked down toward the river as a trail of them was floating in a line that branched off, or maybe began to sort themselves into groups. One group went to the lake; another stood at the bank of the river; another went into the forest. I slowly made my way toward the bank of the river. I tried to stay back by the large tree where I hoped they couldn't see me, but I was able to watch their... what I could only describe as a procession or ceremony of sorts. It seemed like the ones coming out of the river were being sorted by their type or kind. As if they were born in the river, like tadpoles of sorts or mer-creatures, as they were human-like. As these humanoid mer-people grew or were old enough, I guess they go to whatever clan put them in the river to hatch or grow into adults or orbs of light. They were simply beautiful and I found myself unable to peer away from watching them.

A pair of the orbs would float down to the river and a mer-creature would emerge from the river escorted by a really old-looking slender creature. She was more like the orb people but standing in shallows of the bank of the river. She was clad in a white and golden trimmed gown and had a crown or headpiece of sorts. She was obviously the facilitator, queen or someone of importance to be the one conducting the ceremony. She would guide the approaching being from the water to the approaching couple. Sometimes the one in the river would stumble, almost as if they had never walked before and they were unstable at first. She would guide them along to the approaching orb couple and they would eventually travel off together. It was beautiful and I felt myself tearing up from the welts of emotion that were emerging from my throat much like the ones that would cause me to cry during a good romantic flick or drama. It seemed like either the mer-people were sorted by their type or maybe it was an adoption of some sort. It was what I could make sense of from watching them. I wondered if they knew I was there or how long I was standing there for that matter, as it seemed like a lot of time had passed; yet I didn't feel still or tired like I normally would have when one's body starts to let you know, hey, you've been standing here too long. No, I had no idea how long I had been there or even stranger than what I was seeing, how I had gotten there in the first place! In that moment, I sat up in a gasp for air. It was dark. I was in my room in my own bed!

Thank goodness, it was just a dream, a weird and crazy dream. It was probably just my subconscious in a poor attempt to make sense of what had happened earlier in the park. I grabbed my heart and took in a slow, deep breath. I just sat there for a moment allowing the air to fill my lungs as I inhaled deeply from my nose and exhaled it slowly, allowing it to release as a flow of wind as I felt my feet land firmly on the wooden floor next to the plush carpet. The wood felt cool and comforting as it had been smoothed by wear and wax over the years under my walk toward the bathroom. As I quickly made my way toward my toilet, I glanced at the clock on the nightstand I was eye level with from my seat: 2 am. Oh man, what just happened? I was wide awake now from my crazy dream and feeling shaky. Thank God it was just a dream. I had had enough of today and wished I could have just slept it all off and wake up and start over. What were those things? Strangely my dream was so vivid, crystal clear and not the fuzzy haze that lets you know it's a dream. This seemed so real, like I was there. Had I not jumped up from my bed, I would have thought coming home last night was a dream and that I was still at Vines Park. I had to check that place out, in the daytime. No way would I go over there at night ever again. Heck, I was so shaken up right now, I was afraid to go downstairs and make myself a nice cup of hot tea to calm my nerves and hopefully get back to bed. *I have to do it; I'm a grown person.* A manager, well, I was a manger at least. It's not like the skill set flew out the window just because I hadn't been doing it since I'd moved here. A strong, independent woman, I told myself, who is not afraid to go downstairs in her own house just because she had a spooky dream about some little creatures she knows aren't even real. Well, after two more minutes of some mental Scranton spunk and scooping up Jade, I convinced myself to go make myself a cup of Lady Grey Tea I had found in one of the blue and white canisters on the counter. It was good, even better after I'd added some lemon and honey. It was exactly what I had needed and I finally fell back to sleep until the morning.

At 7am, the sun was already shining brightly in my eyes from the window. Jade was curled up at my feet in his cozy spot on the bed. I washed and put on some clean clothes, poured Jade some food and was off in my Subaru before 7:20 am. I found a coffee house nearby, off of Rosebud Road. It was an old house they converted into a coffee shop. I thought it was cool they had a drive-thru but nobody would let me out for at least five minutes from the stream of morning commute traffic, as they all seemed busy to get to work. So I just sat there sipping my latte until one older gentleman waved me the okay to pull out in front of him. I drove through Old Grayson and made a left and drove on Hwy 20 until I hit Loganville again. I drove through my street but didn't stop home but turned instead onto Hwy 78 until I ended up at an Ingles and a thrift store.

Well, I did need some new clothes, as yoga pants everyday didn't seem appropriate for the library. The Goodwill was so much bigger and cleaner than the old Salvation Army in Scranton. I found myself a bunch of slacks and sleeveless tops I'd seen a lot of the locals wear. I was surprised so many of them were silk or dressy with ruffles or other girly things I would never have worn to the warehouse. I picked up a couple of sweaters too, as I noticed everyone blasts the air-conditioning so you freeze inside and sweat outside. It didn't seem natural and I was afraid I would get sick from sweating so much then stepping into the ice-cold buildings, but everyone seemed to do it and be all right, so I guessed I would be too once I got used to it. I put my bags in the car and walked to a tiny Chinese restaurant on the same strip, which I hadn't noticed from the street. The food was okay; my vegetable lo mein probably tasted better than it should have because it was my first meal of the day. I guess I couldn't expect Chinatown quality in a small place like this, not that I had ever been to the one in New York City or even the Chinatown in Philadelphia. Maybe someday I'd get to travel more, maybe after college. College. I slowly walked back to my Subaru filled with the excitement of possibly finishing school and someday seeing places I'd heard about. One thing this move and whole experience in Georgia really had done for me, was it allowed me to see I could change my destiny. To realize that I wasn't stuck but that I had options, even ones I didn't know about.

I drove around the back of the building, past the donation drop-off for the Goodwill and the open kitchen door of the Chinese restaurant and nodded to a middle-aged Chinese man that was sitting on an overturned bucket smoking a cigarette. He was wearing a white chef's hat and white apron over a white tee shirt; I guess he was on break. It took me to a street which I took a left on and I ended up at a stop sign next to a mid-sized house.

A small alley separated me from a run-down playground that was fenced off. I drove ahead and parked in the tiny five-car spot parking lot, which maybe could house six cars if they were little Volkswagen Bugs or Mini Cruisers. Next to the playground sat a small 1950s-era ranch home and an even smaller church surrounded by a graveyard. I opened the gate and sat on the swing that was one of two suspended from the old style metal supports that struck the ground like upside down Vs. Amused by the scene, like a picture stuck in time that allowed me to become a part of it, I slowly meandered my way toward the monkey bars and fort of some kind, built obviously to inspire imagination from the local children. I climbed it and went down the tiny slide and walked the whole length of the fenced-in area of the small park. I did a makeshift lunge off of the picnic table, which gave my legs a really good stretch after what I had put them through recently, and just slowly made my way out of the eating area of the pavilion and back into the designated play area. The park wasn't much, but most moms and small kids would find a nice afternoon here. It was quiet and fenced-in so the kids would be safe and the parents could relax. Barely any traffic had passed along the alley that lined the entrance of the park. It was a gem of a find and exactly what I needed that day after the night before and, well, really the whole thing or whirlwind of life since I got that phone call that led me down here. I meandered my way back to the swing set and lingered a while before choosing which one I would sit on. What now? I guess I just lived, right? Just for one thing… stay clear of those guys! Secondly, just enjoy my beautiful home and Jade, of course, and the start of my new life. The swing was in surprisingly good condition, and it seemed sturdy and strong, even though it now showed its age and wear with every squeak as I went slowly in and out, allowing the wind to move more of me and the swing than my legs. I just rocked for a while, clearing my head, trying to collect my nerves after the series of events that had happened to me since I had left Avoca. It probably wasn't the most hygienic thing to do, but I slipped off my Sketchers and let my feet go into the three or four inches of sand that filled a makeshift box that went around the swing set. I suppose it also served as the local sand box, as there was the remnant of an old sandcastle a few feet away. At least someone had had a happy moment here.

I looked out and saw little cottages whose small structures sat in a row behind a familiar plaque. I knew that plaque; those little homes must be the projects or government housing for the city of Loganville. The area looked old but it was kept up and it seemed like a poor, but taken care of community where people lived and worked. I mean, I had lived in government housing and I wasn't a bad person, and who knows where I would be if people hadn't been kind to me? Heck, not everybody has a grandmother that leaves them a house or knows a good Catholic in Moosic who is willing to give them a chance. I was feeling very lucky and thankful as I turned left out of the alley past the government homes and small white church. I came out onto a major street that was filled with cars, and on the left was the O'Kelly Library. That meant I could walk to the playground during my lunch at the library and eat on the picnic tables, as I usually liked to eat lunch outside. Happy with my little find of the day, I decided to go home as I had to be at the library for my first day of work the next day, and I had to get all of those new shirts washed if I was going to wear any of them tomorrow. The rest of the evening consisted of Jade following me around the house and me loafing on the sofa channel surfing until I went to bed around nine that night.

The next day went well; everyone was nice. From my boss and his wife to all of the locals that came in. I learned how to scan and check in books patrons returned and how to scan books they wanted to rent. I also did one whole cart that I categorized myself, but it took me a couple hours, where I could tell others may have done it in minutes. That was okay; I knew that I would pick up speed once I gained some experience, but I wanted to make sure I was doing it correctly first. The worst thing would be to get into a habit of doing it wrong, then it is so hard to train yourself to do it right. As menial as the tasks were, I actually enjoyed them! Most of it was busy work but it was exactly what I needed. My mind was occupied making sure the books went back into the right place on the shelf, and I had to be careful and pay attention. The place was small and old; everyone seemed to know everyone and they seemed to care, but they weren't too nosy or personal so it was really ideal. I was also secretly glad because I wasn't a big sharer and someone without manners may make me come off as rude, which I wasn't and didn't want to appear as such. I just wasn't ready to open up.

Also, what if some of the weird stuff slipped out? I was sure most people didn't get confused if their dreams were reality and vice versa, especially if they had them about little people with wings and stuff. Heck, they'd probably fire me or think I was crazy or something. That would be the wrong start here, and I wanted them to like me and I wanted to keep my job. This was like a new me, really.

Before, back in Lackawanna County, I was quiet and reserved. I wouldn't have cared if my manager Lloyd and his wife Sue liked me or not. Oddly, it was because I never had a family or anyone really to say I was a part of that family, team, club, tribe or whatever. It was only me and I just tried to survive in a world where everyone had a set they belonged to. I guess it was that here people put me in a set, my grandmother's set or with Andi. People knew us, or they knew her, and were accepting me because of her or her memory, and for the first time I had somewhere to belong and it felt strangely right. If someone had told me I would be living in this fancy house and working at a library, me, the girl who doesn't like to read, I would have laughed in their face. The truth is, I felt comfortable there and I was getting the job. I mean, I wasn't as good at it as Sue, but that was to be expected. I could do it on my own, though, enough that they felt comfortable going over to assist the group of men that came in from the prison for the adult literacy afternoon program. I was the only one up at the desk and it was going fine, I thought, as I handed the little girl the bowl of stickers for her to pick the one she liked best from as I finished out her rental. I left at 1 pm and was so happy with my positive experience at work that I accidently made a right onto Hwy 78 instead of staying straight on Conyers as it changes into Main Street, and then I should have made a left at Broad Street.

Oh well, I had nothing else to do anyhow; I might as well learn my way around. I found another Kroger shopping center that had a gas station and an Applebee's, so I fueled up and parked. Boy, all they seemed to do around here was go grocery shopping. I had never in my life seen so many grocery stores. There didn't even seem to be enough people here to keep all these grocery stores running. How could there possibly be enough demand for the three Kroger's and The Ingles I had seen in not even a five-mile radius? *This place is so weird.* I sat down at a small booth that was designed for only a couple and placed my foot up on the seat. I ate my oriental chicken salad and amused myself by ordering a sweet tea, laughing with my thoughts of *When in Rome... do as the Romans do.* I have to say, though, the iced tea in the south was famous for a reason, and it was far better than the 4C iced tea mix I used to buy back home. I read somewhere that they actually brew it like hot tea, even in the restaurants down here. Maybe I would learn these southern secrets. I'd like to, especially since I'd be living here for a while, at least a year. Plus, it was no exaggeration, it was really good. It was better for you than drinking soda and it seemed to quench your thirst in the heat. I mean, I broke into a sweat just walking from my car to the Applebee's building; soda would just make you thirstier.

*

The weekend went by with no significance. Sunday at 11 am, I went to Mass for the first time at St. Oliver's. The familiar hymns and structure of Mass was a comfort to me as at least some things in Loganville are the same as back home. The congregation was small and surprisingly the priest was from Massachusetts; there was no hiding that accent. I always thought JFK had the best speaking voice. I'd thought so since I was a kid and I had researched that he was from Massachusetts. Usually, you don't hear the smoothed-out, refined accent from the region but my new priest came pretty close but he had to go through the seminary which is equivalent to getting a PhD, or doctorate in religion. I thought. Father Flanagan, he must be Irish, but no surprise as most people from that region were of Irish descent. Not too surprising he was from somewhere else, as most priests are relocated every so often by the archdiocese. I liked the structure of the Catholic Church, maybe it was because I had never really had any in my life, but I also thought it was good as it helps avoid the problems other denominations have with changing the meaning of the verses and stuff. It seemed like just about everyone and anyone opened a church up down here and they were all different. How could that be, and they were all teaching out of the same book? Some of them got weird too with snakes and asking everyone if they 'got saved.' I still wasn't sure what they were asking me when they asked that. I think it has to do with their belief that all you have to do is believe in Jesus and you go to Heaven, which is ridiculous, as any Catholic will tell you; even Satan himself believes in God and acknowledges Jesus. Well, to each their own; I just didn't like them approaching me. I agreed with Mrs. Vendor that religion and politics are your own business. She always said, "You go in that voting booth yourself and ya float up to St. Peter and stand at the gates by yourself attesting to your own soul, not those busybodies." Gosh, I missed her. Walking out of the church, lost in my thoughts, I bumped smack into a lady. She turned around and her eyes were smiling and kind. She said hello as I said excuse me. She had a pretty face and was about twenty years older than me but in good shape, she could easily wear my yoga pants. Behind her had to be the most attractive guy I had ever seen. I quickly looked away so as not to stare. He had brown hair unlike her blonde and had to be her son as he favored her face in some way. She was a little taller than my 5 foot 3 inches and came past his shoulder, so he was maybe 6 foot 1. He glanced me over in a tasteful way, enough to let me know he was checking me out but he was still respectful. It was as though he was paying me a compliment, which I'm sure I should have been offended by, as a strong, modern woman who doesn't need a man's approval. Somehow I really found his approval as he ran his eyes over my form very flattering. I felt embarrassed as he was with his mom and we were at church. He made eye contact and smiled and then his mom smiled at me. I looked both of them in the eye and said, "Sorry," and gave them my best smile and tried to casually walk back to my Subaru. I was a bundle of nerves because I knew he was watching me walk away. As I got into the driver's side and closed the door, he waved to me as they pulled past in a nice-looking black Jeep. I felt excited and conflicted between the hope of seeing him again the next Sunday and the fear of the results of that. I had never had a boyfriend; I had never had a real friend, to be honest. I had chatted with kids at school or at work but had never really had that bond and I wouldn't know what to do.

I guess my close friend was Mrs. Vendor, but she was more like an old aunt that looked after me than a friend. Now Rosa and Jade were my only friends so far and it's not like I had a deep bond with Rosa, and Jade was a cat. I smiled the whole way home and grabbed Jade when I got in and petted him as I told him about my day, my happy day. I tried to calm myself down as I didn't even know this guy; he could be a real turd, like the guys from the RaceTrac. I doubted it but I tried to reason myself to look at things logically instead of getting all excited with feelings. That's how girls get hurt. I saw it all the time on Lifetime. Well, my advantage was I already knew that nobody cared about me, so I had the edge over all those girls who grew up with everyone loving them and taking care of them, so no big surprise or let-down for me. It's just that I hoped that maybe someday I would find someone I could belong to, and I found myself angry for longing for some guy to love me. I told myself that's how you end up abused or pregnant or something that wasn't a great life. I scooped up my cat and went to bed, convinced I needed no one and that I was fine just as I had always been, by myself. Plus, I don't think you are supposed to be eager about going to church in the hopes that a guy will be there and you can see him again.

I worked half a day Monday and Tuesday at the library. Tuesday, around one in the afternoon when I got back home, there was a familiar sticky note on the glass of my oak door. Rosa! Knowing she left me a note made me smile. She left a number and said to call her when I got back. She invited me to the real thrift store, as she called it; tomorrow. She said be outside the front tomorrow at 7:30 am and have five dollars with me. I hung up and thought what could I buy with just five dollars and so early? Honestly, it seemed fun and I liked Rosa, so the curiosity and happiness of having someone to pal around with perked me up.

I made my way upstairs but had the strange sensation that I was not alone. I knew I was being ridiculous and more like a little kid in a big old house than the woman who lives there but I couldn't shake it. As I crept up the stairs, I slowed into caution as the hairs on the top of my arms rose up, matching my fear. I called for Jade in an attempt to normalize the moment or maybe to just not have to brace it alone. As I made my way to the top, I could see that all the doors were wide open and I was pretty sure that I had made a conscious effort to secure them all shut in the new habit I picked up as I left a room. I was pretty sure, with almost certainty, they were closed when I passed them on my way downstairs in the morning. I went through room by room and secured the doors shut behind me until I finally made it to my bedroom. As I confirmed it was empty, I felt myself relax a little, putting out of my mind that I hadn't checked the basement or attic. I said, with a serious effort to convince myself that I was getting all worked up over nothing and would be wasting my time and life, "Checking for what... spooks?" and went into the bathroom and took a long, hot shower instead. I put on my sleep yoga pants and tee shirt and got in bed, deep under the covers in a warm cocoon and turned on the T.V. to put it out of my mind. If they hadn't killed me yet, I thought to myself, they most likely weren't going to, but one thing was for certain: I couldn't let this drive me. I had to get a hold of myself and these feelings. It was no good to be walking around afraid in my own house, and I drifted off to sleep.

Chapter Eleven

A Day with Rosa

She was waiting in her driveway in a brand new Cadillac sedan; she waved when she saw me. I got into the passenger side and thought it amusing that Rosa had it going on with her luxury ride. She said she preferred to drive with the air-conditioning on instead of having the windows down and confirmed with me if that was all right. She had such good manners, like the people back home. Being with her made me think that if she and my grandmother were friends that my grandmother must have been like her too, and I was proud. She told me I was spending too much at that other thrift store in Loganville, which was a good store and she finds good stuff in there herself, but she wanted to show me the 'good place,' which she said with a smirk and popping her eyeballs out at me, making me chuckle. I was just happy to ride along with her. She said she'd like it if we caught a bite to eat afterwards too, which made me happy as all I had had to eat so far was a cup of coffee and a croissant, which I didn't want to eat as I wasn't really awake yet, but I had learned to eat when you can because you never know. We chatted pleasantly as we drove down Grayson Hwy 20 together. She nodded in amusement at my acknowledgement that the roads all changed their name after a while. She said, "Yep, Georgia roads are like her weather, wait a minute and it'll change," and she let out a cackle laugh at her own comment.

As we pulled in a side road in between a big fancy government building and a QuikTrip, the 'good place' sat in the back of a Latino shopping center. Almost all of the stores were in Spanish except Dollar General and the Metro Thrift. A big sign in both Spanish and English read, *Wednesday .25c Everything!* I asked Rosa if everything in the store was really twenty-five cents and she nodded with a smile. Wow! The store was big and it was packed. We were greeted with "Hola!" from a lady sitting at the door checking everyone as they left the store with their bags. I asked Rosa if there was really a shoplifting problem, my goodness, with everything being so cheap. She told me she was surprised too, but it was true. The main problem was two ladies from Ghana who loaded up two or three carts of stuff and then resold it online. At first, they started out like any other business: you buy the product for as cheap as you can get it and then market it for the most that you can get for it, but they got greedy and started stuffing shirts inside pocketbooks and the like. I was trying to listen but my mind was still trying to digest an online thrift store and I couldn't believe it. Well, why not! I guess it was like a newspaper ad or Craigslist but a website. "Maria," as she pointed to the big woman behind the counter, "had them thrown out a couple times but they kept finding a way back so that finally she just warned them verbally to behave, and oh it was a scene! We talked about that conversation at bingo for three weeks. The screaming and yelling between them, it went on, and on. Finally, Maria said okay, but she was calling the police next time they did it." We talked as we walked leisurely down the aisles. I found a couple sweaters and a pair of jeans for a total of .75 cents. They were cute too, and name brand, Old Navy! I couldn't believe it.

Rosa and I made our way toward her car and drove down the street about a minute before she pulled into the Peachtree Café. It was so tiny and sat next to the GOP building. It was yellowish in color, old-looking rectangle single-story, but I was happy it was a diner, as it was the kind of food I was used to as it reminded me of being back home. They seemed like New Yorkers, another surprise, and Puerto Rican. The hostess was friendly and took our drink order and had them out to us before our waitress took our order. They were very fast, as you would expect city people to be. I said, "Rosa, you must like Yankees. I thought you were supposed to hate Yankees and our Yankee ways," I giggled.

"Actually, my best friend, your grandma, was a Yankee, and she had more sense than anybody," she said. "Waffle House was okay, but never quite the same as a good diner for your grandma and with the quality homecookin' and the servin' ya'll get can't be beat," Rosa added.

After I wolfed down my order of French toast and a side of turkey bacon, we just sat and chatted away over coffee. She commented on my hair, how it looked darker since last time and asked if I had dyed it. I noticed my reflection in the light and off the sugar canister and said, "Really, no I haven't. It must be all the stress of the move and me just getting older. I think most people's gets darker as they age," thinking of a lot of children who are blonde but not too many adults are.

"Huh," she chuckled and said, "mine ain't, it just turned white," and we laughed. She went on, "Yep, it sure did get lighter, just not the way I liked it to." She laughed. We had a good time and she dropped me off back at the house and went on to her bingo. I felt light and filled with the good time we shared.

Just as I could no longer see the tail end of Rosa's car and I had one foot up on my porch step, I heard "Haaay" from behind me. I looked. A middle-aged white woman looked eye level at my face. She continued with, "How 'r-uh yewoo?" in her deep Loganville twang of friendliness. I replied with "Hi" and a smile. I had closed the gate behind me and was on the first step and you could tell she was itching for any sign of approval from me that she could reopen it. I turned around to face her. "Yes, can I help you?"

She smiled and made eye contact with her big brown smiling disk of eyes, which reminded me of those Japanese anime characters drawn with the little faces and exaggerated eyes. "Oh haaay. You must be the new neighbor! I just wanted to come over and welcome y...eew," she said. "I'm Barbara and I live a... cross da street there," and she pointed to the yellow Victorian ranch. "I can't begin to tell y... eew how niiiiice it is to have a young new face to say hi to," she went on. "That old woman that used to live here, well, I don't think she was Christian," said Barbara with a clear disdain placed through her words.

"Oh, you mean my grandmother. Yeah, she passed away," I said casually. I turned my back to her as I said, "I'll be seeing ya," and walked into the house and deliberately closed the door behind me with a hard shut. I giggled to myself as I peeked through the lace curtains in the living room to see if she was gone. She stood there looking at where I had stood a moment before for a brief second then she composed her surprised face into a plain scowl. She turned and faced the street, crossed and I watched until she walked into her house. I knew I had continued the 'bad blood' between her and my grandmother, but I wasn't sure that anything could be done about that. This place was so confusing and the people here were as strange as its happenings. I was uneasy because I felt compelled to defend my grandmother, yet I didn't know her. Barbara actually may have. That, for one, really bothered me. Number two, isn't it someone's words and actions that let you know how someone is? You get to know someone and you learn about them and you can kind of tell if they believe in God by how they act, not this *What's your name? Are you saved?* crap. Oh, that woman! Well, if I was anything like my grandma, I could see why they didn't get along, that's for sure. How nosy, and the nerve coming here and insulting her!

What a day! I made myself some hazelnut coffee with extra cream and curled up in my kitchen bench at the table, with Jade peering at me from the opposite chair. Sometimes I thought that young cat was a human trapped inside a furry cat body. I didn't know, as I didn't have much experience with pets, but it was kind of cool and weird at the same time that he liked hanging out with me. I told him about my encounter with the neighbor. I played it cool as I was conditioned not to really talk about personal stuff outside. Actually, no one where I was from did, and I was even more private from my background. This was even stranger since most people in Avoca knew everybody else, and they knew them since they were born. I thought it was silly of that old woman to come over here assuming I was Christian in the first place; not that being Christian was a bad thing, but how can you assume what anyone is in the United States, let alone to start talking about it before you even ask my name? Plus, even if she wasn't talking about my grandma, I wouldn't like her talking negative about someone. I mean, gosh, my first introduction to you is you talking bad about someone. Guess St. Mary's did influence me after all, but they never taught to judge people and speak badly about them if they weren't religious. Plus, we didn't say Christian, we said Catholic. I wondered if there was really a difference. So far, there didn't seem to be. I thought you were supposed to try to get them to come to Mass with you or something if they weren't raised religious, not talk bad about them not being so. Aren't all Catholics Christian? I mean, my grandmother did go to church every Sunday, right? I guess it was that she wasn't exactly what Barbara was, so she must have been bad in her mind. More things to learn, I guess.

Now I was dying of curiosity as to what happened between Barbara and my grandmother to cause her to assume she wasn't a

Christian. Maybe Rosa would know. I bet she did and I couldn't wait to ask her. I felt like a schoolgirl waiting to hear the latest gossip on the playground. I didn't want to get too excited, logically trying to guide myself as it really didn't seem like it would take much to offend Barbara or at least get crossed off of her good graces. Even so it was a story I wanted to hear.

The next day, I found Rosa in the garden, humming and weeding. I brought out two glasses of sweet tea from the gallon of Mayfield I had purchased from the Dollar General and sat with Rosa for the longest time, soaking up all the dirt about our neighbor. Apparently my grandmother had refused to say that 'she was saved' and Barbara swore it was the devil that had a hold of her tongue. Then a series of events caused Barbara to believe it was the devil's doing, such as an influx of cats that kept sleeping on her car, and the day of her and my grandmother's big argument, Barbara's car wouldn't start. Then, a tree fell on Barbara's house and when my grandmother ran across the street to see if she was all right, Barbara accused her of 'admiring her handiwork.' I just kept listening to Rosa in disbelief.

I mean, this was a grown woman saying these things and acting this way. I had never heard such nonsense, well, not since they taught us about the Salem witch trials in middle school. I mean, cats usually have a bunch of kittens at once, and how could she have caused a car to stall or a tree to fall? That was crazy. I was thankful that I asked and would try to avoid Barbara; it was very unfortunate that she was so confused about my grandmother. I mean, I didn't know her to logically defend her. I mean, I would as she was my family, but even if she wasn't, who thinks that way today, in modern times? Like, did she believe my grandmother was so bad that she couldn't be redeemed by conversation, that she had to be avoided, or some evil would come upon her? *Wow, well, happy to know I am the descendant of so much power*, I thought sarcastically. Rosa could tell I was brooding in my thoughts and said, "Don't pay her no mind. Your grandmother didn't," and smiled her Rosa smile and patted my hands that were folded on the table between us. We just sat there for a while enjoying our sweet tea and our spot in between the two gardens. Pretty soon, the Georgia sun grew too unbearable and Rosa and I parted our ways into our houses. Back inside, I found the solace of my bathroom offered me no peace from Barbara's comments. I was fearful at the realization that maybe I was just as bad as she was for disliking her because she thought different than I did. I took in a deep breath as I was removing my clothes and just looked around at my beautiful bathroom, taking in every object and visual until I felt the anger leave me. Rosa was right; my grandmother was really a cool old lady and she had enough sense to know where these comments were coming from and not to let them bother her. I played the part pretty well of being tough but inside I wished I was more like her and strong. I mean, I didn't even know this woman Barbara, and in five seconds she had enough power over me to ruin my whole day, with just some words. Funny thing was, I knew Barbara was wrong. I mean, she was basing her hatred and judgment on something that wasn't even true. That was ridiculous really, and in knowing this, I still got angry. It was me that had the problem; I mean, who gets mad at crazy people? After all, Rosa said my grandmother didn't care, so why was I ruining my day over it?

As the thought left me, I looked up at the reflection in the mirror and saw my face change by the big bright smile that grew across my face. I was startled for a moment as I almost didn't recognize myself. My hair was red! I mean, a true red and thick and full, shaping my face as it hung past my shoulders and down my back. Had it gotten longer too? I had never realized how pretty I was when I smiled. Jeez, I looked unlike myself but yet it was me. I looked better, healthier. I guess Topps really did a number on my looks and I hadn't realized until I left. I guess I just needed to get away from the factory, because I looked great! Huh, I'd heard that sometimes just a change of scenery does wonders for a person. I guess it's true. I really was so fortunate to have this opportunity and

I was being silly for not appreciating it and letting that woman's comments affect me, thank goodness for Rosa. I really was thankful that although I hadn't had a mother, I had always had a wise woman in my life to kind of nudge me along. Even though I didn't have Mrs. Vendor very long, and I barely knew Rosa, they were there enough when I really needed them and brought some guidance and comfort to me. Guess life is like that; it may not be the way you want it all the time, but somehow you get it when you need it and you can just keep on going.

Chapter Twelve

Georgia Gwinnett College

The next two months of summer just went by like that, slow and pleasant. I enjoyed my work at the library and my Wednesdays with Rosa. Before I knew it, it was time to start school. My first day at G.G.C., I was up at 5 am! My class didn't start until eight but my nerves had me all wound up and eager to begin class. I almost didn't believe it; the whole drive down Highway 20 until I hit downtown Lawrenceville was a blur of doubt. It wasn't until I found my class on the first floor of a rectangular building past the Starbucks I got a latte and a muffin from, that it set in that I was here; I was really at a campus. That college was happening for me; I just hoped that I wouldn't screw it up. *It's okay, I'll just be quiet and pay attention and it should be good.* I mean, I wasn't dumb and once I got it, I got it… it was just a matter of getting it, but lots of people went to school, so why was I different? I tried to reassure myself with a small pep talk.

I had cash but some girl with a nose ring insisted I check my student account and dragged me upstairs, had my picture taken and she handed me a card, which she took behind the counter where the register was at the Starbucks and swiped. Apparently she was a senior there and worked part-time at the Starbucks and was dating the guy who just started at the student ID office. Well, it worked out for me. I had one hundred dollars in claw card cash, that had to be used by the end of the semester or I lost it. I probably would have found out about it too late and not have had enough time to use it, so I thanked her and her boyfriend and they assured me that the school was really bad about telling new students it is automatically applied from their tuition. She swore it was a big conspiracy to make money for the school and we had a laugh before I made my way to my first class. More so than for the free coffee, well, I still paid for it but didn't have to that day. I was grateful for the laugh, as my nerves eased up a bit as I pushed open the door to the classroom. I was thankful I wore my sweater from Rosa's thrift store, as it was freezing in the big open room and just about everyone in the class had on a hoodie.

A middle-aged man came into the room wearing a tweed business coat and loafers. *He must be the professor.* Sure enough, he wrote his name and Psychology 101 on the board in erasable marker. Gosh, we had chalk at St. Mary's. Had it been that long since I went to school? The intimidation began to creep back and I felt my hands start to get all clammy. Just then, the professor made his way down my row and handed me the course syllabus and flashed me an easy smile, which kind of helped. I looked over what we would be doing and what was expected of me for the course. Wow, everything that I had to do was listed and how much it was worth toward my grade. I really liked that, as I felt like I knew what was expected of me and it was given to me way ahead of time so I could start working on it before it was due to make sure I got it right.

Maybe this would be okay. I sat back in my chair and thought that maybe I could do this. Listening to the lecture was really interesting and there was no homework; just read and make sure that I understood the material, which I intended to do anyway. I felt super excited and happy for the first time in a while. The next class was College Algebra, which wasn't too terrible, but I definitely would have to do a lot of homework, after that Art and then History from the beginning to 1500. I didn't have class again until Wednesday and I didn't know how to tell Rosa I'd have to miss our date, at least until after this semester was over. Andi had made this schedule for me but next semester I would pick my own classes and times. Maybe I could find classes after our day or on another day, who knows? It was all new to me. I was surprised how friendly everyone was at G.G.C. and how the classes seemed doable. I was so scared that I would fail, but after seeing all the other students, I began to think, well, they're doing it somehow. All of them can't be that much smarter than me. I was determined to pass at least and hopefully do well. Who knows? Maybe I'd learn something.

I got home and ate an English muffin with butter and grape jam and read my psychology book at the island in my kitchen. Surprisingly, it was interesting and I didn't have as hard of a time as I thought I would with the reading. When I had first seen the book, I thought, my gosh, how would I read all of that? It looked really big and like too much reading. This was especially true for me, since I was never a big reader. Well, look at me now, working at the library of all places and reading big textbooks for school. College Algebra wasn't as easy and I ended up having to go to the math lab after every class to get my homework done. One weekend, I went to the lab on Saturday and got one chapter ahead and got my homework done for that class too and was able to read the next chapter and have the math lab tutor explain to me how to do the problem, so that when I got to class on Monday, I was prepared. This was the first time I ever remember enjoying a math class, I mean, ever in my life. So I learned the trick: to be one assignment ahead and read before the class, and it was smooth sailing after that.

*

My first semester flew by and before I knew it, I was starting my second term. I ended my first semester with three As and a B in College Algebra, which I was totally fine with as it seemed like that was the best I could do with working and taking other classes. Heck, for someone who dropped out of high school and got a G.E.D., it was fine. Actually, it felt pretty good because until that point I wasn't really certain that I could do it. I had my doubts that I could even get into a college, let alone pass. Here, I got high marks. I started to think of that cliché saying: *Ya never know what you can do until you try.* Well, I guess that's right. I figured out how to register for classes on my own in Banner, G.G.C.'s chosen software. I just had to meet with an advisor each semester to make sure I was taking the right classes for my program, which was Business Administration. My advisor was a chubby, middle-aged woman who seemed nice but preoccupied. We met for about five minutes and she said it wasn't until junior or senior year that it gets more particular, as right now or for my first four years everyone pretty much had to take the same courses, regardless of their major. It wasn't until after you complete the first two years, they call 'core' or your core classes, that you got specific to your degree. At that point of our meeting, she pointed to area F and the Program of Study area on my required classes form to indicate what she was referring to. She said there was no order but I had to take all the classes in this category first and to just take them at my preference at the best times for my schedule.

I liked that she printed off the form for me, so I could just check off what classes I had taken already and then just register for the ones I hadn't taken yet until I graduate. It seemed pretty straightforward and there was a level of control I felt I had over my course in my life. Now I had to take English 101 and Itec, which was some sort of computer class, the second History which was the period from 1500 to the present day, and World Religions. It seemed interesting and moving at a faster pace than I expected, as I thought it would be boring and drag on. I was surprised at how fast time seemed to be going by. It was the winter already and I was on Christmas break from school. I thought of what Mrs. Vendor had told me once: "It seems like you wait most of your life just to get to the age of eighteen, then you're not a kid anymore. Then it's to be twenty, so you're not a teenager anymore. Then it's twenty-one, so you're legally an adult," she said with a wink. "But we know it's so ya can go out and have a beer with your friends. Then after that it flies by to thirty, then fifty. Before you know it, you're dead." I guess it does seem to go by faster when you get older. I'd been really busy too, where as a kid I just walked around the neighborhood with not much to do. At work, I had a tendency, well, at least at Topps, to watch the clock until lunch. Then watch it until it was time to go home. At the library, not so much, as surprisingly the pace was much slower, but it seemed to go by much faster. I wasn't sure how that made sense, but it felt true.

I decided to stop at the Big Lots store on Hwy 78 in Snellville to buy some Christmas items. It was weird that I was only five, maybe six minutes from my house and was in another town. *I may never get used to the way they do things down here*, I thought to myself. I had found my grandmother's Christmas tree in the basement and decided to put it up and celebrate this year, even if it was just Jade and I. I guess they had got me all excited about it at St. Oliver's and it felt right. I thought I should commit to some traditions and decide now what I wanted to do with my life and how I would celebrate and which holidays. Of course, all of my grandmother's Christmas decorations were blue and silver, which I had never seen before.

Just about everyone back in Lackawanna County used the traditional red, white and green for the holidays. Blue and silver were usually for New Year's Eve, but even then, a lot of people implemented red in the décor too.

Inside, the store was packed with people in a craze for their last-minute Christmas items for their loved ones, and the shelves were overstocked with everything you could think of. I ended up picking up a pair of slippers I thought Rosa would like and a small gift bag for them. I also found a can of cat treats for Jade. None of the decorations looked as good as Grandma's so I ended up not getting anything but the small gifts I picked up for my new friends I had made in my new home. I decided as I was waiting in line to check out that Grandma's ornaments were beautiful and made of good quality and materials. Why shouldn't I use them? After all, they were mine now. Wasn't that what was traditionally done with ornaments? They were passed down to the next generation. Finally, I was part of that tradition and I almost messed it up by not appreciating it because they weren't the norm. Well, what was normal? Why did I have to do everything the way everyone else did? I realized right in that moment that the only reason was because it was a habit I picked up long ago to fit in. To try to blend so no one would start asking questions about me and my family or why I didn't have one. To just look at me and assume I was like them, like everybody else and that I belonged. I realized I had never really thought about me, or what I liked or wanted. I was too busy playing the game to really figure out who I was or was supposed to be, if you believe in all that destiny stuff Mrs. Vendor did. Potential, she sometimes called it. She always seemed interested in trying to figure out who I was or what I thought and why. I really should try to think about those things, 'go find myself' as they say, before I ended up as one of those middle-aged people who never give much thought to themselves and wake up with one of those mid-life crises. Too bad she didn't have more time with me, but I was thankful I could at least see what she was talking about now, even if I was too young to before. I found myself pushing the button of a Christmas Plush Snoopy that danced to the *Peanuts* theme song. I was lost in a happy memory of watching the show one holiday when just in that moment a friendly face peered right into mine. "Well, hello there!" It was that mom of the really cute guy from St. Oliver's. "I'm Ann, we met at St. Oliver's, remember? This is my son, Derrick."

Just as she said it, his handsome face turned around and said, "Hi."

I immediately matched his smile and said, "Aurora, but everybody calls me Rose."

"Derrick and I were just going to walk over to Provino's to grab something to eat, do you want to join us?"

He chimed in while looking into my eyes with an intent and sparkle of a gleam off his blue-green eyes with, "Yeah, you should come. Have you ever eaten there?" I said no. "Oh, you have to try it. It's so good, right, Mom?"

"Oh, it's our favorite," she replied convincingly. They had such a presence and amount of friendly charm between them that before I knew it, I had paid my surprisingly reasonable five dollars and twenty five cents to the Big Lots clerk and the three of us were on the sidewalk of the shopping center that led to the restaurant. Surprisingly, I felt really comfortable with them, even though I really didn't know them and had only met them briefly that one time.

Once inside, a hostess led us through the dark and intimate atmosphere to a back corner table. Ann ordered a Coke and Derrick and I ordered sweet teas. Just as they arrived, Ann's phone buzzed and she excused herself from the table, only to come back and make her excuses to us that she had to go. She apologized to me and promised to make it up to me. I assured her it was fine. "I would hate to ruin this for Derrick. Why don't you two finish and if it wouldn't be too much trouble, could you drop him off at the house when y'all are done? I would really appreciate it. Here, let me buy you dinner since I caused all this trouble," and she handed Derrick a fifty-dollar bill. "That should cover it, son."

I said, "No trouble. Okay," with a smile. Derrick and his mom were both smiling so big at each other and then back at me.

He looked at me. "Sorry about that." I assured him it was no trouble and I was happy to be invited to dinner with them and totally understood; things come up that aren't planned for sometimes. "You're really nice," he said. He asked if I lived around there and he told me he lived in the neighborhood behind St. Oliver's. We talked and talked. I felt so comfortable with him; he was really easy to talk to. I was still conditioned to guard myself so I didn't reveal much of anything to him other than that I worked at the library and went to G.G.C., nothing personal. For me, that was a lot. On the shows I watched on ID TV, the girl always told too much and ended up with a guy she couldn't get rid of, and eventually dead in an alley somewhere. Derrick gave off such good vibes, though, but that's how they do it. I mean, who would go into Jeffrey Dahmer's apartment with him if they knew he was going to kill and then eat them? No one. He had to be pretty charming to convince them to trust him. Well, this guy seemed okay so far. He hung out with his mom for goodness' sake, and we were in public. His easy smile and deep eyes that seemed so interested in me made me want to give more. I knew from my psychology class that I was particularly suitable to guys who were more driven and aggressive in their interest, as I never really had anyone care about me, where most girls had a parent to give them that. I had to be careful or the first guy who came along and was nice or paid me any attention, I'd lose it to. Looking at Derrick, it would be so easy to lose myself into anything he wanted. Gosh, I surprised myself as I had never really been attracted to a guy before. I mean, I had messed around with a couple guys from the neighborhood and even went out to play pool a couple times with the accountant at Topps, but I had never felt this tingle. Like a little spark of excitement that they were interested in me.

Looking back at my experience with the guys back home, it seemed drab and dreary. To go out to go out and just-passing-the-time kind of dates to see what would happen as time went on instead of any real kind of attraction or interest in one another. But this wasn't a date; this was a coincidence, I told myself. A chance meeting, yet it felt so right. Like we had been old friends for a long time already, and I had just learned his name less than an hour ago. He seemed so interested in me and everything about me. I couldn't take my eyes off of him; I even found myself admiring his square masculine hands as he put down his cup of sweet tea on the table. I was so thankful for the distraction of bread and salad, as I needed a distraction. I was pretty sure I was doing a good job of hiding my feelings from him, as I knew enough to not let on how much I was starting to enjoy all the attention he was giving me, and I wasn't sure if he was a good guy or not. I mean, I was new here and had been through a lot; plus, if he was bad, would I be able to get rid of him? This was how girls got into trouble and I had no one to confide in, no big sister, mother or friend. Jade was no help; he couldn't speak English. I excused myself for the ladies' room and almost gave away my feelings as he stood as I rose to leave the booth. I had never had a guy make me feel like a lady before, and he was doing it. Heck, I had never had anyone make me feel like I was of any sort of significance. At Topps, I was the manager, so you would think I was used to feeling important, but the Lackawanna attitude is pretty casual and straightforward. Most people there were hardworking, blue collar and the descendants of coal miners. This treatment was a little bit more refined. I almost felt uncomfortable, but I liked it way too much, especially from him.

My nerves from my experience so far allowed me to actually use the restroom and I then just took a breather and allowed the cool water to wash over my hands and wrists in an attempt to recollect myself. I found my lotion in my purse and lathered up in case he touched my hand; I wanted it to be soft. Oh, my gosh, what was I doing? I was in no position to have a boyfriend, or worse, a guy who was really interested. I wasn't ready for all these feelings; plus, it was dangerous to be living alone and having men I didn't really know coming around. But God help me, I wanted him to; I just wasn't sure about what all that entailed.

The rest of dinner went well, really well actually. I found out he used to go to G.G.C. as well, but he transferred to U.G.A., and he paused to say "Go dawgs!" He looked at me like I was crazy when I didn't know what he was talking about. Apparently you had to be dead and under a rock to live around here and not know who the Georgia Bulldogs were. Here, he got out more information from me, as he concluded I wasn't from Loganville. He told me he was also a business major but said U.G.A. was a better school and that he did his core at G.G.C. and transferred out to save money, it was smart. He went on to explain that if he did at least two years or his last sixty credit hours at U.G.A., he was eligible to graduate from them, and a degree from U.G.A. was the pride of Georgia, even today, he said with an emphasis that brought on a chuckle, and I found myself at ease listening to his deep southern twang at the end of each word. What was wrong with me! I had to admit, though, his accent sounded attractive and educated; not at all what I thought about the south. I was really ignorant to have believed the stereotype about all the men down here, and I guess it was probably why I found it much more appealing now to see that I was wrong. Come to think of it, I had seen statues and flags of bulldogs wearing red jerseys all over the place, now I could relate. He told me the mascot's name was U.G.A., pronounced OOOHGUH. Cute, I thought, and momentarily admired the creative individual who gave U.G.A.'s mascot their moniker. He went on to say his father had graduated from U.G.A. and his grandfather, and hopefully soon, he would too. His dad worked for Lockheed Martin as a lawyer who wrote up the government contracts, and his mom was a manager at the Credit Union that was on base. I felt really stupid when I asked him what he meant when he said, 'on base.' He said, "No, you're fine. The Air Force Base in Marietta, it's about forty-five minutes from here. Lockheed Martin makes the planes for'em. It is a bit of pride around here, just like Coca-Cola, where I work, along with Delta." His tone changed a little bit as he leaned into the table and gazed into my eyes in a flirtatious glance as he said, "You've heard of Coca-Cola, right, Aurora?"

He chuckled as I said, smiling, "Of course."

He nodded with, "Just checking. Gosh," he said, "I was beginning to think Avoca was the boondocks in the pit of the earth." He laughed. I gently pushed his arm as he asked, "What about you? How about your parents?" I opened my mouth, trying to avoid a panic of having to reveal something about myself when I was saved by the bill, as the waitress came to our table and began asking Derrick about his dining experience. Whew! What would I even have said?

We walked toward my Subaru and I pointed to her as we approached. He commented on how clean I kept my car and sadly in a few short minutes he was directing me to turn right onto South Crestview Drive and then go around the turn toward the left. The road was a single-lane paved road that was surrounded by trees on both sides. We passed some entrance to a neighborhood on the right and he directed to keep going forward on the tiny road lined with trees on either side. Traveling the road made me feel like a kid again, driving on some dark path in a fairy tale, soon to encounter a werewolf or other villain at any moment. The trees seemed endless and so dark that I was unable to see anything further into the woods than the first row that lined the road. The scene was beautiful and mysterious, as anything could be hiding in there. We came to a four-way stop and I realized where we were. I was at the four-way stop that led to the tiny church I had mistaken for St. Oliver's my first day, trying to find my way around. I asked him what was down there, leaving out I had been there before in the hope he'd give me an honest assessment as a local.

"Old Raymond Hill. Oh, they say it's haunted," Derrick said.

"Why?" I asked.

"Sure enough, cause of what happened. Yep, way back when, right after the Civil War. You can go see graves from black soldiers who fought during the Civil War on both sides. Pretty cool, huh? I like old historic stuff. I like seeing a place and hearing about what it was like throughout time. Oh, yeah, you asked me something. Right, no, they say it's haunted and if it wasn't hallow ground on both sides, from the church and before it used to be a Native American site for their ceremonies. Yeah, sure was. Them got driven out, though, during the Trail of Tears. They all live up in Cherokee now, in North Georgia. So there was this preacher, Moses Ray. Not sure where the name Raymond Hill came from, no one told me that part, but Moses supposedly tried to stop a mob of men from raping one of the mothers of a boy he knew. They say Moses believed so much in what he was doing in that moment, in that the mob of men was wrong, and he was called on to defend that innocent that day that his very soul froze as an imprint and a testimony to his righteousness."

He said it with such charisma I thought I was on a haunted hay ride for a second, and in the full effect with the dark around us, creating the perfect atmosphere for him to tell the story. "They say every single one of those men from the mob was struck dead within a week of what they did, and Moses himself comes back now and again, a hauntin' us to remind us what comes to the wicked." I felt goosebumps go up my arm and trail down the back of my neck as he finished his legend of Raymond Hill and we drove over the little stone bridge that led into the Summit Chase community.

"Are you serious or are you just trying to scare me?" I asked with a smile. Derrick said he was, with a wicked smile that could have charmed the socks off a nun. He commented that just about everyone knew the story and he was just catching me up as he aught to.' He guided me to make a right at the stop sign onto Brooks Drive, then a right again onto Green Turf Road, past the Summit Chase Country Club sign. *Wow*, I thought, *this guy lives in one of those fancy country club neighborhoods*. He didn't seem stuck-up, though; he and his mom were both two of the most down-to-earth, caring people that I had met so far. He actually reminded me of the people from St. Mary's, now that I was giving my assessment some thought. He looked right into my eyes briefly as he directed me to pull over to the right in front of a white house that sat in front of the lake. It looked nice and well maintained. It had white shutters on the outside of the windows that were actually closed over some of the windows; it reminded me of an old farmhouse you would see in a movie about Savannah or the old south. It would seem almost ordinary if not for the details like the carved balusters and corbels. I could see the water moving in the background from a wide grassy path that led to the lake from the front walkway of the house. Then I noticed a small white statue of the Blessed Virgin, facing anyone who would come toward the house, an old guardian. I had seen so many of these statues in Avoca, but it was the first I had seen here in the south as there were not too many Catholics around here. It comforted me in some strange way to see her, standing in front of the giant tree that marked the entrance of the path to the water, with her arms spread and her hands in a feminine, motherly gesture angled down toward the ground. Like a blend of a saint and King Arthur's Lady of the Lake. Looking back at the house again, it seemed expensive but middle class all the same. He looked at me and said, "It seems like if you'll be here for a while, you'll be need'n' an official guide. You know, a local to fill you in on all the things you should know about these parts. I reckon I'll be need'n' your phone number to make those arrangements," and he shot me a charming grin. He held his phone and glanced at me with an intense look as he said, "Come on, let's have it." I found myself saying my phone number, and he had already input the digits into his phone and was closing the car door before it really sunk in that he had asked and been given my number. I heard my phone buzz and he smiled, saying that was him giving me his number. He leaned into the open window of the passenger side to inform me that he had had a nice time and told me to make a right at the stop sign then a left after

St. Oliver's and I would hit Athens Hwy at the next intersection. He yelled he would call me soon. I watched him make his way into the house and I made my way in the direction he told me to go in, trying not to have a dazed, happy expression on my face. He was so different than what I was used to. I didn't want it to show and hoped my face didn't give me away. Thank goodness it was dark. I was in a blur of excitement and in that moment I realized I had no idea where he had told me to go. Well, I thought, *what's the worst that will happen? I may drive around a bit and maybe even go out of my way but I have gas in my tank.* And I was pretty sure that I would find my way out of the neighborhood and make it to a gas station before I needed to refuel.

I drove home in a huge smile and bundle of nervousness as I realized how smooth he was in getting my number and how he had it in his phone before I realized what happened. I had such little experience and hoped with all my heart in that moment I wasn't being a fool. What if that was just him, how he was and he did this with all the girls? Ya know what, though, so what if I was being a fool? What was the worst that could happen? I thought to myself. I mean, we had a dinner; that was it. Plus, people get hurt, but somehow if I did end up getting hurt, how I felt in the moment would be almost worth the risk to explore the new excitement of this feeling, to find out what this was or could be. Normally, I would not even bother, and if I saw a guy again, so what? One thing was for sure, you definitely wouldn't find me all giddy over an easy smile, but somehow I felt Derrick's sincerity and genuine interest in me and it felt good. This guy had me falling for him over one dinner. Silly how I lapped up all the little attempts to let me know he was making an effort throughout the night. I smiled and was happy. Whether I was being stupid or not, I hoped he'd call me, and soon. I found myself snapping out of a happy daydream of thoughts about my evening as my tires pulled into my driveway. I hadn't even realized I'd made it home!

I made my way into the house and did a couple loads of laundry. As I sat at the kitchen table waiting for the drier to finish up with my last load of clothes, I heard a tap at the back door. What! I thought to myself in a startle. Who would be knocking, especially on the back door, as most people would come to the front, and at night? The only person who would be using the back door was Rosa and it wasn't likely to be her at this hour. I was afraid to go answer it, as if it was someone suspicious, I didn't know how to avoid them seeing me. The curiosity overtook my fear and I thought, *Well, I don't have to answer it, even if they see me. It's my choice if I answer the door or not, right?* I mean, there was no law that said you had to. It was only out of politeness that people did, and then what? I get raped and murdered because once I open the door and they see that I am alone they push their way in? No way. I worked myself up some courage and stayed against the washer and drier of the mud room as much as I could while peeking out the left side of the glass.

There was no one there but there was a bucket or barrel of some kind on the step and it was filled with something. I didn't dare open the door, not yet. I waited a good two minutes and then turned on the back porch light and waited again until I was sure I didn't see anyone before I quickly opened the door and grabbed the barrel of potatoes and brought it inside the house. I looked through it pretty well and it seemed to be okay; just a barrel of potatoes. There was no message, and to be honest, I was glad the secret visitor hadn't made themselves known as I was still spooked and it would have been awkward. Now after the fact and having some time to get over the initial shock and fearful possibilities, I was curious who left me this strange gift on my back doorstep and why.

Chapter Thirteen

Derrick

It was the next day that Derrick called and asked me to have lunch with him. He said he knew the perfect place to begin my official tour and campaign to educate my Yankee ways. He was so charming and spoke with such wit and humor, I was unable to say no to his request. Before I knew it, I was dressed and pulling into the very same RaceTrac gas station that led to my run-in with those bad guys a couple months back. I pulled up to the front and parked on the left, away from the entrance doors but still in view of the cashier at the counter. He flashed me the biggest smile as I pulled open the door handle and got into the black Jeep. He drove across the street, down the very same road I walked home from Vines Park from. No, he wasn't. He was, to my amazement, making a right into the Vines Park parking lot! He looked at me with excitement and a big smile as he reached into the back seat to retrieve a plastic bag that was full of things I couldn't make out, but I assumed was to be our lunch. "We're here," he said cheerfully. "Today, my dear, your education will begin with one of my all-time favorite places. I do hope you like it," he went on, with his elaborate gestures reminding me of a man of modern times playing the role of a gentleman from an earlier period.

He seemed amused he got my smile and acknowledgement of his performance. I teased him with my comment, "Business major my arse, you should major in drama." He made fun of the way Avocanians said ass and added a few more gestures before we arrived at the gates that indicated the entrance to Vines.

Here in the light of day, I took in the gleam that reflected off of her metal entrance. Much again, just like the first time, I was unable to deny her the acknowledgement of her splendor that her gates invoked, that could lead only to the desire of a passage through her entryway and on into the park. The word park really didn't describe Vines accurately. It was more like an entrance into a forgotten time, or a land from a storybook told to you as a child. It evoked all the feelings of wonder and the reality of being lost, even if for a moment off of a trail of a place away from our modern world as you passed beneath her gates you were somewhere else, somewhere beyond a day trip.

I wondered if I felt safe because it was the daytime or because Derrick was with me. It wasn't the right time to tell him of my chase by those boys or the dreams. Those may come up when we were having a more intimate or serious moment; here in the moment with Derrick was bliss. Vines Park was so beautiful. I merged over to his left and took a big helping of water from the old fountain. "Oh, now you've done it," he said in a voice a little louder than before. I couldn't tell if he was serious or not.

"What?" I asked.

"You drank from Vines. Well, you already have red hair, so I guess it won't matter much," he said peering at me from his profile stance.

"Derrick, what are you talking about?" I said, folding my arms and facing him.

"Oh, nothing... it's just that they say if you drink from the waters of Vines, your hair will turn red."

"And why is that?" I asked him.

"Some magical source where the water came from originally, but it's been built over for a while now," he said casually, as if there really was magic.

"Oh, is that so? So will I have powers now or something?" I taunted him with.

"Not sure, I've drank it as many folks have. This used to be some Native American spot of healing or something then they got chased off. There was a big stand-off and everything. Some say they never really left."

"What do you mean?" I asked. "Like they are ghosts or something?" in a questioning tone as I leaned closer toward him.

"Nawh, well, maybe; I'm not sure really how to talk about Vines or what to think. Just telling ya what we know about it, from a local perspective is all," he said, looking into my eyes with the clearest sincerity. "What I do know for sure is how it came to be what it is now. Gettin' its name and all. It wasn't always a park. I'm sure you know all this building around here, I mean, the whole area is somewhat new. Folks my parents' age and a 'lle younger can recall notin' but 'em trees for miles. I mean ya had to drive to get to the store and it was a ways. I remember even as a kid myself drivin' at night and it being pitch-black. The only light for the longest time would be comin' from my mom's car lights. That's just how it was 'round here and a lot of folks really liked the way that we lived. Some say they felt so strongly about the land that even when they passed on, they left part of that sentiment behind, right here in the soil!"

"Oh, come on now! Derrick. You almost had me carried away with your stories again, just like last night at the church," I exclaimed.

"No, really, Aurora," he went on in all seriousness. "Some guy and his wife bought the land and built that mansion on it and lived here until they passed away and then their family sold it to the county. The only condition was that the county couldn't change it or sell it again; it had to stay protected." I looked over to where he pointed and I didn't see how I could have missed it before, even if it was dark last time I was here. It was bright white and grand. It was held up by immense white columns in the front and had so many windows I couldn't possibly have counted them all if I had spent half the day trying. He could see the wonder in my face and he was happy he was able to share that with me. He winked at me and asked if I was enjoying my tour. I nodded and he put his arm out for me to hook mine into so he could guide me along the path that led deeper into Vines.

"Not many people know about this place, believe it or not, as it hasn't been open to the public for very long," he said as he paused to look up at a massive oak tree that had twines of vines interwoven all around its trunk and branches. I heard a racket of scratching and watched in amusement to see two squirrels at the root of all the noise. The base of the tree they were running around was brick-red, as were their coats.

I commented, "Wow, even the dirt here is red."

"Sure is, that there is Georgia Red Clay. It comes from the minerals in our soil, turns the earth red," he confirmed. He led us over the long white wooden bridge that allowed us to cross the narrow part of the lake of Vines. We walked through the Asian Garden, which had Asian-themed statues, and bamboo that offered foliage against the lake and enclosed the area. It had a red gazebo sitting area that was facing a rock garden, and small frog pond. There was a small bridge that led out and was crafted in the Asian-style architecture and led us past Japanese maples and elms. My favorite was the striking weeping tamukeyama, which appeared as though it really was sad and called to us to visit. We must not have been the only ones, as there was a small bench underneath it. We walked on until he led us up a hill past the white woods, which was really a row of white flowered bushes that lined both sides of a grass walking path. It ended at a picnic table in an open area that was surrounded by yellow brick walls and faced a life-sized statue of a boy who had horns and the legs of a goat. He was holding a bunch of grapes in one hand and a horn in the other and was smiling. Yep, Vines Park was just as strange in the daytime, with company. Derrick didn't seem to notice. He thought the place was great, and it was. It was just different than anywhere I had ever been before and my first introduction here, running and hiding from those assholes, wasn't the ideal. I guess it made more sense now that I knew this had been someone's home and it was taken 'as is' for the county to use as a park. I couldn't see the United States government's workers selecting mermaids and goat people as décor, paid for with the local tax dollars. Actually, it all seemed surreal as when you thought of Loganville, Georgia, mythical creatures didn't come to mind at all. I guess they did now. Just then Derrick handed me a hoagie, at which I exclaimed, "Hoagies!"

Derrick started laughing a big hearty laugh. "Do what?"

"I said hoagie, that's perfect! I haven't had one since I left home."

"I knew I'd done right when I ordered from a Yankee place," as he pointed to the brand logo on the bag that said Jersey Mike's Sandwiches.

"Well, I've never had 'em," I said, "but these are the kind of sandwiches you get where I'm from. They're called hoagies. If you go to the deli, you can also get them on rye or on a Kaiser bun." I bit into it and it was delicious, and I was glad because walking had built up a little bit of an appetite, not to mention my nerves from Mr. Gorgeous, my tour guide.

He asked, "Oh, is them the round ones with the seeds on top?"

I said, "Ahhhh," in agreement because I didn't want to stop eating to talk. He seemed pleased with his lunch selection, as I was clearly enjoying it. I had never had a guy try to impress me before, or make an effort to see that I got what I needed.

He handed me a bottle of Snapple Iced Tea. "Sorry, they didn't have sweet tea to go."

"No," I said, "this is the only kind of iced tea I knew about before I moved here." I could tell he was shocked by the look on his face.

"No sweet tea! Bet you're glad you're here, huh?" he said with a smile. I let out a contented "yeah" as I smiled and nodded, but I got the feeling he already knew how I felt, and was pretty sure, or I at least suspected he knew, that he had a lot to do with how I felt, or at least how I felt in that moment. I wasn't one to play head games or anything like that, but I didn't want to seem too eager was all I could say to myself, but the ease of his mannerisms eased my thoughts. We finished up our lunch and discarded all of our trash in the garbage bin at the entrance of the patio. Soon enough, we were side by side and strolling along, chatting and leisurely enjoying our day as it went on. He asked if he could take a picture of me next to the mermaids and I reluctantly agreed. I commented that he must be a pretty good photographer since the picture from his phone didn't look half bad. "You shouldn't be so hard on yourself, Aurora," he commented as he walked toward the roses.

"Why do you call me by my official name?" I asked.

He leant in to catch the smell of the bright pinkish-red roses that climbed up one of the columns of the entrance of the walkway as he said, "Well, roses are beautiful and all but just about everybody has seen 'em. Not you, Aurora. Nobody's seen you. You're different and I guess I want to be different to you too, so I want to call you something that not everybody does, if that's all right with you." My heart skipped a beat and froze at what he said. Lucky for me, he extended his hand in a friendly manner and said, "Come on, you're missing your tour." Thankful for his friendly distraction of the moment, for I was afraid I'd show that what he said to me had affected me.

As we walked past the human-like statues of the four ladies, he introduced them as 'the Guardians of Vines.' He said I resembled the Lady of the Fowl the most. I agreed but said I only recently got a pet. Then I told him about Jade and how he was the first pet

I had ever had. He assured me that just because I had never had a pet didn't mean I couldn't have an affinity toward animals. He went on to tell me, "You mustn't be a very good Catholic, as every Catholic knows St. Francis didn't start speaking to animals until he was grown, sure enough." I giggled at his comment and also at the elaborate way he spoke in his accent so different to mine, yet somehow I didn't want him to stop.

We came to the split in the road and I saw the tiny sign that welcomed visitors to the butterfly garden. He guided us left toward the whimsical garden, where I was so happy to see the giant troll emerging out of the ground, if only to verify that I wasn't crazy and that night did happen to me months ago. He led me through the children's maze and then past the small house that operated the miniature trains and waterfall. He led me back past the trains and through a patio of vines that had overgrown and formed a sort of roof over the verandas that covered our walk, until I saw the table I awoke from in my dream. It looked exactly how it did in my dream, but how was that possible? This would be the first time I had seen it in the light! It was there in that beautiful spot that could have very well been the backdrop for a romantic painting or love scene in a film. I told him I had been there before and what had happened. After I told him every detail, he just grabbed me and pulled me close to his chest. As I rested my head in the dip of his chest for a minute or so, enjoying the safe, warm feeling that came from the firm shape of his arms and his solid comfort, he said, "Don't you worry, I'm here now. They better hope I don't see 'em," he said in a tone that was way darker and more serious than he had revealed of himself before.

I appreciated his reassurance and kind of enjoyed the old-fashioned sort of way he swore to protect me, his female company, from harm. I definitely would have felt much better if he had been with me that night. I also didn't want to see him get hurt, especially because of me. Derrick seemed like a really nice guy and a good person. That group of guys wasn't good and seemed to enjoy just hurting people just because they had nothing else to do. I always hear people comment about there being really sick people in the world, and that was close enough to those kinds of people I want to get. Mrs. Vendor always said, "You've been through enough crap, Rose. Keep your nose clean and try to avoid trouble," and she was right. Sometimes trouble finds you, like that night for me, but for the most part, I tried to listen to her and her advice.

Derrick led us to the wooden tower and bleachers that were designed to overlook the trains when they were set up as a show for the local children. We continued on over a small stream and past the glass gazebo house and back onto the main path toward the parking lot. Before I knew it, we were at my car and he was telling me what a nice day he had had with me and thanked me for a great day. He told me his mom wanted me to come over for dinner, as she felt really bad for having to run out on us like that the other day at Provino's. Since he put it that way, I found it almost impossible to say no, and against the better judgment of my head, which was really mad at myself for allowing him to follow me back to my house to drop off my Subaru.

He had really good manners and I didn't have to ask him to wait outside; he automatically just turned off the engine and sat in his car until I approached his window. "Hey," he said with a smile as we made eye contact.

"I'll just be a minute," I told him. I took off in a dash as soon as I was safe inside and I knew he couldn't see me. I took the fastest cool shower that must have ever been recorded, careful not to get water on my hair or eyes so I didn't have to re-do my eyeliner and mascara. As I pat dried my face to go around my eyes, I ran a brush through my hair and scooped it back up into a loose bun off my face. Huh, maybe he was right; my hair was getting darker and it definitely looked redder. Well, it was winter and I was getting older. I heard stress can affect your hair too. Probably what it was, the stress of my first semester at college and the move here and everything. I rubbed in a light layer of Oil of Olay facial cream onto my forehead, around my mouth and neck. I threw on clean yoga pants, my long grey and black knee-length sweater dress and my pair of black Sketchers slip-on sneakers and was out the door. I ran back in and poured Jade some food, as I didn't know how long I would be out. I gave him a quick pet and told him to watch the house. To my amazement, he seemed to nod as an acknowledgement of his duties. I laughed and thought of how many people would take that coincidence as a sign the cat actually understood what I said to him. Just as I thought that, I heard a door slam from upstairs as I closed the main entrance one behind me. Drafty old house, I thought, as I skipped down the front steps toward Derrick's Jeep.

"Wow! You look great and you were super-fast," he said. I felt good at his acknowledgement of my efforts to be considerate, and I enjoyed that he liked my appearance too. He reassured me that he would call me before he just stopped by and that he could tell that I liked my privacy. I thanked him and we drove off toward Athens Hwy 78 en route to his house.

We pulled in between his and his neighbor's house to park outside the garage that seemed to be under the house. He used the garage door opener from his sun visor to let us into the house. He led us through a glass exterior door that separated the garage from a small basement recreation room. There was a pool table and an old leather sofa and coffee table, with a single end table against the wall that housed a lamp on the left side of the couch. We continued on through to a set of stairs that led us into the kitchen, where his mom greeted us with a big smile and hugs for us both. "Aaah, you made it," she said as she released him from his hug and made her way over to me. "It's going to be just the three of us tonight. Your father had to fly to D.C. on a last-minute business trip. I made fried chicken, biscuits and green bean casserole. I hope that's all right," she said as she pulled a large tray out of the oven.

"Mom, that sounds great," Derrick reassured her. I loved watching him as he was so respectful toward her. Well, actually they both seemed to treat each other the way I imagined people should when they cared about each other. I'd seen it on T.V., of course, in a sitcom of a family here and there, or in a few minute encounter with a family from St. Mary's. Just then I was almost knocked down and slobbered to death by a giant beige dog. I gently pushed him down as they both commanded in unison, "Toby, get down." Ann apologized by saying, "Sorry, honey, he's a rescue and we're still working out all the kinks," she followed with a laugh.

I said, "Oh, that's okay. He looks like that dog from *Annie*, the first movie from the eighties."

Derrick said, "Exactly! Oh, you see it too. Mom wasn't sure about him at first but I think she's coming around," and they both smiled at each other. Derrick went on about his dog for a minute, saying he would have actually named him Sandy, like in the film, but whoever turned him over to the animal shelter had already called him Toby, so they kept it to avoid confusion for the dog. They were even considerate of the dog's feelings, they were really nice people, I thought as I followed them both to the table in the kitchen. Ann was setting down some plates and napkins for us and Derrick was getting glasses from a cabinet over the counter behind us. Their ease and flow of their movements let me know this was their regular pattern they had included me in tonight. I had never had fried chicken before, except from Kentucky Fried Chicken, and it was so much better, I assumed because it wasn't fast food but homemade. The green bean casserole was a southern classic, I was informed, and it was amazing. The conversation kept going at the table and it felt really nice to eat with people for a change instead of the usual solo supper at home. I was determined to learn how to make this great meal and was sure the recipe was online, and if I really needed help there must be a YouTube video, I was sure. Ann would probably have shown me but I was too shy to ask, and the conversation took a pleasant flow of its own that I didn't want to change its course. I offered to help load up the dishwasher after we were finished with our meal, but I was scooted off to the basement for a game of pool with Derrick.

I had played pool enough after work so many times with the crew from Topps to not totally be terrible at the game, but Derrick clearly schooled me in the first match. "Ohhoho, where did our gentleman go?" I teased.

"Why, ma'am, he was certain his lady believed in equal rights and would be appalled at the thought of her gentleman acquaintance holding back due to his belief in his superior pool-playing ability," he taunted.

I played along in an attempt at a southern accent. "Well, sir, I do declare... I'll have to step up the game, indeed."

"Bring it, my lady," he smiled. He of course beat me again, but we had a lot of fun. After I excused myself to use the bathroom, I asked him to take me home as it was getting late.

Right in that moment, before I could even finish the sentence or close my mouth, he leaned in and kissed me. It was a fast, soft sweep-to-the-tongue kiss, intimate but quick so it seemed more natural and casual. I was glad actually, because if it had been any slower, I probably would have tried to avoid it. I felt the tingle and the happiness that he did it, but in my usual way I just brushed back a piece of hair behind my ear that had fallen out of my bun and flashed him a smile. I didn't say anything about it and neither did he. He just called up to his mom he was taking me home and that he'd be back. She acknowledged him with, "Love you. Drive safe, honey. Bye, Rose," which I called back, bye in response, as he closed the basement door behind us.

On the drive home, both of us just listened to the radio. That Justin Timberlake song came on from the movie *Trolls*, that was uber-popular and upbeat. Both of us just smiled and sat in silence on the way home. He pulled up to my house and I felt silly for forgetting to leave the front porch light on. I got out and he leaned over to the passenger side window to call after me, "I'll call you, 'night, Aurora." I said goodnight back and nervously walked into the house, because I knew he was watching me walk away. I was suddenly conscious of my walk, as I didn't want to walk like a robot or a guy, but it would look stupid if I shook my hips too much, so I ended up walking slower than usual and felt even more self-conscious at the thought of holding him up. I was happy he was cool about our kiss and didn't try to overdo it with a big slobbery goodbye kiss before I got out of the car. No, the way it happened was perfect and natural.

Being in a super positive mood still from the *Trolls* song helped me get into the house, and I turned around to wave him off as I closed my entrance door. I just stood there smiling for a few seconds before I scooped up Jade in a whirl and told him about my evening as I petted him. I threw him over my shoulder and we made our way upstairs to my bedroom to get ready for bed. After brushing my teeth, I just lay in bed for about forty-five minutes of excitement, too wound up to sleep. I was still not over my night with Derrick before I finally found something on T.V. to watch and distract my busy mind and emotions so I could drift off.

*

I felt a slight breeze on my face and opened my eyes from a very comfortable sleep to find I was sitting on the lawn in the middle of the patio area of the rose garden at Vines Park. I sat up in wonder right next to the life-sized lion statue. How did I get there? Did I come here last night because I was restless and couldn't sleep? I didn't remember. Fear suddenly crept over me as I knew I was off somehow and hoped it wasn't something serious but I wasn't sure who to talk to about it, but it was something I would have to think about later. Right now I needed to see if I had driven here or if I had to walk home. I suddenly thought of those guys and almost took off in a panic. I looked down and I was wearing clothes, thank goodness. I had on my go-to yoga pants and a light hoodie and my Sketchers. So I must have come here consciously, as most people in a daze or sleep walking don't stop to get dressed and put on a pair of shoes, but why couldn't I remember! The thought plagued me with an inner panic as I slid off of the stone ledge that surrounded the square of yellow bricks that encased some trees and the patch of grass that I found myself in. I looked back at the lion and, funny, I couldn't help but be happy to see him sitting there, so proudly watching all who would enter along that path that led to the rose garden. I really must be losing it to be having carefree moments in a garden when I should be wondering what was wrong with me that I didn't know what I was doing and had lapses now of time that I couldn't account for myself. Strange, though, I felt better and happier than I ever had, standing right there in the entrance of the garden, stronger and more of myself as though I had realized who I was. It must be the move, the stress of the move and a new place. That didn't really make any sense either, as I had been through a lot of crap in my short life and this was actually good. I mean, who would be crying about being handed their dreams? Look at me now: college, a house, and a really cool one at that. I had made friends, and the night before with Derrick was awesome. I really couldn't say I was stressed out. I mean, for the first time in my life I could say I was happy, I mean, really happy. I was on a path that was good. Not that being a manager in Avoca was bad; some people worked at the factory their whole life and never made manager. It was just as if I knew all that time that I was doing just that, buying time… waiting. I was basically handed all of my dreams out of the blue. Yeah, I had to leave my home and all that I knew, but that had secretly been my wish all along, I just didn't have the ability at the time to make it happen. No, this was something else and I wasn't sure who I should go to talk to about these strange occurrences.

Just as the thought left my mind, the red doe stepped proudly out of the surrounding thickets and onto the yellow stone path before me. I slowly followed her as she made her way down the path. She slowed and turned back to look at me and to my surprise she just held my gaze for a second then leapt into the statue of the Lady of the Fowl! What! She must have leapt behind and the bushes covered where she went. I raced ahead but before I could get there, a yellow light began to reflect off of the statue. It wasn't as bright as it was daylight still, but I could clearly see some kind of light shining out of it. A figure began to emerge; a lady I began to recognize as a feminine shape from the slender hand, then arm that ended with the flow of ruffles at the elbow. She was about my height and slender in build with flowing dark hair. She looked at me as she stepped out of the statue. She was maybe a ghost or a shape of pure light; I am not really sure how to describe her as she stepped down onto the bricks that led to where I was standing. As she approached, she began to change again! Her shape elongated and began to form into an animal: the deer! It was her, the doe who led me to safety that night the guys were chasing me. I owed her my gratitude and safety. "Thank you," I said as tears began to well up from my throat and drip out of the corners of my eyes as the emotion of the moment was too strong for me to contain inside.

She approached me and somehow I felt that she understood my appreciation as she nuzzled her head under my hand. I jumped back at the touch of her soft and thick fur; she was real! How could this be? I felt such a whirlwind of emotions that I wasn't sure if I was going to faint or pee myself. She stood in front of me as a real deer. What the heck was going on? Maybe there was glass or crystals or something that reflected off of the statue and I thought I saw a light; no, I knew what I saw, and I just didn't want to admit it. I slowly reached my hand up to her and allowed it to caress her soft coat from the top of her head down the slide of her back. I looked into her eyes and they were green like mine, not the brown you would expect. They seemed intimate and personal, almost knowing, like a person's eyes, and I stepped back in a gasp of recognition. She knelt down on her front knee and turned her head to look at me. What! This wasn't happening… "What do you want? You want me to get on?" I asked. I approached her slowly and mounted her gently by stepping my right leg over her side, and she stood up to my surprise with ease. She was much larger and stronger than I had assessed her to be, and she gently carried me over thickets in a quick and graceful leap. She seemed aware of my presence the whole time and kept a steady but swift gait. I was in disbelief as we traveled through Vines together like old friends. A deer who eventually allowed me to ride her; this was absurd and magical. She dashed through the entire park, leaping over bushes and streams until she finally slowed down and allowed me to get off, and we walked together side by side along the trail until she stopped to drink from the river. As she drank the water, her coat became a dark red until her fur was almost black. She turned to face me and her coat began to shine like a golden light and she began to walk toward me, but I had become afraid and slowly backed away from her. I heard at that moment a bunch of tiny voices exclaim, "No, she rejected the guardian." "No, no, Aurora," seemed to be coming from the bushes and all around me. I turned back to face where the doe had been and it was gone. I became sad as I glared in disbelief at the bush in the hope she would reappear. I looked up as a large bird, maybe a hawk, with what appeared to be a tiny rider of sorts clad in an acorn-shaped hat, soared above until they flew so high I could no longer see them in the cover of the treetops. I readjusted my gaze back toward the bush in the hope that the doe would return.

I walked toward it, and in a jump, I awoke and the television was still on, playing some infomercial marketing skin cream, showing people looking years younger after only one use. I glanced at the clock on the nightstand; two o'clock. I was soaking wet from sweat and so relieved to be in my bed, safe. I looked down at myself and, thank goodness, I was in my pajamas, and the relief to see my bare feet with the shiny neon green toenail polish gleaming from the darkness under my bedcovers. *Dang, what is with these dreams, and always at 2 am when I wake up?* I was going to need more than that psychology class to understand this. I made my way into the bathroom, and as I looked up after sitting down on the toilet, I made eye contact with Jade, who was sitting perfectly upright and facing me from the center of the doorway of the bathroom. *That's weird.* "What is it, Jade?" I asked. "You think that it's weird too, huh?" Not that I would know what was normal or weird since this was my first experience with a cat, or any animal really. Well, in real life anyways. To be honest, all of my encounters with animals seemed to be strange. I finished and washed my hands and got back into bed and tried to get at least four or so more hours of sleep for the day before my alarm clock woke me. Jade jumped up onto the bed and crept close to me before rounding himself up into a cozy ball next to my side. I closed my eyes and just relaxed my whole body, starting with my feet, and it was around my hands where I remember dozing off. I was able to ease back into sleep and, thankfully, had no more dreams of Vines Park or anything else that I remembered.

The next morning, I found a bouquet of purple flowers that were hand tied with string and left on top of my storm doors that led to my basement. It didn't make sense that it was Derrick, as I didn't see him with his big, masculine hands hand tying handpicked flowers. He was sweet but he would probably have bought them if he got me any; or if he were to hand pick them, it would most likely be spur of the moment, while we were walking, in a scoop-them-up kind of gesture, not this. Plus, he would leave them on the front porch, or my car, not out back. Strange! For some reason, the combination of the flowers and my dream led me to get the chills all over my body. It was almost as if someone was trying to tell me something... but who or what exactly? I had gone from being a normal girl to a weirdo in a matter of months, I thought to myself, as this was all too bizarre. Then in an action I couldn't explain, I pulled the handle of the storm door and it was locked. Whew! Well, at least that was in order. Still something told me there was more, and I looked down to see the flash of a white paper that was wedged in between the two massive metal doors that led down to my cellar. I almost jumped back when realizing it was there, as it was a confirmation that someone had been there last night. I was almost afraid to pick it up, but then curiosity overtook my caution. It read: *Happy to find you. You are one of three, come by my shop anytime.* It was signed *Namoi.* It had a Little Five Points address on the back of the card and the name of some crystal and gems shop. Great, I was being sought out by one of those new age crystals and fortunes people. Maybe it was intended for my grandmother, as I hadn't really met anyone, but that would seem even stranger. Huh, it had probably been left there by mistake. Yeah, most definitely the wrong house, I thought, but it didn't feel right to leave the bouquet outside, so I cut the stems and placed them in a glass of water on the kitchen table and tossed the card in the junk drawer.

Chapter Fourteen

New and Exciting

I awoke to my phone ringing; it was Derrick. After telling me what time it was, which I thought was too early at 8 am, he asked me to breakfast. He said he knew it was probably a little soon from last night but he wanted to see me. He assured me he had it covered, so since he was buying, it was a date, officially. He laughed and teased me, ending our call with something along the lines of how he wasn't certain how we did it up north with our Yankee ways, but since "I was asking and a pay'n', it was a date," he informed me to my amusement. I thought it may be too early in the morning for Derrick, as his personality was a lot to deal with in the afternoon. He was considerate enough to say he'd be there at 9 am, so that gave me plenty of time to shower and make myself look presentable, have a cup of coffee and feed Jade before he arrived to pick me up.

When he came to the door, I felt a pinch of happiness and said my goodbyes to Jade and was off. As we walked down my front steps, Rosa waved to us from her porch next door, so I said,

"Derrick, come meet Rosa, my neighbor." We walked to the front of her gate and I introduced them and Rosa gave me a wink as she glanced over him. She threw us a smile, a wave and we were off to the IHOP a couple of blocks over.

He asked me if I minded if we walked and enjoyed some of the beautiful weather with some fresh air and exercise. He quickly added that if I didn't want to, he could drive. "No worries; it's just so beautiful today." I told him I didn't mind the walk or the weather and it was true but may not have been had I not had that cup of coffee before he came. Talking with Derrick was so easy that we arrived at the IHOP in no time. The hostess seated us in a large booth in the back and we pretty much had the whole place to ourselves; there were only a couple of booths that were occupied by some elderly patrons. It was the perfect setting to sit and talk. I suddenly became a little nervous, mostly because I really liked Derrick, but I also wanted to talk about my dream and Vines Park, but it just didn't seem like the right time and I didn't want to just blurt it out. True to his word, Derrick paid for my plate of French toast and potatoes. We had to have been there at least two hours, as I know I had an hour's worth of coffee, where we talked about movies and books we liked. I really began to like who he was the more I spent time with him. I never had really gotten close enough to anyone to really like them. There were adults in my life who I thought were cool, a teacher or someone's mom I had encountered, a clerk I saw at the store. Mrs. Vendor didn't count, as I loved her and she was my caretaker. A few girls here and there that I saw often at work to laugh around with to make the time go by. No, Derrick was the first person who I wanted to share a little bit with and hoped to God he liked it. He was also the first guy that I noticed physically. I mean, I had noticed whether a guy was in shape before, if he took care of himself, if he was clean or worked out, but with Derrick, I really noticed. Strange little details too, like the amount of hair he had on his arms and chest that I could see peeking out over his undershirt from his unbuttoned shirt. He seemed very masculine and he always smelt good too. It was subtle, not like most guys who spray on half the can of AXE and take up all of your oxygen; no, Derrick smelt like black licorice and soap. I began to really enjoy it and welcome the scent when I would catch a faint linger of it mix with my air. He asked me as we walked toward my house if I was going to the Christmas dance at St. Oliver's that Saturday night. I didn't know about it but agreed to go with him. As we approached my driveway, we walked over toward his Jeep and just lingered in a slow, flirty way, saying with our bodies neither of us wanted to depart, but neither one of us seemed to want to ruin the nice time we had had with extended verbiage. "So I'll see you Saturday," he confirmed. "Pick you up at seven, all right?" he said, and he backed out of the driveway, giving me a quick wave that was almost a salute goodbye.

I loved that he was keeping it casual but at the same time kept reassuring me that he was interested. He chalked up his ways as his 'good southern breeding and manners,' but a lot of it was his thoughtful nature and his drive. Although it didn't show itself when you first met him, and you could easily be fooled by his relaxed demeanor; he really was a goal-oriented person. This was going really well. I really enjoyed spending time with him and would say he was the first friend I ever really had. Rosa and I were friends but it was different than getting to know someone your own age, and Derrick was way more intense as a person. Rosa was just a good lady and neighbor, but it wasn't the deep connection that Derrick and I were forming. I think Rosa just had a good sense of what she believed was the right way of doing things and the wrong way of doing things, and it just extended to how she treated people. She was just good to me as she would be to most people, and that made her easy to get along with because I appreciated her for that, her being my neighbor and having been a friend to my grandmother. With Derrick, I got the feeling it was because he liked me, and it just came out in the way he acted around me. He made me feel special and that he wanted to have more of me because he valued what I had to offer him. The thing was, I don't even think it was just the physical attraction; I think I really liked him as a person, which really scared me because I could really get hurt… bad. If he was just some guy who I kind of hit it off with, I could get over him just as fast as it started. When you start to give, share and trust, you can also get let down and hurt if they don't have the same values as you or care. Crap, I really wasn't good at this stuff at all, and I was beginning to think it wasn't just because I hadn't had any practice. I think being open and connecting was easier for some people than it was for others.

I made myself a cup of coffee and sat down to have it with Jade when I heard some noise upstairs. "Jade?" I called, in the hope it was him, and I went toward the sound. It was only for a brief moment, but it sounded like a box was being dragged across the wooden floor upstairs. Oh, he was properly using the litterbox, I rationalized, as I walked toward the small table in the foyer to retrieve my purse. I still felt like being outside, as that short time with Derrick that morning got me going for the day. I guessed I should go try to find something to wear to this dance, but what? I guess I should have asked him for some more details. Even if I didn't like him as much as I did, or was starting to, I would want to look my best. Now I knew I heard something. "Ja… de?" I called out. Huh? What was that cat doing? That clearly sounded like a door shutting. As quickly as I was distracted from my thoughts, I was back to preparing my mind for the party. I didn't used to be like that; last year at Topps' Christmas party, I wore jeans. Heck, a lot of people in the area wore sweatpants most of the time, to most things and places. Getting dressed up meant you looked like you had made an attempt to look nice and was not necessarily a reference to what you were actually wearing.

I turned to put my mug in the sink when I was startled by Jade sitting perfectly erect on the floor behind me! Had he been there the whole time? Impossible! Then how did I miss him, and what was the noise I heard upstairs? Crazy, no, he must have slinked past me while I was daydreaming and I hadn't noticed. Still, I couldn't rationalize away the hairs that rose up on the back of my neck that were urging me to investigate that I may not be alone in the house. I have to do it, I told myself in determination. One, what if there really was someone in the house? What could I do, just ignore them? No, of course not; I had to know. Even if I was just overreacting to an old, creaky house, then that was what it was, and from this point on, I'd know. From there, I could decide how to react. So what was I going to do, go upstairs and check out the whole entire house? *Come on, Aurora*, I told myself. *Let's go, this is your house*, I said, in sheer determination of will and logic, my chosen weapons to banish the fear of the unknown sounds that had been haunting me. This was my first attempt to really address all of the oddities that had been happening to me since Andy called me. I had to address it or at least find out what it was so I knew. I couldn't just be a witness anymore to what had been happening to me. As I acknowledged the shakiness of my right leg as it stepped onto the first stair leading up to the second floor, I wished I wasn't alone right then. As I made it to the top of the stairs, I smelt a wonderful smell, familiar, like a flower mixed with a spice. Someone else was here, a female. It smelt very good and somehow logically I came to the conclusion they weren't thieves or at least murderous burglars, but maybe one of my grandmother's friends coming back to look for something. Then the vision of an older woman scaling the second floor to enter the house through a closed window almost had me laughing out loud at myself and my ridiculous ideas. Well... it was more of a logical explanation than the other options. I felt led to the office so I stood in the doorway and scanned the room; nothing. It was just as I had left it and everything was in its place. I felt the odd sense that I wasn't alone and that someone was watching me as I entered the room. *This is crazy. I am losing my mind and wasting my time,* but as I fought hard to listen to my thoughts of reason, a stronger emotion washed over me: fear. Somehow, deep inside, I knew my intuition was right. Something else was here, and listening to myself, honestly, I was blocking what was trying to guide me out of fear that I was crazy or had 'cracked.' I knew I really just wanted someone else to confirm what I already knew just so I could keep on going and experience whatever this was that was trying to communicate with me, but I was so tapped into this world and intent on making a good place for myself in it that I was afraid to let go, to really let myself see what it was. *Well, here goes nothing,* I said to myself as I called out, "Hello?" I called again, "Hello?" Nothing. I felt the loneliness of the quiet room, and anger erupted within me, and I even found myself stomping my foot at the stupidity of what I was doing. Investigating, hoping, looking for what… and I was knocked down to the floor by a heavy gust of wind! I lay stunned on the hardwood on my side, feeling the very real sensation wash over me. It felt warm and it carried the scent, the spicy familiar floral scent. I opened my eyes and briefly saw a bluish-purple light that could only be described as similar to the aurora borealis, and tears came to my eyes. In seconds, it was over and I opened my eyes, and as I sat slowly up, I saw the brass vent cover on the floor in front of me. There was a slight airflow that could be felt, but nothing of the nature that I had just experienced.

What had just happened? Assessing that I was okay and the house seemed all right as well, I was slightly relieved that it was not a person, as statistics show that homeowners who encounter an intruder in the act usually don't live to tell about it unless they were ready or prepared, which I wasn't. Logically, I should call an HVAC company and have them come check out my vents and make sure my furnace didn't blow up the house or something like that, I don't know. I tried to remain logical but I was pretty shook up. I zipped downstairs and scooped up Jade from the bottom of the stairwell and quickly went out the back door. I just sat outside in the sunlight for about three minutes, holding Jade tightly and stroking the fur on the top of his head. The warmth from the sun and his fur calmed me as I allowed my inhales and exhales to rhyme with his purring. I stepped back into the kitchen, putting Jade down now that I felt that it was okay, and grabbed my phone. I searched for the handyman's number in my contacts that Andi left me and called it, but there was no answer, so I looked up a local HVAC company in my Google Search and found one with 4.5 stars and good reviews, so I called. The dispatcher was pleasant and to my relief she said a guy could be there in thirty minutes. He actually arrived in twenty-five minutes and looked clean and professional. His light blue striped overalls were pressed, and his name patch that was ironed on was clear and legible.

I felt much better oddly with this stranger walking with me through the house as he checked out all the vents and went up into the attic and down in the basement with me; at least I was assured with this big handy guy as my witness that we were alone in the house. He also confirmed sixty-five dollars later that my system was in good working order. Well, if it was foolishness, I felt much better, and that was worth more than sixty-five dollars to me. Feeling relieved that my house wasn't going to blow up or something catastrophic, I decided some fresh air would do me good. I walked over toward the front foyer and froze in my tracks to the front door being wide open! I stood in that second frozen but intently listening to hear if someone had run upstairs or if I could detect any movement, but the door closed shut right before my very eyes! I raced to the door and opened it and looked out, even putting my head out and looking on either side of the porch; nothing. On that note, I grabbed my purse and made sure to quickly shut and lock the door behind me and I pretty much ran to my car and backed out of my driveway haphazardly, all within what seemed like ten seconds. Well, if the neighbors didn't think I was odd before, they had a reason now, I thought, as I reflected on how I would have looked to anyone who just saw me leave the house. Why did I care anyway what they thought, as I may not even be able to stay there anymore with this weird stuff going on? I needed a plan, but what? I was thinking maybe I could get the house blessed by a priest or something, although that didn't seem right either as this whatever it was, didn't seem mean or wish me harm. I know, it knocked me down but I didn't get the feeling it was bad. *Am I listening to myself, am I thinking it is a spirit? I need a shrink is more like it,* I said to myself, trying to keep my thoughts more aligned with what Mrs. Vendor or others from home would have said. *Well, I need to wake up and first realize this is my home now. I definitely need to speak to someone about this but whom?* I asked myself as I drove down Athens Hwy toward the Goodwill thrift store. I didn't want Derrick to think I was nuts and scare him away. I wouldn't know how to begin with Rosa. Plus, she thought so highly of my grandmother and I didn't want her to be sad at her memory by having her granddaughter talking about all this weird stuff with her. I definitely didn't want some pseudo-hippies doing research for their college running tests in my home to 'try and connect.' Maybe a psychologist was the best bet; I could talk to someone at least who was educated and who I could run my ideas by in private without having to worry about them judging me, and it would by law have to remain confidential.

I pulled into the Goodwill parking lot a little eager to take my mind off of what happened that day by looking around for something to wear to the dance the following night. I entered the store and made my way to the ladies' room, finding relief in washing my hands and feeling the warm water run over my wrist. I took in a deep breath and slowly meandered around the store. I spent a lot of time looking down the second aisle of various discarded knick-knacks and other unwanted objects that made their way there. I found myself holding some of them just to ground myself in the moment in some strange therapy to forget the day's earlier events. I smiled at a tiny frog motif made out of seashells that was playing a tiny guitar. After only a few minutes, I felt lighter and made my way over to the ladies' dress section.

I found two dresses and since both were under ten dollars for the pair, I bought them both. I couldn't decide which one to wear as one was more formal than the other. The first one was a black, just-above-the-knee loose cut dress with a hint of silver sparkly fabric sewn into the seams so it seemed very formal. If I didn't wear it out tomorrow with Derrick, it would be a good New Year's Eve party dress, if I found anywhere to go for the holiday. The second reminded me of the dresses you see in old black and white movies from the Second World War. It was the same length as the other, just above the knee. It had a round collar and it completely opened, with a string of tiny black buttons from collar to hem. It was royal blue and pleated with white flowers. From far away, it looked like a blue and white polka dotted dress, but when you got up close, you noticed the prints were actually tiny white flowers.

I guessed I should call Derrick and see what he was wearing so we kind of matched, at least in formality. We would look ridiculous if he showed up in a tuxedo and I wore this floral print or vice versa, if I wore the black formal and he had on loafers business casual. I was starting to get excited and surprisingly not nervous, but rather eager to see him. Usually, my stomach would be in a knot and I would need to eat something, but I found myself smiling as I envisioned his wave salute he gave me as he pulled away from my house the other day, and I felt good inside.

I started wondering what he was doing in the moment and found myself calling him before I knew what I was doing. I felt a small smile start to develop as I heard his baritone "Hello" on the first ring. He was going with business casual, so the floral print it was. I found a pair of black, lace-up heels that fit the period. They reminded me of the pair of saddle shoes I had in the fourth grade, but for me to wear now as a woman because they were heeled. I felt like a little kid in my anticipation, waiting for a birthday gift.

An eager kid was not the vibe I wanted to give off at the dance to Derrick or for a 'smiling idiot' to be my first impression to his friends and family's acquaintances. I took a deep breath and practiced my walk in my new shoes.

When he came to the door, he gently grabbed my hand and tied the corsage he bought me around my wrist. "You look great! Thank you for coming with me tonight," he said as he smiled at me and gave me a formal look over. I smiled back a sincere grin at the compliment. I had never been on a formal date before. Having never gone to high school, I had missed the prom, so this was really special, and I felt myself blush in the cheeks from the novelty of the moment. He looked nice too. Wearing jeans, but they looked new and pressed. He had on a button-up plaid collared shirt and a sweater over it; he looked fresh. You could tell both of us had made an effort to get ready but we didn't look fancy. I said goodbye to Jade and got into Derrick's Jeep and we were on our way to St. Oliver's. I know he had stated we were on a date before, but this really was official. It was a beautiful night, chilly but not cold. The drive over was too short as we barely made any small talk and before we knew it, we had arrived. The small parking lot of the church was full as various couples and small groups of parishioners made their way toward the building. I could feel the excitement of the event as I heard small bits of laughter and caught a smile here or there as we all walked toward the warm glow of light from the dance floor.

I felt the rush of comfort from Derrick's strong hand as he took mine in his to my happiness, as we walked into the building as one. I was so thankful as I had felt my nerves creep up in anticipation of my newness to the group. I felt much better going in with Derrick by my side. He was so charming and confident and already knew people that would be here tonight, and at that realization I felt nervous again as I really hated meeting new people. Well, that wasn't really true; I just hated being the only new person meeting a group of people who were already friends or were already established as a group. It always made me feel like a specimen at the zoo with everyone being so curious to take a look, leaving me feeling naked and exposed. Well, at least tonight I had Derrick to hold onto, I thought, and immediately began to relax as I looked around. He looked over at me with his friendly smile as I slipped my arm around his, interlinking us as we made our entrance through the double doors as one. It was nicely decorated; the volunteers had done a great job arranging banners and balloons. It housed a good mix of about one hundred parishioners of different ages, so it seemed more like a party. The lights were dim, yet you didn't have to strain your eyes to see clearly; the mood was perfect. The long cafeteria-style tables were dressed with red and green tablecloths, and there was a life-sized manger in the corner that had a couple of gifts symbolically set in front of the baby Jesus to be donated to charity for the holiday. Derrick led us over to the table for refreshments.

He poured me a cup of punch and then poured one for himself. He held his small paper cup up to me and said, "Let's make a toast to us, new friendships and beginnings." I smiled as our cups met in cheers. He led me onto the dance floor as we slow danced to *Silent Night*. After an hour of dancing to all the famous holiday songs, we made our way back to the Jeep. He asked if I wanted to go back to his place for some popcorn and a movie. I agreed with "Sure," as I didn't want to leave his company so soon. On the way over to his house, I thought about how comfortable I was with him and realized that maybe I shouldn't be so eager to be alone with him as he may want it to move sooner than I was prepared for. The block and a half drive was over so soon, I felt silly having fastened my seat belt, but that constant ding of the automatic reminder to fasten it up would have drove me to it if I hadn't. We made a joke about the kind of person who came up with the idea at the auto manufacturing plant. "They sure make those annoying so there is no possible way you didn't 'buckle up' if only to prevent you from going insane from the annoying ding of the reminder," and we laughed; and before we knew it, we were back at his house.

The house was nice and warm inside. He opened up a bag of microwave popcorn from the pantry and put it in on two minutes as the bag instructed. He handed me two cans of sweet tea from the refrigerator and took the bag out and shut the lights of the kitchen off as he led us down to the basement. He turned on the television and asked me if I wanted to watch *It's a Wonderful Life* or *A Christmas Story*. I told him I had never seen *It's a Wonderful Life* and his mouth dropped open in disbelief. "You lived in this country your whole life, right?" he teased. "Not sure how that's possible, since they play the dang thing every year," he went on. "Heck, one channel even does a marathon morning, noon and night in case you missed it, or want to see it again," he cited, still in amazement. He hit play and we snuggled together under a soft afghan throw blanket on his sofa and watched the movie. We finished the popcorn and before I knew it, I was lying underneath him in a deep embrace. His kiss was so warm and deep and we lay there fitting perfectly together as he continued with no break in his exploring of my mouth. I had never been kissed like that before. I had deep kissed a couple of guys from the neighborhood, but not like this. This was so comfortable and it began to stir a desire in me that asked for more. I didn't want it to stop but we went on for about twenty minutes before I slowly separated my mouth from his and ended our embrace. He looked at me in such content and comfort and said, "I really liked that; you're a good kisser. You want to go grab something to eat? I'm starving," he said with his typical grin.

"Me too," I answered. I ran into the bathroom really fast and my mouth was all red from our kiss. I fixed the smear of eyeliner that had gone under my eyes from our face-rubbing and washed my hands that were still greasy from the popcorn. After smoothing out my hair and collecting my appearance, I emerged into the room, where he seemed all too happy to see me. He grabbed my hand and said, "You ready? I know a place."

I was hungry too and a little skeptical as he pulled into the rectangular black brick building off of Athens Hwy that said American Tavern, lit up in lights. Outside were parked at least thirty Harley Davidson bikes. I looked at him with a curious giggle. "You have a death wish?"

"Nawh, it's cool. Yeeow trust me?" he asked.

"Well, it's been okay so far. But you know I won't be able to kiss you if you have a fat lip," I flirted.

He patted my butt and whispered into my ear, "I'd make it work," as he led me by my hand into the tavern. That was the difference; Derrick was a man. He was mature and not like the guys I had been with before, even though he was only two years older than me. Maybe it was because his dad was away a lot, so he was used to hanging out with his mom. I definitely liked the way he handled himself; I felt safe with him despite the direct way he often let me know he wanted me. As if his desire for me was the most natural thing in the world, almost an understood truth that was natural and to not act upon it would be the wrong thing to do and not the other way around. I was unsure if it was his upbringing but he seemed to be in control but he didn't come off as controlling or like some guy off of a Lifetime movie. He asked if I minded if he ordered a beer. I shook my head no. I said, "Well, you're driving so like one, right?" He said yeah. I liked that he asked me since I kind of depended on him for a ride home. I liked that he always checked with me and I wondered if it was that he cared about me or if it was southern manners. Guess only time would tell, I thought, as I sat across from him and enjoyed the environment of the laid-back atmosphere. We both had a Heineken and our cheeseburgers came out just as the stage lit up and a band came out. I looked at him. "Wow! What a nice surprise, Derrick, live music."

"Yeah, they have live music every weekend," he informed me. The beer hit me a little faster than it hit him, as I wasn't a big drinker, so it gave me a nice buzz. It just relaxed me and made me laugh a little more at his antics, but it wore off after the food, which I enjoyed. I had never seen the fun in losing control of yourself out in public. I always thought drunken people looked stupid and I never saw one that looked like they were having a good time, only in movies. The waitress brought me a water to wash it down with and we stayed until the band finished at around 1 am. Somehow, without my noticing, he had taken care of the bill, again. I felt a little bad as I had traded the fries out for the onion rings, which was an extra dollar charge. He told me I was being ridiculous and he thought I knew how happy he was to have me and to be able to take me out. He assured me it really was no trouble and it was 'his pleasure to treat me and show me a good time.' He looked down into my eyes as he rose from the table in a gesture to leave. He allowed me to walk in front of him, but he quickened his pace to reach his hand out in front of me to push open the door for us. "Being a southern gentleman is hard work," I said with a flirtatious smile as I brushed past him on my way through the open door.

He smiled back with his wit. "Oh, it's worth the effort," he countered, just as flirtatious. "Plus… it's a sense of pride in being who you are." He unlocked my side of the Jeep first and waited until I was in and he closed it firmly behind me before getting into the driver's side.

"Now you're just showing off," I said, and he just nodded and smiled casually in an all-knowing grin.

He pulled into my driveway and put his Jeep in park. He leaned over toward me and looked me intensely in the eye and asked me, "You had a good time?" I said yeah. "Well, I don't want you to worry about paying and all that stuff; please just worry about having a nice time with me, Aurora. That really would make me happy if I knew you really have a nice time when you're with me." I felt my heart melt then start beating so fast, I thought it was going to jump right out of my chest. I got really nervous as he leaned forward and gently brushed my hair back behind my ear. I could take it if he kissed me again, but I never had anyone in my life talk to me so sweetly and touch me so gently, like I was a little cat so tender. I could have lain down right there and then and allowed him to caress my head as he did; I never remembered feeling anything like it. I didn't want him to stop. I had to stop this. I was falling for him hard, and I didn't know what to do. In a panic, I tried to fake it and tried to look collected as I smiled and said, "No, thank you. I really did. You were... are great," I stumbled but managed to say. Just then I placed my hand on the door handle and he grabbed my other arm firmly but gently. He somehow got my other arm, so now he held both of my arms and kissed me so deeply and with emotion that I was certain how he felt: he liked me. He wanted me. I broke away and looked at him as I closed the door of his Jeep. "Goodnight."

"Can I call you tonight?" he asked. In shock that he still wanted to talk to me and in being happy with the reassurance he didn't want our time together to end, I said yes. He smiled at me as he made his way around the front of his Jeep and got in, watching me the whole time. I got my key in the door and turned back to wave and he pulled out of the driveway. I stood there for a moment in my foyer with my back against the front door, smiling, and realized I should make my way upstairs to get ready for bed.

Sure enough, I had just enough time to take a quick shower and get into bed before my phone rang. It was him. "Gosh, I wish I was over there," he said.

I responded with, "Um, no."

He said, "I know we are moving a little fast, but I like you, Aurora. Look, I don't want to make you feel uncomfortable or anything; I want you to trust me. I just like you, is all," he finished. After that confession, we talked for another two hours about the dance and some of the people he knew from St. Oliver's and how they had been acquainted before I felt myself dozing off, so I ended the call.

*

I woke up at 10 am in good spirits the next day. Somehow Jade knew to just stay curled up next to me in his ball of fluff that wrapped against my ribs on the blanket. I was so happy in my new situation with school and mostly Derrick. Life here in Loganville had become a good one; I just hoped it would stay on this positive course for me. My thoughts continued as I got out of bed and made my way downstairs to put the coffee on.

Chapter Fifteen

The History

After two cups of coffee in my old yoga pants that I slept in, the ones that got too worn and raggy-looking to be worn in public, I smiled at Jade, knowing he loved me no matter how I looked as I watched him make the leap from the kitchen island to a slow trot over to where I was sitting by the window. My legs stretched out onto the opposite chair and the free copy of the *Washington Post* the G.G.C. business department budgeted for and distributed in front of the corner of the building that divides the campus, Starbucks and the library.

I had heard they wanted to promote the school's reputation by encouraging their graduates to be well rounded and able to discuss hot topics in future business settings. I heard one professor say the school was new, only ten years old, and the president worked his butt off to secure the school's position and accreditation. He went on to say he was proud that the school was producing people who could actually give a good PowerPoint presentation, as he knew a

lot of people who went to big Ivy League schools, but because they
were used to sitting among three hundred in a lecture, as they were
paying for that big professor's lecture or expertise, they never got
that opportunity to compete themselves. Those students were used
to being told what to think and weren't given the opportunity to
debate or ask questions with those who were in a higher position
so they could grow themselves. Not that they would need to, as
the Ivy League brand and the connections they would make at the
school would secure them a comfortable future, but most of them
didn't have the passion or grit that comes with the drive to go up
and improve. They were just taught from a young age how to be
successful in their successful worlds or circles. I saw it because I
was never a part of those circles and never would be; you have to be
born into them. So I got the promotion or way of thinking, which
was good since I was part of it now. It was true his audience was a
lot of older students, most of whom already had a family or were
working full-time. It was a totally different demographic than the
college students he was describing. I started late but twenty-one
was still young, and I didn't look old or out of place in a classroom
where some of my classmates were well above middle-age. He was
right in the sense that the concept of college was made for someone
to live in a dorm and do just that: study. At G.G.C., although a lot
of the student body did live on campus, most of its students were
already out in the world living a life, and college was a side passion
or something they'd always wanted to do but life had got in the way.
Well, even though the newspaper was only fifty cents at the stand,
I thought the school was right that most students wouldn't pick it
up if it wasn't free. I remember when people at Topps were talking
about the housing market bust that nearly destroyed our economy;
people called it the great recession and I felt so dumb because I
didn't have a clue what they were talking about. Maybe G.G.C. did
have a clue, as back then I wouldn't have been reading a newspaper
either. I had changed. I rinsed my mug and put it on the counter for

later and went upstairs for a quick shower and found some clean yoga pants and tee shirt for the day. Standing in front of the mirror, I felt an eerie feeling, as though someone was watching me from the bedroom. That was silly, as no one was there. I peeked around and scanned the room, over the bed. Nothing, the room was empty. I continued to dry my hair with the towel before hanging it back up on the ornate silver bar that was screwed into the wall. I picked up my brush and began to slowly brush my hair up off of my face and into a loose bun on top of my head. I patted some gel onto it so it would stay put when it dried, and as I turned on the faucet of the sink to rinse off my hands, I thought I heard something, like a voice coming from the hallway. Fear crept up the tiny hairs on the spine of my neck as I slowly shut off the running water and listened as I dried my hands. It was late in the morning, almost midday, not the usual time for a break-in. No, this was something else my intuition told my rational thoughts as I crept out of the bathroom, checking both directions of the hallway for any sign or movement. I stood completely still and barely taking in a breath in my attempt to listen and remain as quiet as humanly possible. I waited for a few seconds with earnestness and fear for the noise again. I thought to myself how silly, here I was, a grown woman, getting all spooked and caught up in this nonsense, and began to walk toward the staircase to make my way back downstairs when I heard it again! I quickly backed myself up against the corner of the hallway to face whatever it was. Standing in the corner of the hallway, I heard Jade bellowing a meow from somewhere I couldn't place. I went into the hallway and then it sounded like he was in the bedroom, but I didn't see him anywhere. It sounded like he was on the bed, but he wasn't. The meow was definitely coming from the bedroom, but where? He was nowhere in sight! I pushed the bed to the other side of the room as I was certain no, it was coming from there. I pulled the carpet over to one side and to my amazement there was a small brass handle in the floorboard that almost blended into the oaken floorboards. So

I wasn't crazy after all; it was possible that Jade really was making a noise that I did indeed hear while in the bathroom, but it was still unusual. Fear crept up behind the mask of wonder that left my face in small beads of sweat that accompanied my excursion of panic in pushing the bed and carpet out of the way to follow the sounds. It wasn't horror movie fear but more like the fear you have when you get lost or separated from the group you are with and it's somewhere you haven't been before.

I pulled and a small square of floorboard came up easily. I called, "Jade," my young cat, but he didn't come and I no longer heard his bellows for help. I was afraid to leave the top open, like a small child afraid of what may come out of the unknown darkness, so I closed it back up and left the room. I ran down the stairway as fast as I could to the kitchen junk drawer for the flashlight. With it in hand, I went as fast as I could back to the bedroom and opened up the hidden space in my floor. I clicked on the light and could see the silhouette of a box, or a chest, resting in the space between the floor and the ceiling below. I laid down flat on my stomach and extended my arm as far as I could and inched the chest toward me with my fingertips until it was close enough for me to lift it up with both hands. It was a small oak chest! Tracing my hand over the intricate details of the carvings in the wood, it could only be described as beautiful. How cool was this! It was rather dusty but it seemed like flowers or plants of some kind with its vines going all around the box. A child's imagination could amuse itself for some time tracing the different patterns as they intertwined on the sides of the case. The curiosity was too much that I had almost forgotten my cat and the whole reason I had opened the floor in the first place. "Jade," I called again but no answer. The chest was locked, I realized, as the lid wouldn't open to my pull. Just out of some random act that was inspired by a feeling that I could not explain, I grabbed the key from the necklace around my neck and inserted it into the keyhole that sat in the middle of the chest. It slid in the hole with such perfect fluidity that I knew it was the right key and that the lid would open before it had sprung ajar with a creak. Inside, there was a stack of money, large bills of fifty and one hundred dollars that were rolled around into a cylinder and bound with a rubber band. There were also old photographs, an old map and some documents. I was so excited and eager to go through all of the items, but kneeling on the hard wood floor became too much for my knees, so I closed up the floorboard and threw back the carpet and moved the bed over it so the room looked just as it had before my discovery. I picked up the chest and made my way with it to the kitchen. I placed it on the kitchen table and made a pot of coffee with the intention to relax and go through my find. The thought of not knowing where Jade was began to really nag at me and I started to become really worried about him, so I made my way back upstairs. I called him a couple times before I had to use the restroom. While on the toilet, I heard him again. Unable to get up from the toilet because it made more sense to finish and then give my undivided attention to the pursuit of him again, I sat there but called him gently. I finished and washed my hands and from the reflection in the mirror I saw something move behind me.

The hairs stood up in fright on the back of my neck and I jumped and forced myself to turn around to see what it was. Were my eyes playing tricks on me? Did my eyes just not adjust properly to the images I caught from the corner of my eye? Maybe the light reflected off the nickel of the faucet and I caught movement in the reflection; it had to be nothing really, as what could it be? As I faced the wall and my back was to the mirror and sink now, I saw a tiny paw clawing from the silver heat gate in the wall. Its old and ornate swirls of metal that served as both a barrier and elaborate design that allowed heat to come into the room blocked my poor cat from his desired exit. "Jade," I said, "how did you get in there, sweetie?" I asked as tears filled my eyes. "Hold on, Mommy will get you out," I said as I ran downstairs to the junk drawer for the Phillips screwdriver. Just as I turned around, screwdriver in hand,

Jade emerged from the vent gate in the kitchen wall that lay adjacent to the cellar door. "No way," I said out loud! *Well, better you than mice,* I thought to myself as I put the screwdriver back in the drawer. I scooped him up and held him for the longest time until he began to purr in my arms. "You almost gave me a heart attack, you devil," I said as I placed him down on the tile floor. I poured him some food in his bowl and asked him never to do that again.

I was so thankful to sit down and take that first sip of the freshly brewed coffee. I just sat for a moment watching Jade finish up his meal as I sipped my coffee. After that, I began to go through the contents of the chest. I counted the money first, unrolling the bills from the rubber band. Ten thousand dollars, holy crap! The bills were the new edition hundreds too, so that means Grandma had to have put them there soon before she passed away, but why? I personally always have a doubt when it comes to people, and I definitely didn't trust big banks, so I related completely as to why someone would have a stack of cash hidden that only they knew about, because ya never know, you might need it. If you were in that situation where you needed cash fast, and without a trail, how would you get it? I thought this way but I never had the means to have an emergency stash of cash; well, now I guess I did. Old people understood that thought that I had, one that most people today would describe as paranoid or weird. I wouldn't be stupid enough to think it was a good idea to keep a stash under my mattress that could be burnt up in a fire or stolen. Grandma had the right idea but I would have used a fireproof safe; I guess I could now. It wasn't odd, it was smart to plan. Those poor people who had just had all their homes washed away in that terrible storm in Tennessee that plagued the news morning, noon and night that week. Their homes flooded so that the things they'd worked their whole lives to accumulate were destroyed in an instant. Some celebrities, like Dolly Parton, were putting the victims up in hotels, but as nice as it was an act of charity, that was only a temporary fix. Those poor people would have to start again, and in some cases, rebuild their entire lives. Those people wished they'd thought like Grandma. I couldn't talk really; I had always wanted to have a 'what if safe,' as I called it. An emergency plan, or a contingency plan I think I heard it referred to; I just never was able to come up with the funds. I heard some educated people on the radio one time say you need three months' worth of living expenses saved to really have a chance if anything ever happened. I just worked and tried to survive. I had always wished I could save more, but thinking back at myself in Avoca, it was like I was asleep, just waiting for someone to come along and pick me up, to show me. I guess they did. If Andi hadn't called me, I would still be there, working away at a factory, wishing my life was different, just surviving but not really living. Well now, here was my chance. I felt momentarily guilty for being so happy and feeling 'blessed' as they said around here, all due to my grandmother not being there. I quickly told myself that was normal, as I never asked to be put up for adoption and I sure wasn't going to not be happy over some sentiments I should or maybe shouldn't feel.

I rolled up the money and put it inside a zip-lock baggy I retrieved from the drawer in the kitchen. I took one of the empty jars Grandma had washed and dried and put away with the intention to preserve one of her berries in or use as old-timer Tupperware, I surmised, and poured sand from a keepsake bottle that said Myrtle Beach on it and let it line the bottom of the jar. I placed my baggy of money in the jar on the sand, then covered the bag with the sand and sealed it up with the metal lid. I threw the bottle in the garbage and put the jar of sand that was hiding my money in the chest. Happy that there was some barrier of protection for the cash if there was a fire, I proceeded to go through the rest of the contents now that was settled. Well, at least I knew Grandma enjoyed vacations; I thought as I wondered what Myrtle Beach was like.

The letter was written on a paper that was much thicker than the types often used today. Even if it hadn't yellowed from age, I would still have been able to tell it was old. My grandmother's name was written on the front of it: Miss Lauren Lorensen. I noticed that both Mrs. and Kohl were removed from her title, so I had to assume it was written to her before she had married my grandfather. It went as follows:

Lionhawk,

I apologize that I am not familiar with your married name, but I do wish you both much happiness. You have earned my trust and respect as only you have done in these last two correspondences, and I have found much relief from your work and efforts in how you have honored the treaty between your clan and my tribe, one that was made many centuries ago.

Please continue our work to secure the sacred lands do not fall into the hands of those treacherous men, as their interest lies only in immediate profits and they seem to be without honor or spirit. I cannot tell you how much you have lifted the spirits of my people in knowing not all pale faces are without spirit, as you have reminded us of the treaty that was made long ago; and you have honored it. It has been with great pleasure that we have witnessed you awaken your totem and claim your true name and walk among us in the sacred place of both of our ancestors. You bring much honor to them. The document was signed today and there is a copy with the county clerk. I leave Vines in your care and will be leaving to join the rest of my family in Cherokee, North Carolina, now that Sue and I know the lands are under your watch.

Charlie Strongtree

So my grandmother handled something for a Native American friend about Vines Park.

How she would be handling something for them if the park belonged to the county, I wondered. I placed everything back inside the chest and carried it back to its hidden space in the floor. After moving the bed and carpet back for the second time this morning I was ready to lie down and relax to some T.V. for at least an hour, which I did. After an hour of Law and Order's Criminal Intent I got up and decided to go for a walk. I walked until I reached the Lowe's parking lot and was happy when I remembered they had a TJ Maxx next door. I perked up at the thought of finding a new pair of yoga pants. Inside, I just wandered around for a good hour, taking in all the new styles and pretty things for sale. I left with three pairs of yoga pants and a faux gold collar for Jade. I stopped by the Dunkin' Donuts on the way home and got myself an egg and cheese sandwich on a croissant for supper, with a coffee to wash it down, which I enjoyed as I walked down the alley towards my house.

*

The next day at work, I was able to do some research at the library and found out that my grandmother had helped secure the possession of the property and was present at the sale of what is now Vines Park. There was even a picture of her, an old black and white, standing alongside a trio of Native Americans and a white couple – a pretty woman and a man. The Native American woman had long dark hair in braids that hung at her side and the male also had long hair, but it was loose. The other Native American appeared younger and was holding a document. Everyone was smiling in the photo. As I observed it closer, I realized I had seen the exact photo in the chest I found the other day in my floorboard. Huh, this was odd. Well, maybe not. I was sure it was an important day and Grandma was there, so she saved a copy. The Loganville history section also had a copy of the sale of the couple's property to the county, which today is known as Vines Park. So what I pieced together so far must be that the land was special in some way to the Native Americans. My grandmother must have also recognized that the land was special and agreed to help them sell it to someone who appreciated it or saw its value, but not in the commercial way of the 'bad men' that were described in the letter to my grandma. Then, the land was lived on, and Vines Mansion was built by that family and then sold to the county as a park under the stipulation the grounds would remain 'as is' to avoid commercial development on the sacred grounds. The white couple from the photograph must be the original owners that lived in Vines Mansion. Wow! My grandmother had a part in making that beautiful park! It was pretty cool to not only have visited a place she was a part of but to learn she was part of the history there, in addition to it making her 'more real' if that makes any sense. It also felt good to know she helped people and was recognized for it. I felt a moment of pride to be descending from something good, from a person who did something in her community. I guess it was the family and social recognition that I secretly craved, and the need to be associated with something positive.

I kind of already felt that from the people at the library, I thought, as I smiled while categorizing some books in the children's section. I walked by the glass case that housed a map that looked similar to the one I'd seen at home from the chest. It was different and more general, just showcasing the area of what is now Loganville, Georgia. I had to go back into the chest when I got home and check it out again.

After my shift, I went straight home, fed Jade and gave him his five minutes of affection to make up for being gone all day. We jogged up the flight of stairs to the bedroom and pulled out the chest again as I told Jade, "You had better stay put; don't go off and get yourself lost anywhere," as I looked at the vent. I sat on the floor against the bed I had moved for the third time in the last two days and opened the wooden case to retrieve the map. It was an old map and it had blueprints of the land attached. I sat there and tried to make any sort of understanding of it and failed. I closed up the chest and moved the bed back, this time just leaving the jar of sand and money in the floor and choosing to carry the chest to the closet to rest it on the floor. Thinking this was more practical than moving the bed again, I figured it was better to just get all of my curiosity out of my system and satisfied and then place the contents back in the chest in the floor for good. For now, I knew I would end up moving the bed again, so it made more sense to just keep the chest out, but not out in the open. For some reason, I had the strange sense that I should conceal the chest and its contents. I pulled an old sweater down from its hanger in the closet and threw it over the chest, so if anyone took a quick peek inside, the eyes of the busybody would just see usual closet stuff. Maybe it would make more sense after I had eaten something and allowed myself to rest a little from the rush of just coming in after work. I returned to the kitchen with the stack of papers and set them at the table to be viewed after coffee. I fried up some onions, tomato and cucumber from my garden and placed it on two slices of toast, melted mozzarella cheese and a spread of French dressing. My coffee was percolated and ready as I cozied into my small cushioned nook in the kitchen and began to go over the map. It was Vines Park! Crazy, it was almost like Grandma was obsessed with it or something, but why? The blueprints suggested there was a road or maybe a body of water or tunnel or something from Vines to the house. Maybe a long time ago it was a river that had dried up or something. There was clearly a path from the park to here, but I wasn't familiar enough with blueprints or old maps to determine what I should be seeing. Either way, it was pretty cool, I guess, learning about the history of the place you lived in, or any place really. To see what it was from the beginning and what happened to it along the way to make it what it was now, like a story of a place.

Just then, the doorbell rang and brought me from my thoughts back to my kitchen. Who could be visiting at eight thirty at night?

It was Rosa! She had a gift with her. A square blue box wrapped in a silver bow. It looked very beautiful. I welcomed her in and gave her a big hug which she returned with a "Merry Christmas" and handed me the box. I said, "Wait! Rosa, I got something for you too," as I hurried to the closet in the foyer to retrieve her gift! We exchanged gifts and I was happy to see Rosa liked her slippers and they were the right size. I hung my silver bell ornament that had the inscription *To new beginnings* engraved in blue glitter on the tree.

We walked into the kitchen and had a cup of tea with the cookies she had baked and brought over. Looking at the map that was left unguarded on the table, she smiled at me and said, "You know, your red hair does suit you, just like your grandma's did her," almost offhand. "I guess the apple don't fall far from the tree, now, does it?" she said with a grin. "She was always getting into stuff, but she was strong. I'm sure gonna miss her this holiday, hum," she said while looking down. "Oh, I forgot why I was coming over; you is welcome to come tomorrow. We is having ham and all the fixin's. My daughter is bringin' her corn bread and pie. We'd love to have you." My heart swelled and I gave her the biggest hug.

I told her I appreciated it but I was going to hang out with Jade and maybe check on some things and that I'd catch up with her after the holiday. "Okay then," she said, "but I was wonder'n' when you is brin'n' that handsome young man over. I ain't been see'n' him now," she smiled with a nod.

"It's going good, Rosa, just not too fast, but right," I continued as I matched her smile.

I watched her walk across the garden and into her yard and we waved to each other as she went back into her house through her back door. I felt all good inside, love. That was what Rosa was and you couldn't help but to love her as she was just a good person and exactly what I needed to live next door. I was so thankful and I hoped God knew it. *Here comes that Catholic guilt, as they call it,* I chuckled to myself as I washed out our mugs and placed them in the dishwasher. I had to yell at Jade as he tried to climb inside the machine. "You are too trusting, Jade. What if I wasn't paying attention? That would be a bath you'd never forget, now come on, I'm trying to work here." He sautéed with a strut out of the room and finally out of my hair.

I sat back down to look at the map. If it wasn't so late, I would go over there right now, but there was no way I would go to Vines by myself at night. I felt the fear return from the memory of my encounter with those guys. I knew I had to go; I felt compelled and it seemed by more than just curiosity. I felt this should be a secret, though, so my only option for perfection would be to ask Derrick, but I wanted to keep this private. Maybe there was a way I could go with him but not let him know I was checking out the spot indicated on my map. Maybe tell him to meet me at 11 am and explore at 10 am. Plus, I doubted those losers would be even out of bed yet at 10 am, let alone what were the odds of them being at Vines Park? Slim to none. They were probably sleeping in until the afternoon from their night of trouble or doing drugs or whatever they did, breaking more bottles and scaring the new girl in town, I ranted in my head. So it was, I had convinced myself to call up Derrick to see if he wanted to meet me at Vines Park the next day. It figured Derrick had to help his mom by visiting some group of friends at a holiday social in Alpharetta and wouldn't be back until that evening. He invited himself over then, saying he had picked up a little something for me on account of it being my first Christmas in Georgia. He said he was sorry he couldn't stay, but his mom would just swing by so he could drop it off and give me a hug. I said fine and was definitely excited about seeing him, even if it was not going to be until six o'clock that night, and for only five minutes, but somehow I was still eager. I threw on my dark grey long yoga pants and matching hoodie that was thick enough to keep me warm with just a sleeveless cotton tee shirt underneath. I was dressed perfectly for a Georgia winter and comfortable enough for my excursion.

I parked my Subaru in one of the designated parking slots under a big oak tree and made my way toward the gated entrance of Vines Park. At the water fountain, I was greeted by a red-headed middle-aged woman, who greeted me with a big friendly, "Hello there." She stood there, medium build, thick but trim with her head cocked to one side and her hand rested on her hip in an open fist. With her teeth out in a smile, she reminded me of a squirrel as she acknowledged me as she changed the bag in the trash bin that was located next to the fountain. I realized that she was the park attendant from her gloves and Gwinnett County shirt. I said, "Oh, hi. You work here; I thought this was Walton County. I'm Aurora Rose, but everyone calls me Rose."

She replied, "Oh, hey. Nope, we're right on the line here at Vines, but it was Gwinnett County that bought the park from the couple that used to own the land and live here. I can see how you'd think it was Walton, as we are in Loganville, but sure am glad the county stood up to 'em builders. Anyhow... Merry Christmas. I have to get out of here and get that roast in the oven. My Papi will be madder than spit if he ain't eat." I watched her climb into a green golf cart with tools and buckets loaded up in the back and take off down the path toward the back of the park.

"Merry Christmas," I said in a low voice, knowing I'd missed the opportunity to say it to her before she left but said it anyway, mostly because it felt weird not to respond to someone when they say it to you. She seemed likable and I couldn't get over the odd feeling that I had met her before, even though I knew that would be impossible unless she had been to Avoca. I walked down the paved path that meandered around the carefully cultivated beauty of the Vines' master gardeners.

Tree after tree led me to the giant white wooden bridge to eventually crossing the lake. I should have made a left at the end of the bridge but I wanted to explore the Asian garden and wander up to the little structures and admire the statues in my quiet peace.

There was something so calming about Vines that encouraged me to just breathe and wander as I admired her beauty. I eventually made it past the guardians, or the four ladies, as Derrick called them, and past the troll to the children's maze.

When I came to the end of the white lattice that was overgrown with the vines that shaped the maze, I pulled out my map, aware that the entrance, if it was real, would be in this area somewhere. I looked up to the sound of a vehicle approaching; it was the park attendant. She drove past and I could see her on the road that led out of the park from the old servants' entrance. Her white county pickup truck with the Gwinnett circle emblem on the truck door sped by as I briefly stood still to acknowledge her if she had seen me. When I heard the truck make it further down the road, I reopened the map and began to walk toward the indication where the mark began. It led me to the canopy of vines that served as the roof of the trellis that marked the entrance of the stairway. I looked to my left, which was where it was supposed to be, and no doorway, only a wooden wall that also served as a planter for more plants and vines. If I walked along it, I would arrive back at the beginning of the children's maze. If I went straight, I would arrive at the troll. If I went up the stairs, I would be at the road alongside the lake. I could have gone back the way I came and follow the patio to the miniature train station and model city but just sat down on the second to last stair and looked at the map. It should be right here somewhere. Well, it was an old map. Maybe they had built over whatever this was originally. I mean, these stairs seemed old, but wood can look like that in only a couple of years due to wear and the weather.

I looked up from the map ready to head back when I met with a set of stone eyes. I looked longer and they came from a face, the face of a stone bunny rabbit that was placed somewhat inside the plant whose long leaves grew in vines that resembled a hanging head of green hair. I rose up to leave but I noticed the thick wood behind him was a different color than the wood of the giant planter the stone rabbit was placed inside. Curious, I got closer to take a look and there it was; a brass keyhole. I had found it! The excitement and happiness in that moment shot threw my body like an electric shock. I looked around and saw that I was alone, so I pushed aside the vines to reveal a solid oak door that was built somewhat in the ground, almost as if when it was pushed open, I guessed it would have to lead down, as I could only see the wooden planter that led along the staircase that led to the road above. Where could this door lead to? It must be a storage shed, but why the elaborate map and shaded areas that would indicate a tunnel or river? The only keys I had were either my car keys or the key I had found at my house to my chest that now served as my favorite necklace. Why not? I inserted it into the keyhole, and with a turn and a click, it opened the door with a push!

This was unbelievable! Like something out of the *Hardy Boys* or *Nancy Drew* series. The excitement was overwhelming but fear began to resurface as well, telling me to be careful, as I had no idea what was down there, and reminding me that I was all alone. I inspected the inside of the door to make sure it couldn't close and lock behind me. To my relief, it opened from the inside. My cautious nature forced me to shut it but leave it cracked and unable to close completely with a tiny pebble I found on the ground in its latch. No surprise there were those same carvings on the doorframe and on the outside of the door as on my door at home. I wondered what they meant as I entered the dark passageway. To my relief, small lights lit up along the base of the wall, illuminating the cement hallway. It was solid dark grey cement from floor to ceiling. There were little holes carved out and the small lights lay inside the base of the wall. They just went on automatically, like the ones in the Vines' bathroom above ground. If the doorframe hadn't had the same carvings that Andi doted on his silver band, I would just have assumed this was an underground tunnel used for storage for the park, or so they could work on the pipes that lay under the lake, aid in draining it or some government purpose. No, this was something else. As I walked down the path, it began to get cooler and the air more crisp. I surmised I must be walking adjacent to the lake. I had the sudden realization that if the structures of these cement walls cracked in any way, my fate would be sealed and I would suffer a horrible death from the water that would fill this enclosure and drown me.

I thought of Derrick; tonight, if I didn't show up for our date would he be able to piece together what had happened to me? I tried not to think in a small-minded bigoted way, when the thought of the Loganville police department looking for me suddenly made me laugh. A small town force like Loganville would probably find my car at Vines, but I doubt they could find me, even with the rock I stuck in the base to assure me that it wouldn't close behind and trap me inside to my doom, the door most likely was still concealed pretty good by the vines that hung over to the grass. No, it was up to me to make sure that I got back home tonight as no one would come looking, or at least not in enough time to save me if something happened. To my left was another big oak door. *Well, here goes,* I thought, reassured by the silence that it would be safe for me to explore. I tried my key and it worked; I guess it opened all of her secrets. Oddly, I was no longer afraid, as if somehow I had experienced all of this before and I already knew what the outcome would be. Secure in my belief that this was what I was supposed to be doing, like I had done a hundred times before.

My curiosity was becoming dangerous, much like Jade's, who apparently had become a bad influence on me, only that there would be no one to come looking after me as I had done with him in the vents. After pushing the heavy door open, I waited in the entrance, unable to see in the darkness. Inside, the lights came on after a second, again along the floor, but in this small room there was also a gas lamp on a small table that housed two wooden chairs but seemed to have last served as a desk since it sat against the wall. On the other side of the room was a bed that had two sleeping bags laid on top. Two jugs of water dated for next year and a box of granola bars. The doorway surprisingly led to a small bathroom that had a toilet and a small sink. I tried the faucet and it actually worked. This made me think the place was rigged up off of Vines Park, for how else would there be electricity and running water? I began to think scary, dark thoughts, wondering if some weirdo lived here or if this was a place serial killers would lure someone like me down into to torture. No, I told myself, I had the map. It was my grandmother's. It pieced together with the research I had done at work.

The key fit and I had found it accidently, from Jade. No one had lured me here. I was safe. I trusted her, as weird as that may be since I never knew her, I did. It felt right. I began to think that maybe I had watched too much Lifetime and *Law and Order* for my own sanity, as I had really creeped myself out there for a minute. As I walked further along, I came to another door, which I opened, and it led me up a flight of stairs to another door which pushed open upwards. It came out in the middle of the meadow. Wow, and this would have come in handy that night those guys were chasing me. It was right over there where I hid at first, as I could see the brush a couple of feet ahead. It really was a good hiding spot, but the one I had just come from would have been better. I closed the shaft behind me as I descended back down to see where else it took me. It led to another door which opened at the beginning of the woods at the end of the parking lot. I peered out and could see my Subaru in the distance, to my left the Hokie O'Kelly Mill Road. I descended back below to see where else it led.

This was so unbelievable, I thought to myself. This had to be the coolest experience and it was really good to know about if I ever met trouble again, like with those guys. Well, only if they didn't know about it too. Then it just dawned on me that they wouldn't have a key; only I did or people my grandmother knew might. But who would be coming here? Probably no one. I could leave a test, like rice paper or colored sand on the floor to make sure. I laughed at the sound of myself, like a ten-year-old kid who had found a treehouse in the woods. No, I had found something even better; something historic and remarkable.

I even sat down and rested for a few minutes before continuing on, with no change of scenery or any indication the tunnel would come to an end. Finally, it stopped and there were two doors, one I could just open; the other led to a flight of stairs which I went up. I pushed up and I couldn't believe it opened up right into the path between Rosa and my garden! So that means, I thought, as I closed the shaft behind me and took off in an almost run to the other door, that "I'm home." I said it in such an excited and happy tone that Jade jumped back.

The poor cat was waiting for me on the other side, just sitting there on the stone floor of the small room that housed the cellar part of the finished basement. How clever, there was a trio of shelves that hung in front of the door, so from a quick glance or unknowing eye, no one would have noticed this door. Grandma had to be the coolest person, I thought, as I scooped up Jade and turned around to make sure the double latch was locked on the concealed door. I then double-checked to make sure the other exterior door was locked. I froze at the realization. "Jade... how did you get down here if the door was locked?" So I knew for certain that there was another passageway in the house Jade was using; I just hadn't found it yet. Creepy, but as long as only me and Jade were in the house using it, it was kind of cool. I fed Jade and drank a glass of water. I took a small nap on the padded bench at the kitchen table and woke up to take a nice, long, hot shower. I was getting myself dressed in my usual long sweater and yoga pants when my phone rang; it was Derrick. How strange; his call brought me back to this world and away from the strange series of events that I had been experiencing, snapping me back and grounding me to function.

He had gotten out of the social outing with his mom and wanted to come over. I was so excited. I made a pot of coffee and waited for him to come stop by. I hoped my face wouldn't betray my secret. I had to compose myself I thought, as I determinedly and slowly forced myself to complete the motions of getting ready for our date.

Chapter Sixteen

A Shared Secret

After my first cup of coffee, there was a knock at the door. "Merry Christmas," he said as he came in. He was wearing an elf hat and a huge smile. I gave him the most comfortable hug, just enjoying the warm spot in his chest as he embraced me in his well-built arms. What I liked about Derrick was that he didn't look like much, but when you felt him, you knew right away he was strong and solid. I had never been attracted to that beefcake kind of guy; it looks unnatural when a guy gets too big, and I was thankful Derrick felt normal. He produced a small box from behind his back.

It was a small black box with a tiny red bow on the top of it. I smiled so big. "Oh, you are too much, but I like it," as I received the box. "Wait," I said as I retrieved two small snowman bags from the closet. "Got one for your mom too, as dinner the other night was great. In fact, you have both been awesome since I got here, and I really appreciate it since I just moved here." I handed him the bags.

He pulled his gift out; it was a very masculine wooden frame in which I had inserted the photo he had taken of me at Vines, which he had insisted I pose for. You could tell he liked it; his face changed and he looked quiet and happy.

"Aurora, it's perfect. Now, it's your turn." I opened the box and inside was a small, solid silver peach on a tiny silver chain. There was a tiny paper inside that read *Welcome to Georgia*. My eyes immediately watered up; it was just the right gift. This guy was really winning me, bad. I had never felt like this from a guy. Now he was adding all the things about Christmas I had always wanted into the mix. I couldn't put up a guard any longer; I had fallen for him and hard. "Hey, ya don't have to cry. If ya don't like it, I'll take it ba—", before he could finish the sentence, I had kissed him.

He accepted my thank you with all the warmth and affection of his previous hug but with a passion I finally accepted. I was scared in a way, as this was my house. We were alone here and there was no one to stop us from getting carried away, from going too far. Once you take that step, there is no going back. I gently broke away from our embrace with a shy smile to his huge grin. "Well, I'm glad you changed your mind about the gift, as I thought of you when I saw it," he teased. "Let me put it on you," and he gently pulled the chain from the box and stood behind me to clasp the chain. I felt suddenly nervous as I felt him so close behind me; I could feel his presence just a breath away as his hands moved to work the clasp.

Odd, how kissing him felt completely normal, but to feel him so close behind me made my knees wobble. Maybe it was because I had kissed guys before but had never experienced the intimacy of a guy doing these close and personal things, like dressing me, even if it was just a necklace. Who knows, but I hoped it continued. I wondered what that meant for us now. Were we together? For the first time, I wanted to be somebody's girlfriend. I had always wanted to belong to someone, but the idea of belonging to just a guy seemed backward or oppressive. With Derrick, I would get the whole thing, and this sudden longing to be close to him seemed normal, both mentally and, oddly, physically too. Ya hear of guys wanting to mess around, but here with Derrick, I found myself wanting to be close to him, to feel his arms around me, to kiss me. If I had just went with the feeling, I wouldn't have stopped us, but mentally I had to remind myself to not let it go too far. I mean, I just met him really. I didn't really know much about him. At least back home I could ask around about a guy; somebody would know about him or I could watch him at work and see how he was. Things were different here; everything and everybody seemed more remote, more by themselves. I walked over to the kitchen and poured him and myself a cup of coffee and we sat at the table and enjoyed our beverages.

We were having such a nice chat when he asked me if I was going to Midnight Mass at St. Oliver's. He said his mom would be expecting to see him there, and if I came I could meet his dad. I was blushing and I could tell, then he embarrassingly noticed. "What?" he asked.

"Well, it's just that we were just making out a second ago and then you mentioned church. I just thought of Catholic school where we were told to always have a space for our guardian angel in between you and a boy."

He chuckled. "Aurora… there ain't noth'n' wrong with kissi'n' a woman, especially a pretty one like you. What y'd think, when you get married and have kids, you won't be kissin' like that after Sunday breakfast and then going off to church? There ain't noth'n' wrong with being affectionate with someone you care about. Now if you be doing that with everyone, that's different, but God made you to be attracted to women now and ya gots to pay y'r respects in church." He stood up and took my hand to pull me up to him and kissed me. He pulled away to tease me with, "There is something wrong with 'em boys up in Avoca if they don't wanta go to church or kiss you." He chuckled and shot me the biggest smile. I slapped his behind with the dish towel I had quickly rolled up. He said he was hungry and asked me if I wanted to go to Waffle House before we went to Mass.

I was so glad to be out of the house, as I didn't want our evening to end, but I was getting uncomfortable being alone in the house with Derrick because it felt too right. Part of me was scared that hanging out with him seemed so natural and that one day he would just decide he didn't like me anymore. My feelings were getting stronger for him, and I was also afraid, because I could see myself giving in to the feeling and I was afraid it was too soon. Losing your virginity was supposed to be special. I wasn't saying I thought I was going to wait until I was married or something, as I had never really given much thought to having a boyfriend, let alone getting married. That was just it, it was all new and scary and I was afraid it would end before I could really get comfortable with it and enjoy it. The other reason was really odd, and I was sure if I told anyone they would think I was weird, okay, more weird than they probably already thought.

It was just that I had just gotten comfortable in my house, in the whole situation, and I wasn't used to having people in my space. Looking around at my things and relaxing and being in my private dwelling, let alone a really hot guy who I really was starting to like. I cared what he thought too and wanted him to like me as much as I liked him, if not more; so it just added to the weirdness of him being in my personal space. Thinking of it now, I had never had company. No one had ever visited me in either apartment in Avoca, only landlord stuff. Rosa was my first guest, and I wasn't sure if she counted as she was more like an older aunt than a guest. No, Derrick was the first one, and because it seemed so right, it was scaring the hell out of me.

I was just so attracted to him that I found myself pulling closer to him as my reflexes were screaming run away. I was a certain mess, I thought, as he ordered us both a coffee and water. Looking into his eyes, it was hard to judge him, to not trust, as they were so big and clear. I just sat and sipped my coffee, allowing the warm to flow down as he spoke. It was hard to care about getting hurt when in the moment I was so happy. I had never felt safer or more comfortable in my life than I did when I was with him.

Soon we found our way to St. Oliver's. Mass was beautiful and it felt good to sing all the hymns in unison with the congregation. Derrick's dad was his height and build but had more of a golden complexion, with dark hair and more sharp features. He was crisp and professional but very nice. He seemed pleased to see me there with his son and to be enjoying the service with his family. It felt good to share the holiday with Derrick and his family. It had been forever since I was last at confession, so I did a terrible thing and received communion so as not to seem bad in front of Derrick and his family. I thought God knows my heart and knows why I did it; I couldn't bear the thought of them wondering what I had done that was so bad that I had to skip out on Christmas Communion. I just said an Act of Contrition as I allowed the wafer to dissolve under my tongue and was okay with it, as what had I really done that was terrible since my last confession? Nothing that I could think of. It was just the rules and I was fine with breaking this one to save face. I just asked God in that moment to lead me to do what I was supposed to do, as I felt like I didn't know what I was doing. After Mass, Derrick excused us from his parents and said, "I'm going to see that she gets home, love you," and we headed back toward Rosebud.

"Well, it's officially Christmas, so Merry Christmas," he said.

"Merry Christmas," I replied with a smile. "Oh, hey, I almost forgot. Would it be too much trouble for you to drop me off at Vines Park? I left my car there. He said, "Of course not," as we made our way down Athens Hwy. He pulled in and there it was, all by its lonesome self. My Subaru had collected some dew from the cool moisture in the winter air. I got out and thanked him and waved as my car started right up. I pulled out toward the access road and

I made a left with a wave and he made a right down Athens Hwy. The road was completely empty and scattered with the occasional holiday wreath or snowman that the county hung from the street lights. As I drove, I saw a derelict individual, male, clad in a loose jacket with a hood of some sort. It reminded me of a cloth garbage bag as he walked slowly. It would have seemed to be a sad sight to see one walking alone on a cold Christmas night if he hadn't looked so menacing. He was headed for the entrance to the small trailer park that attempted to hide itself from view off of Athens Hwy 78 by a daycare and a group of trees that showed a small resemblance to the forest they were before the mobile homes took residence. As he walked under one of the street lights, I was able to see his face, and it was him, the leader of the group of boys who tried to assault me that night! I tried not to be bigoted and think of course he does, where else would he live but in that run-down trailer park off of the highway?

I hated that I had fallen into a pattern of thinking that was driven by assumptions, but honestly, if he lived next to Derrick in that well-loved and cared-for neighborhood, I would be shocked. Him going in there made sense as it looked as though no one cared about that place, and it was obvious he didn't care about anything either. The screen door that covered the main entrance hung halfway off its hinges and swung in the wind as I drove past in a testament of my assessment of him and his place. I mean, yeah, he could just be a product of his environment but honestly that was just an excuse, he wouldn't act the way he did just because he was poor. Heck, most of the people I knew were poor and didn't act like him. He was just plain mean. Mean-looking, sounding, and most people would just try to stay away from him. To be honest, that trailer that looked like it would fall over if I kicked it was at least a reason for him to be so miserable a person. Well, I may have almost believed that had I not come from the projects myself and knew a lot of good people who were so poor, they told their kids to fill their pockets from the school lunch so they had something to eat later, and they were never unkind. In fact, most of them wouldn't do harm to anyone. Not coming from money isn't an excuse to hurt people. I sped up and was happy to have my Subaru to get as far away from him as I could and took comfort in knowing that he couldn't see me from the street, especially in the dark. I pulled into the driveway and was happy to see the lights from my Christmas tree could be seen from the great window. Well, it looked like an actual home, my home, as I could see Jade peeking out from under the curtain.

I went into the house and went straight to bed, only to be woken up at 2 am by a sudden jump. I had no recollection of a dream and looked at the alarm clock on my nightstand to orientate myself. When I saw the time, it made sense in some sort of weird way, almost as if I knew it was 2 am. I went to the bathroom and when I was finished I was wide awake and not happy as I didn't want to ruin my schedule. Just then, I heard the door downstairs slam shut and I looked at Jade, so I knew there was no logical explanation for it; someone must be in the house.

As still as I could be, I tried to listen to see if I could hear any more movement; nothing. I had to go investigate. I quietly left my room and closed the door behind me, going through each room and shutting the doors behind me as I made my way toward the stairs. At least I knew no one could come at me from behind. As I arrived on the first floor, I glanced around. The front door was locked; all the windows and foyer looked as I had left them. The living room was clear, dining room, only to check the kitchen now, clear. I turned on the light, checked the mud room and double-checked the door. It was locked. The basement latch was locked from this side; no way could someone have gone down there and locked the door, even if they had a key. The latch was locked; impossible. However, I knew I had to go down there because someone could have come in from the basement and found this door locked and gone back out, thus the slam I heard. I was trying to work up the nerve to open the door but found myself frozen. What if it was someone as menacing as the guy I saw last night, the one who chased me into Vines? No way I could fight him off and get away without getting seriously hurt. My only chance with someone like that was to hide. But this was my house and I had to make sure it was secure. I looked down at Jade and said, "Ya know, sometimes dogs have their perks. What, don't get insulted. Okay, you better be ready to scratch and bite then." I removed the skeleton key from the nail and stuck it into the keyhole and turned until I heard the click. I then pushed the latch to the side and with a quiet, slow pull I allowed the door to open. It sounded quiet and was dark. I flipped the switch and made my way down the stairs into the basement; nothing. I opened the guest room, looked under the bed, in the empty closet and bathroom; nothing. I opened up the exterior door that led to the cellar; nothing. I moved an old metal garbage can that housed a shovel, rake, pick ax, ax and broom to sit directly in front of the shelf that hid my secret door. I took some comfort in knowing that if someone did open it, they would make a racket and at least give me a brief warning if they weren't scared off by the noise.

Grandma had put bells on every door but that one. I guess it was so if she had to sneak out, she could pass by undetected, but honestly, if you knew they were there, you could still come and go in quiet. It would take some effort but it could be done. It was there for the people who didn't know about them. To warn the people that were supposed to be there against uninvited guests. Grandma was a funny lady, but I understood her, it seemed. I made my way up into the house from the basement, locking all the doors behind me. I stopped in the kitchen for a glass of water and was starting to feel more secure as I completed my ritual of securing every room as I passed through it.

Guess I just gave myself a scare, not used to living in a drafty old house alone. I mean, I had rented the apartment in Avoca but I wasn't alone. There were still people living below me; and in the projects, the duplexes were set up as units of two, so there was a family living next door in the same building; a single mom and her three kids. There were always landlords or government workers, utility guys, someone who was invested in the place to check in on me. I guess I wasn't used to being all alone, even though I thought I was. I locked up the door behind me, turned out the lights in the kitchen and made my way toward the Christmas tree. I pulled out Jade's tiny present of treats and pulled him onto my lap as I opened the tiny cardboard jar and gave him one of the treats. "Merry Christmas, buddy," I said to him with a stroke as I placed him down. I unplugged the tree and made my way toward the stairs to return to bed now that I was assured no one was in the house. Just as I was about to close my door, I realized he was taking longer than normal to come up behind me. After my experience of freaking myself out and being woken up in the middle of the night, I just couldn't get into bed and fall asleep with the door open. I didn't feel safe. I got out of bed and called him. "Jade." He came running up the stairs and then just sat at the top and began grooming himself. "Come on, silly, its bedtime." I softly beckoned. I stepped out into the hallway to notice the bathroom and den door was open. What! I was sure I had closed them behind me when I checked those rooms not an hour before. I was certain of it. Also, I walked back by them to come into this one. I felt the hairs stand back up on the back of my neck in a cold chill of fear.

I remembered what Mrs. Vendor used to tell me to calm me down: *Fear the living, not the dead, child.* It was so true. I would much rather see some unexplained phenomena than that group of guys from Vines Park any day, but in this moment it was really hard to get over the feeling of fear. Just in that moment, the den door slammed shut, then the bathroom door closed, then in a gust of wind, the bedroom door behind me shut. I felt so scared, a chill of goosebumps covered my body and I thought I was going to pee myself. I could smell the scent of flowers, roses to be certain. Jade came to my feet and I scooped him up so fast and ran into my bedroom and closed the door behind me. I moved the upholstered chair up against it and held Jade, just looking at the door. I said, "Okay," out loud. I went to the bathroom and said at least three Our Fathers before I curled up in a ball under the blankets and fell asleep in a pit of fear.

I woke up at 7 am and it was a bright, chilly morning. The sun wasn't quite up but it was bright enough that I could see, telling me it was going to be a sunny day for the winter. I thought about how silly I was spooking myself out the night before as I moved the chair back into place. If it was anything, a spook or what have you, it didn't seem menacing. I know in most good horror films, that's how the spooks always start out, seeming benign then later in the story revealing themselves to be something more sinister. Even in knowing this, I felt pretty good that morning, and I was happy to enjoy it, not bothering myself to analyze how odd it was to feel this way. I mean, I was woken up in the middle of the night and scared half to death by an unexplainable force. The energy in the house seemed positive, if I was to get all metaphysical and hippie-like. Honestly, if I knew for certain there were spooks, I think it would have been less scary than hearing noises and not knowing what they were. There is something terrifying about a being, person or otherwise, who breaks rules, because you don't know what they are capable of, but ya know they don't care because the usual constraints such as rules don't guide them. I do know for certain if someone is in your house and you didn't invite them in, most likely it's going to end up bad for you. I entertained the thought further until I was finished with my shower and in my yoga pants and sweater for the day.

I made coffee and two eggs with toast and just reclined on the couch to watch *Christmas with the Kranks* when the phone rang. It was Andi wishing me a Merry Christmas and congratulating me on successfully completing my first semester and registering for the upcoming one my own. He apologized for not checking on me sooner and asked if there was anything I needed. We made plans to have dinner on the 3rd of January and he told me his wife, my cousin, would be there too. He wished me a Happy New Year as well and told me to be careful; reminding me that everybody parties that night so I should try to stay off the roads, as there are a lot of people drinking and driving about. We said our goodbyes and I finished the movie in a comfortable mood, snuggled warmly under a throw on the couch.

*

Christmas came and went and the following day Derrick called before noon, asking if he could come over. Before he was barely in the door, he began kissing me and we ended up making out on the sofa of my living room for two hours. It was like a comfortable dream that I didn't want to awake from, but nature called and I had to use the bathroom. Once inside, I saw the area around my mouth was all red from making out and my hair looked terrible, all puffy and going in a mess of every direction. I had no idea where my scrunchy was that had it held up in a secure bun before our kissing session had started. I opened the bathroom door and called to Derrick, "Hey, you want to get a bite to eat?" He manifested with my scrunchy in hand. "Definitely, as you sure made me hungry," he said, approaching me with another kiss. I pushed him back after allowing him to steal a small fast kiss, and said, "All right, let me get cleaned up so we can go."

"Why, you look great. I know you'll be the best-looking one in there, wherever we go," he smiled. He walked over to the foyer and put his leather jacket on. He looked smart; I had never seen a leather coat look expensive before. Usually, bikers and punk rockers came to mind when I thought of leather, but this looked business-like. He still looked casual, as he donned dark jeans and an old navy collared shirt and sweater. I put on my jacket blazer I'd found with Rosa for .25c, which surprisingly looked nice over my sweater and slimming yoga pants which gave the appearance that I was wearing a dress and leggings, but I knew the truth.

We headed down Rosebud and Derrick made a right into the park I had seen when having lunch with my cousin in Grayson. He parked and said, "Pizza okay?" I said sure, but didn't see the restaurant from the trees and playground. I knew the coffee house was across the street and the ice cream place Bruster's, but if we were going there, why park all the way over here? Well, maybe he wanted to get some exercise, as he was really into fitness.

"They have pizza in the park?" I asked.

"Kind of, I think you'll like the New York-style pizza parlor they opened up. It's okay for Yankee food," he teased. "It's just a'ways up," he gestured as he took my hand into his as he closed the car door behind me and led me away from his car.

We strolled through the picturesque park and past the row of old houses whose yards ended at the path that meandered around the enclosure where the rides for the local children were housed. You could see the life that was Loganville and now the newly developed Grayson area, as we passed the aged houses that sat long past their glory. He commented, "Yeah, these were the old families of the area before 'em Yankees came in and developed all this for commercial. They had 'em ideas and proposed all this development, but when I was a kid, none of this was here. Not the Kroger, this park or roads even. This was a dirt road that took you to town, past these houses that had lived here since the time of the Civil War. They just enclosed them in there, one side the park, other side Rosebud Road, and they just kept living there, stuck in time. I heard they were offered a lot of money too. The city could have expanded the park but they were old, stubborn families who liked the way things were and their lives they had built there. The funny thing is, I heard his son, and I hope it ain't true 'cause I'd a hate it for 'im if it was," as he gestured to the old white house with the clothesline that still hung in the back on either side of his beaten-up white picket fence, "went on to college in New York City and is up there living large making Yankee profits." His poor father, I sympathized. "I didn't expect you to understand, being from up there," he said.

"Well, Avoca isn't New York City, for one thing. Number two, I don't have to think like someone to be able to relate to what they're going through. I assume every parent wants their kid to be like them and their family, and share their values."

He looked at me and smiled. "I knew you were okay," he winked. We meandered around the curved pathway that led down a flight of wooden stairs to the pizza parlor.

New York Pizza had a funky, dark college kid vibe with its strung lights that illuminated the restaurant walls and created a cozy, private atmosphere with its high-backed wooden booths and separate bar area where you could get adult beverages. When I went to the bathroom, I realized why they had closed off the bar, as I passed the arcade that was loaded with kids of various ages. After we had finished off a medium cheese pizza and a basket of BBQ chicken wings and two sweet teas, we just sat and talked. Eventually, he ordered us two Heinekens and we talked for another hour before it started to get dark. He paid the check and we walked back to the car. In not wanting to leave each other's company, he said, "You want to go to Vines'? We can sit and watch the sunset at the lake," he encouraged.

I said, "Yeah," with a smile that let him know I didn't want our time to end either.

He parked close to the very spot I usually take up and we walked under the entrance gate into the park hand in hand. I stopped to use the bathroom and found him waiting for me at the water fountain. "I am so thirsty from the pizza. I guess it was the garlic," he said as he took a big helping of water from the fountain. "I'm surprised they left it on. They usually only let it run during the summer months on account of all those people who have heatstroke in the summer; otherwise, those greedy councilmen would have it shut off all year long," he commented.

"This from the guy who lectured me over chicken wings about registering to vote and taking responsibility for your life," I chuckled. He kissed me and then draped his arm around my waist as we strolled to the end of the path to the rocking bench that faced the water. It was so beautiful, sitting there at Vines so close to Derrick on the swinging bench, just watching the sun descend behind the lake and resting my head on his arm. I would probably have been cold had I not been nuzzled against his sweater inside the sleeve of his heavy leather coat, just swaying back and forth.

The beautiful moment was interrupted by the sound of people, who were being really loud. Just then, we heard a crash, maybe one of the tin garbage cans and its chain that held the lid on the can. Derrick pulled me up and led me away from the noise and we walked briskly toward the white bridge and crossed the lake. I looked back to see a group of five or six guys, then I realized it was them. "Derrick! It's them; it's the guys who chased me! What do we do?" He took my hand and walked with me steadily and led me up the grassy path of the white garden. We kept walking when we were intercepted by one of them. He was taller than Derrick but not as broad. He just stood there in the middle of the walkway, smiling. I could sense this wasn't good, but I wasn't sure what the right thing to do was to escape; surely, his friends weren't far behind him.

Derrick kept walking forward but held me a little behind him. He looked the guy right in the eye with determination and said, "Excuse me."

The guy didn't move, so Derrick attempted to go around him, putting me on the right, away from the guy and into the grass so I could pass. Just then, Derrick was shoved by the guy. "Why don't you watch where you're going?"

Derrick shoved the guy back and countered with, "Why don't you?" The guy stumbled back but chuckled and gave us both an evil grin as one of his friends approached from behind him. As we looked at them, Derrick said, "Run, Aurora!" So I did, but not too far because I knew if I left him, they would hurt him bad, maybe even kill him. I made it to the mermaid statue and jumped into the high grass and flowers that surrounded her base. *Oh God*, I said to myself in a whisper of a prayer. I waited anxiously to see Derrick, for him to come. I knew only seconds had passed but it seemed like an eternity. I heard them rumbling, scraping the gravel beneath their feet, brushing against shrubs maybe. They needed to be quiet or else the others would hear them and Derrick and I would have no chance. I knelt on a rock in pain but was relieved to find something to defend myself with, if need be. I held its jagged edges; it was a good one, thick and heavy.

As I crouched up, I could see Derrick throwing punches as he tried to fight them off as the others approached from the distance. There was my chance. As he knocked one down, I threw the rock and it hit the back of the other one's head. His arm went up to touch his head as he fell down. Derrick took the moment to run toward me but he couldn't see me. I jumped out and he followed me. We ran in between the guardians and took a shortcut in between the Lady of the Water and the Lady of the Grain, past the giant rose bushes that separated them, toward my secret opening in the meadow. I looked back to see if we had eluded them and stopped dead in my tracks, frozen, trying to take in what I was seeing. The same style of flowers I had found in front of my storm doors was placed like an offering at the feet of the statue of the Lady of the Fowl! There was no denying the same person must have done this; it was bound in the same twine and same fashion. I shook myself out of the daze, realizing I was soon to be dead, much like a deer that was frozen in the sight of an approaching car's headlights, if I didn't pick up speed and move!

I sped up my legs to run. I wasn't certain exactly where it was but I knew I was in the right spot. Derrick said, "Hey, we have to get out of here. We have to hide." I realized he didn't know what I was doing, but just in that moment, I found it and pulled the door up.

"Come on," I said as I went down the stairs. He followed and we shut the trapdoor. "Hurry," I said. "We have to make sure the other door is shut so they can't get in." I ran down the hall as it illuminated with my steps. I was running in such determination I didn't look back to see his expression. I made it and pulled the door closed to make sure they wouldn't find the entrance by the bunny statue I had left ajar a couple of days ago. Out of breath, we just leant against the walls and allowed our breathing to regulate, looking at each other in disbelief and appreciation that we had made it; we had gotten away.

When we regained our composure, he grabbed me in a kiss of such passion I began to feel faint. "Aurora, what is this place?" he asked.

I told him. "I don't know. I found the map at my house. I think my grandmother had a hand in building it." I told him about the research I had done at the library, and the chest, and Andi. I led him back to the room and we freshened up in the bathroom and I told him everything. I shared all my thoughts about my secret find and even that I had been afraid to tell him at first. "In a strange way, I'm glad this happened, so I could share this with you. I am so sorry you had to get hurt, though," I said as I patted his bloody nose with cool water and toilet paper.

"It's nothin'," he assured me. "I'm just glad you're all right, that you're safe. Aurora, 'em guys are no good. Now I want you to stay away from 'em, yer hear?"

"Believe me," I said, "if I knew of a way to do that, I surely would." He looked at me with such a funny look. "What... were you expecting a 'what, and miss all of this fun' kind of answer? Derrick, I told you I am honest, now cut the crap, okay."

He chuckled out a "Yes, ma'am," with his big smile. Most people wouldn't be able to smile with their face all bloodied up.

It was then, in that moment, that I realized what had happened: I had fallen for him. Right in that moment I knew he cared about me, cared about what happened to me. He was the one that was bleeding and his only thoughts were about me. He wanted to know that I was all right, safe. The feeling that accompanied knowing he wanted me safe stirred something so deep inside me, something that I had longed for, that I kissed him. I had continued the movement by wrapping my arms around him in a close embrace as he slowly backed up and was leading me until he slowly fell on the bed behind us. I still with my arms around him and distracted by all the moment of his kiss, found myself lying next to him on the small cot still in his embrace. He began touching and caressing every part of my body so that I wanted more and more of him until it happened; we were completely naked and didn't stop. He retrieved a condom from his wallet and allowed my feelings to take over the moment with him. He was obviously experienced or at least had done this a couple of times before, as he took over and led me through the experience. Afterwards, we just lay in each other's arms for a while before he asked me if I was okay. He stroked the peach on the chain he had given me and looked at me very contentedly. I got dressed and told him I was hungry. He looked perplexed as he tried to follow me while pulling up his jeans.

I looked at him and said, "I can trust you, right, Derrick?"

He said, "Yeah, of course, what's this about? Listen, Aurora... I know maybe we moved a little fast and maybe I kind of took advantage of the moment of the emotion 'n all... but what I'm train' to say is, well, I like you and I want you to be my girl." He paused.

"What?" I said, kind of half paying attention and it coming out more rudely than I had intended. "No, what I am trying to say is... Well, what I didn't tell you was that this leads back to my place. Like, directly to my basement." There, I got it out.

"Do what?" he said. "Yer grandma was something else, just like her granddaughter," as he grabbed my hand. "I think we should just go back to my house and drive over here in the morning, when it's daylight outside, and check out your car."

"Do you think they'd do anything to it? Oh, I hope not," I said.

"You're right, 'cause if they did somethin', we'd be stuck there defenseless. At least this way we have a clear, safe path back to the house," he went on as we walked as though he and I were just strolling along the street in the middle of the afternoon and not on a crazy adventure in a secret tunnel that only we knew about.

*

Back at my house, I enjoyed seeing his reaction to my secret. It was almost as great as when I had experienced it. It was like reliving it again through watching him go through it.

Watching his wonder at our find and happy to have escaped from those thugs, and our experience that night, was just the best. I looked at him as I made a pot of coffee and said, "You know, you, that was my first time, right?"

"No," he said, "but I kind of figured."

Then a plague of insecurities came up and I commented, "Why, was I terrible or like why did you think I was a virgin?"

"No, no, no, you were great. I mean, you could just tell by the way you were acting and the way you carried yourself, is all." He went on, "What I mean is it was nice, Aurora, and I would like to do it again." He smiled. He walked over to me slowly. "Would you like that?" he teased. "Now that you are an experienced woman an' all, would you like to show me a thing or two?" he said as he nibbled on my neck and scooped me up and carried me up the stairs. He placed me down at the top of the stairs, kissing me and pulling away to find my bedroom as he looked in each room. He finally found my room and led me into the room and took off our clothes, then surprised me by leading me into the shower, where he washed both of us.

Afterwards, we just explored each other under the covers of my bed until we fell asleep, because he said he didn't have another condom. He said if he was with any other girl, he would have left and got some; but he didn't want to leave me alone after all that had happened. "Plus, this is real nice," he said. That was the last thing I remembered before falling asleep in his arms.

*

We woke up and I showered and put on clean yoga pants. I was so happy to find Derrick still there, eager to have another day like the day before with him. Somehow, even having to run from those guys, the fact that Derrick was with me made it impossible that the day would be a bad one. I was just sorry he got hurt but so happy I was able to share my secret about the tunnel with someone. Couldn't believe I had lost my virginity. It didn't seem weird, and I didn't seem any different, just a lot happier. Happy to have experienced it finally and that it was with him. It was perfect. I mean, I guess most girls would want candles and a bed of roses or something romantic, but for me it was real and passionate. Most of all, I cared about him and I wanted it to happen. To share how I felt with him, and he said he felt the same way.

"How is your face?" I asked as he poured my coffee.

"Oh, it's fine. Don't even hurt anymore. Forgot about it, in fact. I had so many more lovely experiences after that to take my mind off it," he said, kissing my hand.

"If this doesn't work out, I don't know how I will ever get over you," I said.

He looked at me with the utmost charming seriousness and said, "You're not. Guess you should just stick around then and make it work," he smiled with a chuckle.

"I believe, sir, you are taking full advantage of my innocence," I chided.

"Well now, I have plans for your innocence later," he said, with a naughty masculine taunt. "But as for now, it seems you are the one who holds all the cards, Miss Aurora." He confirmed his feelings and I melted. There was no denying how I felt about him, no barriers that I could put up anymore. I thought why, it was silly to not be honest. If he ended up hurting me, so be it. I didn't want to miss out on something great or hurt him because I was afraid. So I just gave him a big smile and we went down into the basement and out the tunnel door. We walked the long way to Vines Park, chatting the whole time, enjoying each other's company and our small adventure.

Strangely, I was more worried about him knowing about my secret tunnel to Vines Park than in losing my virginity to him. I am not sure if that was messed up or not. I mean, the sex with Derrick was honest and real; it was beautiful and just happened. Both of us were adults and consented; we wanted it. We wanted to be together. Vines Park was an old secret and I wasn't sure yet whose secret it was to keep. I mean, I wasn't sure yet or why even I was allowed to know. I just hoped that I was right about Derrick. I wouldn't know how to even get it sealed off if I had to, and it would really be sad to have to close this magical and beautiful thing because, well, if Derrick decided to be a jerk, well, what could he do with the knowledge? Tell people, I guess, not keep our secret. I almost had a panic attack as my mind filled with the images of gangs of street kids, punk rockers and worst of all, those guys from last night drinking beer and writing graffiti in the tunnels, my tunnels! Those guys would have direct and hidden access to my home, and they could come and torment me whenever they felt like it, unseen. I would be forced to move and they would ruin it and I knew would take much joy in its destruction. In ruining this beautiful, magical thing my grandmother had trusted me with. Oh no! What had I done?

My face must have revealed my horror as I could not contain my fears inside. My expression betrayed me and now, as he held both of my arms and beckoned me to face him, "Aurora, what is it? Are you all right?"

"Derrick, I just need to know that you won't tell anyone about this," I said. Pain swept across his face as though I had stabbed him in the gut. "Look, I know it's really awesome, I mean, like out of a movie, right? But that is exactly why we have to keep it a secret. I mean, we don't know why my grandmother did this yet. Derrick, you said you cared about me," I said, approaching him until I stood as close as I possibly could to him. I looked at him with a serious earnest so he would know how to take what I was about to say. I looked up at his face, deep into his eyes searching for a commitment, for honesty and said, "Look… you said you care about me. Well this is really important, and I trusted you with this. My secret. I need to know you won't tell anyone, no matter what. Not the police, the FBI, CIA, anybody. Not even your mom."

"Oh, you meant about this. Vines Park and the tunnels," he said as joy swept across his face. "Aurora, I will protect this with everything I got, you have my word."

"What did you think I meant?" I asked. Then I knew; he was sad at the thought of me not wanting anyone to know I was with him, and my heart shot out like a rocket of joy and emotion. We just continued our walk hand in hand along our secret path until we reached the stop.

We made it to the opening in the beginning of the woods that faced Vines Park. I peeked out and I didn't see anyone, so I came out and then Derrick. We made sure to cover up the door so no one could find it if they happened to walk by. We walked to his Jeep and it seemed to be okay. All the tires were intact and it didn't appear to have any scratches or dents. All the windows were as they should be: unbroken. "Maybe they were too dumb to connect that this was our car, but I really don't see how, as it was the only vehicle in the parking lot. You know, if they knew it was ours, they would have done something." He dropped down to the ground and looked under the car and said wait as he came up and opened the car door. He put the key in and started the car; he let it run for a few seconds.

I teased him, "Boy, I thought I was paranoid," and giggled.

"Aurora, 'em guys are bad, there is no telling what they'd do." He asked me to get in and if I would like to get something to eat. We were off to the diner across the street, the Main Street Restaurant. The place actually sat in front of his neighborhood, so if we really wanted to, we could have walked, but both of us were worn out after our last couple days. I got the French toast, and it was large. I thought they must make the bread themselves in the back because I had never seen slices of bread so thick. We just sat for a while, enjoying each other's company in the privacy of the small place off of the highway.

He dropped me off at my house and gave me a hug and a quick kiss and told me he would like me to come to a holiday social with him and his parents at the country club. "Awh, it's no big deal, Aurora. It's just the Summit Chase annual bash, they have it every New Year's Eve and I won't be able to enjoy myself if you're not there. Who will I dance with? You know, I'd just be thinking of you the whole time. Just come and put me out of my misery." It was impossible to say no to him. One, because he was gorgeous and secondly, because I had never had anyone seem like they really wanted me to come anywhere, let alone care enough to try to convince me.

"Guess I should start looking for a dress," I said with a smile. Plus, we were kind of together now. I mean, it wasn't officially said but it was. It wouldn't be right for him to be dancing with other girls, and I wanted to be part of his life. I mean, he wanted to share this with me and this was something he normally would do, and as stupid or pretentious as I thought these kinds of things were, if I was with him, I should show him I supported him and show up to be a part of his life. Even if I didn't agree with or like everything he did. Heck, I could stomach one evening of stuck-up country club snobs for Derrick. Ya know, that might not be fair. I mean, I was wrong about Loganville, right? I mean, Derrick and his mom were like the two coolest, most down-to-earth people, and they belonged to this country club.

Maybe I was wrong about everything and I was the one who was a snob, and the worst kind, because I had no experience to base my beliefs on. I mean, when was the last time I had hung around a bunch of rich people? Like never, so I should have been more open, I guess. I didn't like it but that may have been because I was out of my element. There was only one way to find out and I was super excited that I was going.

Chapter Seventeen

One of Them

I managed to find a beautiful, flapper-style silver spaghetti strap dress for two dollars at Rosa's thrift store. I had to go on Friday, so everything was two dollars instead of our usual twenty-five cents. Hey, who can complain? I found a dress that fit and that I would have paid sixty dollars for at the mall. I had a pair of black suede pumps already and they had already been worn a couple times so they were comfortable. I just pinned on a vintage-style clip-on earring to the top of the shoe and the silver accent matched the shoe, so it looked like they went together. I chuckled to myself as I walked into the country club on Derrick's arm. I knew I looked the part, and none of these wealthy socialites would know I had paid a total of six dollars for my collection of handbag, clip-on earrings and party dress. I had on a black fur coat that Rosa gave me. She said she got it for fifty cents and it was too much for church, so she insisted I keep it. She added that her daughter was an Amazon in stature; it was from her husband's mother's side of the family, so the coat wouldn't have fit her even when she was in middle school. I smiled at the thought of my moment with my friend; I was so lucky to have a neighbor like her.

Two snobby-looking blondes approached us; they were about our age. "Oh, Derrick, so glad you could come. We haven't seen you in ages. What have you been up to?" the taller one on the right almost hissed. She was pretty, but her face was too cruel for her to be attractive. Her friend was almost a replica of her, but more plain in features and appearance.

"Amanda and Gretchen, this is Aurora, my girlfriend," Derrick said as he introduced us. His *girlfriend*; the words were so sweet to my ears but I tried to play it off like it was expected, or casual in my attempt to hide my emotions. I was so happy in that moment I felt like my soul was screaming and had jumped out of my skin. I concentrated on my breathing and tried to copy the plainer girl's mannerisms to cover up what I was feeling. Amanda swooned with an "Ooh" and she gave me the once-over look as she glanced at me, up and down. I knew in that moment, if I had doubted it before, that she liked Derrick and wanted him for herself. She managed a fake all-teeth smile and they turned away as quickly as they had appeared, thank goodness. I wondered if they had dated before, but there was no way I could ask him. He led me to the dance floor and we danced until an instrumental version of *I'll be Home for Christmas* started up by the band. Here goes… "Girlfriends of yours?" I asked as I looked up into his eyes as he held me close to slow dance.

"Them witches? No. Plus, my mom would kill me if I did. If she can't hold a conversation with them for more than five minutes, she doesn't approve. In fact, you just might be the only one she's approved of, possibly liked even," he chuckled.

"Yeah, your mom is great," I commented.

He led us over to the table and poured us some punch and introduced me to "all the right people," as he put it. After an hour of socializing and smiling at all of his parents' nosy friends as he referred to most of them, he led us to our table. "Aurora, I appreciate you coming along tonight. Look, I know it ain't your thing. In fact, I don't want to put on all the necessary charm and social graces, but it means a lot to my dad, so my mom does it, and they really appreciate it when I do it too," he said. "Mom says he worked really hard to get where he is and most of it was for us, so I really am thankful for your company, as there is only so much of the expected manners and conversation I can put on," he commented as he looked at me with such honesty and sweetness that I really appreciated it.

"Well, I value you opening up to me and sharing your life with me, and if this is the bad part, it's definitely doable," I said with a chuckle. I could tell he liked it when I smiled big and he shot me one back, as if they were contagious. He escorted me back to our table as most people were clearing off of the dance floor to find their seats. "What's happening now?" I asked.

"Oh, now we go order our food and mingle with our table before the ceremony," he informed me.

He ordered the lamb chops and I had the roasted hen. It was delicious but nothing I would pass a big cheeseburger up at the diner for, definitely not my French toast, but I guess it was all in what you were used to eating and doing, that was what made it good or enjoyable. A couple people made speeches and spoke about upcoming charity events and I just tried to be a good date and look pleasant. We danced a couple more times before the final dance on the countdown, when at midnight, balloons and confetti shot down from the ceiling upon us and we kissed one long, passionate kiss for good luck. "Happy New Year, Aurora," he said, looking into my eyes as our lips departed from our embrace. "Happy New Year," and I hugged him, leaving with my arm still around his waist. He helped me to my coat and he tipped the coat clerk with a five-dollar bill. It seemed like a lot but yet not enough for this place. It was too fast that I couldn't catch the denomination, but a twenty would have been too much, I'd imagine. He took me back to my house and said goodnight and that he had had such a nice time. "Thank you, Aurora, you saved me. Happy New Year."

"Goodnight, call you tomorrow," I said as I closed the Jeep door.

I waved once I got inside the house and watched him drive away down my street toward Athens Hwy. I took a nice hot shower, mostly to remove the chill that had settled in my bones from the winter air outside. I put the kettle on for a cup of tea in my plan to unwind and get ready for bed. Funny how one wouldn't think someone from Pennsylvania would get cold in the mild Georgia winters. I read about it at the library. It has to do with the humidity in the south and how the moisture sticks, making it seem colder than the temperature reads. Well, I believed it as I was freezing. I even put on my fuzzy socks I had bought the week before at the Dollar Store. I sat at the kitchen table, drinking my tea and stroking Jade until my beverage was gone. It had helped as I felt comfortable and wasn't cold anymore. It was hard for me to relax if I was cold. I made my way upstairs and brushed my teeth and fell asleep in less than twenty minutes.

*

I was up at eight o'clock and dressed and full of coffee by 9 am. I called Derrick and was en route to his house to eat cookies and just enjoy a day of T.V. with him before we had to go back to school the following Monday. It was his last semester and he was so ready to graduate. I totally understood. I had also taken on this 'get it over with' attitude about school. Well, he did it. And it was over like that, so quick I don't even remember much of the three months leading up to the end of the semester. He told me he would like it if I came to his graduation. He said I could sit with his parents and we could all ride back to the restaurant to celebrate. A small group of his friends and his parents' friends would be there. His grandparents on his father's side had passed away a couple years ago, and his grandmother on his mother's side and his cousins were all in Maine. Well, that explained her laid-back attitude, as his mom was what people described as a real down-to-earth kind of person. "Gosh, real climate adjustment for her; I totally feel her pain. But this month was perfect, just needed a light jacket or a sweater and a hat," I added. His dad was definitely what you would call a 'good ol' boy,' southern down to the grits, as they say. I wondered how they'd hooked up. Derrick was too excited from the talk and making plans to celebrate his acknowledgement for me to bog him down with personal stuff right now, especially questions about his parents. No, he worked hard and did it. I wanted to show him support and be happy with him in the moment. I let him scoop me up and give me a big kiss.

After his graduation, we drove over to Texas Rhode House, in Snellville. It was a Texas/Western-themed steakhouse that seemed fun but also like a good place to eat. As we walked in, we were immediately addressed and seated, as his father had made reservations and reserved a giant room in the back for us. It was a cork floor that was covered in peanut shells from the giant barrel in the waiting area that was filled with peanuts. Guests were encouraged to 'eat up' while they waited to be seated. We passed large stuffed moose heads that were displayed on the wall on an actual saddle on a faux horse for the kids to amuse themselves while their parents passed the time with peanuts. We were led past a giant glass counter top where you could select your meat or steak to be cooked specifically for you. We passed a table being sung to and two-stepped for by the staff. Derrick explained they did that when it was a guest's birthday. "Sorry, Aurora, you'll have to wait 'til June," he teased.

I countered with, "That's all right."

His dad chimed in with, "What, she's a June bug! What day? I'm June the 8th," he stated.

"June 1st," I said.

"Well, ain't that something," he smiled, and allowed me and Derrick to pass in front of him to get into the room. The room was packed with about fifty people, all happy-faced, who let out a cheer when Derrick and I entered. I couldn't help but be happy with everyone smiling and shaking Derrick's hand and mine, some patting him on the back as we passed to be seated. Derrick sat at the head of the table with me to his right. His mom sat next to me and his dad sat next to her. He was surrounded by his friends who, apparently, were also University of Georgia alumni. It started to feel like a mix of a giant frat party and old Savannah money mixed into one. Like confirmation that he was a 'Bulldog,' similar to a girl's sweet sixteen where she was coming out into society. It seemed weird, mostly because I didn't understand it, but what would I know about parties or gatherings, as this was probably my first that wasn't a church get-together? I guess any party would have seemed weird, no matter the custom, to me. The other end of the table was a small serving tray on legs that housed a giant white cake that was decorated in his honor. Derrick leaned in to whisper, "Don't worry, no one has noticed your Yankee ways." He chuckled. "Your secret is safe with me. Just keep drinking the sweet tea."

"Am I that transparent?" I asked.

"No, I'm just that observant, especially when it comes to my girl. I'm so happy and glad you're here with me tonight, Aurora," he said and leaned in again to plant a kiss on my cheek.

That night, we made love again back at his place, down on the sofa in his recreation room. We enjoyed each other's company, undisturbed under a quilt his grandmother had made for his family.

In the morning, we ate breakfast at a Waffle House and he dropped me off at home. I didn't want to leave his company but I knew I looked like crap and needed a long shower and my bathroom. From my porch, I watched him drive off beyond my line of sight down my street. As I watched him, I saw Barbara across the street. I waved but she ignored my friendly gesture.

I went into the house and took a nice, long, hot shower and exfoliated my whole body with my Dove body wash and loofah. It felt good to smell like a girl again, not that I didn't like the smell of Derrick, but it was time to take a good shower and scrub off the night before. I happily thought that I was in an adult relationship. I had seen them on T.V. and wondered what it would be like to be serious with someone, care about them. Attend events with them, sleep over at their house. It had all happened so fast and yet, it seemed like the right pace and going along naturally.

I made a pot of coffee in the kitchen and fed Jade and took my cup out onto the back porch to sit and admire my garden. Jade was beckoning to come outside with me but I was so afraid he would get fleas or run off that I ignored his persuasion. After one cup of his meows, I had had enough, so I just had my second cup at the island in the kitchen. "Are you happy, Mr. Annoyance?" I asked him, as I stroked his smooth fur. He just purred away. I told him that I missed him too but he had to understand that I had met someone and would be gone sometimes. He just jumped off the counter, as if to say "Like I care" and left the room. I thought that he seemed to understand me, that cat. I just lounged around the rest of the day, enjoying my time off from school and the library. I wanted to make the most of it as the upcoming semester started in three days. Well, winter break was fun while it lasted, but now it was time to get back to G.G.C.

*

Spring semester had begun and I was eager to be a sophomore. I was told by my advisor that after the summer, I would be finished with my core classes and would start taking the classes for my major and be only taking business classes. I was super excited to be making progress. I couldn't believe I was doing it, and succeeding! I was in college and actually understanding the material. I had met a couple

nice people to form a study group with. We usually met after my
last class on Tuesday and Thursday. We finished our homework or
worked on projects in the library or at Starbucks and then just hung
out. It was nice and I was starting to feel like I belonged here and it
was beginning to feel cozy and comfortable, like home.

It was nice to have friends to study with or just blow time with,
chill after class with people other than Derrick. Don't get me wrong,
no one compared to him, but it was good to just be with others too,
even if we didn't have a serious relationship. I mean, just casual chit-
chat kind of peeps to just enjoy each other's company or to discuss
subject material with. I knew I probably wouldn't see these people
again after graduation or maybe not even after this class with them,
but I valued them just the same right now and it was a pretty cool
experience. I guess it got you ready for the business world where
maybe I would meet someone and have to work on a project with
them for three months then never see them again. It wouldn't mean
I didn't value them or their work, right. I guess it's true that you learn
so much in school and most of it isn't the study material. I guess I
was growing up, I realized, and wasn't bothered by who I was or was
becoming. Avoca had definitely made me but was becoming more
of a memory, like an experience that I had moved past. I knew that I
wouldn't go back there, but I was just walking on secure ground
here in my new environment and it was still too new to determine
where or what my future would be. I just knew right now that it
looked like I was going to finish college and that was a concept that
still surprised me.

Actually, it seemed like the hardest part would be the getting-
in part, how to begin. Especially for someone like me who had no
real guidance. If it weren't for Andi and my grandmother, it would
have taken me years to figure out how to do it and who knows, I
may have felt it was too late then and have given up on myself and
my dream of finishing school. I walked back to my Subaru with a
smile, happy that I was doing it. I also realized it was easier for me

because I came from a group home environment. I thought this was probably counterintuitive, but the kids who had it easy in life found it hard to give the professor exactly what he was asking for. I also noticed the kids who were obviously treated badly by life and their environment, the ones who had a chip on their shoulder, also had it difficult. They were always trying to convince the professor that their paper was good and would be taking up class time to argue why they should have a better grade. I got what he meant when he said to them, "Your paper is good, maybe even a great paper, but it's not what I asked for."

They called him a racist or a dick behind his back or under their breath in class, but I got what he meant because I had had to please so many different people from a young age. Sometimes it was to avoid a problem, other times just to stay unnoticed in the shadows and sidelines to be safe. I had learned to give people what they wanted to get by. It was so easy for me now to size someone up in a few seconds, and I couldn't understand how it was difficult for those kids when the professor was actually telling them what he wanted; they didn't have to guess or figure it out. I felt my first sense of pride when papers were returned to me in class with a red A marked in the corner, and those kids who went to high school and had their parents would get back Cs. Of course, I didn't want them to fail but my pride soared in my ability. It was then that I realized that because of what I had gone through, I was better, and it wasn't something to be ashamed of anymore. I was here at G.G.C. just like they were; we were the same, just students who were admitted, and now it was up to me to determine who and what I was. To determine who I wanted and was going to be. My story was just the opposite of everybody else's. I started off with nothing where most other people had parents to love and care for them, to provide for and guide them. I didn't, but I didn't have to pay for school and would never have a mortgage. I thought now of those kids who had parents when I didn't have to finance school and then a mortgage, so really I now had the advantage. Of course, there were higher circles where it did matter who your parents were and what middle school you went to, but for me it didn't and I felt so fortunate with my situation and my new life.

*

On Valentine's Day, Derrick showed up with a dozen red roses and took me to Provino's, where we ate a romantic Italian dinner by candlelight. He told me he had been accepted into Mercer and wanted to get his MBA. He went on to say they had a ten-month program where he could be finished up in less than a year and that he would have to quit his job to attend full-time, as it was day hours. He said he had thought about going the one day a week where he could still work, but he really just wanted to get it over with and be done with school. I was so proud of him and happy he got accepted into the program he wanted. "So when do you start?" I asked.

"In May, so I have a little bit of time and I want to spend it with you, as I don't think I will be able to see you as much while I'm at Mercer," he said. "Actually, I'm kind of scared, to be honest, Aurora, as I heard it's intense. But I felt that a lot of people have done it, and so can I then. I just gotta buckle down, make that sacrifice for now to get my reward later," he said with a seriousness that allowed me to see his sincerity. This was important to him.

"Well, of course. I know you'll do well. I'll support you any way I can, Derrick," I said, looking into his eyes and placing my hands over his on the table. We spent the night making love at my house and then watching T.V. until we fell asleep. The next morning, we ate breakfast at the Main Street Diner and parted our ways.

*

In March, we went to the famous Cherry Blossom Festival down in Macon. I had never heard of it, of course, but was eager to go and see it. The two-hour drive with Derrick was actually enjoyable. The time just flew by, and before I knew it, we were in the old city that had somehow survived after the Civil War, but you could see it took some damage from the important hub between Savannah, Atlanta and Charleston. They had to burn it, Derrick said, but here it was. I found the small old town comforting as the old brick buildings reminded me of Avoca, with the cobblestone streets in some parts and little shops all lined up in a row. I was amused to see one of the adjacent streets closed off for the annual race, where people dressed up in pink sat on beds on wheels and raced through town. It was the oddest thing I had ever seen, but yet I wanted to see more of it and found myself eager to see what else the day would show me. There was a dog show where all the dogs were either dressed in pink or their fur was dyed the hue. Derrick said, "It didn't hurt them any," as he patted a pink poodle on the head. We walked around, rode all the rides and ate funnel cake and corn dogs until it was time to leave.

On the way back was when he said it. "I love you, Aurora. I love us." I smiled so big and for whatever reason I just couldn't say it back, even though I felt it. I found myself saying that corny line from that famous movie *Ghost* and just let the word "Ditto" fall off my lips as I slowly stuffed a handful of pink cotton candy in my mouth. His face lit up like a spark and he grabbed me in a 'got you' almost playful embrace as he said, "You think I'm a gonna let that fly, Aurora?" and he kissed me with such intent. He let me go only to look me right in the eye with his wicked gleam to say, "Don't lie. I know you do and I want it. I want it, Aurora, just as bad as I've ever wanted anything," and he kissed me again. He dropped me off at my house after a long goodnight kiss on the steps of my front porch. When he was walking off and had gotten into his car and I was waving goodbye to him as he drove down the street, I noticed Rosa. She was sweeping her porch and said loud enough for me to hear her, "Aah. Heh heh heh. Oh, don't mind me, ch'd," with her smile so big as she looked me in the eye. "Go on and be young. Not like you could help yourself; he is handsome. Likes you too, sure does." She smiled and waved. "Now go on," as she went into the house. I went into mine with the biggest smile on my face and felt so light, as though I was filled with air that had lifted me up. So this was what they were talking about, love making you feel as light as a feather. Jade rubbing his body against my ankles in his affectionate greeting was a reminder for me to come back to reality. "What would I do without you, little buddy?" I asked as I scooped him up and allowed our noses to touch briefly. I took a nice hot shower and went to bed.

*

The next day, I worked at the library and had lunch in the park behind the thrift store. I just sat and swung on the swings until it was time to go back to work. Today would be the first time I was given the responsibility of locking up the library by myself, so I double-checked everything, especially the alarm, so they would trust me to do it again. I drove down the alley and made a left at the park and then a right into the thrift store parking lot. I ordered some Chinese food from take-out and killed time until it was ready walking around the thrift store. In twenty minutes, I came back for my vegetable lo mein and spring roll platter and sweet tea to go and was off to my place for T.V. with Jade. I had to read some chapters for school, so I just wanted to get home and relax before I got into bed. I knew I would fall right asleep after reading that much, so I planned on reading it in bed. As I was planning my evening in my head, as I sat at the traffic light before the turn at the old Loganville plaza, I saw him, the leader from the group of guys that chased me at the tire shop on the corner.

As the light changed and I had to turn right, he saw me. I wasn't sure if he would recognize me and I definitely hoped he didn't as then he would know my car. He looked dirty, wearing an old blue jean jacket and tan boots. Then I realized he was helping a lady and that he worked there. Crap, right across the street from the library. That meant the likeliness was that I would run into him again. My good, happy day had just changed into one of possible dread and worry. I tried to reason with myself that he was holding down a job now, maybe he'd changed. But I knew he hadn't. Someone like him, who just naturally thought of ways to cause trouble and pain for others was just like that, and it was better to steer clear of him if I could. That was the thing; how could I in this tiny town? Impossible! I just kept seeing him and I definitely didn't like the idea of having to pass him to get to work. He was too close for comfort now. Never in all my life had I thought about hurting someone, and never would I have left glass for someone to run over, let alone being the cause of it and thinking it was funny. The more that I tried to reason that maybe he was just immature, just acting stupid in front of his friends, the more I kept thinking about my possible attack. He had intended to rape me that night and I knew for certain I had to be ready with a plan to get away if I met him again.

That night, I woke up at 2 am from a dream. I found my text book and reading light on as I meandered from the bed to the bathroom. I dreamt that I was a bear that was awoken from her den that lay hidden deep in the forest of Vines Park. In the dream, I woke up and looked down at my enormous reddish-brown paw as I emerged from my cave of rock that was covered up by overgrowth and bush. I was hungry and angry at being disturbed by the careless, loud voices that carried through the park. I ran toward them in a fury, acknowledging my strength as each paw of mine struck the ground in a thump the shook the ground beneath my steps. In a swift leap I made contact and I felt my powerful paw push down his back with a thump to the ground. I stood on him as he lay helpless, afraid and face down in the high grass that began the meadow. I let out a powerful roar only to see the terror and fear take the shape of the faces of the youths, who awoke me. It was them, the guys who chased me months ago at this very spot! Just as I was backing up off of the guy who attempted to scramble to his feet from the ground, I looked at his frightened face. It was the leader, his face still cruel but afraid. I stood up on my hind legs to reveal my powerful might and they took off in a run down the paved road to the service entrance gate. I did not follow them but hoped they wouldn't return and would leave me in peace. It was in that thought that I jumped up to see the alarm clock read two o'clock and I found my way to the bathroom, thinking over my dream. If I was to think of myself as an animal, it wouldn't have been a bear.

Chapter Eighteen

❧✗❧

Further Down the Path

Before I knew it, the spring semester was over and I was midway into summer semester at G.G.C. Derrick was busy going to Mercer every day and doing his coursework at night. Good thing was that I was really busy too, taking a full load in the summer, but I was happy to stay busy and get my last group of core classes out of the way.

It was almost my birthday! Wow, I had lived a whole year in Loganville. Twenty-two, I was to be a woman. I know at eighteen I was a woman, and some would say I was long before that, on account of that I had to take care of myself. I don't know, there was something about twenty-one, like it was official you'd arrived into adulthood, but being twenty-two just confirmed it. I felt pretty good; I owned my own house where most of the other students still lived at home, and after this semester I was only two behind what I should be if I had finished high school and enrolled like most other kids at eighteen. It looked as though I would have my bachelor's degree soon after Derrick graduated with his Masters, and we could go back to spending more time together. I missed him but was so busy with the heavy summer load that it made it bearable. The summer courses were shorter, a semester only being seven weeks long, but they were as intense, as they held the same amount of content and coursework. In a way, I kind of enjoyed it as I was eager to start my business classes and get past the required courses. I sat through the required Political Science; it was so dry and boring but I was happy to understand the basic differences between a Republican and Democrat.

The class did remind me that I needed to register to vote and that I should exercise my right to do so as a citizen. I hated those people that complained about things but didn't vote to change them. I just didn't really know much about politics or what they meant when they referred to policies in their debates, so I didn't watch them and I never felt comfortable just voting for a candidate if I didn't know what they stood for or what they were going to do. Mrs. Vendor always said they'll promise you the moon to get your vote but seldom keep their word, no matter what side they represented, blue or red. She always voted for the person and not the party. I was not so sure that I would be able to figure it out in time to vote for the right candidate. I mean, if they're all lying, how can you tell? I read somewhere that George Washington was the only honest candidate we ever had and will ever have, as he's the only one who didn't want the job. I kind of started to see why people stuck to their political party as even if the candidate is lying he still stands for the basic principles of the party, so it's like a synopsis of what you're getting. It would take me some time, if ever, to decide which party to believe in. I really didn't know enough to comment, but I finally registered to vote and made it to the DMV to get my Georgia driver's license. I had been meaning to get it done sooner but was caught up in school, work at the library, Derrick and my new life that time just flew by and I never got around to it. Well, it was official; I was a Georgia resident.

On the morning of my birthday, Andi called to congratulate me and then Derrick called to say he was coming over to take me out for my birthday breakfast. He stood at the door with an enormous bouquet of yellow and pink roses. He scooped me up into a big hug and then kissed me before we were out the door and on our way to Denny's. "They just opened up," he said.

I said, "I like Snellville but it seems to lack the old charm that Loganville seems to have, plus, I read that in the last two years, over twenty thousand people moved into the area. That's more than the population of the entire county where I'm from!"

"Yeah, it's crazy. It was as if they kept doing things the same old way as before, even though all these people came in. No way to grow and improve, develop," he said. "It's funny you bring that up because we were kind of going over that in one of my classes, how a company which is supposed to be competing in a global market keeps making the same choices it has for the last ten, twenty or even fifty years and is surprised when a young start-up surpasses them with ingenuity, or a great new process or product. You have to grow, stay current, innovative to remain competitive," he went on. "That's why a lot of people think we're backward in the south, it's stuff like that," he said, "even though there is a lot of money to be made here, especially in Atlanta."

I got my breakfast platter for free in honor of my birthday and we talked for hours. Long after our plates were cleared away, we kept the coffee coming. He paid the check and we were off, driving further down Athens Hwy, which I noticed had become Hwy 78. He pulled into a parking lot that faced a small structure that could be a bait and tackle shop. The sign read, *The Yellow River Game Ranch*. He looked at me. "I know it ain't much, but Happy Birthday." We walked inside and he purchased two tickets and bought me a bag of peanuts to feed the animals with and a stuffed beaver plush doll. I was surprised at the set-up. It almost resembled a run-down Vines Park in the way all the roads curved around and were surrounded by trees. Two deer approached me and I fed them some peanuts and was surprised they allowed us to pet them. We just walked around and talked amongst the foxes and beavers, flamingos, turtles, lamas, raccoons. The bears were in a giant pit that was securely dug way down below us. In our view from the top, I recalled my dream as I threw down the rest of my peanuts to their delight. We drove back to his house and we parked the Jeep, but it was such a beautiful day we decided to walk around a bit.

We followed the sidewalk all the way to the playground, where Derrick pushed me a couple times on one of the swings. We continued up the road until we reached the parking lot of the antique store off of Athens Hwy. Inside, we were greeted by a sweet older lady. She was a Yankee transplant like me, but her daughter, who must have been twenty years older than me, had more of a southern twang. Derrick said, "Get anything you want, it's on me. You only turn twenty-two once." I kissed him in a quick peck of delight but knew I would overextend his eagerness to please me and overspend just because he offered. I found a beautiful stained-glass window someone had repurposed and framed in white beech wood and painted on it, *Welcome Friends.* I thought the two blue butterflies in the stained glass reminded me of my home and my grandmother somehow and I liked it. "So you found something, cool. Let's go get it. I'm starvi'n." He took the window up to the front, holding it by the silver metal chain the crafter had secured on top of the wood so it could be hung, and paid the two ladies at the counter. I stood there watching him with pleasure as I admired the various scents and natural soaps that were homemade and placed on display at the counter. I intended to research how to make soap at home at the library the next day when we got slow. He handed me my gift and we both said goodbye to the ladies. I pulled him close when we got outside and said, "Thank you, it's great."

He replied, "So are you," as he patted my behind in a teasing spank.

I said, "Derrick, what will those ladies think?" as I thought public displays of affection outside a small kiss or hug were distasteful.

"That I like you... or at least your butt," he chuckled.

"Oh, you're bad," I said with a smile.

"No, you know what's bad... how hungry I've gotten. It must be this heat," he said as he led the way behind the parking lot of the antique shop to a small path. You could tell the path in the dirt was from people walking to and from the antique shop, but where did it go? I assumed he was taking us to some short cut back to his house when we arrived at another parking lot.

Wow, it was the Main Street Diner. I guess I didn't think about the set-up or layout of the area. In thinking about it, when you weren't on Athens Hwy, it was all pretty close. It just didn't seem that way because it was undeveloped land. We went in and it was my first time ordering pizza instead of my usual French toast. Derrick had them bring out a piece of chocolate cake with a candle in it, and the whole staff and patrons serenaded me with *Happy Birthday*. I made a wish that this wouldn't end and that my life would continue on like this as I blew out the candle.

Everyone cheered and I found myself getting a little watery. "Derrick, I've had a great day. Thank you. I'm happy I had you to spend it with," I said as a sweet smile passed between us.

We walked back toward Rosebud Road from the diner. I didn't feel as safe being in plain sight of all the cars that zoomed by us off the road. It was such a busy street, but honestly, I feared that the bad seed from the tire shop would be in one of them and pelt me with a bottle or something as he passed. I tried to speed up and just look at the back of Derrick's shirt until we made it to Rosebud Road. Only once we'd passed the old farmhouse and made the right from Rosebud onto Brooks Drive, did I relax. It's funny how I never was scared like that walking around Scranton even. I guess it's really just because I wasn't from around here and felt like I wasn't one of the locals, so I didn't understand all of the possible dangers, where

Derrick seemed at ease. We found the sidewalk that began at St. Oliver's Church and followed it, as we walked leisurely hand in hand toward his house. When I could see the top of the white fascia and carved brackets that were on the top of his porch, I reached for the window which he had carried the whole way for me. "Sir, I would like to relieve you of your gentlemanly duties," I grinned.

"Not on your life," as he leant me against the door of the Jeep to kiss me deeply as he unlocked it for me.

*

Back at my place, I got into bed and thought about the amazing day I had had with Derrick, which had to be the best birthday ever because he showed me he cared. It had been a great year so far. I had definitely warmed up to Loganville, but I still wasn't sure if I could see this as my forever home. I think most of it had to do with the concept of living in the south, especially a nowhere place on the map like Loganville, Georgia. Number two, since my first group home, I had had my mind set on that I was going to be somebody and visit all these cool and exotic places. I would see the world and do all of these amazing things. What exactly they were going to be, I didn't know, as I just wanted to do them so I didn't have to be the girl without a family who had nowhere to belong. Now as I lay in my bed, with a home of my own, and a beautiful one at that, did I want the same things? I wasn't sure. I had a home and somewhere to belong. I could make a place for myself here and find a good job in Athens or Atlanta if I wanted, as neither would be a terrible commute. Lots of people worked in the nearby Norcross or Lawrenceville if I wanted a career. Honestly, what would be so bad about staying at the library? Nothing, except the expectation that I should be pushing for a career, that I needed to find my place in the world, define myself. Those were things I had believed before I was given a house and going to college, before Derrick and G.G.C.

To be honest, I was pretty happy the way things were, even if I was pretty much handed all of it. Maybe that's why I couldn't sleep; I felt like I hadn't worked for these things. To defend myself, I quickly thought that getting this house was no different than a good mother and father steering their kid to a scholarship or their connections getting them a six-figure job. I lay awake with my thoughts until before I realized what had happened and that I had fallen asleep, my alarm rang and I was up and taking a shower to go into work at the library.

I came in and scanned back all the books that had been returned to the library from the night box and helped a couple older gentlemen find the books they were looking for. I made a pot of coffee for myself and the boss and immediately collected all the books on soap making I could find. Some of them were in survival guides or historical books from the colonial period, informing the reader how early colonists lived.

After reading for enjoyment for a change instead of the usual textbooks, my spirits were lifted, although I was sure I would never be able to make my own soap, which I was totally fine with. It really was the same as cooking; you just read it the first time and after one or two times of combining the same ingredients, you knew how to cook or produce the desired product. It seemed cool, though, and I liked the idea of knowing I could do it if I had to, but I didn't see the need since it was relatively easy to buy a six pack of Oil of Olay bars of soap. I also found out some people make their own soap because they have really sensitive skin and have allergic reactions to the perfumes and various chemicals in the modern products. Others just like making their own individual scents that are unique to them or have jumped on the whole all natural, go-green holistic bandwagon. I like Oil of Olay, but I had to admit some of the handmade ones smell awesome. In that shop Derrick took me to by his neighborhood, I could recall the scent of some of the soaps on display even now. I remember really liking the fragrance of the patchouli and lavender handmade soap and thought it was even more attractive when I read some lady made them herself in her home. There was something really cool about it being her personal craft, that she put something of herself in there and made this product from her idea, not a big factory. I still didn't buy it, as one bar was the same price as six Oil of Olay bars of soap at the store.

Thinking about it, it must be hard to compete with a big company, and I regretted not getting them. Enough melancholy, and I convinced myself to feel better with the thought of not knowing what ingredients she put into the bars of soap, convincing myself I had done the right thing because of the health regulations and brand protection the big companies offer the consumer. That convincing logic should hold me over until I got back over there and picked up a couple bars or learned to make my own, whichever came first, I thought casually. I read a couple magazines before it was time to close up the library and I was free for the rest of the day. It was my last week of classes before the end of the summer semester, so I had to head back to the house to study for final exams.

Derrick wasn't available and had become so busy that for the last three weeks he would just randomly text me and make a phone call on Sunday night and we would talk for an hour. I missed him and was becoming sad that I couldn't see him as I was finished with classes until August and had a lot of free time. I took two extra days at the library and was still restless. I drove out to the mall on Sugarloaf Parkway a couple times but just couldn't see myself spending that much money after going to the thrift store with Rosa.

*

It was one day after work. I had decided to eat at Sonic's. While parked and sitting in my car waiting for the hop on roller skates to come back with my burger, tater tots and chocolate milkshake, I noticed the sign, *Taekwondo* in big, bold black letters.

After I finished my meal, I drove through to the adjoining parking lot and parked in front of the small brick building. I finally got up and out of my Subaru and walked inside, where I was greeted by an Asian man only a few inches taller than myself. He introduced himself as Mister Kim but said the owner was Master Nam. He smiled and his body language was confident but he had friendly eyes. He gave me a tour of the facility, which was the small entrance room and two smaller rooms with mats, and the large room with shiny polished wood floors that had a wall of mirrors. He addressed me, "You want to learn self-defense, I can teach you self-defense. It is good to know body and control body with mind. Control body control environment from mind. You like?" I had never met anyone like him before. I had seen martial artists portrayed on T.V. of course, but Mister Kim really portrayed the image I had always had of a karate instructor. If nothing else, it was going to be good exercise, so I decided to give it a try and I signed up for two days a week, Tuesday and Thursday nights at 6 pm. I could easily make it here after G.G.C. and my study group. I would just have to make sure I ate before the study group or during so as not to be full when I got to Taekwondo, mostly because I wasn't sure what a lesson entailed. What if they punched me in the stomach, who knows? It was better to not be full when I went to class, just in case. I actually ended up really liking martial arts and moved up from white belt to yellow within four weeks, mostly because I practiced the basic moves in my living room each morning as my coffee percolated. I was honored with the yellow belt but now I had to spar with another student in the second half of every class and I was really unsure of myself and uncomfortable. Mostly because I was unsure of how I looked, and in my prior experience with fighting in Avoca or Scranton, it was more ferral and I was just striking to injure the person bothering me to escape. Here, those in the class seemed to love sparring and practicing their skillset. I had none and a couple times even ended up on the floor of the mat. The most embarrassing thing was I couldn't tell you how, didn't even see how they got me down. Mister Kim suggested I try meditation to focus. He said I wasn't connected to my energy and showed me some breathing exercises he wanted me to try.

It was true; I was upbeat but I still longed for Derrick and I felt displaced even though I knew I belonged here. For the first time in my life, I was a part of a community with a job, enrolled in school and had extracurricular activities, but I wasn't here. Mister Kim was right.

I added some deep stretches to my routine every night before bed and afterwards I started my meditation from a lying-down position on the floor, as the bed was too soft. Mister Kim said I would eventually be able to do the breathing sets from a sitting position but it was okay to start lying down. I also found out Mister Kim is not called Mister as the title we Americans give a male. It was actually a rank, with the highest being Master. That totally blew my mind and I was happy to be thinking about something new and not Derrick.

By the time I was a green belt, it was time to enroll for fall classes. I was so excited to be focused on my major that I treated myself to Applebee's. I went to the one in Snellville instead of my usual because I was on my way home from class and just wanted to grab an oriental chicken salad and be on my way to Taekwondo. The place was occupied but not full. I sat at the bar and was eating my salad and ordering a cookies and cream milkshake when a guy approached me. He was in his late twenties, face scruffy like he hadn't shaved in two days but it wasn't a full beard, but his nails were short and clean. Maybe it was a conscious choice not to shave. He was wearing a leather jacket, a longer black one, but it wasn't as nice as Derrick's. He asked if he could sit down and I said, "Suit yourself," in my typical Avoca. I found it stressful to be approached but I guess I should lighten up; he didn't know that. No harm in being friendly, right.

"Hi," he said. "I'm Tom."

"Rose," I said with a smile. I finished my salad and told the bartender I wanted my check.

"Let me take care of that for you," Tom offered.

"No, it's okay. I can pay for myself, thanks," I said firmly but with a smile.

I paid my bill and finished up my milkshake when Tom continued, "Well, can I get you next time, maybe dinner and a movie?"

I said, "Thank you, but no, I am really busy. Maybe I'll see you around. Nice meeting you."

He smiled. "Hey, can I get your number?" I was out the door and in my Subaru before he could get a response from me and off to Taekwondo. Traffic was terrible so I had no concerns about going to class full as my meal would probably be digested before I turned onto Athens Hwy from Hwy 124. I was sad Derrick wasn't at Applebee's with me, but he'd be finished soon and then we'd have more time together.

*

By October, Derrick had only texted me four times, mostly to check in, but his brain was completely focused on his studies. He said it was doable and that he was doing well but that he had to give it his all. He assured me that he missed me and was thinking about finishing up the program and spending his free time with me. He said it was what was keeping him going because it was really hard and he needed the motivation sometimes. He told me he'd showed my picture to some of his friends he'd made at Mercer and they said I was pretty. I soared inside that he was showing me around. I was happy to know I was also in his thoughts if we couldn't be together. I Face Timed him once but our schedules didn't match up this semester so I had to settle for a text.

I tried to stay busy with school and buying pumpkins to carve on Mischief Night, but Halloween didn't seem to be as big of a thing in Loganville as it was back in Pennsylvania. I gathered from talking to my boss and doing some research at the library the main reason was that until five to ten years ago, Loganville was pretty rural. It would be kind of hard to go trick or treating if you had to walk a couple miles from your farm to reach the next farm. The second thing was most of the residents were Southern Baptist and thought the concept of dressing scary and the whole holiday was about the devil and that people should be using their time to spread good and not the spooky nonsense. Plus, it was a holiday of Irish origin, a lot of which settled in Scranton, so it just made sense the culture stuck and developed into the commercial monster it was today, marketed to develop profits just like Christmas or any other holiday today. I liked it myself, the dressing up and getting candy, as I grew up poor and didn't have many opportunities to have fun and get treats. But I totally understood the weariness of the holiday, because if I wasn't familiar with the culture and lived in the middle of nowhere and a group of people showed up at my house dressed as monsters yelling trick or treat, I'd probably be scared and think it was the devil too. I laughed to myself at the personal account of Mrs. Jackson, a local patron from the library who had had a similar experience in Monroe about sixty years ago. She said she had at least heard of Halloween but had never been exposed to it until that night on her farm. I couldn't help but laugh as she told her story of her first Halloween as I scanned in the day's book returns.

*

I spent Thanksgiving watching the parade with Jade and the next day did some Black Friday shopping I didn't need. In my solicitude, I became restless and put on my jacket and ended up in my Subaru at Vines Park. I walked the trail for a good thirty minutes before resting on the bench that faced the lake. I just sat there for the longest time, enjoying the quiet and the wind flowing over the water to make waves dance. It reminded me of a painting, the one in my house. It led me to believe that maybe my grandmother used to do the same thing that I was doing right now. It comforted me to know she found peace or possible inspiration at the things I did. I hadn't realized how long I had sat there as the sun began to set behind the lake. It was magnificent and I found it hard to take my eyes off of its glorious cast of red-orange rays that kissed the water, although I knew I shouldn't be in the park alone, especially at night. I stood up on that thought and turned to make my way back, when out of the corner of my eye I saw a splash plummet in the middle of the lake.

What was that? I immediately turned around to try to catch a glimpse of what was in the water. I peered as hard as I could and made out what looked to be like a large reddish-orange tail swim beneath the surface. It was larger than I had expected but I at least saw something and wasn't spooking myself out. If not, I would have convinced myself it was a turtle, even though they don't usually make a splash like that. For my sanity, I tried to remain logical when I could. So as not to linger in the park alone any longer, I turned to face the mansion behind me and chose the path that meandered around the high bushes and ended at the massive tree that was overgrown with vines. I wasn't as worried as I was five minutes at the most from the entrance gate of the park and close to my car at this point. Just then, a large red-furred squirrel stood in the middle of the path with its hand on its hip. In that moment, I looked to my right out of physical habit when I needed to address something absurd, which was totally odd coming from someone who was used to solving problems alone. The habit of looking around when something is odd is to see if there is anyone else around seeing what you do. I wasn't sure how I ever picked up the habit, but it was part of my mannerisms.

In that moment, I saw something sparkle in the vines that grew up the massive wooden wall that accompanied the walkway in front of the Vines Mansion and stopped at the old servants' house. I walked toward the wall which was entirely overgrown with hanging vines and then further obscured by the row of high bushes planted in front and then a row of smaller bushes in front of that, followed by a row of various flowers and plants. The master gardener had clearly landscaped this with the intention of keeping Vines Park guests away from the manor house as they enjoyed their visit to the park. Just then, I saw the golden illuminance from a small opening between the leaves of the vine.

As I moved the vines aside, I saw it, a keyhole. I took my key from my chain that hung around my neck and stuck it in the hole in the wall. To my wonder, it clicked, again another find. I pushed against the wood with the click from the keyhole and found myself in a dark stone tunnel. To my disappointment, there were no lights to guide my path this time. I followed the path until I came to a door which, as quietly and slowly as I could, I opened, to see what was on the other side.

Chapter Nineteen

⚭

The Royalty of Vines Needs No Mansion

It was a beautiful room, which was ornately decorated. Old-world ballrooms and afternoon parlor tea in a grand palace came to mind as I quietly entered the forbidden space. What was this place, was it another dream? But as soon as the thought left me, I knew I was inside the Vines Mansion. What a delight! I wandered through room after room, exploring each until I was content. I imagined it was my home and I was just strolling in from my leisurely daily walk through the grounds. I viewed every grand bedroom on the third floor and was making my way back down to the second, stopping by a small parlor that housed a piano and a painting similar to the one I had in my home. It could have been its twin had it not been much larger.

I relaxed as I gazed into the same calming power of the purposeful strokes that manifested as the waves of the Vines lake.

The artist had really captured the moment in this masterpiece which seemed all too real; it was as though I was still outside gazing into the water as I was a couple of hours before. I was surprised at how much more vivid the details seemed in this one, maybe because it was larger, I thought. I noticed the inscription on the bottom; it was a signature. I had seen that most artists do that to receive the credit that is due for their work. After a few moments of staring, I could finally make out the name signed on the bottom: Claire Cottontail. What a kooky name, I thought, like a character in a children's book. I was eager to go home and see if the same signature lay on the bottom of the one I had at home. There was something about this painting, but I couldn't put my finger on what I was supposed to see or realize. Not wanting to dally, I continued my forbidden tour, trying to be as quiet as possible, even though I was pretty sure I was alone. My only fear was if there were cameras, but even in seeing me, would they be able to place who I was, I thought as I made a mental note not to disturb or touch anything to leave evidence.

I ended my tour in the kitchen, which didn't suit my taste as it looked like it belonged in a restaurant. My imagination was hoping to find an old Hampton's style French beachfront whitewashed wood with marble countertops. No dice, all industrial. On that, I thought I would just take a peek in the basement to see if it had any more surprises for me. I made my way down the cement stairway to a wine room and a couple of storage rooms that were neatly categorized as a laundry room and a small room with a cot that was facing an old T.V., which I assumed was employed by the staff while waiting for laundry or something. Crap! Now I would have to make my way back up to that room, if I remembered which way it was, and go back out the way I came, as I was pretty sure if I went out the back door it would sound some sort of alarm. I was assuming that the room I came in from was on the first floor, so I went toward the general area I felt was the right direction and soon found it.

I made sure to close up both doors behind me and quietly emerged from the tunnel behind the wall of vines. It was completely dark with just a sliver of a moon above. I listened first to make sure there was no one else close by and made my quick walk back to my Subaru. When approaching the gate, I was happy to see that I was alone and quickly entered my car and locked the doors. Wow! Vines Park never ceased to amaze me. I had never got to see the inside of a house like that and I was sure I would never be invited inside. I was lucky to have found my secret way in. In a way, I was sad that a family didn't live there anymore and that it was only used when rented for formals and banquets now. All the walking had made me hungry, recognizing the need long before my stomach started to growl on my way back to my car. I wasn't as excited as I should be, I guessed, as I put my key in the ignition to start my car. Maybe I had been through too much already and was immune to the shock of yet another unbelievable experience in Loganville. I pulled out of the park onto the tiny road that led out onto the main road and headed to find something to eat.

Back home, if you had had a night like this, you would go to Crazy 8's. All its patrons were either trying to get over a crazy night or they wanted one for themselves. I hadn't found my Crazy 8's down here yet but Waffle House seemed like the closest thing, so I stopped by Waffle House on the way home and ate. As I sat in the booth, I was happy to be brought back to reality by two customers who were in serious competition over the jukebox. Their battle became so intense, as one would slip in a quarter and play Garth Brooks' *Friends in Low Places* and the other would immediately follow and play Nelly's *County Grammar*. The contrast in both customers and their song choice was both comical and exactly what I needed after another unbelievable find at Vines. My section's waitress, with her blue-streaked hair and quick grin that lacked a couple of teeth commented that they would "start a race war if 'ey don't quit!" So, her customers stopped playing the jukebox and one of them paid his tab and left. She came over to me with a smile and refilled my coffee. I noticed her name tag had Wanda written in purple sparkle glitter and was decorated with stickers. I placed a ten-dollar bill on the table and told her she had saved the day. I didn't usually tip that well, but that night I did. I left a good tip as I knew what it was like to run tables from my days at the Blue Oyster. I had it, so why not? I wouldn't make a habit of it, but I think she appreciated it. I know I did when someone threw a little extra my way.

As I pulled out of the Waffle House parking lot and made my way through the connecting lot of the CVS Pharmacy to come out at the light, so I didn't have to pull out into the traffic of Hwy 78 or worse, and waited until it cleared so I could pull out, I felt peace. Odd, as I thought I would be more excited from my experience but I wasn't. It was eerey as if I had already experienced this, or maybe that I kind of knew this was going to happen. I tried to scratch my brain as to why I felt that way; maybe there was more of a logical explanation. Maybe Andi had mentioned it and I hadn't realized what he was referring to when he said it, so I had blocked it out. So now that I needed the information, my subconscious had stored it, leaving my conscious mind to think it was new information. No, I was sure Andi had never mentioned it or anything to do with Vines. Even so, but wait… he had to be connected somehow. I mean, first of all, he wore the same markings on his jewelry that were at Vines. Yeah, but that could just be our family name or something significant in Danish. It didn't mean he was involved in my grandmother's dealings with Vines, I quickly shot down. It could just be that my grandmother was really involved in Vines Park but deep inside I knew differently, but what? What else could it be? What were these pieces that kept emerging, and was I the only one who was finding them? Was I supposed to know something or do something, what? The most nerve-racking thing was I had no one who I could discuss it with to run ideas by and to help me try to make sense of what I was seeing and experiencing. I mean, it would sound absolutely nuts to most people, or even scarier was the kind of person who would believe me, but they may have motives of their own and I had my grandmother to think about. I mean she trusted me for some reason with this secret, I only wish she had told me about it herself. In not knowing, I may have missed something or the whole point all together and screw it up. Why would she risk all of that? Risk something that was so obviously important to her and her friends? There must be a really good reason as to why she couldn't tell me. Maybe she was sworn to secrecy, or worse, protecting me or herself. Jeez! Well, she seemed like a smart lady. I didn't think she would have put us in any danger, and from the image of her that I got from Rosa, she seemed like the kind of person who knew how to handle herself, but what then? Before I wasted any more time letting my imagination run away with me, I should probably just assume it was exactly what it appeared to be and work with I knew for sure to be true or real.

The light changed so I had to focus on the road as I pulled out into the four-way intersection, and never was too careful as more than once I'd seen drivers run the light or not even notice it because they were looking down at their cell phones instead of the road. The ride home was quiet and somewhat peaceful and the mood was right. I didn't even turn on the radio or listen to a CD or anything, I just drove. I pulled into the driveway and was mad at myself for not leaving the porch light on for myself again. "Planning, Rose, planning," I said in a somewhat curt tone to myself as I made my way out of my car.

I had one foot on one of the cobblestones of my driveway and one still in my Subaru as I was attempting to grab my purse from the passenger side floor when the realization that I was not alone nearly killed me as I shot up and almost hit my head. I jerked so high in fright at the sudden, unexpected sound coming from the voice of the person standing outside my car: "oung lady such as yerself shouldn't be out so late at night, it's dangerous," she said. As I was composing myself still from the fright of her sudden appearance while I was distracted, I realized it was Barbara. Barbara, my neighbor, who had called my grandmother a witch, had come over to tell me to be careful.

What the heck, I thought, as I said, "Barbara, besides you not minding your own business, you nearly scared me to death. Is that what you came over here for?" I asked.

"Well, yes, I mean, no," she went on to say. "What I'm a'tryin' to say is... Rose? Was it? Look here, I know we started off on the wrong foot but I don't mean you any harm. In fact, I am part of the neighborhood watch 'round here and just thought you should know about what has happened."

"What happened?" I asked as I stepped completely out of my car and hit the lock button on my keyring, so I heard the confirming beep that she was locked up. I stepped back so as to let my back rest against my Subaru to face her as she continued to tell me her news.

"Well, when I say trash, I mean trashy folk come out'a that trailer park and come and assaulted that poor girl."

"Who?" I asked.

"Oh, don't you worry, you don't know her on account of you being new and all. It was Stacey Lyn, Deloris's niece. I know 'em from church. Anyhow, Stacey Lyn was vistin' from Alabama, that's where she goes to school now. Gone to college, was gonna make somethin' of herself, yes ma'am, yes she was. Anyhow, she pulled into the Chevron up a ways and a group of young hoodlums assaulted her, right there behind the store! Can you believe it! They didn't even take her no wheres to do it. They just raped her right there on the cement behind the store. Thank the Lord Bobby Ray came out with the trash and ran 'em off and got her help. They caught two of 'em but the police said there was more of 'em they hadn't caught. The good sergeant came tonight to our safety meetin' and told us all to keep watch being they's a still out there, and most definitely still up to no good," she concluded with.

"Oh, Barbara! That's just awful. Thank you for telling me. Please tell your friend I am sorry what happened. We had better get inside ourselves. Goodnight," I said.

"Night, honey," she replied as she made her way across the street to her house.

Oh my God! I thought to myself as I closed the door behind me. I scooped up Jade as he approached my feet to greet me as I came into the foyer. I just know who it was too! It had to be those no good guys from Vines Park, I'd bet ya. That poor lady, I thought, and fear crept over me as I realized that was almost me. Some of them were still out there, I thought, as I secured the double locks behind me but most likely they'd got the ones who actually did the deed. Maybe the others would straighten out if the ringleader was behind bars. *I hope so*, I thought, as I took off my shoes.

*

The next day, I immediately went to inspect the painting. I poured my first cup of coffee for the day and took the mug with me upstairs to view my tiny replica of what I had seen the night before at Vines. So, it was the exact same artist! Another Vines Park mystery! Claire Cottontail, but who was she? Maybe Google would help me find out. I sat at my desk and searched. As soon as I typed in her name, a whole bunch of links to Cherokee, North Carolina came up. On one site, a picture of a young and beautiful Native American woman came up. It was an old black and white photo and she had her hair fixed in the traditional braids on both sides and was wearing the traditional ceremonial dress. The small information box said, *Claire Cottontail, local artist*. There was a link to a website of a store in Cherokee that sold various types of silver jewelry and Native American cultural items. There was a modern picture of a woman on the site. I could see a resemblance to Claire and assumed the woman must be a relative. I pulled up a map and Loganville was only two hours away from the shop, so I made plans to take a drive up there Thursday night after school and Taekwondo. I booked a room in the nearby Cherokee Grand Hotel because it had a pool and free breakfast. Why not make a day of it? I planned to check out a couple shops, the famous waterfall on the reservation and visit the Native American History Museum while I was there. Why not, right?

*

The six days' wait for the day of my trip was complete agony. I had changed the litter box for Jade and left four bowls of water in the kitchen and one giant bowl of ice, so if he decided to be fussy, the ice would melt and he would think it was fresh water. The great thing about cats, I thought, as I was pouring him an extra bowl of food, was that they were so independent. You could never do this with a dog. Having a cat was becoming a great joy in my life. If I had a dog, my house would probably be torn to pieces and there would be poo everywhere. I read somewhere that some dogs could be trained to go on puppy pads or newspapers so you could leave them alone for a while, but the dog still seemed to suffer from being left alone, not cats. Maybe I was wrong, I don't know, but was happy to go and know he was going to be okay while I was away. I grabbed him and gave him a big hug and told him to watch the house and that I would be back. I locked up the house and I was off on my first vacation. Even if it was only a day, possibly two, it was my first getaway and exploration of a different place just for fun. I was really excited.

In a short couple-hour drive, I was there. The surrounding area was beautiful but the actual town was run-down and much smaller than Loganville. I checked into my room and took a quick shower and was off to explore the gift shops, and in particular the one from the website. When I got there, I knew it was the right one because of the huge carved Native American Chief that was painted to his real likeness and guarded the doorway of the shop. The woodworking and carving in the area was amazing and the whole place smelt of cut wood.

Inside the shop, there were a couple paintings for sale by Claire Cottontail; here was my opportunity. Just as the realization came into my mind, the woman from the website came from behind the counter. "Excuse me, what can you tell me about this artist?" I asked.

"Oh, my grandmother," she said. "She was a very talented painter. Do you like her work?"

"Oh yes, it is beautiful. Actually I am asking because I have some of her work already, it was left to me by my grandmother before she died, but I never had the chance to ask her about it, Aurora Kohl," I said while extending my hand in a friendly gesture. "My grandmother was Lauren Lorensen Kohl," I said.

"I'm sorry. Oh yes, my people were very fond of your grandmother. She was a friend to us when no one else was," she explained as her long dark hair shimmered against the counter. "Beth," she said as she extended her hand to mine in a friendly shake. "Her animal spirit was a deer and it was predominant that she was given the name cottontail. I can see her spirit walks with your totem. Your spirit grew strong in the sacred place just as hers did many years ago, but I can sense power and cunning within you. A bear and maybe a fox, but you will have to search inside yourself to release your other spirits. I think you are strong like she was, and will find one is more dominant and maybe also take the name and accept your destiny," she said with such a truthful intensity. It was obvious she really believed what she was saying.

I was just quiet and listened, just as I had learned to do years ago when all I heard was crazy stuff and crazy things from the different group homes I was shipped off to.

This time, it was different; Beth seemed like a really nice person. She came off warm and open. I mean, her religious beliefs did seem crazy but I guess really no different than some of the stories in the

Old Testament. Plus, she mentioned a bear and I thought of my dream, and something inside me agreed with her and what she said. I mean, as crazy as it sounded, it fit together somehow. I mean, she did know my grandmother or know of her, and a small amount of research had led me here from my home. I asked her what else she could tell me about my grandmother and she said all she knew was that my grandmother was the one who convinced the couple to buy Vines and make it what it was today.

"She helped my family because we believed the land was sacred and it held special powers from the magic that flowed in the waters. No one would listen to us at the time. My people had no power and our reasoning for why the land shouldn't be developed seemed strange and displaced from the reality the people of Loganville wanted to live. How could my family convince anyone in a town hall meeting? It was the first time any of them had met someone like us, and our ways seemed strange to them. We dressed differently, were darker and seemed out of touch with their lives. Our beliefs seemed impossible, and the investors were eager to buy the land and get it developed and had done a good job of showing the town what it would gain from their plans. A generation after the Civil War, people had lost a lot of pride and money and were eager to get it back. If it wasn't for your grandmother's help, our voice and our lands and all of the magic that lay hidden inside her would be lost forever. It was most unusual for a white skin to see, especially as much as your grandmother could see, but she was different," said Beth in a serious but warm manner, making me recall that Rosa used the exact same word to describe my grandmother. Beth continued, "She wasn't from Loganville and was taught the old ways before she came, or maybe her family had kept them and passed them down within your family. I do not know. It was said for a long time, many generations of our people, both yours and mine, had the honor of seeing, and that when your grandmother met my people we were both just really happy to find others who remembered the ways."

She handed me a book on animal spirits, which served as a guide book on how to find your totem. "Waking Bear, please take it as a gift," she said with a warm smile.

"Thank you, it was nice meeting you." I smiled in return and placed the book as a hug in my arm as I walked out of her store.

I did the tour of the remaining shops and the museum. I went back to the hotel and took a swim in the pool. I did some laps and swam underwater once and back to get a good workout. It helped in releasing some of the energy I had picked up from the excitement of finding out more about my grandmother and Vines Park. I got dressed and made sure to blow-dry my hair because it had become rather cold outside. I put on the hat I hadn't worn since Avoca and laced up my tall Sketchers boots and made the short drive to the Native American reserved lands to check out the famous waterfall. I sat there in peace for the longest time, just allowing my mind to clear to the sound of the flowing water eventually hitting the rocks below. Eventually, with my spirits calmed, I made the walk back to my Subaru that was parked at the end of the trail. I had paid for an extra night at the hotel so I went back to my room.

I became restless again, so I went out to the tiny town and walked around the shops again. I didn't purchase anything; I just took in all the different sights and sounds and enjoyed looking at all the cultural pieces of artwork and jewelry that were distinctive to the Cherokee people. After an hour or so, I made my way back to the hotel and took a nap for four hours and woke up, took another swim and went back to the room to pack. I checked out and returned my room key and enjoyed the complimentary breakfast. I made sure to use the restroom and took a coffee and extra water with me to go.

My drive back was quick and I was back home before ten in the morning. It was now Saturday, and a lonely day because Derrick would still be occupied with graduate school. Jade was super happy to see me and he still hadn't eaten all of his food, which made me happy because then I knew he had had enough to eat while I was away. I put all of the dishes in the dishwasher and set his usual porcelain food and water bowl back in their usual positions in the kitchen. I did all my laundry and wrapped myself up in yoga pants, woolly socks and a long sweater on the couch and covered myself with the throw I usually had hanging off its back. It was a dark and cold day and the chill went down to the bone. I made myself a cup of hot tea and went back to my cozy spot. It helped warm me from the inside; I felt as though I was thawing out.

I eventually fell asleep for an hour and woke up warm, which was a relief. The heat must have kicked in while I dozed off, I thought. I began to read the book Beth had given me and soon realized it made sense. I really was enjoying the read and soon identified with the bear and fox, like she had suggested, but was uncertain of my other totems. This, to my relief, was normal and it took most people a long time to figure them all out. For some people, it took a whole lifetime before they really got to know and understand and support who they really were and allow their spirits to walk their chosen path and fulfill their destiny.

It said to begin by sitting quietly, just like Mister Kim had instructed. Open your mind until you are totally relaxed, allow all of the incoming thoughts to pass and eventually you will be somewhere. Where is that place? Is it a forest, in the mountains, the plains, or the river? From there, you will be able to see hints emerge of your spirit. Do you climb onto the bank from the river? Are you landing on a tree branch?

I continued on with these exercises until I realized that I was in Vines, deep in the forest almost to the start of the meadow. I could see my paws; they were black and hairy. My claws; large, and they felt heavy as I found my way into my cave to return to my sleep as it was not time for me to awaken yet. I was hibernating! I was a bear. From that thought, I realized I was really half asleep, cozy in the in-between of sleep and awake. My body lay on the couch so comfortable and warm I didn't want to emerge, but I did, as I had to eventually use the bathroom. Amazed that I had experienced yet another dream about Vines Park, but this time I was actually awake. It was not a daydream, but more like an induced trance, but it felt important and I felt so much calmer now that I had experienced it. I was curious as to whether I could do it again, but this time on purpose. I felt kind of silly as an adult imagining, or whatever it was, but I thought what harm could it do? Plus, no one would know I was sitting on my couch trying to recreate an experience I'd dreamed to see if I could become the bear. I had heard of people doing this, but it wasn't to be an animal. In the dreamscape I'd heard about, it was to imagine wealth or to project yourself into seeing the success you wanted or to visualize what you wanted to happen. I guess I would be happiest free and in Vines Park. I guess if I was being really honest, I would imagine that I was making out with Derrick right then, but that was not where I wanted my mind to go. Plus, there was so much Catholic influence, I feared it would smut up my brain and it wasn't healthy to think about sexual urges, as God intended them for you to enjoy your partner and eventually have children, not watch it as porn or think of it. I eventually got my mind off of Derrick and back on to my meditation as I slowly began to relax and clear the thoughts that raced into my head.

One by one, I allowed the thoughts to pass, like a silent witness to my own mind. I reminded myself that I was safe and that the thoughts were okay, no matter what they were, and that they couldn't harm me and that I was not here to judge them, only to let them pass. Eventually, as my body became completely relaxed, I became more and more solid, it seemed, as if not distracted by my body's various tensions or twitches. I began to lose consciousness and allowed myself to spin around and around until eventually I began to drift off into a dark blue that may as well have been black.

*

Asleep; I must have fallen asleep because I found myself the next morning staring at the ceiling of my living room. I guess I fell asleep on the sofa and somehow ended up on the floor throughout the night. I put on a pot of coffee and went upstairs to shower and get ready for the day. I was eager to finish up the last two weeks of the semester before winter break. I was hoping to spend some time with Derrick as he had become a dull ache that I carried with me inside as the days passed without him. I had tried with all of my might to not become one of those girls who were consumed with their boyfriends, and had done well to have a life separate from him, but on the inside I knew what I craved and what I needed and it was only him. I almost felt like it would be easier if we had broken up, as part of my torment was that we were together, yet that we couldn't be together. The feelings never stopped, just our ability to express them. I hoped he still felt the same way about me. I told myself that I was being silly, one of those women I hated who were full of insecurities. What was next for me, to start checking his phone and emails to make sure there was no one else? Honestly, even if that was possible, which it wasn't because he wasn't ever here for me to have access to his communications, it wouldn't have given me more time with him. Oh, I was miserable. I got ready to go to work at the library; hopefully, it would offer me the distraction that I needed.

*

The day came and went without much excitement; it was just a busy day. Tons of kids were in and out all day and we had two full adult reading groups. I had double the amount of returns to check back in, and before I knew it, it was time to lock up and go home. I stopped by the American Tavern and got a Philly cheesesteak as I guess I had the blues, and having something from back home made me feel better. Cheese was definitely a comfort food for me, I realized, as

I eagerly wolfed down the meal. I went home and went straight to bed to get ready for the next day, when I was scheduled to open. That meant I had to be there by 7:30 am to unlock the doors and retrieve all of the books from the outside drop box before the library officially opened at 9 am. I was not looking forward to it, although I enjoyed the fact that I had finally earned the responsibility of running the place alone. It was just that the cold air made me want to sleep in.

There was just something about November that made me want to snuggle up with a good book and stay in, even if I wasn't always a big reader. Watching T.V. was too loud and distracting for getting cozy under the blankets, but I didn't mind relaxing to a good movie either. It was just one of those days where I wasn't feeling like leaving the house and lacked the motivation or desire to get up. Like the cold had settled inside me, straight through to my very bones, urging me to just bury myself somewhere or hibernate. Just as I realized the thought, I flashed back to my daydream as the bear. Maybe there was a connection; well, they say where the mind goes, the body follows. This was what I got for exploring and thinking this new age weird stuff, so open-minded my brains fell out, I scolded myself. Hopefully, by tomorrow morning, I would feel better, maybe after I'd showered and had coffee.

The next morning, I didn't feel better but I wasn't tired or what felt like I had been moving along really slowly. No, I was in a terrible mood. I wouldn't say angry, because no one was there to make me mad. I had just woken up on the wrong side of the bed, as people say to describe what I was feeling. Nothing could go right as I nearly tripped over Jade and spilt my coffee and had to wipe down the spill off of the table and chairs. Then I had to mop the floor before I was even awake yet. I dropped my keys right before the front door of the house closed behind me, locking me outside. I had to get my spare that I had left under a flowerpot in case of moments like these. I ran over the curb as I was backing out of the driveway and Barbara was standing there behind me as I tried to back up onto the street, who was the last person I wanted to see in my moment of angst. I finally made it to the library and opened up, taking extra precaution to do everything slow to avoid any more hold-ups. After a pot of coffee and just doing routine work such as checking in the returns, I began to relax and the rest of the day continued as planned.

A couple of patrons enquired about me, saying, "You aren't your usual self today," but for the most part it was just a normal day at work. I was annoyed with the various books I kept noticing such as *Grumpy Bear*, *A Guide to Happiness* and *Girl, What You Need Is*. I hated the concept of signs from the universe or psychology's suggestion that you notice things your subconscious is trying to address, whatever. I just found the whole day to be annoying and I couldn't wait for it to end so I could go back to my bed. Finally, at 6 pm, I locked up the library and set the alarm. I couldn't get out of there fast enough and within fifteen minutes I was in my yoga sleep pants and under the covers of my bed.

*

By December 9th, I had finished all of my final exams and was home on winter break. I baked a bunch of holiday cookies, which I shared with Rosa. I was so happy to have coffee with her and confide in her my feelings for Derrick. She was exactly what I needed in the moment. She was so happy to talk to me about my 'young people problems' but said, joking aside, "Love ache is real and it can kill, so you's got to listen to it, c'ld."

Chapter Twenty

Awaking the Bear

I was antsy so I drove over to Dick's Sporting Goods, which was in the back of the Lowe's parking lot. I purchased a punching bag and stand and sparring gear for my hands and feet so I wouldn't hurt myself while I practiced. It was nice having a little extra money to spend on myself. I guess trying to keep busy and working all the extra hours paid off. I would normally feel kind of weird purchasing this fighting stuff when having to ask for the stuff to be loaded and brought to the front and facing the young male clerk and have him know I spent my free time punching stuff. I guess I felt that way because I was a woman and traditionally fighting was a male sport, but today I didn't care and just smiled, as I could tell the clerk was dying to ask me if it was a gift or why I was buying these macho items but was obviously conditioned in his store training not to pry. I know people would like to say that today we don't have these concepts or stereotypes, but the truth is we have stereotypes for a reason. We have them because people are used to seeing things a certain way and they assume it was always that way. I mean, if I saw a guy buying lipstick, I would at first assume it was for his wife. It's because women usually use it more often than men. It is associated with women. That doesn't mean that some men don't use it, but it's safe to say that it is usually used by women.

I read briefly the other day in this Navy SEALs book, as I was checking it back in from the return bin, that *A woman's best self-defense is that her attacker will underestimate her*. I thought about it and it was true. What if a bad guy, like one of those guys from the park, attacked me but didn't know I was taking martial arts? What if I looked soft but when they attacked, I was ready and quickly employed some moves? Because they weren't expecting me to defend myself and be able to fight, I had the advantage and would be able to get away. I hoped this would be true if I ever met those guys again. That was the second point in the book, not to hope that by some miracle of the universe you would be able to escape. You had to make sure you got away, alive.

The author went on to say that it was absolutely foolish to believe that the kind of person who would attack me would also have mercy on me and stop hurting me at some point and let me go in peace. He said they might, but logically that didn't make sense because what kind of person would be attacking me? A bad person! What do bad people do? Bad things, and letting me go or live for that matter would be classified as a good thing most likely. He also said don't put your hopes in the fact that someone will come and rescue you, whether it be a neighbor, the police, your husband, whoever. Most people are dead within three minutes. It really isn't enough time for help to get to you, even if they knew about your situation and wanted to help you. This made sense from all the *Law and Order* episodes I had watched over the years. I knew it was up to me to make sure that I was safe. I was angry that I had to worry about someone messing with me at Vines Park, but I was also angry that Derrick wasn't here either to make sure I was safe.

No, if I was going to make any kind of life here, I couldn't let the fear of what almost happened to me govern what I did or how I felt. Vines Park was mine, not theirs, I thought, in some twisted sort of animalistic unspoken territory. I was going to change how I felt when I drove by the tire depot and stop worrying about the what if I run into them. It was a horrible feeling to be afraid that there was someone out there who would hurt you if they had the opportunity, and the feeling that maybe there was nothing that you could do to stop it. That had to be nonsense, and if not, I had to figure out a way to make it so that it was.

In that moment, I knew I was determined to let them, or anyone else who had the idea to mess with me, know that I wasn't going to let it be so easy for them. I was going to care enough about me to figure out a way to not get hurt and be vulnerable anymore. I wanted to be strong and confident like Mister Kim but was afraid that was a long time ahead. I needed to do something now to prepare myself, but what? I mean, there was no way any amount I could do would guarantee my safety or at least not anytime soon; self-defense training took years to master. I was scared I would meet those guys before I was ready, because with certainty, if they were given the chance, they wouldn't stop hurting me. I would totally be at their mercy and I hated that.

I ate at the Italian restaurant next to the Petco and afterwards brought my training equipment into the house. It took me forever to get the bag into the house and down in the basement. After it was set up, I took a coffee break and then got into my gear and practiced punching and hitting the bag like I had learned in class. I also added a couple knees and things that felt comfortable as I worked the bag. I became tired within a half-hour and realized that I was nowhere near the level of fitness I wanted to be, so I made a plan to do an hour of yoga every morning and to work the bag every night. Fused with the excitement of taking positive steps to making small improvements to myself, I decided to drag the Christmas tree box upstairs that I hadn't set up yet. I had really procrastinated this year. I should have had it up the day after Thanksgiving, but with my new find at Vines and final exams at the end of the semester and in longing for Derrick, I hadn't felt like doing it. Today was different and for the first time in a while I began to feel awake, like strength was returning to me. Strange because I had never felt strong before, not really, but I was and I had the feeling that it was there all along, just waiting for me to acknowledge it. I went back for the two boxes of ornaments and the box of the porcelain nativity set. I opened the box and set it up on a red holiday runner in front of the fireplace. I felt my face get flush with brief anger as I thought of Barbara calling my grandmother a heathen. She obviously didn't know her, I thought to myself as I looked at the scene that stood in height up to my knees. It was a beautiful set; it seemed old and hand painted. Boy, they didn't make stuff like this anymore, I thought, as I paid homage to its craftsmanship. I was too tired to hang the decorations up but I did manage to finish assembling the tree. I started to unravel the string of lights and gave up. Deciding it was time to wind down for the night, I got in bed and made a mental note to put it on my agenda for the next day to finish putting up the Christmas decorations. I went to bed tired but feeling better than I had in a while. At least I had a plan for myself, and it was a good plan. It seemed to be intuitively what I needed to maybe more of what I had been lacking up until then. I dozed off thinking about buying the instant just-take-out-of-the-fridge-and-throw-in-the-oven type of Christmas Cookies I'd seen at Kroger.

*

The next day, I did my morning routine of yoga from a video I had ordered online. I took a quick shower and ate breakfast. That day, I forgot I was supposed to help Rosa clear out the garden and to cut down the branches of various bushes in our yards, but she didn't and was asking me if I wanted her to make another pot of coffee before we got started. We sat in the kitchen and chatted for a while before we got on ladders and trimmed tree branches and pruned all the hedges. I was glad I had her to teach me this stuff, as I'd never had to care for a yard before, and doing it with her made it enjoyable and not seem like work. Afterwards, she said, "I got three dollars, want to go?" So we did, and made our way to our thrift store where we made out like bandits. I got a couple long pullover sweaters and some leggings, and she bought a ton of books. Even after going with her all this time, I was still amazed at what we found, and so cheap. I mean, I knew all these items were donated, so the store was operating on profit but still, this was hard to believe. After shopping, we made the drive home, as Rosa said that was too much excitement for an old lady like herself. "I ain't no spring chicken no more, c'ld," she smiled. "I needs to rest," she exclaimed.

She dropped me off and that was the last time I saw her. Her daughter came by later that night around 10 pm to tell me when she stopped by she had found her on her recliner in the living room. She had passed away in her sleep. She must have went home and took a nap just as she said she was going to do, and died. I gave her a big, long hug and told her I was sorry for her loss, that her mom was a good lady and my friend. I was comforted that she wasn't in pain but went while at rest. That seemed to ease her daughter some and she gave me the information about when the funeral would be. I closed the front door and found myself sliding down onto the floor as giant sobs released from my chest. I cried for a good five minutes, unable to stop. Once I was able to compose myself and stand up, I went upstairs and washed my face and got into bed. I dozed in and out of sleep for what seemed like a while. Jade slept with me, lying against my side as my support. He rested with me, allowing me to occasionally find comfort in running my fingers through his fur before nodding off.

*

The funeral was three days later over at the small graveyard that was next to the playground by the library. There were so many people there; we all barely fit inside the tent. I was the only white person at the service and I got a couple inquisitive looks but everyone was very nice and acknowledged me. Her daughter was unable to hold back her tears and cried heavily; you could tell they were close.

After the service, everyone went back to Rosa's house, where her family had put out a lot of food. I had stopped by Ingles that was next to the thrift store to pick up a Dutch apple pie so as to not go over there empty handed, I knew enough to know that was rude. I sat with them for a while and met a lot of her family members and ate a plate of food before I left. I asked her daughter what she was going to do now and she said her brother and her already had homes of their own, so they were probably going to put the house up for sale.

Something inside me became really sad at the thought of someone else living next door. I gave her a hug and told her to come by and visit sometime and that she was always welcome. "I loved your mom," I said as I was leaving the porch.

"And she loved you too, and your grandma," she said with a sad smile. She put her arm up in a wave as I walked over to my house next door. As I made my way up my porch steps, I turned and saw Barbara sweeping her stoop and I knew she was just doing it to see what was going on across the street. I know I was taught at St. Mary's not to speculate negatively about people, but I knew she was. I waved to her and she just looked with what people describe as a 'deer in the headlights' big-eyed blank stare. Come on, I hadn't ever been rude to her where she would be surprised that I acknowledged her when I saw her and waved. Maybe her mind was so full of dark thoughts of my family that she couldn't see good in me, even when I was doing it right in front of her face. It wouldn't seem as strange if she hadn't come over that night to warn me about the assault on the local young woman. I mean, why care enough to come by then, even if it was just to be Christianly? Well, why not keep up the pretense, why stoop again and go back to not being friendly? I swear that woman was so weird. Well, I guess I wouldn't really know unless I go asked her myself, but today was not that day. I locked the door behind me and went upstairs to take a nice hot shower.

I worked the bag for thirty minutes that day and was proud of my extra ten minutes that I was able to do. I wanted to get out of the house, so I ended up going for a walk. I walked to IHOP and ate dinner then made my way home. I had forgotten to plug the Christmas tree in before I left and I came home to a dark house. It looked sad but I thought it was just because of Rosa. I told myself I was being selfish, as it was her time to go. I was only sad because I missed her and I should be happy she went in peace. I tried to think of the great day we had together and I kept thinking it was her last day and ended up bringing myself to tears. I was in the middle of a deep sob when the phone rang. I tried to compose myself and answered the phone.

It was Andi. "Hello, Rose," he said.

"Hello, Andi." I felt happy to hear from him. I wasn't sure why, but his voice had calmed me somehow. Maybe because I knew I still wasn't alone and as I felt the choke in my throat as the thought developed and left me, I knew that's what it was. I had loved Rosa and now she was gone and I felt she was all that I had since Derrick had been away.

"I am sorry to call you so late in the evening, but something has come up. I have mishandled something and it seems I had to make a split decision concerning the contents of your grandmother's storage. They are dropping off its contents to your front porch tomorrow. If there is anything you don't want, I have arranged for a charity to stop by the following day and pick up whatever it is you decide you do not want to keep. I apologize if this is an inconvenience. Forgive me and I will treat you to dinner when I return to town from New Orleans after the holiday," he said.

"Oh, no problem, Andi," I said. "Actually, I am happy to do this for you and am eager to see some of her things, no worries," I assured him. "If you want to show me around New Orleans sometime, that would be great too. I always wanted to see the city, it sounds cool," I told him with eagerness.

"Done," he replied. "Let us wait until after spring semester in your school, yeah. As it is better to tour in warmer weather," he confirmed. "Thank you, goodbye," and he hung up his end. I was eager to see what would arrive the next day. I made a hot cup of tea and began to relax for bed.

*

The next morning, I was up and ready but no one came and I had to be at the library for work, so sadly I had coffee and a blueberry muffin and left the house for the day. I was reminded with pain that I couldn't call Rosa and ask her to look out her window and see if anyone came to drop off the stuff on my porch. I guess I would just have to wait until after work to see what it was, if they even came. I had a feeling that it was going to come that day, though, and would most likely be there when I got home. I could barely take the suspense of waiting until it was time to go. The last hour of work from five until six was total agony and I managed to distract myself with an old book about pirates and the seas they were known to sail, mostly because it had great illustrations and it got my imagination going. If I hadn't paid to get my nails done, I know I would have bitten all my nails off in waiting and watching the clock drag on that last ten minutes. Finally, the little hand clicked onto the six to my freedom and I was out the door.

When I arrived at home, there was the silhouette of stuff on my porch that I could see from the driveway as I pulled past the house toward the garage. I went into the gate and got a better look as I walked up the stone path. There was a metal clothing rack on wheels, a large wooden trunk and a gargantuan white metal birdcage that stood taller than me in height and was on cat claw legs. I just stared at it in amazement; it was beautiful. There was something else behind it that I missed and now looking at it, I didn't see how, as it was taller than the birdcage. It was covered by a dusty black cloak which released what must have been years' worth of the filth as I pulled it down to reveal a totem pole! It was intricately carved and painted, afterwards covered in a thick glaze to protect the craftsman's handiwork. It was beautiful and frightening at the same time, as the fangs of the bear appeared as though they were coming down on the viewer. The top one was a giant black bear and the second a hawk, the third a wolf, the fourth a beaver, the fifth a bobcat. Each image was done so purposively that it seemed to come to life. My mind raced back to my time in Cherokee and to Beth. It was all surreal and I wondered if I was ever going to make any sense of it, yet somehow it made me happy. It had to be that I myself was also strange; there was no denying it as all of it felt very comfortable. As I unlocked the front door, I wondered if I should make another trip to North Carolina. I hadn't realized how long I was standing outside in the cold staring at the masterpiece. So as not to damage the threshold I first backed my way into the doorway then laid the totem pole down halfway inside the house. Then I placed the end of the totem pole on the cloak and allowed that to drag as I grabbed the front end and pulled it into the house. This way I wouldn't damage the pole or my wood floors. I did the same thing with the chest. The birdcage wasn't heavy and so moving that and the coat rack was easy; I just had to tilt them to get them into the front door. Once inside and behind the locked door of my home, I delighted in the possibility of what was inside the chest. First, I decided to find homes for my new things. The totem pole was wrapped in a throw from the living room and a cloak, so I decided I would be able to get it upstairs if I used them to maneuver the pole. I grabbed either side of the throw and slowly dragged it up the stairs by sitting on the stairs and grabbing it up between my legs and arms like a hug and using the power of my legs to push up with the totem pole, one leg at a time. When I finally made it to the top, I was so proud of myself for having gotten it up there alone. I continued to walk backward and dragged it with the help of the blanket and cloak until I finally got it into the den. I stood it up in the corner of the room on the right side of the window behind the desk. It looked grand and I knew I had found the perfect spot for it. I wondered why she hadn't placed it there before. I thought it was cool and also very strange that all of her totems were of predatory animals.

Usually, you see a bunny or deer in there, but in a sense, Grandma seemed powerful too, so I was not surprised that her spirits weren't softer, quiet animals. I had hoped to explore my meditation more and discover my own, but with all that had happened lately, I wasn't able to sit quietly. I placed the birdcage in the kitchen and washed it until it looked almost new, amusing myself with the tiny latch door. I left the coat rack outside for the charity to pick up tomorrow and took a shower to relieve myself of all the dust I had carried in off of the old cloak which I would be too embarrassed to donate that filthy, so I carried it and the throw to the laundry room. I put it through the washer machine two times and it finally came out usable to my standards. I folded it and left it on the clothing rack. There was no way I could have donated something that filthy. I tried the trunk and it was locked, and to my surprise, the key I wore around my neck didn't fit the opening, so I was out of luck, to my disappointment.

I Googled how to pick a lock and tried various instructed methods to no avail. I was really disappointed and thought I may have to break the chest but it was solid wood. It would be a shame to damage such a beautiful, old chest and I wasn't sure if I could be successful in getting through, it may take half a year even. What would I use, an ax, as there was no way I felt comfortable using power tools like an electric saw? I knew my capacity and thought I would probably hurt myself or damage the contents inside the chest. There had to be a way to get inside. I made myself a tuna salad sandwich on white bread. As I enjoyed the smell of the green onions that masked the tuna, my mind refused to accept that Grandma wouldn't provide a way into the chest, as she had helped me each time so far. Maybe I expected too much from her and was beginning to take her thoughtfulness for granted. Maybe it was time for me to figure things out on my own, but how? I guess I could hire a locksmith. I knew of one off of Hwy 20 in the Dollar General shopping center across from the old elementary school. That didn't seem right, letting a stranger into the house and paying him to pry into Grandma's chest, to reveal the intimacy that she had locked up and hidden away. I finished eating and washed my plate and hands and put the dish into the dishwasher. I took my water bottle with me, as surprisingly I hadn't finished drinking it, and made my way to the den upstairs. I sat down in the chair at the old desk releasing *What do you want from me?* in a sigh to the universe. I sat in the chair at the desk for the longest time, not thinking about anything, when Jade leaped from the top of the totem pole in a hiss and landed on my desk in front of me. "What, well, Jade... stop it. That isn't nice. Come on, man, you're my buddy. Look, whatever I did to offend you..." realizing that it wasn't me he was hissing at. "What is it, honey?" I asked, looking behind me to see what it was that he was looking at. He looked back at the bear and hissed again and hopped down onto the floor and trotted out of the room. "Jade... honey... It's okay, it's not real, it's stuffed..." but before I could finish my sentence, the door slammed shut behind him and I jumped in my seat. "Spooky old house," I said out loud as I looked up at the totem pole behind me and right into the mouth of the bear, when I saw it. A small brass skeleton key, similar to the one I wore as a necklace but smaller and slim. I knew it; I knew Grandma wouldn't let me down. I stood up on the corner of the desk and reached over and put my hand inside the bear's mouth to retrieve it. I was off down to the foyer to see if it fit; I knew with certainty it did, although I had nothing to support what I felt. I slid it in and it clicked. I popped open the chest, eager to discover what was inside.

First lay folded a white wedding dress and veil that must have been hers when she married my grandfather. I thought this was a nice family heirloom to have. Something of importance to her and to my family, a piece of our history; I had always longed for that and got a little watery. I guess it was too much emotion, still after Rosa's death. Inside, there was also an old leather book that had some of the symbols on the front like the ones on my front door. It was in another language, Danish, I assumed, so I had no idea what it said. Further contents were a stack of papers, two of which had my name on them. They looked official. They were Delta and Disney stocks purchased for me. I had better hold on to these; I knew they were worth something. I felt so happy in that moment, knowing that she had been there the whole time, and even if she hadn't been able to take me in physically, she had thought of me and looked after me in her own way. There were some other things that seemed insignificant, such as a tiny metal pot I'd seen Arab people use to make coffee in movies, and a black and white photo of a man dressed in a suit with his hair slicked down, as well as a stack of letters, which I assumed were in Danish as they weren't English. There was also a map of Loganville, a map of the land that was now Vines Park. Grandma sure loved Vines. I tried to imagine an old woman walking around the path as she must have. Then it occurred to me why she must have built the tunnel. If she made sure the property was sold, she would no longer have had access to the lands, which I gather were special to her. Maybe she enjoyed walking the grounds, but once the couple had made it their home it would seem odd for her to be wandering around the grounds so she had to do it in secret. That also explained the hidden entrance to the mansion, as she had to keep an eye on the couple to make sure they were not doing harm to the sacred land so she could keep her promise to Claire and her people. I mean, I'd never really be able to know the truth as that secret was lost with my grandmother, but it was as good a guess as any and it was the only one that made sense so far.

I made a pot of coffee and researched for a couple hours on the five totems that were carved in the pole. I looked up each spirit animal and their meaning. I was disappointed to find a lot of other Native American beliefs were mixed in from other tribes, and some distinctly Cherokee beliefs were lost as different tribes mingled during the Trail of Tears. None the less, I felt more of a connection to my grandmother as I read about her animal spirits.

I thought for a moment that I was being silly, and that Grandmother wasn't Native American, she was Danish. They probably just gave her this as a gift for helping them secure the property, and there was no evidence to support these were any representation of her or who she was. It was just a hunch, somehow inside I knew that it was, and I felt almost as though I had known her now. Some sort of connection to her that I hadn't felt before, with anyone. I must be losing my mind. I mean, the whole thing was like a made-up tale and not normal; none of it was, from tunnels to dreams, doors closing on their own, drafty winds, cats and trips out of state to learn about a culture when I didn't even know my own. Grandma knew about me, though. I felt that she knew enough about me to know my secret wish, or maybe she just planned for her granddaughter to go to college, as many others did. Who knows, but whatever it was, it gave me a peace of mind that most other things did not. It was more believable to accept these signs as truth than try to make sense of them as mere coincidences. As I learned in my psychology class, if it's not maladaptive, why not, right?

Chapter Twenty-One

Alone

The next day, the Kidney Foundation came by and picked up the clothing rack and cloak. I had stepped out of the house to do some quick shopping and stopped by the Lowe's shopping center and bought a large houseplant to put inside my new birdcage. I would have liked to place two small parakeets in there but something about keeping them in a cage bothered me. I know it was probably silly, as a life in my kitchen would most likely be a better one than the one they lived in PetSmart, but it felt wrong somehow and I always tried to listen to my feelings, as weird as they could be sometimes. Plus, Jade would most likely torment our new guests anyhow, not the best idea as much as I liked it. The lush plant would have to suffice. I liked the concept of the large green leaves emerging out of the white bars of the birdcage; it would look great, I thought, as I imagined it in the corner wall that rested as a little nook in between the basement door and the mud room. I could probably benefit from more oxygen in the house anyhow. I got back to the house and set up the plant in the birdcage. It looked perfect there and was exactly the piece that was missing from the room. I loafed around the house until it was time to go to bed.

*

Spring semester came and I was going through my second semester of business classes. I liked them a lot more; it was less homework and more lectures. I had to do a paper here and there or project every now and again, but it was for the most part enjoyable. Weeks went by without any word from Derrick. I would have almost gotten used to him not being around had the dull pain not crept up every now and again to remind me that I missed him from the very core of myself so that it ached. My own body would remind me that it needed him, it wanted him and that I would be left with the feeling of void and a faint emptiness even though the rest of me carried on. When February 14th came along, a dozen roses arrived at my house from him. I had heard the doorbell ring and to my sad realization it was a carrier and not him. I signed for them and placed them on the kitchen island but wasn't pleased; they almost saddened me in some way. Almost as though they angered me from within, they sat there as a reminder of what I wanted, but he wasn't there. Would I see him again? It seemed that I would if he was making an effort to send flowers, but could he be that busy that he had no time at all to even text me to say hello? I hadn't even seen him at church on Sunday, and this comforted me in some way, I guess, to know that maybe he really was strapped down with his schoolwork. I mean, he was going at an accelerated pace in the ten-month program as opposed to the regular sixteen months to two years it usually took other cohorts to complete an M.B.A., but I missed him.

My desire for him overrode all logic, even though my mind was telling me that he was doing exactly what he'd said he was going to do. He was doing what he was supposed to be doing: finishing his education and pursuing his dream. I mean, if I really did love him as much as I thought I did, I would be supporting him, right? I mean, what were a couple months away from each other; if the feelings were real and genuine then it wouldn't matter, it would be worth it. If he was separated from his mom or cousin or something like that, he would feel exactly the same way about them when reunited. No amount of time will erode love, if it's honest. Just then, the reality hit me in the pit of my stomach; I wasn't sure what his feelings were. I doubted that he cared about me, that he was sincere. So this was about me and my insecurities and not him at all. What the heck! Then why did it hurt so bad, way down inside? In a way, I was glad if he had to be away he wasn't just coming around out of obligation. Plus, I didn't think I would be able to face him on Sundays if we weren't on good terms or if he was there just because he felt he should be. I couldn't just turn off how I felt about him; it was too strong, and knowing he really wanted to be somewhere else would drive me mad. I knew I would end up making a scene at St. Oliver's as my feelings would compel me to find him and seek him out. If I saw him, there was no way I could not go over to him. I smiled at the flowers, knowing at least he had thought about me. I picked up my phone and dialed his number. "Aurora, hey. Glad you got the flowers. Do you like them? Listen, I hate to do this but I have to meet up with my group to finish our project that's due in two days. I am really sorry I can't be there today. I didn't forget that it was Valentine's Day. I am so sorry and will make it up to you, okay? Please try to forgive me, I love you. Please, wait for me. I'm going to be done soon, okay," and he was gone. I totally understood him and that he needed to go. That he couldn't come and be with me but I hated the situation. I was just fine before without him but now that I had all these feelings and he wasn't around for me to share them with, to at least get rid of some of them, I was furious. I couldn't help it either.

Normally, I was a very calm person and could probably count on my hand how many times I had actually got mad, let alone angry. I was just numb from growing up in foster care, and maybe a little of it was that I didn't have high expectations in life or from people. If you don't expect anything great or aren't used to people being good to you, you can't really get upset because you didn't get the big letdown. I didn't know my parents to be angry that they weren't there to tuck me in at night or to teach me how they did things, and how their parents did things, so I didn't have that bag of wrath I had seen other people carry with them and throw out in rage. They had something and lost it and it ate them up inside until they couldn't stand it. I thought of little Becca, one of my foster sisters. We had been placed in my second foster home together. We woke up one night and she had dug through the wall in her room, right through the wallpaper, the Sheetrock and insulation until she hit the support beams. I don't think she would have stopped if we hadn't come into the room. She, of course, was sent away for someone else to deal with and fix. I mean, I get it, those people weren't equipped to help her but all she took away from that was more anger. I had been very fortunate up until now to have never lost anything, or at least anything that I was aware of.

Well, I have, but it wasn't unrightfully taken from me so I knew it, missed it and wanted it, because it was mine and because it was supposed to be there. No, Mrs. Vendor left me because it was her time to go. Just like Rosa, she loved me but she had to go. I realized I viewed her death like an appointment or a bus schedule you don't want to be late for. I wasn't sure if it was proper canon but it made sense, and I was happy with my view and it left me with peace as I remembered my loved ones. I used to see a lot of kids who I thought had everything; both parents to raise them. Someone took the time to pack them a lunch every day and was there to make sure that they had the help they needed with their homework or were shuffled off to any one of the various clubs or activities after school that they wanted to participate in. I watched them be prone to anger because they expected good things to happen to them and were disappointed or angry when their life didn't go the way it usually had for them. I had never had that luxury and just usually accepted things as they were and floated through life. Then I met Derrick and his mom and they were great, and I wanted more of them in my life. I had grown to love him and began to feel as though I were part of him and his family. For the first time, I had wanted something so badly and I knew how it felt to be angry that it wasn't there. The ache was more than anything I had ever felt in all my life and I needed him so desperately but grudgingly I just woke up and went through the motions in the hope that it would end soon. That soon he would be finished with school and we could be together. He wasn't even in my mind anymore; he had consumed my entire soul as a heavy weight that dragged me through everything. He wasn't even in my thoughts anymore, yet my spirit yearned for something that wasn't there and my body slowly carried me throughout the day and I silently knew it was because of him.

Fortunately, I had made myself get into the routine of doing the yoga video each morning until by now I had memorized the routine and could do my daily practice in quiet. Beating the bag at night also helped me let off some steam and get out some of the negative emotions I had been fighting to overcome. It helped me to the point where I was still pleasant in my exchanges with others outside, but the ache still lingered for Derrick as my silent secret. Leading me to sometimes wonder if he forgot me, if he hurt the same way each day that I did.

*

I continued throughout the rest of the spring semester just going through the motions of my set routine – yoga, class, Taekwondo karate, school, homework – until finally the day came when he called me to invite me to his graduation. I was so excited! One, I was really proud and happy for him but also happy that now maybe things could go back to the way they were. To when everything was right because I was with him. He was finished with his courses so why wasn't he coming to see me? The dread and fear crept up like a whisper of pain I didn't want to face, afraid that the answer may not be what I wanted to hear. I told myself that I had to know and move on if need be, but this had to stop.

He wasn't working at Coca-Cola anymore and not going to class; he was finished. The graduation was just a formal ceremony. He could actually write M.B.A. on any application and it would be true; he had a Master's degree now and had probably received a copy of the diploma in the mail already. What was the deal? If we were over, he wouldn't be calling me to invite me to his graduation, but why avoid me then? I called him up to ask him but it went straight to voicemail. I left a message saying call me, let's hang out, I want to see you.

After an hour of him not calling me back, I was so tempted to call him again, but I thought of Mimi, a girl I knew from Topps. She was so sad and would just sit in the break room at lunchtime and repeatedly call her so-called boyfriend who either didn't answer or he would say things that would upset her to the point that she couldn't control herself, even at work. She would cry sometimes throughout the day on the assembly line and ignore most of the other workers because she was consumed with her bad relationship. No, it took everything in my power to not call him again, but I didn't; I wasn't going to be like Mimi. I went down to the basement and beat the crap out of my bag for at least twenty minutes before I sat on the floor and had a good cry. Afterwards, I did some deep stretches, which helped my mood a little bit, and I just allowed my thoughts to wander until I found myself in a very relaxed state and lying comfortably on the floor. My spine was aligned and straight. I could feel the curve of its arch as my shoulder blades and sit bones rested against the floor. I eventually drifted off to sleep…

I was standing at the gates of Vines Park but oddly, they were closed. It was dusk, yet the light off the polished bronze and iron illuminated the path. I walked toward them and pushed gently and the one on the right gave way for me to enter with an eerie creek. The path was not the paved road that I remembered but dirt, which felt cool and soft under my bare feet as I walked further into the park. I could smell a campfire burning in the distance long before I could see its yellow-orange glow dim on the other side of the lake. I made my way toward it like a fool, I told myself, as I wasn't sure who was over there, and the fact that someone had lit a fire in the park should probably serve as a warning and not an invite but I felt no fear. In fact, I was so relaxed as if it was the middle of the day and I was briskly walking to meet an old friend at our agreed meeting place. I passed the stone wall that separated the rolling green hills from the path between the forest and the start of the lake, but I hesitated as the bridge was gone! Who could have taken the bridge in the short time since I was here last? Down a little bit further was an older bridge, one I had not seen before. It was much smaller and looked handmade and old, very old. People don't make stuff like this anymore, I thought as I noticed the details in the carved wood along the beams. It began at the shallow part of the lake by the old beaver dam and crossed at the river that went around the old, big trees in the Asian garden, but wait... The Asian garden was gone too! I made my way across the much smaller bridge and stood in the forest that should have been the Asian garden of Vines Park. Huh, I looked around and took in my surroundings. There were still the marshes that I'd seen ducks and other waterfowl wade in, but it seemed like a larger area that kind of eventually emerged into the start of the forest. It was so dark and growing darker as the night began, I made my way toward the firelight to avoid becoming lost. I could hear the soft hum of drums beating in a rhythmic flow, becoming clearer as I approached.

There was no longer a path so I had to walk toward what should have been the white garden, but it wasn't. I kept walking, knowing at any point now I would hit it, but I just kept walking further into the forest and closer to the light and hum of the drums. Surely even if I missed the row of white bushes in the dim light, I would have caught their sweet fragrance by now. I looked to my left for what should have been the lion statue and giant set of massive brick steps that led as a second entrance to the rose garden but they weren't there. I slowly made my way up a small hill, where I could see them. They all sat around the circle of fire, about twenty of them. Most of them were Native American but some were white, mostly women in their early twenties and thirties and two African-Americans; an older woman in her early to mid-thirties and a younger one who was thinner and strikingly pretty in the face. Both of them had their heads wrapped in those traditional headscarves and wore long skirts. Looking around, all of the Native Americans were dressed in traditional clothing, feathers, silver jewelry, deerskin boots; and the other two white women wore their long, dark red hair loose and were in long skirts as well. I couldn't make out the other white men in the group as they were on the other side of the fire. As I crouched down to make myself more comfortable and to lie still so as to see what was going on, she emerged in a slow rhythmic movement toward the crowd. She was slender and strong, with her muscular limbs carrying her form through each expression. She occasionally leapt with what would be described as a fawn-like expression I'd seen only in ballet or Broadway performances had it not been so earthy and sexual in its womanly movements, as if she were asking the ground itself to become a part of her. No, it was more like she was a symbol of the park itself, partaking in some exotic ritual of Vines only she could perform. She slowly lowered her head in a thrusting movement, allowing the antlers of her headpiece to act out some part in this play of a dance she was performing for us.

The long, flowing pieces of the top of her garment hung past her knees on some parts to reveal a slit in the deer skinned skirt she wore under the sheer garments that somehow allowed her arms to be bare. Her long hair occasionally complemented her movements as it swayed in unison with her, shaping her form for us to see.

I tried to look at her face to make out her features. The more that I tried, the more that I was distracted by the grace and feminine power of her movements, but then almost as if she could sense me as I lay there, stunned by her enchantment, she turned and looked right at me, straight in the eyes. I almost screamed but quickly muffled my cry of shock with my hands, all the while realizing it was me! It was my face there dancing. What the heck! Not giving me a second even to take in what I had seen, she began to slowly turn and turn and spin around so fast that only a yellow light, which must have been the glow of the fire cast off of her skin in the movement, was the only shape besides an occasional antler that could be seen as she spun around. As she slowed and her form began to emerge once again, it was no longer her but the red doe of Vines! She gracefully stepped out onto the soft grass ahead and placed her left hoof first in front of her and lowered her head as a form of acknowledgement of sorts and turned to enter the forest in a swift leap. She was gone. I slowly crept backward in an attempt to leave undetected. When I was down the hill enough to rise without being seen by the others, I did, and made a swift run for it back toward where I assumed the bridge was. I knew the general area but it was a little harder to see as my back was now to the fire and I was moving away from the light toward the dark of the woods. It was amazing how dark it was. I mean, there was no light to be seen anywhere! How was that possible? I mean, the lamp post from the parking lot should be seen, even if very dim from here. I opened my eyes; I was asleep! I had been dreaming this! I put my hand down to feel the floor of my basement! Awh! I must have fallen asleep down here after working out.

I awoke in complete darkness and made my way out of the room and up the stairs to the kitchen. It was eleven thirty; maybe I could watch a couple of *Law and Order* episodes and fall back to sleep. I thought even if I went back to sleep at 2 or 3 am, it would still be a good night's rest because of my long nap. I wasn't even tired; I knew my body needed rest because I had been upset. Sleep tends to be the best medicine for most ailments, whether they are mental, physical or otherwise; well, at least for me. I put the kettle on to brew myself a strong cup of tea as I made my way upstairs to take a nice hot shower. It was almost as if I was washing away all of the hurt and aches of the day as the water flushed over me. It was amazing what a nice long shower could do for your spirits. I had taken way too long and could hear the whistle blowing from downstairs. I quickly dried off, lotioned up and jumped into a pair of yoga pants and a long tee shirt and was downstairs to finally pour my much-needed cup of tea. I dried my hair with the towel as the tea bag soaked in my mug. I was still fascinated by the osmosis process as the tea and water became one the longer they sat together in my cup. Even this realization of how tea was made carried my thoughts to Derrick. Oh, I had it bad for him. I didn't want to – well, my self-respect didn't – but I checked my phone and he hadn't called me back. I was furious, and then I felt bad, as what if something had happened to him? Why were my first thoughts rejection and anger, to judge so harshly a guy who I supposedly loved, because he didn't do what I thought he should? There were a hundred possible explanations; maybe he was sick or had lost his phone. Who knows? The point was I didn't know and I didn't believe the best about him because my own needs and expectations weren't being met. Really, it was that I just missed him, but it was also that I was afraid because of how strongly I felt for him. I was afraid because I liked him so much that he could easily take advantage of me and not treat me right, or that I just wouldn't care, like Mimi, because I was just so crazy about him. Was it really possible for me to love someone so much that I would look past everything, even how they treated me? That thought frightened me down to the bone and made me angry. No, I thought, I'd been through enough crap; I needed someone who really cared about me. That is what I'd been waiting for and I was proud of myself for being able to say it. Some people couldn't admit how they really felt, or what they needed because honestly, everybody's needs seem stupid but to them they are the most important thing. I just wanted it to be true that he felt the same way about me. Now I knew what people meant when they said, "Time will tell," as I guess I would have to wait and see if that time we'd spent apart had changed how he said he felt about me. Would fate be that cruel and allow me to desire him so much to the point where I could almost see him, sense his presence only reserved as a memory from our time together? Saved and stored deep inside me because I valued it so much, that I longed for it again, only to find that he had changed his mind? Would life deal me another bad hand for me to sit through as all the other players got to finish theirs? It really hurt. I had to know how he felt, to kiss him again, to be near him. To feel the strength of his arms around me in that embrace that would hold me in such contentment I would feel as though time had stood still for only me to be in his arms that moment.

I broke down and sent him a smiley face emoji as a text but stopped myself from anything else. This seemed okay; he would see it and it was communication but still light. Most people would respond to it, so I had made the first move without being pathetic. I was satisfied. I had texted him but it was within a certain boundary. I hoped with all my might that he would text me back, respond. God, it would be complete agony if he just sent me back a smiley face in response.

Within five minutes of *Law and Order: Criminal Intent*, I was absorbed and fully distracted to my happiness. It was a new episode that I hadn't seen and I was so thankful to be distracted and that my misery had come to an end, for at least that night. I soon fell asleep and slept a long, restful sleep that was void of any dreams, or that I could remember, until the next day. I woke up and went to work and came back home again without any sign or call from Derrick. It was driving me nuts. I had to calm my mind a couple of times, telling myself that Derrick's mom would come find me and let me know if something had happened to him. He had to be okay. He just needed his space, and no respectable girl would go and chase after him. If I really wanted him for good, I had to let him be but it was becoming unbearable and it was rude not to return my calls. I mean, who does that? Even professors will call you back within forty-eight hours, as that is what is considered professional. He had an M.B.A., didn't he? Well, he should have known the protocol. I began to feel my anger resurface again. I needed a good long chat with a girlfriend to really hash this out but was glad I didn't have one, as I didn't want to be one of those stupid girls who only talks about her boyfriend, always asking, "What should I do?" No, Mrs. Vendor always said, "If you don't like something, change it. And don't ask other people what you should do with your life; you should know you and your life better than anybody. Be an expert when it comes to you." I'm not saying people don't need help every now and again, and you should have people in your life that you can talk to, but I guess I was afraid of being overrun and governed, maybe even consumed, by Derrick and my feelings for him. They were so powerful and I wasn't sure where this was going, and the man was making no sense right now.

Why didn't he call? After work, I drove to Vines Park and just walked. I stopped at the entrance of the rose garden and found that I couldn't face the first guardian. It was weird that when I made eye contact with her, I had to look away. Compelled now, I forced myself, all the while knowing I was being absurd, as she was just a statue. I tried and was not successful with any of them, even the one Derrick and I had confirmed resembled me – the guardian of the fowl. She was the last one and seemed younger than the rest. Her other three companions seemed more mature and worldly. She had a wistful and almost free spirit about her as she called for the bird to rest upon her hand. How I wished to be like her now. No, I knew who I wanted to be more like, but I didn't have the courage to say it. Her, or me, I should say, from my dream. I pushed the thought from my mind only to have it resurface again with why? Why was she so bad, forbidden almost? Crazy, I was standing outside alone, afraid to actualize a thought. Telling myself I was safe and it was okay for me to think something, even if it was bad, because I had the free will to act on it or restrain myself if need be, assuring myself that I was in control. I allowed myself to fear becoming her, to develop and explore this raw womanly power of sexual beauty that was free to dance outside, for others, deep in the forest at night. Nope, I was shutting it down; she was pretty much the opposite of everything St. Mary's and Avoca stood for and I didn't want to go down a dark path; I seemed lost often enough already. Even in resisting the rising thoughts from my mind, I felt awakened and felt the spark of a new interest growing. She was what I wanted to feel like, to have the freedom to just dance by the fires of Vines, to let go. To have this heavy burden lifted from my spirit, to be free but still able to love, yet not to be consumed with the desire to possess. This was like a crazed passion that had sprung up from my depths, one that had been awoken that I myself was not aware I could carry and satisfy. Maybe it was because I was older and now alone. Maybe it was just the life changes and then losing Rosa and finding out all about me and my past through my family's history, to believing I had something special finally and it just wasn't there. It made me miss it and to have grown dark and angry that it wasn't there. Finally, I looked up at her face.

That was so young and smooth in the shape of her defining features which held a slight hint of carefree joy in engaging with her animal friend. Firm, defining details that shaped her face, yet feminine at the same time, realizing as I met her eyes that I had overcome this pain I had held inside me for so long. What a release that came from the gasp and smile as I exhaled and let go of all of it into my stone friend, who watched over me as I meandered through her beautiful garden. I leant over to inhale the sweet, yet faint fragrance from her small light pink roses that crowded around her grand stature. Hers smelt the best out of all of them, but the peach-colored ones that framed the pillars of the exit path were a good second. I made my way back to the Subaru and back home.

As I pulled out of the parking lot of Vines, I was shuffled by a police officer and a commotion of cars. There had been an accident and I was rerouted in the opposite direction. Crap! I had never been this way before and had no idea where I was going. The road led me to a four-way stop, at which I took a left. It was a single-lane road that went past a rural area of homes and a lake, which took me back to Hwy 20. Yea! I had found an alternate route to the road that took me to school, which was always pretty neat as you never know when a road may jam up and I would hate to be late to class. Plus, after those guys messed with me at Vines, knowing other possible escape routes may come in handy. As I drove through the small assembly of tiny brick buildings that lined the streets of downtown Loganville proper, the light changed and I was forced to sit for a moment and wait.

Something caught my eye in the glass window of the tiny shop that was squeezed in between a barber shop and the old antique mart. It was her! It was freaking her from my dream! Holy crap! Did I just see that? The light changed and the big Ford Bronco behind me beeped. I had to go but the wonder drove me to pull into the small parking lot that was housed behind the row of buildings as my foot still wasn't fast enough on the gas for the Bronco, who honked again. Jeez! My heart raced and I felt all of the anxiety from the sudden blaring sound and from the possibility of a real encounter with her race up from my stomach to my throat. Jerk! I thought, but I wasn't really worried about him. I had to see if I had lost my mind and if the woman I thought I saw dancing just now was really there and, more importantly, was she the woman from my dream at Vines?

I found a spot right in the front and I parked right in front of the back of the Clock World Café and antique shop. What a weird concept: buy a watch and get a cup of coffee. Well, the locals must like it because it seemed to be doing okay as a business, strangely enough. Maybe there really was a dancing lady, as this place was revealing itself to be as weird as it gets. My mind raced and I couldn't get to the window fast enough, but I definitely didn't want to run or draw attention to myself. I wasn't quite certain if I was more afraid of seeing her in there or of the possibility that I was seeing things and may not be as okay mentally as I had thought. "Here goes," I whispered to myself as I took a deep breath and came to face the red painted wooden frame that encased the giant glass window. I wondered what this shop had been originally. I looked inside to see an empty studio, most likely a dance studio, as indicated by its smooth wooden floor, entire wall that was a mirror and ballet bar in front. Huh! I noticed a flyer on the door that advertised *Amira, Gypsy Fire Dancer* and a list of class times for tribal fusion belly dance lessons. So this type of dancing had a name, it was a thing? Just then, she emerged. Her face, like in the dream, bore a resemblance to mine but she was real! Thank goodness, whew! Oh, the relief. I smiled as I walked back to my car and made my way the couple blocks home. I distracted myself from the afternoon by working on some homework and then watched some T.V. before falling asleep with Jade at my feet in a ball of contentment.

*

The next day, I went to school then my Taekwondo class. I had forgotten to eat after G.G.C., so I stopped by the Waffle House on my way home and ate. I made small talk with the waitress and a couple of patrons before leaving, and they seemed to satisfy my need for company, at least for now. Only two more days before Derrick's graduation, and he still hadn't texted me or anything. I went to sleep and woke up happy as I saw a text from him on my phone. It was the address of Mercer University and where the ceremony would be held and the time. I was furious but still excited about going. I got depressed thinking about what to wear, as I wanted to look good when he saw me. No, I wanted to look better than he had ever seen me, and much better than any other girl he had seen either but I didn't really have anything like that in my closet, and two days wasn't a lot of time to pull myself together. I stopped by the thrift store after work and wasn't happy with anything I saw in there, so I went to the TJ Maxx in the Lowe's shopping center and found a basic black dress and long sweater to wear over it. It was nice but not formal, so I would be comfortable and look respectable but not too much and out of place. I began to realize that looking good a lot of the time was just not looking out of place, funny how that was true. I was so thankful that I had stuck to my workouts in his absence, as my body was a lot more toned since he had last seen me and I was a little more confident than I usually was when I slipped on my new dress. I was so excited; I wished that now we could go back to normal but I wasn't sure how he felt or what he thought. I felt so angry that he was withholding himself from me, from us. I wanted him to be mine and for us to be a couple, a team with no secrets, no walls.

I was finishing up the process of getting ready and heading over to Mercer for his graduation when the doorbell rang. I put the earring I was about to put on down on the counter of the sink in my bathroom and made my way downstairs to see who was at the front door. I pushed the lace curtain aside of the glass cut out in my large oak door and was shocked; it was Derrick! "I was just about to head out to watch you graduate," I exclaimed.

He said, "Can I come in?" I stepped aside to let him in the house. "Of course." I walked toward him to give him a big hug.

His embrace was shorter than normal but still warm and affectionate. It felt as though he cared about me, but I began to worry. "Hey, what's this about? Should I still finish getting ready to go?" I asked him.

"No," he said as he looked me in the eye tenderly. "Listen, Aurora, I just came by because I wanted to tell you that I wouldn't be going to the graduation today and I wanted to swing by and try to catch you before you made the trip over there and wasted all that gas," he said.

"Why, Derrick? What is all this about?" I spat out.

"Now don't you worry, everything is all right. I actually have an M.B.A. I finished the program, and this was just a ceremony. I, well… what happened was my dad is stuck in Chicago on business. The negotiations are taking longer than expected and he has to stay until it's worked out. Mom and I decided last minute to bail and I just wanted to catch you because if I didn't, I'd have to go through with it, as I couldn't do that to you. I'd feel terrible. I'm real glad I caught you as I was kind of down that my dad couldn't make it. I know that sounds silly, right? It's just that I had already graduated from U.G.A. and had the big hoo-ha, so this was just finishing up. I have my degree; the ceremony would just be to celebrate, but since he couldn't make it, I guess I didn't really feel like celebrating. Please forgive me. I know I probably caused you some inconvenience. Let me buy you lunch or something like that or reimburse you for the cost of getting your hair done or for the cost of the dress or whatever y'all women do," he said sweetly.

"Derrick, that is totally understandable and I appreciate you thinking of me and making sure I was in the know so I didn't drive over there and sit by myself and watch you not graduate. I love you," I said with a soft smile. He could see my pain that came across my face as the words left me. He took my hand and looked me deeply in the eyes as though he was looking for the right words or trying to read my thoughts. I thought, *Just say you love me, stupid. Just say it.*

He went on, "No, I mean that you stopped everything just now for me and you really care. Aurora, you see me. I've never had that before, well, my mom, but that's different. She's supposed to be like that. I mean, I found a stranger—"

He stopped because I cut him off with, "A stranger, huh," as I teased him in a flirtatious interruption. Realizing he was serious and trying to tell me something, I stopped talking to listen. "Naw, what I mean is you ain't kin, like related and you do care as if you were family. That moved you into a big place in my life."

"I thought you felt that way before, but you have been so distant lately that I wasn't sure how you felt about me. I was alone and I missed you. If you needed me to wait and be strong, that is fine. I would do that for you, for us, but you didn't. You didn't say anything. You just weren't there." I realized that I was yelling. I didn't mean to scream at him and that wasn't normally how I talked to people, especially to those that I cared about but it was all coming out. Like a big powerful wave and I have to say I felt better. Before I could close my mouth, he caught it in his. He forced me backward in his embrace of passion. I felt him, all of his emotions from the day. His dad, his worries, and how he felt about me. There was no denying his feelings for me as he deeply sought my tongue with his over and over again until we just merged in the moment as one. Two people who connected first by their feelings as it slowly led to this undeniable desire that was finally being answered in this moment. How I had waited for him and had wanted this to happen. We left and made our way over to Waffle House where over many pots of coffee and a cheese egg plate we solidified our relationship. I admitted to him that I was afraid that he would be coming around to make out and then leave me again, and he assured me that he was going to be distant for a while to find a job but that he was serious about me and us. "Aurora, you have to know how I feel about you, to know what I want," he said as he took my hands into his from off of the table. "Look, I'm not in a position to show you, I mean, really show you but please, just trust me and know that I'm a good guy. I ain't one of 'em, so please know you are special to me. I know it's been hard on you and I'm really sorry I couldn't be there; I wanted to be. Know this was better for me and for us. Now I can get a really good job. We have options now, for our future. It's gonna be all right, y'll see," he said. I tried the exercise I learned from one of the girls back home who showed me to just take in deep breaths, as you can't convince anyone that you are tough and that they should leave you alone if your eyes are full of tears. It didn't work; he noticed. "Hey," he said. So gently, like he was calming a horse. He rose and crossed to my side of the table and slid into the booth next to me and put his arm around me and began patting my arm. "Hey, whatever it is, we're gonna be all right. Look, it's been a lot lately, is all. I'm gonna do a better job of being around, okay." He took my chin with his hand and forced me to look into his eyes. "I promise," he said as he planted a quick kiss on my lips. It worked, I felt much better, like I had been emptied out from the inside. As if someone had come in with a big scoop and emptied me out, and he poured in a little warmth. I smiled at him as he slid back into his side.

When he made eye contact, I said, "I'd like that," and smiled again. "What'd you get a psychology degree while you were over there too?" I teased.

He said, "Nawh, but maybe I should of," screwing up his face in a quiet laugh as he stuck out his tongue. Either he was a remarkable negotiator like his dad or I just really loved him, but somehow we were okay again.

He drove me back to my house and lingered on the porch for a while saying goodnight. He looked up at me from the stone walkway as I stood a few steps up, in a sorry attempt to leave. "Aurora, give me some time. I have to find us a good job. Okay?" I could feel the fear creep back up again. I guess I didn't do as good of a job as I thought of hiding it because he said, "Now don't go a worr'in' again. Please, look, it shouldn't take that long." He placed his hands on either side of my arms as he looked up at me. He walked up the three steps and kissed me and turned me around to face my front door and patted me on the behind and said, "Goodnight."

I turned to face him as I was unlocking the front door, not even attempting to hide the giant smirk he had put on my face. That man was magic and he sure held a power over me, I thought, as I waved goodnight and watched him get into his Jeep. I slept soundly with the feeling that everything was all right, but nothing seemed like it had been before; I couldn't explain it. Although Derrick had confirmed his commitment to me, nothing seemed the same. Something had changed and I couldn't quite put my finger on it. I could only hope it was for the better as I drifted off to sleep.

The next day, I worked at the library and was in good spirits. The day passed by pretty quickly and I almost enjoyed it, even though I was at work. I found that I liked being there. It was small and it gave me a sense of community, as everyone knew everyone else. Even though the population had increased by four times over the last twenty years, somehow the place still kept its small town values. I also liked that it housed programs that helped people. I knew I'd had a hard time with not attending high school like everybody else, and I felt good when I saw older people who would normally have given up on themselves, come in and learn to read or practice for their G.E.D. It was as if we helped them switch on a light they had inside them they had believed to have been blown out. To see them light up and start believing in themselves again and to be a part of seeing people make themselves and their lives better was really rewarding in a way most other things were not. Allowing the kids to pick out a sticker from the sticker jar as they checked out always made me smile too. I guess I just wanted an outlet to be nice to people and didn't really have that before the library. I mean, it's easy to be nice to people that are good to you, but I really wanted to be nice. It's really not that difficult to be in a good mood when everything is going your way. I was happy I was over my angst and

I wanted to be over it, no matter what happened with Derrick and me.

That feeling of loss and anger had just consumed me and I didn't like the way that I felt or the person who I had become. I wanted to be good. To be a nice person and live somewhere nice and I guess I finally got it, accidently but nonetheless, it felt good. I say by accident because I didn't plan for it, not that I didn't want it. I just didn't know how to. I thought some people were just born into those great situations, and they are. I know in school I was taught in the United States I could do almost anything that I wanted with my life. I just wasn't sure what I wanted to do or how to get there. By some miracle, I was given exactly what I had always wanted by a lady I had never met. I mean, how weird is that? Maybe not so weird, as she was my grandmother; and maybe blood is thicker than water, as the saying goes, and that it runs deeper than I thought. I left work content with my life and feeling good.

Chapter Twenty-Two

❦

All Is As It Should Be

I t was May and the summer semester had begun. I had figured out a way to squeeze in six classes by taking a full load and doing two as a mini-semester. I was taking more classes and somehow I had a fierce momentum to keep going. I couldn't believe how I was even doing all of this and keeping my grades up but it was falling into place. It was as though I was supposed to be doing this and honestly, I was happy to be as busy as I was since it kept my mind off Derrick. I plunged through the summer, and the seven weeks of struggle were over before I knew it. I was walking out of Building B happy I was finally finished with final exams for the semester. I decided to get the registration for the fall over with so I could really just enjoy some downtime for the remainder of the break. I needed a break.

I was afraid to stop doing so much, though, as I had never thought I could get so much accomplished as I was doing right now and I was afraid if I let go, I wouldn't be able to gain that momentum again. I made the long walk over to Building D, to register. There was a small line of like-minded students eager to get all of their affairs in order. I tried not to stare at the girl in front of me, but her nails were ridiculous. I mean, there was just no way for me not to notice them. They were acrylic like mine but as long as at least four of my nails if they were connected tip to tip. They were painted a dark blue and so long they curled under. They were something out of an old horror film, and I wondered how she took a shower or cooked as they seemed to be impractical. Finally, it was my turn at the window and I was able to register for a full load of four classes but was denied my request to take an extra class, making it five classes for the upcoming semester. The clerk, who knew me from my first semester English 101, told me in a hushed voice that the hold was lifted off my account in the Banner system; I could just go home and register for it myself if I wanted to add the class. She said that she wasn't allowed to register students for more than four at a time, for that I would have to actually make an appointment with my advisor or do it myself and she handed me my receipt with a wink. She made sure to mention that she would do it right away before the system re-set and the hold was back on there or the classes filled up, as there were only two slots left in the one I said I wanted. I smiled at her big thanks and was on my way back to the newly added parking lot next to the daycare.

I hated that parking lot, as it wasn't paved and the lot was just a bunch of dirt and rocks. The school thought it was a good idea to make a maze of sorts with farm-like fencing to 'guide' students into the lot from one exit and out the lot through another. This was intended as a way students would be driving only one way when navigating throughout the campus, but the parking lot was anything but driver-friendly. Also, since students were often not as experienced as drivers, they tended to park awkwardly in the small spaces, making leaving the lot a stressful mess that usually consumed a lot more time than it should have to back up out of your chosen parking space. I myself had been shaken up a couple of times when in my stressful struggle to navigate out of the parking space some student who was on their cell phone and not even looking at me as I was attempting to back up, just suddenly walked out in front of my moving car. My nerves were shot from that parking lot, but the summer semesters were always less crowded and seemed to have a more relaxed feel to them, even though ironically the loads were heavier.

I wasn't sure how it worked at a traditional school. I had heard a lot from movies and people just talking that a lot of college kids come home for the summer and have the semester off. Maybe they did the seven weeks also and came home for the remaining month and a half. This would only apply to traditional students, though, who lived on campus in a dorm or those who attended out of state. G.G.C. was definitely not a traditional school, as a lot of its students were older and attended at night. A lot went in the summer because they had a life already and were going to school at the same time and just wanted their piece of paper to get the promotion at work or whatnot. There were dorms and student housing on campus, but those were the usual straight-out-of-high-school students. I liked the school as it had surprisingly earned its accreditation and good reputation in such a relatively short time. I think part of its charm was like its mascot: a fighting bear. It wasn't fancy like the already established U.G.A., whose reputation would get you a job because you were a member of that polished 'you're one of us' kind of reputation. No, the school was smack set in the middle of two already known great towns, Athens and Atlanta, who already had their respective schools. To make it out of the middle of nowhere, you had to have something. Somehow the fighting bear had earned that status. It was just then, in that moment, I realized the pattern of the G.G.C. Grizzly and mine and my grandmother's totem animal. "Surrounded by bears," I said to myself.

I wondered if my dream was my subconscious trying to tell me something. I had to be projecting something, some unresolved issue or feeling, I thought, further knowing that okay, that could explain my dream; but what about the fact that Grandma had a totem, an actual totem of the bear carved out of wood? The Cherokee had the most dominant animal spirit as the top animal represented first on the piece. Grandma's first animal was a bear. Also, what about that strange connection with Beth Cottontail in the shop? My subconscious couldn't explain what others say or do. Well, not unless they were just a dream and my mind was controlling what they shared and projected. No, unfortunately the totem and Beth were real and the whole experience actually happened. But why and what did it mean? I hoped this wasn't one of those times in life where you are supposed to not know and be content and just accept that life doesn't always offer explanations. I recalled one time in Catholic school our teacher was explaining to a student who had asked why dinosaurs weren't mentioned in the Bible. I thought her answer was a good one; it was logical but it didn't give the questioner that 'this is how it is' solution to the uncertainty we as people need from time to time. I mean she could have went on about what is time? She spoke more as a question back to him, "Is it the same as time for God, or why in Genesis is light mentioned then animals? There is no way every single one that existed was to be listed. Why are the dinosaurs considered more important than other animals that they are to be specifically listed? Just look at the geologic timeline; it seems to flow in order with our teachings. Why do we need to be told every specific thing, to have everything explained to us? That is not the purpose of the Bible," she went on. "The purpose is to teach you how to have the best life here, the one that was intended for you and it's a guide for the here and afterlife. It teaches you how to have a good one and make it to the next. Why is anything else needed, as I feel like even if we were told, we wouldn't be capable of understanding it, so why waste valuable time?"

In recalling what she said, I was comforted some but still unsatisfied. I needed to know what all of this meant and I would go crazy from the inside if I didn't get answers or at least some to come peaceful conclusion.

I found myself driving down Hwy 20 in a daze of wonder. What was I supposed to do? I felt almost guilty in not being satisfied with what little Catholicism had given me. It was mostly that I wouldn't get that giant voice from the sky telling me what I needed to hear in the moment. Was it guidance that I wanted? I was sure I could find a priest or psychologist but what? I guess I wanted to know what to think of it all, to know if I was on the right path. The thing was I had never had a path or someone to show me and now I had been given this awesome path by my grandmother and I didn't know what to make of it. I felt unsatisfied, as I wanted to know if what I was hearing and seeing were signs. What was I supposed to make of them? Was it God, as I knew the God from the Bible didn't come down and talk to people or burn bushes anymore, did he? Was there a correct path for everyone? I thought there was. I mean, pretty much everyone said there was, from fortune tellers reading your palm to token sayings of God's Path and finding the truth or fulfilling your destiny. Just about everyone and every religion taught some form of it, calling it different things. I just wasn't sure what I was supposed to see or find here. I was very confused. At first, I just couldn't believe my luck; my grandmother had pretty much handed me everything I could have ever dreamed up and more. People work their whole lives and never own a house like mine and I met good people and Derrick. All of it was because of her, because she cared about me. If someone had told me two years ago that I would be living in an old Victorian house in a Podunk town, going to college, working at a library, studying a martial art and was consumed by the thoughts of a guy who didn't call me, I would have laughed in their face. I would probably have even made fun of him saying, "Oh yeah, what do we call each other... y'all?" The truth was my life had become so foreign, such that the unbelievable had happened and it had all fallen into place so perfectly I thought I was losing my mind from it. I knew a good sign was that I was actually questioning my sanity, as it is true that those who are actually mad cannot. Yet, I was tormented nonetheless by it and wasn't able to relax until I found my car parked in front of Vines Park.

I walked under her steep parting of wrought iron. Such delicate power displayed as her entrance way wrapped around entwined. So subtle, yet all who looked at her had to acknowledge her strength and mystery. As though she was inviting you in to see some forbidden treasure that was locked away inside. Upon entering, one's mind escaped to some far-off place built by their imagination that had been blocked away by the mundane obstacles of daily life.

Here, it was free to wander and become whatever it wanted or needed to be. I needed her. I didn't know what I expected a park to do. I thought of myself in the projects in Pennsylvania; what would I say to this person now? Would I have laughed at her walking around a park looking for answers? What, did I expect the statues to speak to me, for little fairies to come out and answer all my prayers? I felt so sad now. I knew I had crushed the only thing that had ever made me feel whole inside. The one place that I felt I had belonged to and had given me the answers I needed about who I was, my family. I had a connection to this place, and it was real. As stupid as my old self might still try to convince me it was, but what did she know? She wasn't anything; she barely got her G.E.D. and was only able to get an apartment through lies or the piety of others.

That was when the lights in my head went off and I realized I had felt bad because I didn't like her. I saw her as weak and hated that she felt bad all the time, but she was too scared to change it. Honestly, I was being way too harsh on myself. I needed to practice that cliché saying of 'love thyself' because it was me. If I should love anyone, it should be me first. Why didn't I see myself as a survivor who did the best she knew how to do with her circumstances, that always tried to better herself but didn't know how? There was nothing wrong with not knowing. I mean how could I have? I guess it also bothered me that I should be so happy with the way things were now and I found myself to be miserable. How could this be true when I knew of all the nights I'd lain in bed wishing for a life like this instead of the next opening in the system that was willing to take me in for profit? I also hated that I'd allowed a guy to wreck my world. I always said I wouldn't be that girl who was sitting around waiting for her boyfriend to call, but here I was, exactly that.

In my defense, I had never known love back then, and once I had a little taste of it, I had become addicted. I was driven by it. I woke up wanting it and hoping in angst and with yearning for the next embrace of it. I never wanted to leave his side and I found myself wanting to do everything with him. Just having coffee with him or a walk through Vines made me happy. He had made even the most normal, ordinary things light up with a sparkle that people wait their whole lives for. One moment with him was one that I found myself lingering on past all the millions that passed without him here. How could a moment's caress across my hand from him bring me to life when others passed me all day with no significance? It could only be my love that determined its value. Could it be only that my desire for it made it so great? Why not the clerk at school or the gas station, my friend in class handing me my book, the mailman, the hundreds of patrons I checked in at the library? Not the same! No one's hand was like his; in that moment when it touched my skin, I died and became reborn as something else. How could I have known back then what power he would have over all of me when I passed that judgment so long ago? It was only two years, not a long time, yet it seemed like a lifetime ago, and I was someone then. Different, as though the whole world had changed yet it had stayed the same. Maybe it was just that I had grown up, that simply I was a woman now. Not just in age but I had come to know myself and was choosing to walk through life with my own eyes, not just the ones that had been given to me. To say that I could determine my life, the events around me and not just believe that I had no control or ability to affect any of the circumstances in the world was difficult to contemplate.

Coming from a place where people were sad and shuffled off and paid to be taken care of somehow didn't shake me as it did others. I was just practical and accepted my lot and tried to make the best of what I could. I was never a cynic until now I doubted the logic in what I knew could heal me. Was I smug? Could it be that I thought it was okay for that group of girls to find peace in the daily rituals of Mass under the good Father's watchful eye? For them to be happy they had found something to do that filled them up and drove out their need to 'do something' that would most likely ruin their lives or someone else's in the neighborhood. Why was it not okay for me? What was different in them finding their peace from me? Didn't the rituals of Mass look as strange and hokey as any other practice of faith? Why was dancing with smoke and a tail feather different than the robed walk of the altar boys blessing the congregation with incense? I don't know why I did it in that moment, but I grabbed a handful of dried mud from the base of the rose garden and took my hands and allowed them to streak lines with it across my face. I felt alive. I was certain anyone who saw me would think I was being strange or silly. Labeled as one of those new age artsy people who weren't grounded in this world, but I felt strength from it. If I didn't care what anyone thought, I would do it much like a child plays open with their imagination, free of the constraints of what was acceptable but rather fulfilled with what felt good for them. I finally felt good now, after a long time of suffering. Again, in following my grandmother, I had found my own path, one of my ancestors. I realized now, I was even thinking things that were a little off and that had scared me. But why was it considered off, because it didn't fit into the neighborhood that I grew up thinking I would never be able to live in? Did it seem strange because I wasn't a Native American or more because I was finding my way alone? I did not have anyone to guide me and show me the right path and I had become full of doubt because I was asking for someone other than myself to confirm what the right path was for me. As my totem book called it, I was trying to awaken my spirit guide to lead me to my path but I doubted that I should be traveling on this journey alone. I had let fear and doubt define who I was instead of accepting the signs that I was asking for. Did it matter where they came from, or who, as long as I wasn't hurting anyone or myself, and if it helped me, why not let it be? I was so judgmental of my own needs but understood that it made perfect sense when others did it. If I believed a candle could save someone's soul in Mass, why couldn't my Vines face paint strengthen my spirit?

I had seen adults dress up for Dragon Con in Atlanta just for fun or in weird S & M outfits because they wanted to, but I couldn't accept some mud to soothe my spirit. I walked past the butterfly garden and found myself wandering into the meadow. I was drawn by the transfer of aroma from the roses in the garden to the lavender at the beginning of the field. Soon I felt the urge to sit down and found the tall grass to be taller than my head, so I just gave in and lay myself down in an alcove of grass, completely hidden from the world. Safe, as it surrounded me, and I lay for a long time just resting.

My mind began to wander to escape from the soft ground I found to choose to rest upon. Its solid bed kept bringing me back to Vines as I followed the curve of my spine as it settled on the floor of the earth. My body began to relax and I became more and more aware of my physical self as it was just resting there, a part of my park. My ears listened to the rustle of the wind as it carried past me and the blades of high grass. The ends of the blades were soft as they graced over my hand, being carried by the wind to caress my skin. The water from the river by the children's mini-train station washed the rocks, which surprisingly I could hear from way over here in the field now that I was being still. I found solace in my much-needed release of all that I was holding inside. Everything escaped as I allowed my lungs to fill up with the cleansing air of Vines and released as I exhaled out all of the thoughts and feelings that had been haunting me. Almost in thanks, my body fell asleep and was allowed to accept that it was finally in a state of peace, restored to its rightful state of being. I opened my eyes to complete darkness until my eyes were able to adjust to the dark blue-black that was Vines at night. I remained perfectly still, hoping I was well hidden in the tall grass. I heard smashing and loud noises coming from the bridge and it was headed toward this direction. I listened more closely and realized it was a group of guys laughing and being rowdy. My instincts told me it was probably the same group of bad guys who gave me trouble last time. I mean, who else would it be? Either way, people who were loud like that were inconsiderate of others and their surroundings. People who were inconsiderate of others almost always hurt people, whether intentionally or not; they should be avoided. The good thing about my silly face paint was that it would offer me some camouflage in the high grass. Oddly, I had no sense of urgency to flee. This was most likely the stupidest thing I had ever done, but somehow I wasn't afraid. It was almost as if I was just witnessing them and I was perfectly content to just sit there, unbeknownst to them, in the grass, watching.

I was motionless as I steadied myself, still just observing them being loud and rowdy, unaware of me as I sat and watched, safe in my spot in the meadow. When my thoughts crept back for a moment that it was possible that they could see me, then what would I do? Fight them? Run? No, I knew somehow they would just pass me. Go by without noticing, and I was happy. When they got closer, I realized the noises were them finishing up bottles of beer and then throwing them at various designated marks throughout the park. When one of them finished up a bottle, he would chug it, trying to hit a declared spot then the rest of them would laugh. This went on until they had eventually finished the beer they had brought with them. I noticed the whole park was quiet just as I was, trying not to be seen by them. All of us in Vines were trying to convince them that they were alone, as I was. The group of about nine young men came closer as I sat in silence. I wondered if they had gotten some new recruits or if the ones Barbara had told me about had been released back to their pack, assuming it was them. I just sat and watched them meander through the park, consumed by their pranks and senseless noise and violence as they fought and destroyed as they progressed deeper into Vines. One of them punched another's arm as he jumped up onto the bench that faced the lake. The guy laughed as he held his arm. Demented, that was the word that came to mind looking at them. An old word from my neighborhood that would adequately describe what I saw from the idiot laughing as he held his arm in pain from his friend's punch. No sooner had the thought left my mind than I realized I was sitting in a meadow, in the dark, alone, wearing makeshift Native American face paint. I had to laugh at myself. Yep, it was time to go home. Enough of this silly nonsense, I thought. Oddly enough, I still wasn't afraid. I just casually began to walk through the meadow toward the dark forest that separated me from my Subaru. I figured it was a safer route to my car than the open path. I wasn't going to just walk past those guys on the sidewalk of the park and say, "Beautiful night, huh, guys?" and expect them not to harass me. No, those guys were clearly bored and up to no good and I wasn't about to let them take it out on me. I would normally be too afraid to walk through Vines alone, especially at night, and especially if I knew that group of guys were there.

I could have taken the tunnel but I wanted to enjoy Vines. Why should I let someone else determine my fate? No, I wasn't going to. I just had to still be aware of my environment and be careful but I didn't have to run and hide; I just had to be smart. After a long time, I finally came out of the meadow and was into the woods. It was easier to walk in instead of the high grass. I would hear the occasional faint sound of the guys from behind me so that I wasn't worried of running into them up ahead. When I made it to the edge of the forest, to the clearing that marked the beginning of the pavement for the parking lot, I just stopped and listened for a while. I looked at my car from the distance and my tires seemed to still be okay and full of air. To my relief, the car seemed untouched. I was apprehensive to click the sound of the alarm on my car to unlock it, to only be alerting the guys as to where I was and not be able to escape due to some malice they had inflicted on my escape vehicle. I made haste to the door and got in quickly, locking the doors and shoving the key into the ignition quickly to leave in safety. I suddenly felt like one of those graceful does, making her escape from the meadow in light of seeing a visitor to her environment. Done, my Subaru started right up and I was on my way out of the park.

What time was it? I glanced at the dashboard. It said midnight. I wanted to stop by IHOP to get something to eat but I realized I had mud smeared on my face. I parked my car in the IHOP parking lot and pulled a wipe out from my purse in the car and removed the streaks I had made to free my spirit. I was escorted to the back of the restaurant to a small booth in the corner. I sat facing the room; the only other patron was a woman a couple of booths away. I ordered a coffee and water and went to the restroom to wash my hands a couple times and my face. I was careful not to wash off my eye makeup and just wash my face and neck. This had taken years of practice, but I was content to see that I had finally mastered it. I checked out my reflection and I now looked like I would have on any other day of the week. Content with my appearance, I left the bathroom and sat at my table just as the waitress was bringing out my coffee and water. I didn't have to look at the menu to tell her I wanted French toast with a side of potatoes and turkey bacon. As I waited for my food, I made eye contact with the woman at the other table.

She was about twenty years older than me but still very beautiful. If we were both at the club she could definitely hold her own with her slim figure and graceful movements. I studied her as she poured herself another cup of coffee from the carafe and she met my eyes with hers. Who was this strange woman who also sat alone at night and ate her meal in solace like me? She seemed controlled and content to just sit and watch and just be. Those mannerisms seemed out of place here, as most people in Loganville were friendly and not as refined. She spoke to me in a clear, loud but not offensive voice, as if she was projecting her voice to speak in an auditorium so I could hear her, "Mind if I join you?"

"No, please do," I replied with a smile and hand gestured for her to come over. When she got closer to the table, I could see that she was even more striking in appearance, which was odd for someone older to be as usually, up close, one begins to notice wrinkles or dark spots that are masked by makeup. Not with her; I had to look away from her eyes, they were so unique. They were such a dark blue they were almost violet. In fact, I would say they were purple.

"Hi, I'm Julia," she said as she extended her hand for me to shake.

I met her handshake with, "Aurora."

Her hands were smooth and bony, but firm. *Why did I say Aurora and not Rose?* I asked myself. "I'm sorry, I don't mean to stare; it's just that your eyes are so different, so beautiful. Are they contacts?" I asked her.

"No, and I get that all the time. Just an uncommon shade of blue. Liz Taylor had them. Have you heard of her?" she responded.

"The actress? Oh yes. I thought she was great," I said.

"Do you know why I came over?" she asked. "I'm a psychologist and you looked sad to me for some reason. I know I don't know you and it is pretty rude of me to assume you want to talk but, I don't know. Something about you just compelled me to ask you about how you are. Is that weird? Okay, I'm sure that it is but that's what happened," she said with a friendly smile. All of her was warm and open, yet she looked so put together as she shifted in her seat to display her sharp grey business suit, with the skirt fitting her form subtly. Yeah, she had it figured out, so why was she here alone like me?

The waitress returned with my plate of food and sat it in front of me. "Are you going to eat?" I asked as I buttered my French toast.

"I already have. I actually would be taking off, but for some reason I just wanted to talk to you, had an urge to do so actually. I am not sure why," she said.

"Trying to determine if I should be locked up, most likely," I said with a chuckle.

"You have a good sense of humor. No, actually we don't usually do that. Mental health today is resolved much differently than it used to be, but it still drags up some frightening images for people, even those who were born way after those practices. I'm not saying there aren't facilities where people live to be treated, but most people's ailments are not so maladaptive that they prevent them from leading a normal daily life. You definitely seem to function well," she said with a mirthful smile. "So why do you give off this sad vibe?" she asked.

"So will this be like a *Law and Order* episode… anything I say can and will be used against me," I said with a short laugh.

Still smiling but looking her in the eyes, asking is it safe for us to be friends even if it is just for a moment of our lives? It would be beneficial to speak to someone right now, especially if they were educated and trained like she was, a psychologist, but I was very wary. I mean, what if she wasn't good? Shrinks can do a lot of damage. They study how to get inside you and if they don't care, you get hurt, and I don't know of anyone who could have put me back together. I knew I was having a hard enough time with myself as it was. She took a sip of her coffee and smoothly tipped her head like a cat would and smiled at me gently. That's what it was; she reminded me of a cat. Boy, I really had to get over this seeing people as animals thing I had picked up. If I was accurate, maybe there was a logical explanation that somehow science could explain. It was probably that I was picking up traits off of the people I was observing and equating the animal with them who was known to possess those traits. So what was a cat…? Clever, quiet and a survivor, or known for having nine lives as people say. Julia came off as intelligent or educated, quiet in the sense that she seemed composed and had manners in the way she danced around words to make her company feel welcome and she seemed to have been through some stuff and came off as collected, like she survived or handled it. So maybe I wasn't crazy after all, now I guess I would have to tell the shrink, I laughed to myself. So the signs I was afraid of were just my combination of the street smarts I had acquired throughout my life combined with the new information I had picked up from my new environment. I guess I had a hard time because my new home was so different than what I was used to, so my old methods of making sense of the world didn't make sense here. I decided she was okay; after all, I was pretty fond of cats.

"Well, I'm new to the area, kind of. I moved here not quite two years ago, about a year and a half to Loganville from Scranton, Pennsylvania. I actually lived mostly in a smaller town, a suburb of Scranton, but I'm sure you would be more familiar with Scranton. While adjusting to my new home, one of the only friends I had made here died. Then the boyfriend I met and hooked up with here got accepted into an M.B.A. program that was really intense because it was condensed, so he hasn't been around. I would say as much, but he hasn't been around at all and I began to doubt his feelings for me and wasn't sure what to do. I missed him so much and it hurt, which led to a lot of confusion because if he was staying away because he needed to work, I wanted to support him. I mean, I care about him, I want to help him, but my need to have him around was making me sick. It was really scary because I was used to being alone and not needing or wanting anyone; and my desire for him was really strong. Like crazy strong. I had never felt that way before and I wasn't sure if it was normal or what to do. I was afraid if I went after him to ask him about it to get some clarity, I would seem desperate and I hated myself for being pathetic, even though I knew I wasn't and was being logical. It's been crazy for me, having all these feelings. What really drove me nuts, ha ha," I laughed, "no pun intended," I added with a smile, "was that I actually had everything that I had ever wanted in my life. All of my prayers and dreams had been answered and my life was really good but I was feeling so bad. I tried to tell myself how lucky I was and how I should be thankful for what I had but I couldn't shake it; the feeling was too powerful." She sat across from me, relaxed and just listening with an open look on her face. Allowing me to know she had heard what I had said and was being my friend in accepting the experience I had shared with her.

"You went through a lot in a short period of time. You know, what you are feeling is actually pretty normal, and you are handling it pretty well, I must say. I did some consulting for a local business a while back that had the opportunity to expand internationally. They jumped at the possibility to grow into a global company but they were having a hard time with their employees dealing with the culture shock of living and adapting overseas.

"There are some books out there on the subject that you might like. They say adaptation to a new environment comes in stages when you are changing in a healthy way," she said.

"Wow, yeah, no. Now that you say it like that, it makes sense. Yeah, I could check the library and see what they have on the subject. I guess I never thought about it like that. Thanks," I said.

"But you know, that's not what I think is really bothering you, now is it?" she asked but kept talking. It was almost as if she asked to soften what she was going to say. "You were sorting out who you are and who you want to be, am I right?" she asked. "Some sort of perception or accepted truth you were trying to face? Yeah, those can be difficult and take some time. Just know that you are safe to explore your thoughts and that you have the power to decide what is best. It really is that simple, Aurora; just decide what is best for you and choose it, that's it," she declared.

"That is what my dilemma was, it's just that for me it was more difficult because most people have someone to tell them how to do it, what the norm or accepted practice is. I had to pick out everything and wait and see if it was a good choice or not and that can be scary, because if I am the only person looking out for me, what if I miss something? I can get really hurt. I just wanted to know I was doing okay, and it was hard, having to determine that for myself. After some thinking, I realized I did have people to guide me along. So now I have a religion, a good place to live, an education and friends. My guides just weren't traditional but nonetheless they were still there," I concluded.

I admired her blonde hair that somehow looked natural when I knew that was most likely impossible. I determined she must go to a really good salon and spend a good deal to look the way that she did. As if she could read my thoughts, she said, "Aurora, you should be your number one investment. I'm not saying be greedy or selfish. I am not advising you to not help people or to give, but you should always be number one. I go to this local gym; you are welcome to come work out with me if you'd like," she said, sliding her business card across the table. "I get my nails and hair done and I work out. I don't spend a lot of time on myself but enough so that when people see me, they know I care about me. That I invest in me so they realize when dealing with me that I am my number one priority. It is actually a really good self-defense mechanism and it works. Think about this… studies have shown that crime has decreased in areas or neighborhoods where new plants were planted throughout the area, homes were repaired and garbage picked up. Why did this happen? Psychology will tell you that it is because people care and invest in that area so it becomes a place of value. Think about that research, Aurora, it's very interesting.

There is an old saying: people get their cues from you. You are in charge, my friend," and she put a twenty on the table and shook my hand goodbye and was gone.

I left, feeling a mix of inspiration and calm, thankful I had someone to clear my head with. Sometimes you just needed to hear your thoughts out loud to another person to know that you were on the right track. Even just sharing your experience with another person and hearing what you think out loud could keep you on the right track. I think it's healthy to hear what you think aloud sometimes, even if it is just to see if it sounds crazy as it goes by your ears. My problem was that I usually didn't have anybody or it was too weird or personal to share.

Thinking about Topps and what she was saying about culture shock, if I had tried to open up on the assembly line, even before the distinctive line of me being the manager and employees was drawn, we wouldn't talk like I just had with Julia. People here were different. I wasn't sure if it was because she was a shrink or educated or just not from the hardworking class of people from my neighborhood who stuck to their own and just kept going. I guess when you're working class, you don't have time to work through your feelings; that won't pay the bills. You just keep going, don't stop to look around or ask questions. Here, this place was different. I asked for help and I was helped.

"Thank you," I said out loud, unsure if it was God, the universe or who exactly I was thanking, but I was happy to have had it. My hair had come undone from the bun I had it wrapped up in. Some of the strands had fallen onto my hand as I held onto the steering wheel and they were almost unrecognizable as my own. So dark, a rich red; my hair had darkened from strawberry blonde to this murky color almost identical to the Georgia red clay Vines Park calls her earthen floor. What was happening to me? I had changed and was no longer the girl I had been. Somehow I saw this happening but was more curious and eager to grow stronger and evolve, as I knew if I continued hiding and just sifting through life, I would fall and no one would notice.

I knew enough to know that when someone gives you their hand to get up, take it. I just didn't know how unstable I would be when I stood up. I hoped to grow stronger. I think school and karate and painfully that even Derrick had helped me become this person. I convinced myself on the way home that my hair had grown darker due to some genetic disposition, like Andi. Maybe it was a Danish thing and I just didn't know how I was supposed to look because I was an orphan. Like the ugly duckling, maybe I'd find out this was how I was supposed to be, and the story would end happily ever after for me too.

*

Life continued on for me after that night and soon it was time for the fall semester, in which I continued by signing up for six classes. I had to get special permission from the Dean to take two extra classes on top of the regular load, but it was doable because they were all business and leadership classes. Two of them were online and I worked at my own pace and before I knew it, I had made it through the semester with all As except ironically in the Women in Business course. I got a B because she was really harsh in grading my papers, saying she demanded excellence and that we would thank her someday. I doubted it but was happy to have still done well in the course and proud of myself that I had done it while taking five other classes and still holding down a job. Working at the library had helped actually, because I was able to write most of my papers during my downtime at work in between helping patrons who usually just needed a few minutes of help when they did ask for assistance here and there. I met with my advisor and signed up for my last five classes and was ready to graduate in the spring. It would be in May.

May came around and I had finished up my classes a week earlier and was making plans with Andi for my graduation. I think he was happier than I was about me having finished college. So what now? I was kind of embarrassed that I had no plans for myself after school. I was actually kind of happy working at the library and meandering through the thrift store after work once a week to spot that great find. I guess I wasn't normal; everyone else in my class had this great job lined up or was going on to graduate school or to travel somewhere. Some were opening up a new business on their own or were finally going to get that promotion since now with a degree their company could confirm advancing them would be risk adverse. No, not me. I just wanted to make red belt in Taekwondo, which I did the Thursday before, so I was pretty stoked. Life would go on as it had for me, and I was enjoying it. I guess I would finally be able to read something for fun at work instead of just homework or the boring research for the course. I looked forward to seeing what that was like.

A young dentist from the office next to the library kept coming in and had finally asked me out, but I told him I had a lot going on with my upcoming graduation. I politely declined him without rejecting him. I had learned this southern etiquette and I found it to be a better way than what I probably would have said three years ago had he asked me. I was learning that a lot could be said about southern charm and people paid a lot of money for soft skills these days, so I was thankful to have had these good graces rub off on me. The truth was, he was handsome, had a good job right next to mine and he seemed to really be interested in me; he just wasn't Derrick.

I could look at him and see he was a good-looking guy and that he and I could probably make a good life together; I just didn't love him. I had heard people say that the reason arranged marriages worked was because two people were put together who had the same values and goals in life. That love would come after living a life together, from sharing struggles and children, from having meals together, but then I would remember the first time I saw Derrick at St. Oliver's parking lot and I knew I had felt all of that from a split-second glance, long before I even knew his name. I knew that I should probably give up on the thought of him calling me and

of us. That I should move on with my life, that I was young and in my prime. This was when people meet each other and start a family. I knew that women were having children much later now, even in their forties, but I just wanted a family.

I didn't have some career or was doing something great like discovering a cure for a disease or something grand. I was just a girl from a small town who had waited her whole life for a family and I guess he kept walking over from next door but I didn't want to believe that me and Derrick were over. I just didn't want it to be but I had to grow up, I guess, and face the facts. It was better to accept them than to try to force something to happen that wasn't there. Especially if I wanted kids; I didn't want to hurt them by a divorce or some crap later that I knew was true now. Dang it, what happened? How could he just turn off feelings like that and disappear?

*

After my graduation, Andi came up to me and congratulated me. He handed me an envelope, "A little graduation gift." It read *Welcome Home*, and it had a round-trip plane ticket to Copenhagen and a travel book on Denmark.

I grabbed him and hugged him. "Thank you, Andi."

"My pleasure, Aurora. I knew you could do it," he said with a gleam in his crystal blue ice eyes. "The arrangements have been made for fourteen days. Our family will pick you up at the airport and you will stay at three different family homes until your last three days, then arrangements have been made for a tour of the museum and city proper and a stay at the hotel. A cousin, it hasn't been decided who, will take you on your last day from your room at the hotel back to the airport for your return home. Everyone is very excited that you are coming. Best regards, Aurora, and call me if you need anything. Oh, and use this card overseas, and here are a couple prepaid phonecards just in case. I know you will be with family and it is a safe country for the most part, but I like to stay prepared," as he handed me a small bag.

I couldn't help but feel happy and excited. I called the Summit Chase Animal Hospital and arranged for Jade to board with them while I was away and also to get caught up on his shots while he was there. I gave him a big hug and promised him that I would be back before he had a chance to miss me. International! I couldn't believe it but I was more excited about finding a possible link to Grandma and Vines Park than in seeing my family's homeland.

*

My trip was great and a lot of my family spoke English so the trip was very enjoyable. I had made connections that otherwise would have been broken and I felt as though things were set back to the way they should have been had my parents not died. I had finally been on a vacation, like a real trip and out of the country.

Well if I had had a bucket list, that would have been on it. My family was so warm and openly affectionate and just invited me into their homes and made them mine as well. They treated me as though they had known me my whole life. I had never been around people who weren't guarded and treated others as if they expected to be hurt. No, my family treated me well and expected me to be well as they expected. It was a strange concept, but it worked, as the results were fantastic. I had a great time and added all of them to my Facebook friends list so we could stay in touch.

*

I picked up my mail from the post office and got Jade out of the animal clinic. He wouldn't stop purring and looked as though he had put on some weight. "Don't worry; everybody puts some on while on vacation. You'll burn it off when you get back into your regular routine," I told my little friend as I scratched under his chin.

When we got to the house I was so happy to be home. I saw Barbara was straining her neck to see me as she pretended to be getting her newspaper from the stoop. I waved and she ducked me as usual. I guess some things never change. As I made my way up the porch steps, I noticed a bouquet of flowers lying on the doormat in front of the door. I placed Jade, who was inside his kitty carrier, down as I scooped up the flowers to read the card. It read, *Sorry I missed you. Call me when you get back into town. Love, Derrick.*

Love, Derrick, I thought sarcastically. Where had he been all this time if he loved me? I couldn't help but feel good at seeing the flowers and knowing he had come looking for me.

Inside, I was happy to be able to say that I was out of the country, busy and not available, so he didn't think that I was just sitting at home waiting around for him to show up with his love whenever he felt like it. I wanted the flowers but when I let myself and Jade in, I threw them in the garbage. No, I was not going to be taken for granted. If he really wanted me, he could buy more, but I was not going to allow myself or him to think some ten-dollar bouquet was going to make everything all right. He had some nerve but I wanted to hear what he had to say. I hoped he would come again, that he would call me and see where I had been. To come after me and show me that he was wrong for staying away but he had had a good reason for doing so. That he hated it but he had had to, but now he had taken care of it and he would never stay away again. Now we could be together. I knew better this time and wasn't going to hold my breath; in fact, I was going to make sure I stayed busy so if he wanted to see me, he had to make plans. He would have to make me important and arrange his time to see me. Let's see how he felt. I knew I would hate to have to go through this again with him, but spending time in Denmark with my family had filled me up somehow. I saw how my cousins treated their wives and how happy the kids were, and I knew that was something worth fighting and waiting for. It gave me hope and their good treatment of me and the rest of our family made me fill up inside with a kind of decency that now had no tolerance for anything else. No matter who it was, even Derrick. To my relief, I was exhausted and fell right asleep. It was so good to be home in my own bed.

*

The next day, I slept well over twelve hours and enjoyed every moment of it. I woke up holding the tiny gold alarm clock that I couldn't make quiet fast enough as my still-asleep mind and eyes searched for the button on the back to click off the ringing hammer. As my eyes adjusted, I noticed words encrypted on the case of the bell which read, *Always believe, never forget* in really fancy cursive. "Believe what?" I made my way downstairs and had coffee with Jade and watered all of my houseplants. Then I went out into the garden and started working the way that Rosa and I used to. I hoped that she was somewhere good, that she was happy. She was such a good lady and friend. When I was satisfied with the work I had done for the day, I sat on my porch and had a nice cool glass of sweet tea and just admired my yard. I thought about removing the friendship gate that sat between my yard and Rosa's, as who knew what the new neighbors would be like? I decided a better solution would be to put a bench there against the gate door so they couldn't open it and come over but it wouldn't be permanent. I could rest flowerpots on top and make it seem less imposing and obvious. I put my glass in the dishwasher and ran upstairs to take a quick shower. The shower ended up taking longer than expected, but I felt better after the good scrub with my exfoliating sponge and body wash.

I did my eyeliner and mascara and wrapped my hair up in its usual bun, which was already drying from the Georgia heat. Tomorrow was my birthday. I was going to be twenty-four I thought as I sat in the summer day. I'd never get used to the summers here, no matter how long I lived here. I had to say I was pretty impressed that I had not only graduated but had done it in three years instead of four. It was mostly thanks to Derrick, as I was trying so hard to keep busy in his absence that I had doubled up on my classes, and to my benefit. Andi had honored my grandmother's wishes and my name was printed on the deed of the house, so she was mine free and clear. I had found my family and had started a good relationship with them. Life was being kind to me and I appreciated it. I slipped on some yoga pants and was on my way downstairs to grab my purse when I heard a knock at the door. I saw the familiar silhouette shadow his image behind the lace of the door. It was him. He had returned again. Derrick.

My heart raced in excitement but my attitude was coming out cross. I opened the door and said, "Oh hey," in acknowledgement of him but locked the door behind myself. I stood facing him on the porch. "I was just about to step out for a minute," I said politely but trying to sound rushed, like I had to be somewhere.

"Oh… where were you going?" he asked, seeming disappointed.

"Oh, I have to go to either Home Depot or the family farm down the street to look for a bench for my garden. You know where I'm talking about… the small family-run place that sells the tress and flower pots and stuff," I continued.

"Yeah, my mom got a gnome garden there. Apparently they're all the rage now, little tiny gardens you put on your coffee table or desk in the office," he said.

"You mean fairy garden," I corrected him.

"Yeah, maybe, but I know where you're talking about. After QuikTrip on the left but before John Deere and my neighborhood," he confirmed. "Hey, let me come with you. I mean, the bench might be heavy," he said enthusiastically.

"Oh, so glad you're finally concerned about me and decided to show up and offer your services. What a guy," I said with a cool sarcasm as I unlocked my Subaru.

He hurried behind me. "Look, I know I wasn't here for you. I'm sorry." He grabbed the car handle on the passenger side and got in quickly as if he was afraid I would take off without him and he would miss his opportunity. "I love you, Aurora. Did you get my flowers?" he asked.

I looked him in the eye as I pulled off from the driveway. "How did you know I was gone?" I asked.

"How was Denmark? Wow, that must have been amazing," he stated.

"How did you know I was gone, Derrick?" I said with my voice getting a little louder and more serious.

"I have this job now, well, anyway, I was at a party and I started talking to this guy, and well, he's a researcher for a big P.R. company in Atlanta. I mean big time, Senators and C.E.O.s use him; he's supposedly really good. Well... he helped me out and confirmed what I was thinking that you were gone," he said in a quiet voice.

"You were spying on me, like stalking me. You were so sorry that you couldn't even stalk me yourself; you hired someone to do it. What, were you too busy?" I screamed. Of course it was as we were passing Barbara's house, and of course she was outside to hear the whole thing. Why not embarrass myself on top of it?

"Look, I know it's creepy—" he said before I cut him off.

"You think?" I said, not as loudly as before but still yelling.

"Look—" he started to say but I interrupted him again.

"No, you look. The fact is you haven't been looking at all. You were gone. Off living your busy little life without me," I said, my voice full of anger and passion.

"Aurora, please. I'm sorry. I know I haven't been here. School was really hard. I love you. You are all that I ever wanted. I just had to finish school is all," he said with the utmost sincerity.

"What about after? you liar. Where were you then, huh? What was your excuse for that, you jerk?" I said, gritting my teeth in a fierce snap of words that seemed to flow from the pit of me. I pulled into the Family Farm and he had me against the driver's side door before I realized he was out of the car. He tried to kiss me but I avoided his lips as they made the dive for mine. He then caught the left side of my face in his hand and directed it against his so his mouth could find mine. There was no resisting his desire for me, as it matched my own need for him. All of the emotions just traveled between us in one long embrace. I pulled away and started walking toward the store. He quickly followed and caught my hand to hold it in his. "You think that changes anything, Derrick? You know I'm crazy about you. That isn't the issue. You think you can make me love you then just leave like that, abandon me? Is that what you think? You sack of shit that meant something to me. "Those nights we were together meant something to me. I wasn't playing around when I said that I loved you. You assured me that you felt the same way, and you left. You fucking left," I said as tears filled up in my eyes. My throat began to swell in acknowledgement of how he made me feel. He grabbed my arms and pulled me toward him. He looked down into my eyes and I saw that his were watery too. I felt the intensity of the moment come over me like a wave of thick feelings that ached deep past the muscle, into the very raw core of me as I stood there facing him. He crept closer and before I could resist, he said, "It meant something to me too," and he kissed me deeply until we were interrupted by an older lady trying to pass us with a giant shrub.

Derrick paid for my bench and loaded it into the back of my Subaru. He placed it in front of the gate door and I arranged the flowerpots until I was pleased with the project. He instinctively made a pot of coffee but before we had finished the last cup, we were making love upstairs in my bed. How I had missed him so much. Being with him was a little different now, I guess, because I was older. Maybe because I realized and accepted how I felt about him. After we showered, we lay in each other's arms and watched *Law and Order* until I fell asleep.

Chapter Twenty-Three

Vines Park, the End and the Beginning

I woke up happier than I had ever been, or than I could remember. I looked to my right and Derrick was gone but there was a note on my pillow. I assumed as I was gesturing toward it to retrieve it that he probably had to go to work. *Aurora, took your house keys so I could get back in. Sorry. Be right back. Love, Derrick.* Okay, where did he go? I got up and went into the shower to get ready for the day. I came out, did my makeup and put on clean yoga capris since it was too hot to wear the full-length ones I usually dote. I found a comfy knee-length sleeveless shirt and was set to go make coffee. On the second cup, I heard a fumble at the front door and Jade took off to investigate. "Okay, watch, kitty; it's only Derrick," I said with a smile. I didn't even get up and my comfort was confirmed as I heard the reassuring click of the latch behind the sound of the front door closing.

"Aurora," he called.

"Hey, honey," I responded, letting him know I was in the kitchen. He jumped into the kitchen holding a teal and silver birthday balloon, a bouquet of flowers and a plastic bag. "Happy Birthday," he exclaimed as he grabbed me into a hug.

"Oh, Derrick," I said as he gave me a quick peck on the lips. We sat down and he opened up the bag revealing two to-go plates of French toast and turkey bacon. "You are the best," I said.

"Well, I was hoping that you'd say that," as he got down on one knee in front of my chair on the kitchen floor. He pulled out a black box from his pocket and opened it. It was a silver band that had a good-sized white diamond in the middle of it. "Aurora, will you marry me? If you say yes, I promise I won't ever leave you like that again. I don't ever want to be without you again."

*

The next month, there was a small ceremony held in the white garden in front of the entrance that began the path toward the guardians of Vines. I wore my grandmother's gown that I had altered but I had to buy the floral lace veil and crown to match at Macy's that I wore underneath a floral wreath I had made by a local florist. It was a mismatch but it somehow fit together, much like everything else seemed to for me. Honestly, as I walked up the brick stairs that led to the entrance of the rose garden, I was so happy that if the veil had cost a thousand dollars, I wouldn't have cared. Some people had gathered to watch us seal our union and they began to crowd at the bottom of the steps and scattered in various parts to show their support in a circle around us as they witnessed our happy moment that was the official beginning of our life together. We took our vows from a local judge who knew Derrick's parents in front of the lion statue that guarded the entrance to the rose garden. His parents, my boss and his wife were our official witnesses but there was also a good number who gathered.

One in particular I kept noticing, but I was unsure why until I overrode my instinct to be discreet and got a good look at her. She was African-American and slender in build with long feminine features. She was about my height and she wore her hair long and in braids that were held off her face in some kind of cloth. She looked like an urban gypsy and was clad in a lot of silver jewelry. One piece in particular held my gaze: a giant crystal that hung from a silver chain around her neck. In realizing I was staring at this woman, I moved my eyes to her friend that was standing next to her. She was Asian, most likely Chinese, and she was approached by a white woman with darker features than my own. She handed the Asian woman a bouquet of flowers, my flowers! The same ones I found at my storm door all those nights ago, and now they were here!

Before I could think any further about it, my boss approached and asked if I was ready. He was holding a set of rings Derrick had brought over as he had bought the wedding bands as a set and was having them engraved. The ceremony was short and everyone gave us a big cheer before departing back to their own adventures in Vines Park. I looked for the ladies, but they were gone. I was rushed away in a state of bliss and excitement so that I didn't get to look at the Lady of the Fowl to see if an offering had been made. I quickly forgot my enquiry from my strange exchange as Derrick and I made it back to my home, our home, as husband and wife to pack for our honeymoon. Derrick was so eager to carry me over the threshold in the time-honored tradition that he quickly distracted me from anything else as we entered the house that had been left to me as man and wife. *Thank you*, I thought to myself, knowing she didn't get to see how it had all turned out but I was appreciative just the same. From the sounds of it, it had worked out just the way Grandma had intended.

"Look, I know that maybe you're supposed to buy me mine," he said, speaking of our wedding bands, "but as a seeing how I wanted 'em to match and I got such a good deal on 'em, I was a hoping you could overlook this here indiscretion," he said as he handed me a paper.

"Derrick, you found out what it means," I said. He had had the marking from the outside of my doorframe engraved into our silver wedding bands. "Derrick, that is the sweetest thing." I kissed him and followed with, "You are the sweetest man."

"Oh, I know," he said as he passed my eyes with a teasing glance. It read in runes, which looked exactly like the markings over my front door. "Well, we can only translate roughly but it's something like this. Well, you know them is what y'all spoke before Danish, right?" he asked.

"You think your wife is an idiot," I said, smiling and reading the paper: *Victory in life and battle, bringing honor to your name and family, protecting it always.*

"How did you find out what it said?" I asked. "I took a picture of it and sent it to this professor in Minnesota I found online who studies ancient runes, more specifically, Viking writings and artifacts. I also asked Andi," he said with the biggest grin and in the most casual manner. I forgot how much I enjoyed his humor as I felt the water creep up in my eyes as he said, "Come on. You don't want to be late for your own wedding party, do you now?"

We finished loading up our suitcases into his Jeep and I made sure to say goodbye to Jade. We drove over to the Summit Chase County Club where we danced, ate our wedding cake and celebrated with a lot of Derrick's and now my family and friends. After I threw back the bouquet, which was caught by a young cousin of Derrick's, I handed his mom the key to our house. "Mom, take good care of Jade. Thanks," I said with a hug.

"Bye, honey," she called. "Have fun in Ocean City. I love you!," and we were off on our honeymoon.

For the Love of Vines is the first of three stories written by N. L. Hurtic. The stories were shared with the intent to honor Vines Park and the many people and creatures that make her what she is and has been to all who have encountered her. She would also like to thank the town of Avoca, Pennsylvania, which is a lot like Vines Park in the sense that both seem small and insignificant until one really takes a look.